A Bird-Finding Guide to CANADA

May 12/84

Cam Finley

A Bird-Finding Guide to CANADA

Edited by
J.C. Finlay

Hurtig Publishers Ltd.
Edmonton

Hurtig Publishers Ltd.
10560 - 105 Street
Edmonton, Alberta

Canadian Cataloguing in Publication Data

Main entry under title:
A Bird-finding guide to Canada

  ISBN 0-88830-255-X (bound).—ISBN
0-88830-244-4 (pbk.)

    1. Bird watching—Canada—Guide-books.
2. Birds—Canada.   I. Finlay, J. C. (James
Campbell), 1931–
QL685.B57 1984   598′.07′23471   C84-091150-5

Illustrations by Terry Thormin.

Front photographs by R.E. Gehlert. *Left, top to
bottom*: Eared Grebe, Bohemian Waxwing, Sage
Grouse, Wilson's Warbler, American Kestrel, Eastern
Kingbird, Ross' Goose, Tree Swallow, Killdeer. *Right*:
Northern Saw-whet Owl.

Edited by Anne Leobold.
Designed by David Shaw & Associates Ltd.
Typeset by Attic Typesetting Ltd.
Manufactured by Gagné Printing Ltd.

Printed and bound in Canada

Contents

For Joy whose ideas, encouragement, faith and
support ensure dreams become reality.

For Brett, Warren and Rhonda who have supported
and encouraged their father to do his project.

For Muriel and Hugh Finlay who encouraged their
son to keep his enthusiasm and to grow in the
direction of his choice.

Preface

Joy and I, in our travels, have tried to search out those special places where nature is at its best. Many people have helped us to find those spots. In the same spirit of cooperation, and with the same willingness to share their knowledge, individuals across the country have helped to make *A Bird-Finding Guide to Canada* a reality.

Recognizing that no one person could know of all the places to find birds in Canada, Terry Thormin and I decided to use the same approach as we had in preparing *A Nature Guide to Alberta*, that is, to contact people and request their assistance. The response was both swift and astonishingly enthusiastic. Individuals from each province and territory agreed to coordinate their regional material: R. Yorke Edwards and Wayne Campbell in B.C.; I handled Alberta; Dr. C. Stuart Houston and Dr. J. Bernard Gollop in Saskatchewan; Rudolf F. Koes and associates in Manitoba; Dr. Chip Weseloh, Linda Wesoloh and Arnet Sheppard did Ontario; Mabel McIntosh and Real Bisson in Quebec; David Christie looked after N.B.; Jim Wolford saw to N.S.; Winnifred Cairns in P.E.I.; John Pratt and Bruce McTavish oversaw Newfoundland material; Dave Mossop and Robert Frisch in the Yukon; and Dr. Tom Barry in the NWT. A special thanks to all of you for the many hours spent obtaining and writing contributions, revising and upgrading material, and then cheerfully undertaking that final major edit in early 1983.

Many others willingly provided specific material for selected sites. Their names appear at the ends of their contributions. Others did not want to be listed in the text but provided excellent data, or helped in the provincial editing in the last round, including: Manley Callin, M. Cobus, Joyce and Bill Anaka, Mary Gilliland, Bruce Linegar, C. A. Wallis, John Wells, C. R. Wershler and Al Wiseley. Several other people have provided information that I have not been able to use, but which was certainly appreciated, including: from Alberta, Greg Wagner; from Ontario, Christopher Harris; from New Brunswick, Stanley Gorham, Don Kimball, Louis Lapierre, Ron Weir and Doug Whitman. Thanks to all of you, including Wayne Harris who had to redo his material because Canada Post lost the originals.

To those who encouraged me near the start, including Diane Griffin, Arnet Sheppard, Dr. Robert Nero, Bob Carswell and David Christie, I say a special thanks.

Thank you to friend, adviser and colleague Terry Thormin, who prepared the drawings for the book, and to those who provided slides to assist him: Yorke Edwards sent one by David MacKenzie; Terry Pratt sent one taken by J. R. Graham; Real Bisson supplied some including those by J. R. Coulouche; David Christie contributed several; and also Richard Fyfe and Bob Gehlert, who supplied slides to assist Terry, plus pictures for the cover of the book.

Thanks to Stephanie Kucharyshyn and Inge Wilson, of the cartographic staff at the University of Alberta Department of Geography, who drew the maps.

Many of the historical items, natural history notes, special activities and other gems of particular interest have been taken from that excellent book, *Canadian Book of the Road*, by the Canadian Automobile Association and The Reader's Digest Association (Canada) Ltd., 1979.

Thanks to ornithologist and good friend Dr. Martin McNicholl for reviewing the manuscript in its early stages, though I, of course, take full responsibility for any errors and omissions.

Anita Moore spent many hours, including weekends and evenings, typing the draft and several revisions. Thanks Anita. To my mother-in-law, Marie Barton, whose gifts over the years of reference books on birds and other natural history subjects have been invaluable as I wrote this one, a special thanks.

To Mel Hurtig and the entire staff at Hurtig Publishers I say thank you for making the production of this book possible. A very special thanks to Anne Leobold, my editor, who tightened up the manuscript, did the necessary cross-checking, and finally picked up those gremlin-caused errors that always seem to creep in. And finally, I appreciate the cordial and helpful relationship established with Ms. José Druker of Hurtig, who worked with me to ensure this book would meet the high standards of the trade.

Joy and I have been married nearly thirty years. She has continually encouraged me to develop and broaden myself. It was she who gave me the necessary moral support when I left my job as a geologist to become a naturalist. Without her ideas, enthusiasm and, most of all, her special consideration and commitment to each of our children and myself, we could not be doing the things that we are. Thank you, Joy.

And all you keen birders out there, send me corrections and additions to the choice spots that have been missed, to be included in the revised edition within the next five years. Let's make the second edition more complete.

J. CAM FINLAY

Box 8644
Station L
Edmonton, Alberta
T6C 4J4

December 1983

The Plan

The book covers Canada from offshore Vancouver and the Queen Charlotte Islands on the west coast to St. John's, Newfoundland, on the east; from Point Pelee in southern Ontario to Fosheim Peninsula on Ellesmere Island in the Arctic. The text is designed to help the beginner, the average naturalist and the keen "lister" to find new and not-so-new species while visiting interesting places. An attempt was made to select the best birding areas, most national and many provincial parks, and nearly all major urban centres.

The arrangement of chapters by province overlaps ecological boundaries and is not very scientific. However, such divisions worked in similar guides done for the United States, and we hope the arrangement works well here too.

Birds covered (approximately 550 species) include those of general and specific interest for an area. The more common species, such as American Robin or White-throated Sparrow, are seldom mentioned. Colour phases or races are noted where they are known to be present. The 34th Supplement to the American Ornithologists' Union Check-List of North American Birds has been followed for terminology. Certain terms are used as follows:

waterfowl: swans, geese and ducks
water birds: all species associated with water and marshes
waders and *shorebirds*: those with longer legs found on beaches and shores
alcids: seldom used, but when it does occur includes Razorbill, Dovekie, murres, guillemots and puffins
pelagic species: mainly shearwaters and petrels
land birds: those not usually associated with water.

To find a specific species, look it up in the checklist, then turn to the text to determine how, when and where to find that and other species in the region you plan to visit. The introductions to each chapter provide highlights. It would be useful to read the text with a provincial road map in hand. These maps usually provide information about parks, campsites and other recreational opportunities. When writing for a map, request a complete tourist package for that province. You can often dial toll free for this information (see text).

Helpful Suggestions

Clothing and Safety Equipment

In parts of Canada the temperature can change in a few hours from above freezing to –20°C. In spring and fall you can encounter anything from temperatures of 20°C to a snowstorm. Carry a wool pullover sweater at all times. A light jacket or windbreaker is useful. Bring a parka, mitts and warm headgear (about one-half of your heat loss is from the top of your head).

In summer, from June through August, the weather is generally warm with some rain showers. Bring a light rain jacket and that pullover wool sweater. Also, make sure you bring insect repellent.

Winter brings the cold. These freezing temperatures occur from central British Columbia to Newfoundland. In Victoria, Vancouver and the southern tip of Ontario, the cold temperatures are not too extreme. To go birding during the winter in most of the country make sure to carry in your car, at all times: lined parka and boots, wool pullover sweater, warm headgear, woollen mitts with an outside shell, warm trousers and long underwear (pyjamas will do), matches, a candle in a can to use as a stove for heat and to melt water, a sleeping bag, food, a flashlight, a shovel and a heavy rope or tow chain. If possible, all equipment should stay in the back seat. Trunks freeze up! And always carry a first-aid kit in your car.

Special Equipment

Special equipment is not necessary to enjoy watching birds, but it does help. Three items that will add to your enjoyment include field guides, binoculars and backpack.

Field Guides. Several guides are available in most bookstores. The ones recommended below are all compact and available in paperback. I prefer the Golden Field Guide, *Birds of North America*, by Chandler S. Robbins, Bertel Bruun and Herbert S. Zim, illustrated by Arthur Singer (New York: Golden Press, 1983). Two other guides, both by Roger Tory Peterson and published by Houghton Mifflin in Boston, are: *A Field Guide to the Birds of Eastern and Central North America* (4th ed. and completely revised, covering areas east of the 100th meridian, the Manitoba-Saskatchewan boundary) and *A Field Guide to Western Birds* (areas west of the 100th meridian).

Binoculars. There are many styles, makes and models on the market, with prices ranging from $50 to over $1000. I suggest you avoid the very inexpensive pairs, as these will reduce rather than increase your enjoyment. Check with your local camera store for help in selecting a pair to suit your eyes and pocketbook.

Backpack. We all need something to carry our lunch, rainwear, tuque, pullover sweater, mitts, extra film, camera, insect repellent and field guides. There are many good day packs on the market. The size of pack depends on how much you carry. I usually have quite a bit of material and so the past Christmas our three children gave me an excellent backpack, "Outbound" by Taymor. It has side pockets, back pockets and top cover in which to stuff a jacket.

Attracting Birds

Most of us want to bird-watch all year. There are three main points to consider if you wish to bring birds to you: water, feed and shelter.

Water. Dripping and/or running water does wonders. Even a plastic pail with a small hole that allows water to drip into an upside-down garbage can lid will bring birds. Another technique is to place a garden hose with a slow drip above a birdbath or lid. A spraying fountain is, of course, much better (and more work to build) as are small waterfalls.

Food. Feeding birds can bring its rewards (and expense if you go overboard). Eastern Canadians usually prefer a mix to attract a wide variety of species. Those of us in the west generally feed sunflower seeds; even House Sparrows love them. Hummingbirds occur across southern Canada and can be brought in with a simple feeder. Use one part (or less) sugar to two parts water, no colouring added. Carry a hummingbird feeder when you travel and set it up in a campground. You will be surprised at how often you attract hummingbirds, June through August. Carrying a small bag of birdseed to put on a plate at your campsite also brings in the sparrows and finches.

Shelter. Birds require a place to hide, nest and rest. In landscaping your yard, try and balance open sites with small clumps of bushes. Such a plan provides "edge effect" which the majority of birds prefer. If you are travelling, look for such edges and carefully check them out. They are usually the most productive.

Further Information

Lists of references for each province have been incorporated into the appropriate chapters. For those who wish more information or plan to get in touch with keen birders, a new magazine, *Bird Finding in Canada*, has recently been started by Gerry Bennet. This is an excellent, all-Canadian bimonthly publication, something long overdue. For a subscription contact: *Bird Finding in Canada*, R.R.2, 10780 Pine Valley Drive, Woodbridge, Ontario L4L 1A6.

For those of you interested in birds and broader natural history subjects, the Canadian Nature Federation is by far the best organization to join. They put out a beautiful magazine quarterly, *Nature Canada*. Further information and a subscription may be obtained by writing: Canadian Nature Federation, 75 Albert Street, Ottawa, Ontario K1P 6G1.

Several provinces have their own publications. Refer to the text for these.

A Code for Using the Out-of-Doors

Make all visits to a site instructive and productive, not destructive.

The birds, mammals, insects and other natural objects are for all to enjoy — in place. Take notes and photographs; refrain from breaking branches for a better look or picture; don't collect.

Nests, eggs and young are to be left alone; it is an offence under law to remove them.

Avoid approaching colonial nest sites too closely. Disturbance of these birds prevents them from defending eggs and young from predators.

Stay well away from nests of birds of prey during the early and mid-stages of the nesting cycle. These species, if disturbed before the young are partially feathered, often abandon the site.

Leave family groups of young waterfowl and game birds alone. Splitting them up could result in losses.

Avoid use of powerboats to explore marshes and lakes. A canoe causes much less disturbance.

Observe dancing grounds, or lecks, of grouse from a distance. Place your photographic blind on the edge the night before and enter well before dawn; depart after all birds have left about midday.

Avoid the use of a tape recorder to attract singing males on territory in city parks and other urban sites. Heavy use of tape recordings by bird watchers can substantially reduce breeding success.

Trails are for your use; stay on them when on foot or in a vehicle. Alpine and arctic tundra and even very dry prairie vegetation are particularly fragile. Such environments will take hundreds of years to recover (if ever) from one passing of a set of vehicle tires.

Tens of thousands of dollars are spent each year to pick up trash and litter. What you bring in you can take out!

Carry your own lightweight tent and sleeping mat. Building of a lean-to, or cutting spruce branches for a mattress, was useful fifty years ago when few people camped and equipment was heavy.

Parks and other public areas have special sites for open fires. Use the wood provided. Dead upright trees provide homes for chickadees. Practise axemanship in the woodpile! Bring your own wiener sticks (wire coat hangers make excellent ones).

Ask permission to enter private land. These landholders are often very helpful and will show you their private birding spots.

Close and fasten all gates. They are there to keep valuable livestock from wandering.

Safeguard all water supplies. Avoid dumping scraps and rubbish into streams, ponds and lakes. Don't drive through streams if it can be avoided, as you could disturb fish spawning grounds.

Keep dogs and cats under control at all times. These urban pets have become the most ruthless of city predators upon small wildlife.

Leave wild plants for others to enjoy. A picked flower wilts in a few hours and the plant will not be able to reseed. Transplanted flowers usually require special soil and conditions not found in your yard.

British Columbia

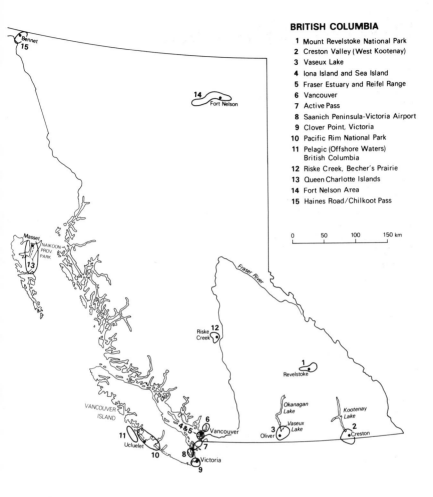

BRITISH COLUMBIA

1 Mount Revelstoke National Park
2 Creston Valley (West Kootenay)
3 Vaseux Lake
4 Iona Island and Sea Island
5 Fraser Estuary and Reifel Range
6 Vancouver
7 Active Pass
8 Saanich Peninsula-Victoria Airport
9 Clover Point, Victoria
10 Pacific Rim National Park
11 Pelagic (Offshore Waters)
  British Columbia
12 Riske Creek, Becher's Prairie
13 Queen Charlotte Islands
14 Fort Nelson Area
15 Haines Road/Chilkoot Pass

0   50   100   150 km

15

British Columbia

Our most westerly province contains more life zones than any other political unit in Canada. This variety results in birders from east of the Rockies adding dozens of species to their life lists per day upon first arriving. Where else can you find huge colonies of petrels, murres, auklets and puffins; Gyrfalcon, large numbers of Bald Eagles, the largest concentration left in North America of Peregrine Falcon; White-tailed Ptarmigan, Heermann's Gull, Barred Owl, White-throated Swift, several hummingbird species and Eurasian Skylark?

Covering 948,596 km², the lands range from sea level to 4663 m at Mount Fairweather. Habitats and birds to search for include:

Boreal forest with spruce and Balsam Fir, cold; in the north and east, with the usual cross-Canada birds, including Spruce Grouse, Boreal Owl, both three-toed woodpeckers, Blackpoll Warbler and Dark-eyed Junco.

Subalpine forest similar to above and occurring in all southern ranges of mountains, with many boreal species and others, including the Franklin's race of Spruce Grouse, Gray Jay, Varied Thrush, Hermit Thrush and both crossbills.

Alpine meadows, dry tundra, rock barrens, cold; and found at different elevations, dropping as you proceed north, with Golden Eagle, White-tailed Ptarmigan, Water Pipit, Rosy Finch and Golden-crowned Sparrow.

Montane forest with Douglas Fir, Ponderosa Pine, dry; featuring Swainson's Hawk, Black-billed Magpie, Clark's Nutcracker, Lewis' Woodpecker, Mountain Chickadee and Lazuli Bunting.

Grassland/steppe consisting of Bunchgrass, bitterbush and sage areas, very dry; with Sharp-tailed Grouse, Long-billed Curlew, White-throated Swift, Rock Wren and Western Meadowlark.

Dry coastal forest with Douglas Fir, Oak, dry/moist; home to California Quail, Bushtit, Bewick's Wren, Black-throated Gray Warbler and House Finch.

Wet coastal forest of Hemlock and Red Cedar, wet; hosting Pileated Woodpecker, Steller's Jay, Swainson's Thrush, Chestnut-backed Chickadee and Townsend's Warbler.

The sea and its shores, impossible to generalize, containing the famous Queen Charlotte Islands seabird colonies (petrels, murres, auklets and puffins, etc.); offshore cruises produce albatross, shearwaters, phalaropes, Sabine's Gull and members of the auk family; seashores can be very productive in rich areas such as some right in Victoria (but *not* in June); wintering water birds include Harlequin Duck, California, Mew, Heermann's and other gulls, Common Murre, Pigeon Guillemot, Marbled Murrelet, Ancient Murrelet and Rhinoceros Auklet.

If you wish to watch seabirds, come in spring (May/June) to the nesting colonies. These birds are often numerous along the coast in fall and winter. Shorebirds are best observed in May and again in August and September. Most lowland species nest from late May into July. Mountain birds usually nest from mid-June into July. A caution — snow may be deep into June and July in the high country.

The "hot spots" include: the Okanagan Valley, particularly Vaseux Lake, south of Penticton, for the Great Plains desert species, such as White-throated Swift, White-headed Woodpecker and Canyon Wren; the Queen Charlotte Islands for large numbers of seabirds in their colonies and Peregrine Falcon, but watch weather; Victoria for Eurasian Skylark on Saanich Peninsula and other sea and land birds at Clover Point year-round; Iona and Sea islands and the Fraser Delta, south of Vancouver, for rare birds and the largest concentrations of winter waterfowl in Canada; high elevation species in Mount Revelstoke National Park, Manning Provincial Park and Mount Seymour Provincial Park near Vancouver.

For a rushed visitor who wants to see the most species in a week: spend two days in the Okanagan Valley south of Penticton, around Vaseux Lake; one day in Manning Provincial Park after mid-June when the timberline road is open; two days on the Fraser Delta at the Reifel Refuge (Alaksen National Wildlife Area) and near the beaches at Iona and Sea islands, with a spotting scope; two days for Victoria, including Active Pass enroute by ferry for seabirds, Saanich Peninsula and airport for Eurasian Skylark, Mount Douglas Park on the north side of the city for dry forest, and Clover Point and Victoria Golf Club shores for wading and water birds.

Any one of these spots is worth at least a day or part of a day, but Victoria probably produces the most "looking time" for the least travel time. The next best site using this criterion would be the Okanagan Valley from Vaseux Lake south to the U.S. border.

The Vancouver rare bird alert telephone number is (604) 734-4554. The number in Victoria is (604) 478-8534. These numbers will give you information on rare or unusual birds in the area and also supply numbers of those birders "on call" to direct visiting people.

People in British Columbia are exceedingly friendly. For specific help, ask at the numerous local museums. Most communities throughout the province have one. Vancouver has several nature centres operated by the different municipalities and there are naturalist programs in many provincial and national parks. The provincial museum in Victoria contains a core of active birders. Drop in to see the best natural history displays in Canada. While there, check with the bird people to see what is around. For specific clubs, write The Federation of British Columbia Naturalists, P.O. Box 33797, Station D, Vancouver, B.C. V6J 4N8. Further information and maps are available from Tourism British Columbia, Parliament Buildings, Victoria, B.C. V8W 2Z2.

YORKE EDWARDS

Mount Revelstoke National Park

Mount Revelstoke offers some of the most accessible bird watching in the wet, rugged interior of British Columbia. A drive from the valley, with dense rain forest at 600 m, to the summit, in alpine tundra at over 1900 m, during late June should produce up to 50 species of birds in a day. Try for the grand slam of chickadees: four species in one day, one of the few accessible spots in Canada where you can accomplish this feat.

The area's mountain scenery and the wildflowers on Mount Revelstoke were so enjoyed that local citizens approached the federal government to have the area preserved as a national park in 1912. Two years later, a section of the rugged terrain in the Columbia Mountains was set aside as Mount Revelstoke National Park. The impressive Clachnacudainn Snowfield dominates the central region. A road linking the city of Revelstoke to the summit of the mountain was opened in 1927. The road provided access to three distinct natural areas: Columbia forest at the base; subalpine forest above 1300 m; alpine meadows and tundra which provide colourful floral carpets above 1900 m in August.

The park, with 260 km², lies adjacent to the city of Revelstoke on Highway 1, 80 km west of Rogers Pass. Greyhound bus and VIA Rail on CPR both make daily runs east and west through Revelstoke. The nearest commercial airport is at Kelowna, 200 km southwest, but you can land in a private aircraft at an airport at Revelstoke. Private transportation is necessary to explore the roads. Car rentals are available in Revelstoke. More than 65 km of established hiking trails wind through the park.

Motels, hotels and campsites are available in Revelstoke. There are no campgrounds within the park; however, Albert Canyon Hotsprings has wooded campsites at the northeast end, just outside the park. All services including police and hospital are available in the city.

Further assistance concerning the park is available from the Rogers Pass Centre. Telephone (604) 837-6274 and ask for a park naturalist. There are a variety of brochures, pamphlets and books on the park. Ask for them or write: The Superintendent, Mount Revelstoke National Park, P.O. Box 350, Revelstoke, B.C. V0E 2S0.

Birding Features

The Summit Road is generally open from late June to early October. Snow depths determine if it is partly or wholly closed the rest of the year. The best time for birds is late June, when up to fifty species may be observed in a day. This road provides an opportunity to achieve a grand slam in chickadees — Black-capped, Mountain, Boreal and Chestnut-backed. Begin at the bridge over the Columbia River at Revelstoke; proceed east for 1.6 km to the junction of the Mount Revelstoke Summit Road. Drive up this road making frequent stops as the elevation increases. Turn right at the sign for trailer parking, 3 km from the junction. Proceed to the end of this short road to explore the old fields in the abandoned ski development area. Many species present here, such as Nashville Warbler and American Redstart, are restricted to the valley bottom. Find Black-capped Chickadee here.

Move back to the main road and continue climbing. The next 6 km should yield typical wet-belt forest species, including Chestnut-backed Chickadee (your second species) and Townsend's and MacGillivray's Warblers. Just past the Five Mile Picnic Area at 8 km, watch for Blue Grouse along the road.

The forest and birdlife will change dramatically as you move into subalpine forest, 16 km from the bottom. Swainson's Thrush are replaced by Hermit Thrush. Pine Grosbeak and Red Crossbill are to be expected. Stop at the small wet flats opposite the cabin at about 19 km from the base. Mountain and Boreal Chickadees (to complete the grand slam) have been recorded here. This is also a good spot to look for Black and Vaux's Swifts, Three-toed Woodpecker and Olive-sided Flycatcher.

Continue to the summit, 26 km from the base. This area has a spectacular flower show in early to mid-August. Explore the many trails, including the Balsam Lake Picnic Area, just 1 km below the summit. Gray Jay and Fox Sparrow are sure to be around from June through early August. Hikers may want to continue into the alpine tundra on the trails to Eva Lake to the north and Jade Lake to the east. Northern Hawk-Owls have nested along the Eva Lake Trail in recent years. The hike to Jade Lake Pass, of 8 km and elevation 2160 m, is strenuous, but can yield such alpine tundra species as Golden Eagle, White-tailed Ptarmigan, Water Pipit and Rosy Finch.

The Trans-Canada Highway route begins at the bridge over the Columbia River at Revelstoke. Travel east for 18 km to the western park gate. Watch for Band-tailed Pigeon along this stretch. Continue for 13 km through the southern fringe of the park. Columbia forest habitat lines the highway. The first 8.7 km of this stretch, to the Skunk Cabbage Picnic Area, is a good spot in May and June for Steller's Jay, Chestnut-backed Chickadee and Western Tanager. At the Skunk Cabbage Area on the right, there is a small creek in which American Dippers are usually active. Check both up- and downstream, and use the footbridge. Skunk Cabbage Trail starts at this point and loops through a variety of wetland habitats. Magnolia Warbler and Black-headed Grosbeak are often found in the willow-alder bushes near the start of the trail. Rufous Hummingbird and several warblers, including Yellow, Townsend's and Common Yellowthroat, are regulars on the walk. Impressive skunk cabbage swamps make the hike worthwhile. Several species of *Empidonax* flycatchers call from the lowlands. Proceed east on the highway for another 2.6 km to the next picnic area on the left. Turning your car into this area across traffic is too dangerous, so proceed further east until you can make a safe U-turn. Go back to the picnic area and follow the signs into the Giant Cedars Picnic Area. The small creek nearby should produce American Dipper. A hike along the Giant Cedars Trail, beginning at the edge of the picnic site, will result in viewing several species of typical Columbia forest birds. Both Skunk Cabbage and Giant Cedars trails are snow free from early May to October, with ideal birding in June. High-country hiking is best done in August. There are few birds in winter, except the occasional influx of finches along the highway.

Some banding is done by the park naturalists. Watch for colour-marked Gray and Steller's Jays and report their colour combinations to the park naturalists.

JOHN G. WOODS

Creston Valley (West Kootenay)

The wetlands immediately west of Creston, surrounded by dry hills, provide opportunities to see over 238 species of birds. Even in the coldest month, January, a diligent search could furnish up to 80 species. Good all-weather roads, a checklist, a bird-finding driving guide for the area, Elk (Wapiti), White-tailed Deer and Coyote all add to the experience.

The Creston Valley Wildlife Interpretation Centre provides an excellent base from which to operate. Operated by the Canadian Wildlife Service (CWS), the centre is adjacent to 6480 ha of wetlands set aside for wildlife by the Creston Valley Wildlife Management Authority Act of B.C. The federal government, in cooperation with the B.C. government, built the interpretation centre. This complex of centre and site is part of the CWS plan to interpret the major regions of Canada.

The centre lies about 10 km west of Creston on Highway 3, the Crowsnest Pass route. Daily Greyhound bus service passes through Creston. Visitors can also be dropped off the bus on Highway 3, 0.5 km north of the wildlife centre.

Accommodation, groceries and gasoline are available in Creston, which has a good selection of visitor services. Several campgrounds exist in the region. The closest one is open in July and August at Summit Creek, 2.5 km north of the wildlife centre on Highway 3.

Drop into the interpretive centre for further assistance, including free copies of "Bird Finding in the Creston Valley" and "Checklist of Birds, Creston Valley Wildlife Interpretation Centre," and a book entitled *Waterfowl of the Creston Valley*, available from: Creston Valley Wildlife Centre, Box 1849, Creston, B.C. V0B 1G0, Telephone: (604) 428-9383.

Birding Features

In the early spring, from late February through March, waterfowl are abundant. They occur on the open water at the centre, in marshes off the Creston–Summit Creek Road, in Leach and Duck lakes and at the south end of Kootenay Lake. These sites contain dark vegetation and circulating underwater springs, both of which speed up the melting of ice. Shorebirds arrive later at these spots on spring and fall migration.

From mid-April to late June, the use of the local bird-finding guide (mentioned above) is most useful. The total driving time to cover the roads shown in the guide is about one hour, with no stops. It usually takes at least half a day if you want to get out of the car and look. At Summit Creek campground, at the start of the drive, Ospreys have a nest near the bridge at the picnic area. Pileated Woodpeckers live in the forest with Winter Wrens, Hammond's Flycatchers and others. At the wildlife centre, look at the variety of waterfowl. Upland birds nearby include Black-headed Grosbeak. At the next stop, on Lone Pine Hill and Corn Creek Dike, two species of hummingbird, the Rufous and Calliope, may be found, with Lazuli Bunting a rare possibility. Driving further along watch for Bobolink in the fields. At the Wynndel turnoff, Turkey Vultures are sometimes observed. Proceeding on, be prepared to spend some time at Duck Lake, which is one of the better

Flammulated Owl

birding spots in the valley. The tower, on site, provides an excellent viewing platform from which to look over the water and adjacent marshes. Birds of particular interest include Cinnamon Teal; the characteristic buzzing calls of Forster's Tern can be heard from cat-tail nest sites south of the road. The guide lists several additional species.

From August to late November, there are many birds in and around the water. As the ice begins to form near the end of the year, freezing is delayed in several sites because of dark vegetation, underwater springs and running streams. Birds concentrate at these open-water sites, making them quite productive for the bird watcher.

In the winter, from December through February, the key to finding birds is to locate feeding and shelter sites. Open water, caused by springs and running streams, is often teeming with birds. Other areas to search include livestock feedlots, orchards and back yards with trees and shrubs bearing fruit and seeds. Don't forget bird feeding stations. In the coldest month, January, there is still good birding from Highway 3A up to the south end of Kootenay Lake, on the road to Duck Lake, the Creston–Summit Creek road south to Twin Bridges; and north on the Nicks Island road. Observations from the Canyon-Lister Highway 21, South Creston circle route are worthwhile, too. Wild Turkeys are often seen in winter as well as the rest of the year. Short-eared Owls (nest locally) and Northern Pygmy-Owls are often seen in winter. Mountain and Chestnut-backed, as well as numerous Black-capped Chickadees are usually present.

Other birds found in the valley include Bald Eagles, which remain all year and nest locally. Virginia Rails are sometimes seen in summer. Vaux's Swift at times hawks for insects. Three of the four hummingbird species found locally have nested. These are Black-chinned, Rufous and Calliope; the fourth, Anna's, has been reported in the winter. The area is great for swallows, with six species reported to nest: Violet-green, Tree, Bank, Northern Rough-winged, Barn and Cliff.

ROBERT BUTLER, ED McMacKIN

21

Vaseux Lake

The Vaseux Lake area, south of Penticton, has been known for over a half a century as one of the prime birding areas in Canada. It has a high species diversity including migratory waterfowl. In addition, birds of the intermontane Great Basin to the south, such as White-throated Swift, White-headed Woodpecker and Canyon Wren, rare or unknown in other spots in Canada, may be seen here. This is one of the best places in B.C. to see Yellow-breasted Chat. The nearby cliffs are home to California Bighorn Sheep and the Pacific Rattlesnake.

The east shore, from Vaseux Lake Provincial Park south, is privately owned, together with some of the area south of the gravel road that leaves the park heading southeast. The island at the south end of the lake is also private property. The remainder of the shoreline belongs to the federal government and is administered by the Canadian Wildlife Service (CWS) as a wildlife sanctuary. The cliffs to the east are also administered by the CWS as California Bighorn Sheep range. There are no restrictions to hiking on the cliffs. Motorboats are prohibited on the lake.

The first settlers arrived around the turn of the century, including the well-known naturalist and writer, H. J. Parham. Early ornithologists, including Taverner and Brooks, led collecting expeditions to the area in the 1920s. The lake and adjacent shoreline were made a wildlife refuge in 1923. The Okanagan River was channelled in the 1950s resulting in a lowered water table and a reduction in the size of the marsh at the north end of the lake.

The good birding area around the lake is about 12 km^2, with the lake 4 km long and 1 km wide. The lake and park lie 16 km south of the Penticton International Airport and 6 km south of Okanagan Falls, on Highway 97.

There is one motel, the Sundial, at the south end of Vaseux Lake, with others nearby on Highway 97 and in Okanagan Falls. The Okanagan Game Farm, with a wide variety of big game animals, is near Okanagan Falls. Vaseux Lake Provincial Park contains nine camping spots. Okanagan Falls Provincial Park, with twenty units, is about 6 km north of the lake. There are seven camping sites at Inkaneep Provincial Park, about 5 km south of the lake. The nearest gas and service stations are at Okanagan Falls to the north of the lake, and Gallagher Lake to the south. Specific tourist information on the region may be obtained from: OK Corral, P.O. Box 240, Okanagan Falls, B.C., Telephone: (604) 497-8252.

Additional reading on the area is available: H. J. Parham, *A Nature Lover in British Columbia*, 1937; R. A. Cannings, R. J. Cannings and S. G. Cannings, *Birds of the Okanagan Valley, British Columbia*, Occasional Paper, B.C. Provincial Museum, in press.

A checklist of the birds of the Okanagan Valley is available from: South Okanagan Naturalists' Club, 465 Ellis Street, Penticton, B.C.

For a contact and additional help, get in touch with: Steve Cannings, 705 Sunglo Drive, R.R.3, Penticton, B.C. V2A 7K8, Telephone: (604) 492-2303.

Birding Features

Habitat for birds in this area includes *Typha/Scirpus* marsh and wet meadows at the north end of the lake; birch, alder and willow thickets at the

Pygmy Nuthatch

northeast corner, along the west shore and at the southwest corner; dry Ponderosa Pine forest with grassland on the northeast side below and above the cliffs near Vaseux Lake Provincial Park; and the cliffs overlooking the park. The most productive birding can be done in a day or less on the northeast side of the lake where all habitats are readily available to a hiker. The gravel road that goes southeast from the park provides easy access to the cliffs and dry forest. Climb up the cliffs via the powerline right-of-way at the point where the gravel road crosses Irrigation Creek.

A number of birds are year-round residents. For Canada Geese this lake is a major breeding site; Golden and Bald Eagles are often seen; Sharp-tailed Grouse, once extirpated, are now returning but are seldom seen; California Quails are common, as are Chukar; White-headed Woodpeckers are rare but can be found; Black-billed Magpies, Clark's Nutcrackers, Mountain Chickadees and the three nuthatches (the White-breasted, Red-breasted and Pygmy) are all common; Marsh Wrens are common in summer, but uncommon in winter; Canyon Wrens are fairly common along the cliffs; Townsend's Solitaires and Cassin's Finches are common; Red Crossbills are irregular but fairly common.

Winter visitors include a great variety of waterfowl if all or part of the lake remains open. Tundra Swans are uncommon and Trumpeter Swans are rare. Bohemian Waxwings are uncommon; Northern Shrikes are fairly common; Rosy Finches and Snow Buntings are rare and irregular visitors.

During the peak times of migration in April and November, large numbers of most fresh-water Pacific Flyway waterfowl pass through. There are no mudflats, and thus few migrating shorebirds stop. American White Pelicans rarely pass through. Snow Geese are casual visitors, as are Harlequin Ducks which sometimes overwinter.

Summer birds arrive in late March and April to breed. They include the odd American Bittern and Osprey; Caspian Terns sometimes are casual visitors; Common Poorwills appear along the gravel road near the cliffs and White-throated Swifts are common here. The following four hummingbird species occur: Calliope is the most common, Black-chinned is uncommon, Anna's is rare and Rufous is fairly common. All hummingbirds are best observed along Irrigation Creek. Lewis' Woodpeckers are fairly common and Williamson's Sapsuckers occur in the larch forests to the east at higher elevations. To see the latter species travel the gravel roads either to the north or south of Shuttleworth Creek canyon, which lies east of Okanagan Falls. The south road from the canyon is usable with permission of the logging company; the office is located at the base of the road. Say's Phoebes are fairly common; Dusky Flycatchers are common. Look at the base of the cliffs for the fairly common Rock Wren. Veerys are fairly common in the thickets along the lake shore. Two bluebird species, Western and Mountain, are fairly common. Yellow-breasted Chats may be found in the dense thickets, especially along the old railroad right-of-way at the southwest end of the lake. Bobolinks are sometimes seen on the meadows at the south end of the lake. Black-headed Grosbeaks inhabit the thickets along the lake shore. Lazuli Buntings and Lark Sparrows are fairly common.

ROBERT A. CANNINGS, RICHARD J. CANNINGS, SYDNEY G. CANNINGS

Iona Island and Sea Island

These islands are best known as the place where the largest number of rare birds have been seen in B.C. Tidal marshes, upland fields and the sewage lagoon attract them. Even the rare Burrowing Owl has been spotted here.

Once two islands in the mouth of the Fraser River, they are now joined by a causeway. Most of Sea Island on the west belongs to the Ministry of Transport and has been developed as the Vancouver International Airport. Most of Iona Island is owned by the Greater Vancouver district and has been developed into a sewage treatment and settling pond project. A 1.5-km-long causeway projects northwest out to sea and serves to divert the flow of effluent into the Strait of Georgia. There is no access to or from the airport grounds, but bird watching is encouraged in the sewage lagoons and on the causeway. Bird watchers are requested to use the sign-in register, which also serves as a guide to the latest rarities that have been noted.

The causeway and islands have extensive mudflats which are covered completely twice each day by tide. Make sure to check tide tables before coming out. The 0.8 to 1.2 km accessible waterfront has soft mud. Be careful!

You reach the area by car, south from Vancouver on Highway 99, over the Oak Street Bridge. Take the *first* exit to the airport. *Do not* take the new Art Laing Bridge to the airport. Alternatively, coming from the south, follow the airport signs from Highway 99. The road in leads past some motels and factories, over the Middle Arm of the Fraser River. As soon as you leave the freeway, start watching for Crested Myna (an import). Take the first right past the bridge (flashing light) and drive beside, and then under, the new bridge. Keep adjacent to the airport property and watch for raptors such as Rough-legged Hawk and Northern Harrier, especially in winter. The road turns sharp right and becomes MacDonald; continue on it until at about 0.8 km further you pass the intersection of Ferguson Road. In winter watch for raptors including several owls and Northern Shrike. Continue on and after curving right and crossing a causeway, you'll be on Iona Island.

With no car, take the bus to the airport and then hitch-hike from the entrance in. Numerous birders use the area, so you should be able to obtain a ride easily.

The Canadian Wildlife Service operates a banding station here in spring and fall. If you'd like to volunteer, contact them at: Canadian Wildlife Service, 5421 Robertson Road, Delta, B.C., Telephone: (604) 946-8546.

Birding Features

This, the best-known birding spot in the lower mainland, has produced Spoonbill Sandpiper, Ruff, Curlew Sandpiper, Rufous-necked Stint, Sharp-tailed Sandpiper, Hudsonian Godwit, and Red and Red-necked Phalaropes. Stints and other Siberian and Eurasian shorebirds have also appeared. Water birds like Common Moorhen show up from time to time too. Anything can appear. It is a treat to search the flocks for something new. The sewage lagoon draws thousands of gulls; the mudflats bring shorebirds and the Iona Island sewage jetty hosts a horde of water birds.

This is the northern limit for wintering Dunlin and Sanderling in large numbers. It is also the southern breeding limit for Semipalmated Plover and the western record for nesting Yellow-headed Blackbird.

Fall migration begins in early July and continues through October. August is a bit slower than the other months. Fall is the best season for shorebirds. Up to two thousand Dunlins and many Sanderlings have been found here in late October. They are also the most abundant shorebirds in winter. Spring migration is much shorter, lasting from late April to late May.

Winter birding can be good for raptors, including Red-tailed and Rough-legged Hawks, Northern Harrier, Gyrfalcon, Peregrine Falcon and Short-eared Owl. The largest number of waterfowl in Canada overwinter along these shores and further south. Watch for Lapland Longspur and Snow Bunting on the nearby fields.

A visitor to Iona should try to have a spotting scope as birds are often far out on the vast mudflats at low tide. At high tide, they congregate in the sewage ponds, making identification much easier. Upon arrival, go through the gates into the plant. If the gates are closed, open them, drive in, and then close them, as special arrangements have been made to accommodate birders. Park in the visitor area on the right and sign in on the birders' register. On your way out, write any rarities in the book to alert newcomers.

Most of the smaller shorebirds will be Western Sandpiper, but check for Least, and possibly Semipalmated and Baird's. Both species of yellowlegs and dowitchers should be here. Most of the latter should be Long-billed, but there are some Short-billed too. From mid-September to October watch for Stilt and Sharp-tailed Sandpiper. Red-necked Phalarope comes in the fall.

Scrutinize the many Bonaparte's and Mew Gulls for the rarer gulls. Franklin's are generally present in September. Examine the large pond outside the fence for a variety of waterfowl. Tufted Duck has turned up at times out here. Caspian Tern has often occurred in late summer.

WAYNE CAMPBELL, D. MARKS

Fraser Estuary and Reifel Refuge

The Fraser Estuary, south of Vancouver, provides the most important wintering waterfowl habitat on the West Coast. The area also supports the largest number of wintering waterfowl in Canada. Birds come from three continents: Asia (U.S.S.R.), North and South America. The marshes host 20,000 wintering Snow Geese and 100 Tundra and Trumpeter Swans. Over 20 species of birds of prey have been reported. Many are attracted to the George C. Reifel Migratory Bird Sanctuary, or as it is more commonly called, the Reifel Refuge. Over 250 species have been recorded at the refuge.

Most of the estuary, including Westham Island on which the refuge is situated, is privately owned, diked and farmed. The extreme northwest end of Westham Island, including Reifel Island, is owned by the federal government. Part of these holdings are leased to a private organization, the British Columbia Waterfowl Society. They operate the public area within the refuge. An admission charge to enter their facilities helps offset costs. Visiting hours from May through October are from 9:00 A.M. to 5:00 P.M. and from November through April are 9:00 A.M. to 4:00 P.M..

The approximately 400-ha refuge lies on the centre-west side of the estuary. You reach it by driving south from Vancouver on Highway 99 to Highway 17; then west on Highway 10 to River Road; continue west on River for about 2.8 km to the Westham Island Bridge on the right. Cross the bridge and stay on the main road. In winter, this road is good for raptors. Continue for about 4.8 km to the turnoff to the refuge on the left. Alternatively, if coming in from the east, proceed west off Highway 99 to Highway 10; follow it to River Road and take River to the refuge gate. The site contains ample parking, a nature interpretation house, feeding stations where waterfowl congregate, walking trails and viewing towers.

Bus service from the downtown Vancouver bus station (pick-up along the route too) takes passengers to the Tsawwassen ferry landing. You can be dropped off at the intersection of Highways 10 and 17, which is about 14 km from the refuge.

Motels, shopping centres, RCMP and a hospital are all available at Ladner about 11 to 16 km away. There are several private campgrounds along Highway 17 near the ferry dock site. Environment Canada has produced an excellent booklet on the estuary, *Explore the Fraser Estuary!*, by Peggy Ward. The book is available for $3.95 from most bookstores and: Canadian Government Publishing Centre, Supply and Services, Hull, Quebec K1A 0S9. Some of the material for this site was taken from this publication. Information on the refuge and trail maps may be obtained by writing to:

Interpretive Section, Canadian Wildlife Service, Box 340, Delta, B.C. V4K 3Y3, or Waterfowl Manager, British Columbia Waterfowl Society, 5191 Robertson Road, Delta, B.C. V4K 2N2, Telephone: (604) 946-6980.

Birding Features

The variety and abundance of suitable food at the mouth of the Fraser River attract millions of waterfowl and shorebirds each year. Staff at the refuge feed these birds, making the spot a veritable hive of activity in winter. In spring and fall shorebirds are numerous and raptors winter in abundance.

The migration influx begins in late August, increases through September and October, and peaks in November and December. Birds begin to leave at the end of March, with most gone by May. June and July are very quiet with few around.

For the past few years almost a hundred Tundra and Trumpeter Swans have used the marshes off Brunswick Point, immediately south of Westham Island and Canoe Passage. The Trumpeter Swan, largest of the world's waterfowl with a two-metre wingspan, and weighing up to 18 kg, will stay here all winter before moving inland to breed.

Local groups and clubs have raised and released 2900 Canada Geese in the Fraser Valley since 1973. Today, there are between 5000 and 6000 of these birds resident. Snow Geese winter feed on the bullrushes, sedges and agricultural lands near the marshes. Arrivals begin in late October, with peak numbers of 20,000 or so in late December. They depart in March-April on their way to Wrangel Island, off the coast of northeastern Siberia. Brants are seldom seen during the fall migration as they pass through further offshore. However, in the spring, in April, they come close to land, in numbers of 20,000 to 30,000.

Dabbling ducks are attracted to the tidal marshes for the abundant food in early fall. During the hunting season of October to January, they use the estuary, particularly the refuge, for loafing sites in the daytime. At dusk, they fly inland to feed on the unharvested crops and weeds in flooded fields. During the very cold periods when the fields freeze, the ducks go to the marshes, which are relatively ice-free because of salt water and tidal action. In March, they return again to the marshes because of decreased rainfall and resultant dry fields. Several species breed in the estuary, including Mallard, Gadwall and Cinnamon Teal. The Wood Duck is common on the refuge, but seldom seen outside. This is probably the best place near Vancouver to spot the Eurasian Wigeon.

Diving ducks prefer the Boundary Bay region, south of the Boundary Bay Airport, immediately south of the intersection of Highways 99 and 10. At high tide you can observe, close at hand, White-winged and Surf Scoters, Common Goldeneye, Greater and Lesser Scaup, and Oldsquaw; Harlequin Ducks are often seen in numbers as are Hooded and Common Mergansers. Another good spot for diving ducks at high tide is along the ramp to the ferry at Tsawwassen.

Over 20 species of raptors are comparatively abundant. This is one of the few wintering sites for these birds in B.C. Bald Eagles congregate in large numbers in February prior to moving inland in April. One or more pairs nest on the refuge. Red-tailed and Rough-legged Hawks and Northern Harrier are common. Peregrine Falcon and Merlin are seen often. Owls, including Snowy, which sit on fence posts in green fields in winter, are fairly common. The Great Horned Owl nests on the refuge. On the way to the refuge, or on a drive in the estuary area, stop at any farm for Common Barn-Owl. Many of these buildings are sanctuaries to these birds of prey (38 on Westham Island).

The extensive mudflats provide feeding sites for an estimated five million migrating shorebirds of 38 species each fall and spring. Thousands spend the winter. From May to early June and again from July through October are the best times. Sharp-tailed Sandpipers may be found in late September and early October. Flocks of 5000 to 10,000 Dunlins are noted regularly all winter. Great Blue Herons have at least one rookery in the area and are quite common wherever you drive. Nesting marsh birds are best spotted from May through July and include American Bittern, Virginia Rail and Marsh Wren.

WAYNE CAMPBELL

Vancouver

A metropolitan community of more than a million people, greater Vancouver contains parks, forests, beaches and lakes, all close to mountains. This habitat diversity attracts at least 238 species of birds regularly. Of these, at least 140 nest. An additional 70-plus species have been sighted less than twenty times. The maritime climate allows a birder to list over 50 species quickly at any time of the year. Wintering water and shore birds include Western Grebe, Pelagic Cormorant, Harlequin Duck, Barrow's Goldeneye, Black Turnstone and Pigeon Guillemot.

Founded in 1862 as Gastown (after "Gassy Jack" Deighton, who built a saloon in twenty-four hours with the help of lumberjacks), the ramshackle frame-building settlement prospered. Incorporated in April of 1886, the community was wiped out by a forest fire in June of that same year. By the end of 1886, citizens were erecting more permanent brick and stone structures. The large influx of Europeans after the Second World War turned the city into a cosmopolitan community. The zoo, botanic gardens, art galleries, museum and the revitalized Gastown shopping area, in combination with bird watching, make a three-day visit worthwhile.

The major international airport on the southern fringe, and the western terminus of VIA Rail and Greyhound international bus service all provide easy access to the city.

Vancouver contains a variety of accommodations. If you plan on visiting Stanley Park and Zoo (see below), the Denman Place Inn is recommended. A visitor to Seymour Provincial Park (see below) could stay at the Coach House, which is medium priced and recommended.

The Vancouver Natural History Society operates a "Bird Alert" (hot line): (604) 734-4554. When you dial this number, you obtain an extra service (in addition to location of rare birds) — the telephone numbers of members "on call" to help visiting birders.

Major contacts: Jude and Al Grass, #202 — 6444 Silver Avenue, Burnaby, B.C. V5H 2Y4, Telephone: (604) 437-7194, or Al Grass, Naturalist, B.C. Parks and Outdoor Recreation Division, 1610 Indian River Drive, North Vancouver, B.C. V7G 1L3, Telephone (604) 929-1291. For Mount Seymour Provincial Park, contact the above or: Wayne Weber, #303 — 9153 Saturna Drive, Burnaby, B.C. V3J 7K1, Telephone (604) 421-2020.

Birding Features

Stanley Park. Named after the Lord Stanley of Stanley Cup hockey fame, the park is owned and operated by the city of Vancouver. The park has a zoo with a collection of exotic birds and mammals, and includes the Vancouver Public Aquarium. The total area of 2470 ha is located on a peninsula at the mouth of Burrard Inlet. A half-hour walk northwest from the downtown core will get you there. By bus, you catch the Stanley Park bus from downtown and disembark at the main entrance next to Lost Lagoon. An automobile driver would take Highway 1A and 99 and watch for the turnoff on the right from the freeway at the main entrance on the south end of the park. Be careful that you exit at the park entrance or you'll get onto the causeway — there is no getting off until you are over the Lions' Gate Bridge. Before entering the park, pick up a map and brochure at the entrance.

The park was logged selectively in the early part of the century, with hazardous trees still being removed. Logging has resulted in the creation of forest edge habitat. Extensive areas are cleared for gardens, which attract urban birds. Habitats include rocky shores, sandy beaches, offshore waters, forests, gardens and a lake. The best birding walk (two to three hours) is from the bus loop at the park entrance, along the south side of Lost Lagoon, over the stone arch bridge, then to the sea wall on the edge of the inlet; take the sea wall north, about halfway to the lip of the peninsula to Ferguson Point, and then cut east via a forest trail, back to Lost Lagoon and the park entrance. This walk usually produces 60 to 70 bird species with no trouble. You may wish to continue beyond Ferguson Point, right around the tip (a total of 11 km) to Lumberman's Arch on the east side, and then back through the zoo to the entrance. Take another shorter walk east from the main gate along the shore to Brockton Point, then northwest to Lumberman's Arch and again back through the zoo to the main entrance. You can drive around the periphery of the park, stopping for a short stroll.

There are other trails that crisscross through the forest. A good inland hike may be taken to Beaver Lake and then around the shore. The lake is reached by road or pathway, from the sea wall about halfway between Lumberman's Arch and the Lions' Gate Bridge to the north. Beaver Lake contains the only bit of real marsh in the park.

Stanley Park is probably the best birding area for wintering waterfowl around the lower mainland of B.C. Look for Western Grebe, Pelagic Cormorant, Harlequin Duck, Barrow's Goldeneye, Black Turnstone and Pigeon Guillemot. Nearby forests contain Red-breasted Sapsucker, Winter Wren, Brown Creeper, and Black-throated Gray and Townsend's Warblers. Species diversity is best from mid-November to mid-March. Summer is fairly

Black Turnstone

Harlequin Duck

quiet. Rarities are showing up continually, including Ruddy Turnstone, Rusty Blackbird, Tufted Duck and Black Phoebe. Great Blue Herons are common as they nest in the area of the zoo. Look for these birds on the mudflats at low tide. Lost Lagoon has a good variety of wintering waterfowl, including Redhead, Canvasback, Ring-necked Duck, Lesser and Greater Scaups, Wood Duck, Common and Barrow's Goldeneyes, Mallard, and Red-breasted and Common Mergansers. Double-crested Cormorants often rest on the fountain. Gulls include Ring-billed, California, Herring, Glaucous-winged, Mew and Bonaparte's.

Burnaby Lake. Located east of downtown Vancouver, between Highways 1 and 7, off Sperling Avenue (on the west side of the park), or off Cariboo Road (on the east side), the lake and surrounding park have been known by bird watchers for many years. The area became a regional park in 1972. You'll find the nature house on the north side. This centre is open in summer. You can pick up brochures here or write: Burnaby Parks, 2294 W. 10 Ave., Vancouver, B.C. V6K 2H9, Telephone: (604) 731-1155.

This is one of the few fresh-water lakes and marshes near Vancouver in which large concentrations of waterfowl are observed. During the fall, hundreds of Green-winged Teals stop on their way south, with many overwintering. American Coots and Mallards are there in large numbers, with some Northern Shovelers, Wood Ducks and a scattering of other species, until spring.

Mount Seymour Provincial Park. The 3508-ha park lies immediately adjacent to Vancouver. Take Highway 1 (the freeway) over the Second Narrows Bridge. Turn east shortly after the bridge and follow signs for 3 km to the park entrance. Ask for a bird checklist, park brochure, tree information and other material at the park office at the entrance. Elevation rises from 100 m at the gate, up the twisting and turning road to 1000 m at the base of the chair lift to the top. Lower slopes of the park were logged in the 1920s, with a resultant present growth of cedars mixed with Western Hemlock forest below 900 m. Above this height, Mountain Hemlock prevails.

The excellent checklist and park brochure provide good information about birds to see at several stops, and about trails to walk along the road to the top. This area gives ready road access to coastal subalpine habitats adjacent to the city. The snow usually does not leave the higher elevations until mid-June. The lower elevations are therefore the best sites in late spring, from mid-May to mid-June. You should spot a Gray Jay, Rosy Finch, and Red and White-winged Crossbills. You may also sight a Solitary Vireo and several warblers, including Black-throated Gray, Townsend's and Wilson's. Bring along a tape recorder to call up the Northern Pygmy-Owl and Western Screech-Owl. At Deep Cove Roadside Lookout at the start of the Perimeter Trail, look in summer for Black and Vaux's Swifts. Watch along the way for a Red-breasted Sapsucker.

If you are in the area from November through May, try exploring on snowshoes or cross-country skis. Check at the park office for recreation brochures.

JUDE AND AL GRASS

Active Pass

Active Pass, a channel of public, navigable sea, lies between Galiano and Mayne islands on the ferry trip between Vancouver and Victoria (Tsawwassen to Swartz Bay). Waters often race and boil through the pass, influenced by the tides. These upswellings make the pass a place of outstanding biological richness, attracting spectacular concentrations of water birds. The entire channel is worthwhile; however, the western third is usually the most prolific. There can also be significant concentrations of birds up to 0.5 km beyond the mouths of the channel.

California and Northern Sea Lions are often spotted in the water on the south side just as you enter the pass from the west or coming from the east. The California Sea Lion has increased in this area in the past ten years.

The pass is most easily accessible by the car ferry. Ride the windy bow through the pass. Dress warmly from September to May. Local island ferries also ply the channel to visit the many islands. Seasonal timetables are available from the B.C. tourist offices along the highways or by writing to their headquarters in Victoria. The more leisurely approach is to rent or charter a small local boat from people in the small communities on either side of the pass at Saltspring Island or near Swartz Bay. However, watch carefully as these are dangerous waters, both from the churning tides and the big ships that regularly ply the channel. These big boats cannot stop or turn quickly!

Visitors usually stay in Vancouver or Victoria. However, the B.C. Ministry of Tourism publishes an annual list of motels and hotels in the province. Accommodation on Mayne and Galiano islands is detailed within this tourist booklet. Tiny communities on these islands also offer most village services, such as groceries and gasoline.

For further help refer to a weekly study from September to May on the area: "Birds Seen in Active Pass, British Columbia," by R. Y. Edwards, in the British Columbia Provincial Museum Annual Report for 1964, pp. 19–23, now out of print.

Birding Features

The best birding is when ebbing or flooding tides produce strong currents. Few birds feed during slack water, appearing to scatter to other sites. The area is a favoured wintering location for a number of species. The dominant species, in season, are: Arctic Loon, Western Grebe, Brandt's Cormorant, Glaucous-winged, Bonaparte's and Mew Gulls, and Common Murre. The Brandt's Cormorants are especially interesting, since almost all of these birds nest south of British Columbia, some as far away as California. Storms bring in and hold occasional pelagics including Sooty Shearwater, Fork-tailed Storm-Petrel, Sabine's Gull and others.

In summer, June and July, there are few birds. Pigeon Guillemot are resident throughout the year. Bald Eagles nest locally and are seen in numbers later on in winter, with a dozen or more resting on trees or fishing in concentrations of feeding seabirds.

The greatest numbers of seabirds occur from September to May, with

March the best month. In September and October, Bonaparte's Gulls peak in abundance (as many as 5000); Heermann's Gull arrives from Mexico and is most numerous. As fall moves into winter other birds come to feed. White-winged Scoters are there; Glaucous-winged and Mew Gulls remain high in numbers (200–400) all season. Pigeon Guillemots are numerous. With luck, you can also see Parasitic Jaeger, Marbled Murrelet, Rhinocerous Auklet and other pelagic species. If you are good with gulls, try for Thayer's; they are sometimes numerous in winter. By February, Brandt's Cormorants reach maximum numbers of up to 4000, as do Common Murres, with up to 1500 seen. By April, Arctic Loons climax in abundance (1000–2500), as do Western Grebes, with as many as 1000. Bonaparte's Gulls reach their record peak in April and May.

YORKE EDWARDS

Saanich Peninsula — Victoria Airport

The Saanich Peninsula, on Vancouver Island, is the only place in Canada where a Eurasian Skylark can be seen. Transported from Great Britain near the turn of the century, the birds quickly adapted and were once much more common than they are today. They still can be seen in numbers, especially at the Victoria International Airport. Human activity has modified the landscape somewhat over the past one hundred years, but the impact has not been excessive. Haying is the only disturbance within the airport property. Nearby farmland is mainly pasture and hayfields. Thus the whole area is good habitat for upland birds.

Victoria International Airport lies 24 km north of Victoria and west of Sidney. Private vehicle access is via Patricia Bay Highway 17, north 24 km from Victoria to the traffic light in Sidney at Beacon Avenue. Turn west to the loop road around the airport (see below). Visitors from the south can arrive from Port Angeles, Washington, on the Black Ball Ferry to Victoria, and then proceed north on Highway 17. Those coming from Vancouver and the mainland arrive at the dock at the Swartz Bay ferry terminal. Proceed south on Highway 17 for approximately 4.5 km to the traffic light on Beacon Avenue and turn west to the drive around the airport. Bus travellers take the airport bus from the downtown terminal in Victoria to the airport terminal building.

Air travellers may come in via Air Canada, Pacific Western Airlines or CP Air.

Accommodation is available near the airport at Sidney. There are numerous motels, hotels and trailer parks on the road to and in Victoria. Check with the B.C. tourist bureau for a comprehensive list of these, plus provincial campgrounds. The campsite at Goldstream Provincial Park just outside Victoria, on Highway 1, is recommended. Automobile service is available at a variety of stations around Sidney. Emergency police service may be had at the RCMP detachment at Sidney, telephone (604) 656-3931. To locate other sites in the area or for further information dial the Victoria Bird Alert number at (604) 478-8534.

Birding Features

To see skylarks throughout the year, take the roads that circle the airport. Turn west off Highway 17 on Beacon Avenue; proceed west to the end of Beacon and turn north to Mills Road; travel west along Mills through good skylark habitat that persists to West Saanich Road. Make frequent stops on this stretch of Mills; get out, look and listen. Continue west to the end of Mills; turn south for a short distance on West Saanich Road; turn left or southeast on the first private road that lies adjacent to the airport fence. Follow this road around to the terminal building area. Skylarks are quite numerous on the last stretch of this road, east, west and south of the terminal building. After exploring the area continue on southeast, then swing north on Canora Road; proceed to the far north end of Canora. The end of Canora, at the airport fence, is probably the best single spot to see and hear skylarks, both inside and outside the airport. Return south to McTavish Road; swing east to Highway 17 and back to where you are staying.

Other birds to be seen are of course seasonal. In summer, Killdeer and Savannah Sparrow are common. At the southwest corner of the airport, in marshy places, look for Mallard, which are year-round residents, as are Red-winged Blackbirds. The woods to the south of the creek, outside the airport, are good for Yellow Warbler and White-crowned Sparrow in summer, and Golden-crowned Sparrow in winter.

In winter the airport is productive, particularly when heavy rains flood the fields. Watch for Black-bellied Plover and Dunlin, which sometimes occur in hundreds. Raptors are abundant in winter. Look for Northern Harrier and American Kestrel. Short-eared Owls are seen often. In some years, Snowy Owls too may be observed. The nearby ocean, on both sides of the peninsula, provides good birding in winter. On the west side, at Patricia Bay, White-winged, Surf and Black Scoters all may be seen. The bay is good for Common Loons, with the occasional Arctic or Red-throated Loon. Look for Red-necked, Horned and Western Grebes and a variety of ducks, including Mallard, American Wigeon and Common Goldeneye. On the east side, at Bazan Bay, all of the above birds may be spotted. This east side is one of the better sites in the region to observe Black Scoter. From late March through April, both bays are good for Brant.

HAROLD HOSFORD

Clover Point, Victoria

Clover Point, the southernmost piece of land in the city of Victoria, is part of the Beacon Hill Municipal Park shoreline. The point is one of Canada's best urban sites to view a variety of birds, with well over 160 species reported. An impressive number of rarities have been sighted through many decades of careful observation.

Once a military preserve and rifle range, the point later became part of a roadway with cropped grass and some wild roses around the edges. A sewage outfall and pumping station were installed inconspicuously. However, landscaping around the station destroyed the point as habitat for a few upland passerine species.

Land at the point is flat, but high enough above sea level to deflect all but extremely severe storms. The areal extent is small: a triangle perhaps 100 metres across the base and 400 metres from base to tip. A commanding view of the rich waters surrounding the point and its projection seaward are its attractions to birders.

Access from the Provincial Museum, in the centre of the city, is either a quick drive or a pleasant 3-km walk. Drive to the south (sea) end of Douglas Street, which happens to be Kilometre 0 of the Trans-Canada Highway. Proceed east on Dallas Road along the sea to the point. The walk through Beacon Hill Park to the sea should produce Chestnut-backed Chickadee and Bushtit; hike east 1.5 km along the scenic sea cliff, walking to the point.

Accommodations, including motels, hotels and campgrounds, are scattered throughout Victoria. Check with the local tourist office near the museum for specifics.

The nearest pay telephone, groceries and service station lie west on Dallas Road to Cook Street and north 1.5 km on Cook.

For further information on the site, including an excellent article giving specific months for many species, refer to: "Birds Seen from Clover Point, Victoria, B.C.," by R. Y. Edwards and David Sterling, in the British Columbia Provincial Museum Annual Report for 1962, pp. 19–26, now out of print.

Birding Features

Water birds are the species to be found at Clover Point. The site is noted for rare species and as the place for people from east of the Rockies to see western birds. Rich waters, and shelter provided by the point, attract waifs; the point is also an area of winter residence for an impressive assemblage of birds. It serves as a place for migrants to stop and feed. After heavy storms, pelagics such as Sooty Shearwater and Sabine's Gull may occur.

June and July are the quiet months with few individuals and fewer species. August to May is the season with a constant base of grebes (Western and Horned), ducks (Greater Scaups dominate, with numbers up to 500 in December and January; Harlequin, scoters and Bufflehead, etc.), Pigeon Guillemot, shorebirds (American Black Oystercatcher all year, Black Turnstone, Surfbird, Rock Sandpiper, etc.), gulls (Glaucous-winged and Mew); more seasonally and for shorter time periods you'll see Common Goldeneye, and California and Bonaparte's Gulls. In September, look for Heermann's Gull up from Mexico. With luck and the right season, there may be Wandering Tattler, Red and Red-necked Phalarope (Red mostly seen in mid-October), Common Murre, Marbled Murrelet, Ancient Murrelet and Rhinoceros Auklet. Many of these birds will be further out and are best surveyed with a spotting telescope.

While most rarities are seen irregularly, a few are noted annually, like the Yellow-billed Loon around December, and Franklin's Gull. Less frequent are such occurrences as Short-tailed and Flesh-footed Shearwaters, Emperor Goose, Marbled Godwit, Common Black-headed and Little Gulls.

YORKE EDWARDS

Pacific Rim National Park

The first national marine park, Pacific Rim is located on the west coast of Vancouver Island and includes islands, seacoast and long beaches, deep forest, bog and muskegs. Nearly 260 species of birds have been reported, with 57 breeding residents and an additional 17, including all three scoters, Harlequin Duck, Black-footed Albatross and Northern Fulmar, present throughout the year. Spot the Northern Sea Lions at the Sea Lion Rocks and watch a Gray Whale as it feeds or "plays" in the bays.

The Nootka people, who were here when James Cook landed at Nootka Island about 90 km north of Long Beach in 1778, were wealthy compared to inland tribes. The forests, and particularly the sea, supplied an abundance of food. They had established more or less permanent villages that changed with the season. The excess of food allowed time for them to become skilled at basket-weaving and design. Warfare was common between villages to obtain slaves, booty, prestige and revenge.

Cook found Sea Otter and brought back a few pelts. The rush was on to obtain these silken trophies that could be had for a few pennies and sold in the Orient for $120. Within a few years, the otters were gone. Then came the whalers, who nearly exterminated the Gray Whale. In the 1870s sealskin became fashionable. The huge herds of fur seals migrating from California to the Pribilof Islands, in the Bering Sea, were decimated. At about the same time, smallpox and other white man's diseases took most of the native people. White settlers moved in to use the salmon, and a major fishing industry was begun which continues today. Tofino and Ucluelet are both major fishing centres. The road between these two communities was completed in 1942. Highway 4, linking this road to the main traffic artery on the east side, was finished in 1959. The sandy beaches were now accessible and quickly became very popular. Public pressure was exerted for a national park, culminating in the establishment of Pacific Rim National Park in 1970.

This national park comprises three sections of land and sea. The Long Beach unit consists of 55 km^2, with two major beaches stretching 16 km and 6.4 km long. The Broken Islands Group consists of about a hundred islands and rocks located within Barkley Sound. They, and the adjacent waters, comprise about 58 km^2. The third unit, the West Coast Trail, is primarily a hiking trail, 73 km long, and contains the historic Lifesaving Trail, built for the use of shipwrecked sailors who survived this "Graveyard of the Pacific." Over forty ships have gone down off this coast.

The park is reached via Highways 4 and 105 west of Port Alberni, or by boat or airplane. The Orient Stage Line operates a bus service from Port Alberni to Ucluelet and Tofino year-round. The Alberni Marine Transport Company in Port Alberni runs the MV *Lady Rose*, a 100-passenger mail and cargo vessel, from Port Alberni to Ucluelet from June 1 to mid-September. There is an airfield operated by the Ministry of Transport at Tofino, behind the north end of Long Beach. The field is not lit for night flying. There are three concrete runways, each 1525 m. Aviation gas is available. Float planes can obtain aviation gas and mooring at Ucluelet and at the Pacific Rim Airline dock in Tofino. Several firms provide sea charters out of Tofino and Ucluelet. Boat rentals and charter air flights are available. Marine charters are provided by: Canadian Hydrographic Survey, Box 6000, Sidney, B.C. V8L 4B2.

Telescopes are available in various locations for free public use. Naturalists are stationed at the park throughout the year, with formal programs from June to September. The rest of the year they may be booked by groups as requested.

The 92-unit campground at Green Point is the only serviced one in the park. You may walk to a 100-unit campsite on a 1.25-km hike along the Schooner Trail. Both Tofino and Ucluelet have a variety of commercial accommodation and most other amenities. The hospital is at Tofino.

This park has produced a wide variety of material, including a bird checklist, park brochure and pamphlets on hiking. *West Coast Trail, Rain Forest Trail, The Gray Whale* and *Geology of Pacific Rim* are all available free from the information centre on Highway 4, year-round at the park office on Ocean Terrace near Wickaninnish or by writing: The Superintendent, Pacific Rim National Park, Box 280, Ucluelet, B.C. V0R 3A0, Telephone: (604) 726-7721.

The British Columbia Provincial Museum has published *Birds of Pacific Rim National Park*, Occasional Paper No. 20, which may be obtained by writing their bookstore in Victoria. This is a very complete work. Material from it has been used in the preparation of this section.

Birding Features

Pacific Rim is the only readily accessible area on the Pacific Ocean with long stretches of hard-packed sandy beaches and huge breaking waves. The highlights are seabirds, shorebirds and water birds. Notable species include Red-throated Loon, Brandt's and Pelagic Cormorants, Great Blue Heron, Bald Eagle, American Black Oystercatcher and Glaucous-winged Gull. Several forest species to locate include Steller's Jay, Hermit Thrush and Townsend's Warbler. The population of Pileated Woodpeckers is denser here than at any other national park in Canada. Chestnut-backed Chickadee, Golden-crowned Kinglet, Winter Wren, Brown Creeper and Red Crossbill are all present year-round. Notable birds that winter elsewhere but move into the park to breed include Fork-tailed and Leach's Storm-Petrels, Marbled Murrelet, Rhinoceros Auklet, Tufted Puffin, Band-tailed Pigeon, Rufous Hummingbird, Swainson's Thrush and Orange-crowned Warbler. Four species of shearwaters and the Caspian Tern appear in summer, but do not breed there.

There are 23 species of primarily winter birds that use the waters, including 3 species of Grebes, 8 of diving ducks, the Double-crested Cormorant and the Trumpeter Swan.

The islands off Long Beach support breeding populations of Pelagic Cormorants and the only Canadian colony of Brandt's Cormorant, American Black Oystercatcher, Pigeon Guillemot and Glaucous-winged Gull. Sometimes boat trips are made available to see the birds, Gray Whales and Northern Sea Lions. These mammals may be observed by using the telescope from Green Point at Long Beach.

In winter, from November to the end of February, look for loons (especially Yellow-billed), grebes, scoters, scaup and Bufflehead on the waters. In the woods search for Steller's Jay and a rare Blue Jay, Winter Wren, Dickcissel (rare), Song Sparrow and Dark-eyed Junco. By March, Varied Thrush and the Song Sparrow are singing on territory and juncos seem to be everywhere. The numbers of gulls and diving ducks also peak in March. They come to feed on the herring that spawn in local bays.

Spring migrants peak in numbers during April and May. Look for the shorebirds, including Snowy Plover (only accidental), Buff-breasted Sandpiper and Hudsonian Godwit. June is the slowest month. The Caspian Tern appears in summer. The fall movement of shorebirds begins in early July and peaks in August. This latter month is also good for migrating geese and dabbling ducks, especially offshore, and for Heermann's Gulls at Long Beach. Fall migration continues through October. Look for Brown Pelican then. The last to arrive near the end of the year are the Trumpeter Swan and goldeneyes.

Specific spots worth visiting include McLean Point, near the north tip of the Long Beach unit. Here you can find Common Loon, which is a resident; a possible Red-throated Loon; in the fall look for hundreds of Greater Scaups. Spring brings many Buffleheads. The above-mentioned publication, *Birds of Pacific Rim National Park*, describes in some detail a transect on McLean Point Road taken throughout the year. There are 78 species listed. Watch for the Common Yellowthroat in pine bogs here.

There are several good forest trails in the park. Some have been used as transect study areas and reported in the publication mentioned above. On these trails, watch and listen for the common cooing of the Band-tailed Pigeon from June through August. The Western Screech-Owl is a frequently heard bird. Watch for it on the highway in winter near Long Beach. Of course, the Rufous Hummingbird will challenge you on these woodland hikes from April through August. When you reach the shores of water bodies, watch for a Belted Kingfisher. The Western Flycatcher is the most conspicuous of its family from June through August. Listen for the "quick-three-beers" of the Olive-sided Flycatcher, which becomes a familiar summer sound in the park. When you come to a shrub site, check carefully for the Orange-crowned Warbler, the most frequently seen warbler. The Golden-crowned Sparrow is spotted from mid-April to mid-May and mid-September to mid-October. In recent years Palm Warbler, Northern Oriole and Harris' Sparrow have shown up in fall.

Barkley Sound, with the approximately 100 islands in the park, has also been surveyed carefully in the above-mentioned book. Look for a variety of seabirds, including the regular but uncommon Buller's Shearwater; Sooty Shearwater; a breeding colony of Leach's Storm-Petrels on Seabird Rocks and Cleland Island; the northernmost colony of Brandt's Cormorant on Sea Lion Rocks, Starlight Reef and at times other spots; the Pelagic Cormorant is a common resident on the islands. The Bald Eagle is everywhere and stays all year. It is most abundant at the northeastern end of Barkley Sound. The Osprey is seen most easily off Long Beach and nests on Vargas Island, near the north end of Yarksis Beach on the east side of the island. Also look for this bird in the Grice Bay area. The Surfbird is an abundant migrant through these islands, particularly in April and from mid-July through August. The Heermann's Gull is a likely bird on the offshore reefs and islets. Look for small flocks of Common Murres in protected waters from October to April. Pigeon Guillemots nest on Seabird Rocks and Florencia Island. Marbled Murrelets occur in pairs among the islets from April through September. The Rhinoceros Auklet has a small colony on Seabird Rocks, as does the Tufted Puffin. Listen for the Western Screech-Owl on Turtle Island from May through July. Nearby islands may also contain breeding birds. The Rufous Hummingbird probably breeds on every vegetated island and islet in Barkley Sound. Search for clumps of *Rubus*, which supply it with nectar.

The park is an important wintering area on Vancouver Island for Trumpeter Swan. They are best seen from late November to early January in several spots, including Grice Bay, Sandhill Creek, Swan Lake, Kichla Lake, Kieha Meadows, Hobiton Lake and Cheewhat Lake. Swan Lake appears to be the best site from mid- to late November. Areas to search close to the park include Megin Lake, the estuaries of Tranquil Creek and the Cypre, Moyeha and Bedwell rivers, all draining into Clayoquot Sound; several locations in the Kennedy Lake area may have these birds too.

The Peregrine Falcon usually appears in the park in August when shorebirds are passing through and begins to decrease from January onward. The best site to look for them is among the waterfowl wintering areas in southern Clayoquot Sound.

WAYNE CAMPBELL

Pelagic (Offshore Waters) British Columbia

Oceanic birds such as albatrosses, storm-petrels and shearwaters are often the most inaccessible birds to all but the very keen searcher. To attain the goal of more new species, British Columbia bird watchers began to take organized trips off the west coast of Vancouver Island in spring and fall in 1979. These special trips are no longer undertaken regularly, but can be arranged if a group is interested. Northern Sea Lions, seals, Gray Whales, sharks and marine fish are all good possibilities.

The area usually visited on an offshore trip lies between Tofino and Bamfield. Just north of these communities, west of Gold River, Captain James Cook first landed at Friendly Cove in Nootka Sound in 1778. Fourteen years later, Captain George Vancouver, who had been a twenty-year-old midshipman on the Cook expedition, returned and gave the large island his name.

Access to Tofino or Bamfield is usually by car. Bus transportation is available. Both communities are reached off Highway 4 west from Parksville. To reach Bamfield, take the gravel road southwest from Port Alberni. Watch for signs, as there are numerous lumber roads on which you can get lost. There are two motels in Bamfield, a garage, groceries, police and medical help if needed.

Tofino sits at the end of Highway 4 beyond the Pacific Rim National Park complex. There are several motels and more than 500 commercial campsites available in the area. Garage services, groceries, police and medical assistance are all here. Offshore trips are now handled commercially by Swiftsure Tours Ltd., 645 Fort Street, Victoria, B.C., Telephone: (604) 388-4227. Arrangements can also be made privately, but a boat must be booked well ahead of time. Tofino is the best bet.

Bamfield has a special research centre, funded by several universities. By requesting permission, a visitor can usually arrange to see their excellent collection of local sea life in the aquariums used for research.

With the recent trend of taking trips off the coast, there have been a few papers published! They include papers numbered 358, 719, 1072 and 1102 in the Bibliography of B.C. Ornithology. All are available from: Museum Bookstore, B.C. Provincial Museum, Victoria, B.C. V8V 1X4.

Caution: dress warmly and be prepared for a variety of weather. Sometimes trips do not even go out because of heavy winds. Bring sea-sickness pills!

Birding Features
The purpose of the trip will most likely be to locate marine water birds. From May through October can be a good time. The peak spring period would be from the first week in May through mid-June. July is the best summer month. Fall is best from mid-September to mid-October.

Species to be expected include Arctic Loon, three species of grebe, Black-footed Albatross, Northern Fulmar, and Pink- and Flesh-footed Shear-waters. In fall, look for Buller's Shearwater. Throughout the seasons, you'll spot hundreds of Sooty Shearwaters, Brandt's and Pelagic Cormorants; White-winged and Surf Scoters are common; Bald Eagles are always present. Red-necked Phalaropes are usually spotted where warm and cold currents converge or on patches of floating seaweed. Look for a variety of gulls, with Glaucous-winged the most common; Sabine's Gull and Black-legged Kitti-wake are usually present. The trip should produce Common Murres in numbers, a few Pigeon Guillemots, Marbled Murrelets, Tufted Puffins, and Cassin's and Rhinoceros Auklets. Watch for other species.

WAYNE CAMPBELL

Riske Creek, Becher's Prairie

Becher's Prairie near Riske Creek in south-central B.C. contains the best mix of dry plateau grasslands and pothole marshes in the province. The wetlands provide habitat for high concentrations of migrating and nesting waterfowl. The area lies in the Cariboo-Chilcotin region, which contains the highest densities of breeding Barrow's Goldeneyes and Buffleheads in the world. Riske Creek is also the northern limit of Long-billed Curlews in B.C.

Becher's Prairie is mainly crown land; the northern half is a military reserve used occasionally in summer as a training ground by CFB Chilliwack. The whole area, including the military reserve, is under grazing lease. Vehicles must stay on the roads as the grasses are easily damaged by automobile traffic.

The area was originally settled by cattle ranchers and has been grazed for decades. The lands are relatively flat-rolling, and covered with grasses interspersed with scattered clumps of Trembling Aspen, Lodgepole Pine and Douglas Fir. The lakes show a wide range of salinity; some of their margins have extensive bullrush stands, others are bare and salt-encrusted.

The Riske Creek site of approximately 100 km² lies 40 km southwest of Williams Lake on Highway 20. Greyhound bus, British Columbia Railway, and Pacific Western Airlines all regularly service Williams Lake. Travel from there to the birding site is by automobile, which may be rented at Williams Lake. A short day's driving time is sufficient to cover the loop. Be sure to make regular stops for exploratory hikes at potholes, open fields, and woods. Begin at the Riske Creek Store–Post Office; take the gravel road north for about 7 km; bear right or northeast onto the dirt track for another 2 km or less; turn sharply south on the gravel road and angle southeast for about 11 km to Highway 20, then back to Williams Lake.

The closest commercial accommodation is at Chilcotin Lodge and trailer park at Riske Creek. There are several motels and hotels in Williams Lake. B.C. Forest Service campsites are nearby, a gas station, telephone, store and post office are at Riske Creek, and there is a hospital at Williams Lake. Additional tourist information on the area is available from: B.C. Tourist Office, Williams Lake, B.C. Their office is located at the junction of Highways 97 and 20 on the south entrance to Williams Lake. Ask them for directions to the local nature centre.

Further birding help can be provided by: Anna Roberts, South Lakeshore Road, Williams Lake, B.C., Telephone: (604) 392-5000.

Birding Features
The mix of dry plateau grasslands and pothole marshes provides a wide diversity of bird habitat. Uncommon residents include Northern Goshawks, Sharp-tailed Grouse and Three-toed Woodpeckers; Red Crossbills are fairly common, but White-winged are irregular.

Winter visitors include Northern Hawk-Owls, Great Gray and Boreal Owls, all of which are rare but possible; Rosy Finches and Snow Buntings are irregular.

On migration, most Pacific Flyway waterfowl are common; Sandhill Cranes use the prairie as a staging area and many shorebirds stop on their way through.

Summer species start arriving in late March to early April. Birds found from then until September include four species of grebe — Red-necked, Horned, Pied-billed and Eared — which are abundant and have a colony at the north end of Rock Lake (south of the back road, about 2 km north of Highway 20 on the east leg of the loop). Mallards and Northern Pintails are present, as are Gadwalls and three species of teal — Green-winged, Blue-winged and Cinnamon. American Wigeons nest, as do both Redheads and Canvasbacks. Ruddy Ducks, Lesser Scaups, Barrow's Goldeneyes and Buffleheads are common (see above for abundance). Golden Eagles are uncommon; Bald Eagles nest nearby and are fairly common. Sandhill Cranes nest in very small numbers in the marshes. This is the northern range-limit for Long-billed Curlews in B.C. Greater Yellowlegs are fairly common breeders, and are near the southern limit of their breeding range in the province. Long-eared Owls are found in conifer groves. Common flycatchers include Willow, Least and Dusky. Horned Larks are common breeders on the grasslands. Mountain Chickadees occur in the woodlands, and Mountain Bluebirds nest along fence rows. Yellow-headed Blackbirds are abundant in the *Scirpus* marshes. Savannah and Vesper Sparrows appear in numbers on the grasslands.

ROBERT A. CANNINGS, RICHARD J. CANNINGS, SYDNEY G. CANNINGS

Queen Charlotte Islands

The rugged mountains and lush forests on the Queen Charlottes are often shrouded in rain and mist. These lands sit on the edge of the continental shelf. To the west, the drop-off is almost 3050 m to the ocean floor; to the east, the floor of Hecate Strait in places is only 15 m below sea level.

Peregrine Falcons breed here in larger numbers than anywhere else in the world. Subspecies of the darker Northern Saw-whet Owl, Hairy Woodpecker, Steller's Jay and Pine Grosbeak add to the interest. Ninety-one breeding colonies of seabirds have been identified. Mammal species are few. The Western Toad is the only native amphibian, and no reptiles are present. Weather is very unpredictable. Don't venture out to the islands unless you have prearranged accommodation and are in the hands of competent tour guides.

These islands were the ancestral home of the Haida people. Their carvings were, and still are, beautiful pieces of art. After the Europeans arrived in 1774, the Haida, very susceptible to white man's diseases, abandoned their ancestral villages and moved to missions, and later to reservations. By the 1820s, after the discovery of argillite, a soft rock found only at Slatechuk Mountain, on Graham Island, they began using their carving skills to make sculptures. This art lives today in the fine pieces still being produced.

The two main islands, Graham to the north and Moresby on the south, are separated by a narrow channel. Most visitors come in by plane to Sandspit Airport on Moresby. Pacific Western and Trans-Provincial Airlines both serve the airport. Trans-Provincial also flies out of a water strip at Queen Charlotte City on Graham Island. A bus or rented car from the airport will then take you to Alliford Bay. Cross on the ferry to Skidegate. Cars can also be rented at Sandspit and on Graham Island at Masset, Queen Charlotte and Port Clements. The only paved road connects Masset to Port Clements and Queen Charlotte City. The logging roads can lead you into the interior.

A regular ferry service by B.C. Ferry Corp. runs between Prince Rupert on the mainland and Masset on the island. A Sandspit sea service runs to Vancouver, and Mitco Marine at Queen Charlotte City operates a boat service to the mainland.

One provincial park, Naikoon, 707 km², preserves a large block of wilderness on the northeast corner of Graham Island. A road leads from

Masset into the park, to Tow Hill, a lookout where Peregrine Falcons often brought prey to consume.

Accommodation on the islands is limited. There is one motel-hotel at Sandspit on Moresby Island, four at Queen Charlotte City, one each at Tlell and Port Clements, and two at Masset on Graham Island.

Contact Tourism British Columbia (see above) for a free copy of the lists of accommodation or write the Chamber of Commerce in the appropriate community mentioned above. Camping is available in Naikoon Provincial Park.

Information on the wildlife of the Queen Charlottes is limited but increasing all the time. The "locals," other than the Chamber of Commerce people, tend to be sensitive about tourists "invading" their homes and hence it is difficult to obtain a local contact to assist. A few publications have appeared over the years. One, a map entitled "Sea Bird Colonies of the Queen Charlotte Islands," by the B.C. Provincial Museum, Victoria, B.C., gives an excellent description of both colony size and location of these numerous species. Other papers, numbered 50, 187, 484, 652, 737, 1016, 1218 and 1395 in the Bibliography of B.C. Ornithology, are also available from the museum.

Tour companies often arrange special trips for birders to the Charlottes. The expeditions usually originate from Victoria and are run by Kytan or Swiftsure Travel from that city, and the University of B.C. Continuing Education Department in Vancouver.

Several of the above-mentioned ninety-one seabird colonies are ecological reserves and special permission and a permit are required to visit them. Write: Director, Ecological Reserves Unit, Ministry of Lands, Parks and Housing, B.C. Provincial Government, Victoria, B.C. V8V 1X4.

Birding Features

The islands have been poorly birded. A visitor has an excellent chance of adding new species for the islands, B.C. and even Canada. These lands have been close to both Siberia and Alaska for a long time. You expect the unexpected, such as Brambling, Cattle Egret, Great-tailed Grackle, Magnificent Frigatebird and Rustic Bunting. They all have been seen. Of course there is a great variety and number of seabirds, including Cassin's Auklets, Rhinoceros Auklets, and other stragglers from northern colonies such as Parakeet Auklet and Least Auklet. Eiders occur regularly in winter.

Ancient Murrelet reach their southern limit here and are common to abundant in April and less common to late May. Horned Puffins now breed here. With the abundance of seabirds, Peregrine Falcon reap a good harvest. These birds of prey, and Bald Eagle, are at their peak of breeding abundance for B.C. on the islands.

Birding in the Charlottes depends so much on the season, and on weather. Rain, wind and fog are very common at times. Prediction of weather conditions, and consequent bird abundance, is very difficult. For example, thousands of turnstones can be seen in the fall off Sandspit some years; in others they are rare or absent. However, you can count on the regularity and abundance of the seabirds at their colonies.

Ancient Murrelets (in their thousands) come in May and June. The seabird colonies are best from May to July. In winter, water birds are around the entire islands in protected waters. Skidegate Inlet is often a good spot. The main birding areas easily accessible are as follows:

Dekalta Slough at Masset. In the spring and fall, scan for Canada and Greater White-fronted Geese. The latter come in flocks of several hundred to thousands on their way through. Sandhill Cranes also come through in numbers.

Rose Spit, at the northeast corner of Graham Island, is an excellent spot to observe migrating shorebirds in spring and fall. Some seabirds may be spotted from the point.

Port Clements, on Masset Inlet on Graham Island, is good for water birds.

Skidegate Inlet, between Graham and Moresby islands, should be carefully examined from both sides, and while crossing on the ferry, for seabirds, all year. In particular, keep watch for Pelagic Cormorant, American Black Oystercatcher, Glaucous-winged Gull and Pigeon Guillemot.

Sandspit, on Moresby Island, at the end of the road, is another good spot to watch shorebirds in spring and fall.

Langara Island, about 8 km long and 6.5 km wide, lies off the northwest corner of Graham Island. The shores are steep, with the interior partly forested and partly muskeg. The island is best known as one of the few remaining strongholds for Peregrine Falcon; they prey on the large and varied population of breeding seabirds that nest on the island. Bald Eagles are abundant as year-round residents. The islands are reached by boat, and this can be a very tricky trip, so be cautious. Peregrine Falcon nests on Cox Island on the southeast side of Langara. At the south end of Langara, north of the Indian village of Dadens, Ancient Murrelet have riddled the ground with burrows.

The ninety-one seabird colonies are best checked out from April to August. They contain nearly half a million pairs of breeding birds consisting of: over 50,000 pairs of Leach's Storm-Petrels; over 50,000 pairs of Fork-tailed Storm-Petrels; more than 400 pairs of Pelagic Cormorants; greater than 2000 pairs of Glaucous-winged Gulls; 50 pairs of Common Murres; over 1000 pairs of Pigeon Guillemots; 203,000 pairs of Ancient Murrelets; nearly 160,000 pairs of Cassin's Auklets; more than 3500 pairs of Rhinoceros Auklets; and more than 3500 pairs of Tufted Puffins.

WAYNE CAMPBELL, YORKE EDWARDS

Fort Nelson Area

The Alaska Highway descends from the foothills to the lowlands near

Trutch, passing through 200 km of flattish country around Fort Nelson before once more entering foothill country. A visitor often speeds through this flat country without stopping to check for birdlife. A study published in 1976 (see below) reported 157 species of birds recorded below 610 m. This includes 30 breeding species, with an additional 76 probably breeding. Look for Barrow's Goldeneye, Broad-winged Hawk, Varied Thrush, Common Grackle, Rose-breasted Grosbeak, and warblers, including some eastern species: Black-throated Green, Bay-breasted, Connecticut, Mourning and Canada. This spot lies in the corner of the northern, southern, eastern and western limits of several species (see below).

A fur-trading post was built at Fort Nelson around 1800. The post was destroyed and some inhabitants killed in 1813. The Hudson's Bay Company rebuilt the post in 1865 and continues to operate it today. The area was opened up with the building of the Alaska Highway of more than 2436 km. Today the highway serves as the tourist route, oil company access, and general link between the south and the north, including Alaska and the Yukon.

The Alaska Highway begins just west of Edmonton, Alberta. Kilometre 0 lies in the middle of the community of Dawson Creek, B.C. Greyhound runs a daily bus service along the highway in the summer from Edmonton to Whitehorse. Service is reduced to three times a week from late fall to spring. The Department of Transport maintains a major airport about 5 km east of Fort Nelson. There are motels and campgrounds at scattered communities, and at Fort Nelson there are several to choose from. The highway is gravelled for most of its length, with few service stations present. As a precaution, carry an extra spare tire, emergency rations, lots of warm clothing and a sleeping bag.

The British Columbia Provincial Museum published a paper on this area from which most of the following information was taken: "Birds of the Fort Nelson lowlands of northeastern British Columbia," by A. J. Erskine and G. S. Davidson, *Syesis*, Vol. 9, 1976: 1–11.

Birding Features

The lowlands are largely forested with White and Black Spruce. Trembling Aspen forms pure stands on the warm south-facing slopes, especially on the poplar hills from Fort Nelson west to about Kilometre Post 520. Balsam Poplar is the pioneer tree on river gravels, where it attains a huge size. Black Spruce muskegs are common, but seldom visible from the road.

Birds that are at their limits on these lowlands include:

Northern limit: Broad-winged Hawk, Osprey, Black Tern (breeding), Barred Owl (breeding), Yellow-bellied Flycatcher, Solitary and Philadelphia Vireos, Canada Warbler (breeding) and Rose-breasted Grosbeak (breeding).

Southern limit: Surf Scoter (breeding) and Rough-legged Hawk (summer).

Western Limit: Broad-winged Hawk; Cape May, Black-throated Green, Chestnut-sided, Bay-breasted, Connecticut, Mourning and Canada Warblers; Rose-breasted Grosbeak.

Spots to visit include:

Fort Nelson Community. The town dump and mixed woods behind the dump are good places to start. Check near these woods for a Bank Swallow colony and behind the dump for Canada Warbler. Look for a Herring Gull at the dump. In town, watch for a Common Nighthawk, Western Wood-Pewee, Tree Swallow and Cliff Swallow on the high school; Common Raven, House Wren, American Robin, Varied Thrush, Mourning Warbler at creeks; near town look for Brewer's Blackbird, Western Tanager, Purple Finch, and Savannah, Vesper, Clay-colored and White-crowned Sparrows.

Parker Lake. To reach this site, go 11.2 km north of Fort Nelson on the Alaska Highway and then left on an unmarked dirt road for about 1.3 km. From late May to July, you may find Red-necked and Horned Grebes, a variety of ducks, including Barrow's Goldeneye, White-winged and Surf Scoters, Sora, Bonaparte's Gull, Common Tern, Western Wood-Pewee, Common Yellowthroat and Le Conte's and Swamp Sparrows. This is also the best spot for spring and fall migrants, particularly water birds.

Muskwa River. Just north of the Tompkins Esso Service at Km 468.8, take the dirt road to the east, as it follows the Muskwa River. Travel at least as far as the first bridge. This road or trail continues on for over 130 km, with a maze of dirt trails along the way. When exploring, be careful that you remember your return route. There are no services, so travel with a full gas tank. Look for American Kestrel; Hermit and Swainson's Thrushes; a variety of warblers, including Black-and-white, Tennessee, Orange-crowned, Magnolia, Connecticut and Mourning; Ovenbird; Rose-breasted Grosbeak; and Savannah, Fox and White-throated Sparrows.

At the mature aspen forest around Km 512, look for American Kestrel, Common Snipe, Pileated Woodpecker, Yellow-bellied Sapsucker and Philadelphia Vireo; warblers including Black-and-white, Orange-crowned, Magnolia, Blackpoll, Ovenbird, Mourning, Wilson's, Canada and American Redstart; Rose-breasted Grosbeak and Swamp Sparrow.

In bottomland White Spruce forest around Km 538, search for Sharp-shinned Hawk, Bald Eagle, Ruffed Grouse, Barred Owl calling in the middle of the night; Belted Kingfisher near the Muskwa River, southeast of here; Pileated Woodpecker, Three-toed Woodpecker, the difficult flycatchers of the *Empidonax* group, Western Wood-Pewee, Gray Jay, Boreal Chickadee, American Robin, Varied Thrush, Swainson's Thrush, Golden-crowned and Ruby-crowned Kinglets, Bohemian Waxwing, Solitary Vireo, warblers (including Black-and-white, Orange-crowned, Yellow, Magnolia, Chestnut-sided, Bay-breasted, Blackpoll, Ovenbird, Northern Waterthrush, Mourning, Wilson's and American Redstart), Western Tanager and Rose-breasted Grosbeak.

In the Black Spruce muskeg at Km 542 and at Kledo Creek campsite, a short distance farther south, check for Sharp-shinned Hawk, Spruce Grouse, a possible Common Nighthawk overhead, Hermit Thrush, Palm Warbler, White-winged Crossbill and Chipping Sparrow.

In the hillside Black Spruce forest at Km 614, explore for Ruffed Grouse, Gray Jay, Red-breasted Nuthatch, Brown Creeper, Winter Wren, Varied Thrush and Golden- and Ruby-crowned Kinglets.

WAYNE CAMPBELL

Haines Road/Chilkoot Pass

The Chilkoot Pass area in the extreme northwest corner of B.C., bordered by Alaska and the Yukon, is one of the only accessible places in Canada where all three species of ptarmigan occur. The area is adjacent to one of the largest gatherings of Bald Eagles in North America. Gyrfalcons are year-round residents and Wandering Tattlers are rare breeders.

You reach this area by road. Travel to Whitehorse in the Yukon and then take Yukon Highway 1 west from Whitehorse, for 158 km to Haines Road No. 3 and south to B.C. At the border the road becomes B.C. No. 4 over the Chilkoot Pass. This is crown land with some seasonally operated guiding settlements, mostly used in the fall hunting season by guided groups.

A highway maintenance camp is situated on the west side of the road, about halfway down the B.C. stretch on the way into Haines, southwest of Kelsall Lake. There are no really good roads off the highway, but there are some crude trails into such places as Kelsall Lake and Three Guardsmen Mountain.

No motel or camping facilities are present in the pass. The closest accommodation and service is Dezdiash Lodge, with a restaurant and gas station about 24 km north of the British Columbia–Yukon border. Groceries and other supplies should be acquired before leaving Whitehorse, at Haines Junction or down at Haines, Alaska. The closest hospital and medical service is at Haines Junction. Minor car repairs, such as on tires, may be handled at Dezdiash Lodge. For help or a telephone in the case of such emergencies as illness or accident, contact the road maintenance camp mentioned previously, about mid-way through the pass. The highway has fairly heavy traffic because of the movement to and from Haines. There is a ferry service at Haines that will take you down the straits, with regular service to Prince Rupert, B.C. This ferry trip is well worth the money for the scenery alone, not to mention the dozens of Bald Eagles seen en route.

The nearest naturalists or contact people are at Kluane Park in the Yukon. For more information, obtain the article by Robert B. Weeden, "The Birds of Chilkoot Pass, British Columbia," in *Canadian Field-Naturalist* 74(2) 1960: 119–29.

Caution: carry winter clothing and a warm sleeping bag at all times. There are regular unseasonable snowstorms. The low areas are very damp, so wear rubber boots. Carry a full five-gallon can of gasoline.

Birding Features

The landscape is covered with alpine willow and in places is difficult to walk through. The real alpine areas are about one-half to one hour's walk from the lower elevations. However, you are in the alpine area at the summit of the pass. The views are magnificent, with snow-covered mountains and glaciers dominating. Much of the area around the smaller lakes is very damp and wet, typical of shallow bog sites.

Because of the high elevations, birding visits should take place some time from May through September. In early May, and again in September, the birds pass through in great numbers. Blizzards occur regularly and happen very suddenly.

There are three major routes along which birds pass through the coastal mountains from the Pacific to the interior of the Yukon and eastern Alaska. The Chilkoot Pass is the largest and most northerly of these. Birds in large numbers are often seen flying very low through the pass because of the adverse weather so often encountered.

The chief attraction during the nesting season is the Golden Eagle and a possible nesting Gyrfalcon. These falcons are more common in the fall (October). There is a large concentration of Bald Eagles at the mouth of the Klukwan River and Chilkoot River in Alaska. This is one of the largest groupings of these birds left anywhere in North America. They feed on the salmon. This region is the southern limit of nesting by Lesser Golden-Plover, Wandering Tattler, Least Sandpiper, Short-billed Dowitcher, Arctic Tern, Smith's Longspur and Snow Bunting. Common and Red-throated Loons also nest here. Gray-cheeked Thrushes are fairly common throughout the area. Smith's Longspur nests near Kelsall Lake. As mentioned above, all three species of ptarmigan are observed easily. The most abundant, Willow, has a range that almost exactly coincides with the shrub-tundra zone. Northern Hawk-Owls are frequent visitors in the fall. Redpolls and White-crowned and Golden-crowned Sparrows breed here. Scan the hills for Stone Sheep, Grizzly Bear and Caribou.

WAYNE CAMPBELL, DAVE MOSSOP

Alberta

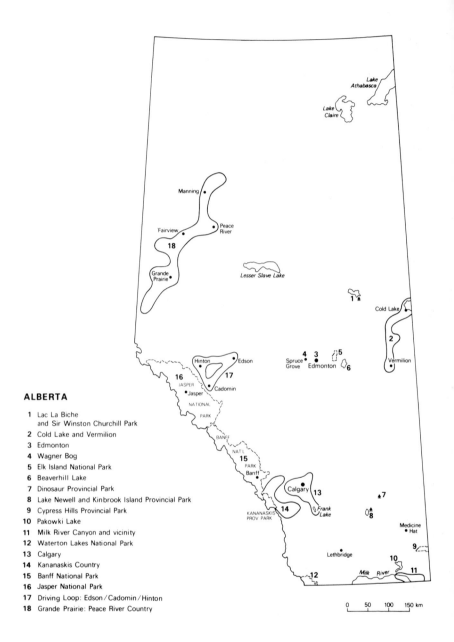

ALBERTA

1 Lac La Biche
   and Sir Winston Churchill Park
2 Cold Lake and Vermilion
3 Edmonton
4 Wagner Bog
5 Elk Island National Park
6 Beaverhill Lake
7 Dinosaur Provincial Park
8 Lake Newell and Kinbrook Island Provincial Park
9 Cypress Hills Provincial Park
10 Pakowki Lake
11 Milk River Canyon and vicinity
12 Waterton Lakes National Park
13 Calgary
14 Kananaskis Country
15 Banff National Park
16 Jasper National Park
17 Driving Loop: Edson / Cadomin / Hinton
18 Grande Prairie: Peace River Country

Alberta

From mountain peaks through parkland to prairie, Alberta provides nesting habitats for everything from Trumpeter Swan, Willow Ptarmigan, Northern Pygmy-Owl, Rosy Finch, through Three-toed Woodpecker, to Sage Grouse, Ferruginous Hawk, Burrowing Owl and Mountain Plover.

With an area of 661,185 km^2, Alberta has a population of 2,160,400, less than one half rural, the majority living in Edmonton and Calgary. The Rocky Mountains are the southwest boundary, with Alberta's highest point, Mount Columbia, at 3747 m. These highlands are capped with tundra and home to ptarmigan, Rosy Finch and other upland species. The northeast corner of the province contains a small piece of arctic tundra. The northern half of Alberta is boreal forest, with Black Spruce bogs being dominant. A piece of prairie is inserted into this boreal forest in the Peace River Country in the northwest. Boreal forests grade south into aspen parkland (interspersed bluffs of Trembling Aspen and open grasslands) around the Edmonton area. Farther south, the parkland becomes prairie from about Red Deer onward. The remaining southeast of the province consists of short grass, very dry country.

Boreal forests in the north support the same birds as does this type of habitat in the rest of Canada. The parklands contain thousands of sloughs which host pothole ducks from May through September. The prairies contain similar species as in southwest Saskatchewan, including Sage Grouse, Ferruginous Hawk, Burrowing Owl, and in the extreme southeast along the Milk River, Mountain Plover, the only place in Canada where these birds nest.

The top birding site in Alberta, in most seasons, is Beaverhill Lake. Within an hour of Edmonton, you can see thousands of geese in spring and a wide variety of shorebirds from April to October. Dinosaur Provincial Park offers prairie birds. The Lac La Biche area provides boreal nesting species and many birds on migration. Pakowki Lake, south of Medicine Hat, has hosted the more southern species and contains a few White-faced Ibis each year. Waterton Lakes National Park often has western birds that slip over the low passes from B.C.; mountain species and prairie birds can also be found in this park, all in one day. Finally, Grande Prairie is a sure bet for nesting Trumpeter Swan.

A visitor to Edmonton could explore Beaverhill Lake and Elk Island National Park in one day. In Calgary, try the Shepard, Priddis and Radio Tower sloughs for water and shore birds and perhaps a Burrowing Owl.

Whitemud Park in Edmonton, Beaverhill Lake, Elk Island Park and Wagner Bog can all be covered easily on a two-day trip. Two days around Calgary could include the above-mentioned sloughs, plus a quick day-trip through Kananaskis Country. Banff requires at least one long day, preferably two. To explore Jasper, you need at least two days, as you do for Waterton.

There are no real bird alert numbers in Alberta. In Edmonton, telephone Terry Thormin at home (403) 482-1389, or the John Janzen Nature Centre

White-faced Ibis

(403) 434-7446; in Calgary, telephone Don Stiles at home (403) 271-4689. The Federation of Alberta Naturalists, Box 1472, Edmonton, Alberta T5J 2N5 will provide a list of clubs to contact. The Natural History Section of the Provincial Museum, at (403) 427-1731, can also provide information.

Detailed maps may be obtained from Alberta Energy and Natural Resources, 2nd Floor, 9945 — 108 St., Edmonton, Alberta. A good road map may be obtained from any Travel Alberta office or by writing: Travel Alberta, Alberta Tourism, Government of Alberta, Edmonton, Alberta.

Bird watchers intending to spend much time in the province would be well advised to purchase a copy of *The Birds of Alberta*, by W. Ray Salt and Jim R. Salt (Edmonton: Hurtig, 1976). Papers published to 1979 have been listed in a bibliography: *A Bibliography of Alberta Ornithology*, by M.K. McNicholl, P. H. R. Stepney, P.C. Boxall and D.A.E. Spalding, Natural History Occasional Paper No. 3 (Provincial Museum of Alberta, 1981).

Lac La Biche and Sir Winston Churchill Park

Southeast of Lac La Biche in north-central Alberta there is a rich diversity of boreal habitats, including spruce forests, abundant lakes, fen and bog systems, south-facing open slopes and ravines with aspen. This is an excellent location for numerous summer resident boreal birds, as well as migrants which utilize the lakes for staging areas to and from their northern breeding grounds. Of Alberta's known birds, 222 species (67 per cent) have been reported in and around this area.

The best route from Edmonton into the region is north on Highway 2 to Athabasca; then east on Highway 55 to Lac La Biche (a total of 220 paved km from Edmonton), where motel and hotel accommodations, gasoline, food and services are available. There are adequate camping facilities at nearby Sir Winston Churchill Provincial Park.

Information is available from the regional offices of Alberta Fish and Wildlife, Alberta Recreation and Parks and Alberta Forest Service, in Lac La Biche. A bird checklist is also available for Sir Winston Churchill Park.

Birding Features

The larger lakes in this area support diving ducks, such as Common Golden-eye, Lesser Scaup and White-winged Scoter. Surface-feeding ducks, such as teal, Mallard and American Wigeon are also common in the bays and on the smaller water bodies. In May and June, and August and September, these water bodies are important staging areas for hundreds of migrating water birds. Lac La Biche, the largest lake, and Sir Winston Churchill Park are the recommended spots (the former for water birds and the latter for land birds, including boreal warblers). For other sites, ask the staff at the park.

WAYNE NORDSTROM

Cold Lake and Vermilion

East-central Alberta offers opportunities to explore the transition between the boreal forest and aspen parkland. The Cold Lake area, with over 198 bird species reported, lies adjacent to Saskatchewan's Meadow Lake Provincial Park. Since Cold Lake is easily reached by car, two other spots which may be passed en route from Edmonton have been included: Vermilion Provincial Park, near Highway 16 to the south of Cold Lake; and the Whitney Lakes Provincial Park to the east of Elk Point.

The region is noted for Virginia and Yellow Rails, Barred Owl, Sedge Wren, Blackburnian and Chestnut-sided Warblers, and Sharp-tailed and Lincoln's Sparrows.

Vermilion Provincial Park, with 769 ha, is located adjacent to the town of the same name, 189 km east of Edmonton on Highway 16. The main east-west bus route through Edmonton passes Vermilion.

The Whitney Lakes Provincial Park is found about 64 km north of Vermilion along paved Highway 41. To reach the lakes travel east from Elk Point for 32 km on gravelled secondary road No. 646. There are few good roads within the lake complex, but several tertiary roadways are found around the perimeter. A good road skirts the southeast and east sides of Laurier Lake. A number of trails provide access to areas near the shores, but be wary of soft spots during spring and in wet weather.

To reach Grand Centre and Cold Lake, continue north from Elk Point on Highway 41; then northeast on Highway 28. An alternative and usually travelled route from Edmonton to Cold Lake (292 km) is northeast on Highway 28, then 28A, and back onto 28 into Cold Lake. This route is also used for a three-times-daily return bus from Edmonton to Cold Lake. The 400-ha Cold Lake Provincial Park contains a good variety of habitats that are readily accessible and provide excellent birding. To reach the park, travel east from Grand Centre (5 km south of Cold Lake) for about 5 km on a good gravel road, then north; or east from the town of Cold Lake to the lake. This Grand Centre option provides additional access to lake shore and birding opportunities.

Visitor accommodation of various sorts, plus gas and groceries, are available at the villages and towns along the routes. Camping facilities are available within Vermilion Park and at several locations around Cold Lake. Visitors are advised to stay at the provincial park site on Lund's Point, the only location that is regularly patrolled.

An unpublished, annotated checklist of birds of the Cold Lake area may be obtained from Alberta Recreation and Parks. For further information on these parks, contact the ranger-in-charge.

Birding Features

Vermilion Provincial Park lies adjacent to the Vermilion River. The south bank is wooded with aspen, whereas the north side is primarily exposed grasslands. Marshlands are found at the west end. The park and adjacent region are good locations for water birds from late April to mid-September. The marshes and the numerous sloughs in the region contain a variety of ducks. The woods host a number of Cooper's, Red-tailed and Swainson's Hawks, with several nesting. The northern grassy slopes support typical grassland birds such as Sprague's Pipit. The aspen woods along the south bank host many typical parkland birds.

Whitney Lakes Provincial Park provides excellent habitat for migrating waterfowl from late April to mid-June and again from late July to early September. Greater White-fronted and Snow Geese travel through the area in large numbers. Hooded and Common Mergansers are seen also. Whooping Cranes are reported occasionally during migration, as the area lies on the western edge of their migration route. The lake shores and adjacent marshes provide good habitat for an abundance of migratory shorebirds. In the adjacent woodlands, watch for Barred and Great Gray Owls, and other boreal and parkland species. Great Crested Flycatcher and Chestnut-sided Warbler have been noted.

Farther north towards Cold Lake, there is a great diversity of aquatic, wetland and upland habitats. The best birding spots are in the vicinity of the Martineau River delta, on the north side of Cold Lake, and along the south shore at the provincial park, as well as at French Bay. Large colonies of Western Grebe have nested just east of the park in Centre Bay for many years. EXTREME CARE must be taken during breeding season to avoid disturbing them. American White Pelicans nest in a colony of up to 2000 pairs at Primrose Lake, to the northeast in Saskatchewan, as do Double-crested Cormorants and Great Blue Herons. All of these birds, therefore, are readily observed on Cold Lake as they travel to and from their nesting sites. Both Cold and Primrose lakes function as staging areas for large numbers of ducks and geese. The shoreline also provides nesting habitat for waterfowl. Turkey Vultures have been observed flying over Cold Lake Park. Yellow Rails are common and breed in sedge fens, with little to no standing water. Forster's Terns raise young in the Centre Bay area. Barred Owls have been found nesting in thick conifers within the park. Sedge Wrens are fairly common, making their homes in sedge/grass fens having scattered shrubs. Blackburnian Warblers are fairly numerous, with breeding territories in heavy stands of spruce and fir in mixed-wood forests. These birds have been seen within the park and at Sandy Point, on the northeast side of French Bay, east of the park. Black-throated Green Warbler is also found in similar forests. Look for nesting Chestnut-sided Warblers in fairly open but mature deciduous forests with thick shrub understory. Sharp-tailed Sparrows are relatively abundant and nest in wet grassy meadows throughout the area. Look for these birds in the fen area south of Centre Bay. Lincoln's Sparrows are abundant and breed in marshes/fens/bogs with extensive growths of willow and alder. These sparrows may also be seen in fair numbers in the Centre Bay area.

WAYNE NORDSTROM

Edmonton

Edmonton, the capital of Alberta, straddles the North Saskatchewan River valley. The south-facing slopes of the river bank contain some prairie vegetation and north-facing ones have boreal forests. Several deep ravines containing a mixture of Trembling Aspen and White Spruce cut through the city. The more than twenty pairs of Merlins nesting within city boundaries make for the highest density of this species known in the world.

Edmonton began as a fur-trading post in 1795. Settlement started in 1870. With the arrival of the railroad in 1891, agriculture became the main business. Oil was discovered just south of Edmonton, at Leduc, in 1946. Edmonton then became the field headquarters of the oil industry. Today Edmonton and the nearby dormitory communities have about 600,000 people. Of these, nearly two-thirds are relative newcomers or were born after the discovery of oil — a city of young aggressive people!

Several national and international airlines service Edmonton. Buses come from both east and west on Highway 16 and north from Calgary on Highway 2. Trains arrive from Calgary on the main CPR line. Hotels and motels are spread throughout the city, but mainly on the south side on Highway 2 and west side on Highway 16. A campground is found at Rainbow Valley, off the Whitemud Freeway, in the southwest sector. Provincial Highway campsites are placed on the east side along Highways 16 and 14, and on the west end along Highway 16. There are several hospitals, with the university the main research, patient and outpatient centre.

The Edmonton Bird Club has recently published bird checklists of the area, together with several bird-finding guides to special spots. For copies, contact the John Janzen Nature Centre, c/o Edmonton Parks and Recreation, 10th Floor CN Tower, Edmonton, Alberta T5J 0K1. Telephone: (403) 434-7446.

Birding Features

There are several good birding spots. The ravines are the best areas, with Whitemud Park the outstanding place for diversity and numbers of birds. Drive to this park in the southwest section of the city, off Fox Drive, or take any of a number of city buses from the university. Other city ravines contain fewer birds. Check the city map for locations.

The woodlands along the river banks serve as a major stopover during migration. The north-south alignment of Whitemud Ravine funnels many birds through, particularly in the fall. The numerous fruiting trees planted in the city, mainly Mountain Ash and small crabapples, attract thousands of overwintering Bohemian Waxwings. The waxwings provide food for Merlins.

Spring begins in late February, with Great Horned Owls on eggs in the Whitemud Valley. Various waterfowl and occasional grebes turn up on the river as it breaks up in March or April. Golden and the more common Bald Eagles use the river as a main route on their way to nesting territories. Gulls start congregating on the river in late March. Juncos and sparrows move through by mid-April. The main migration of land birds takes place in mid-May. Watch for flycatchers, thrushes, vireos and warblers.

From late May to mid-July, some ducks, including Blue-winged Teal, Common Goldeneye and Mallard, are around. They nest in the less frequented parts of Whitemud Ravine. For some years, Peregrine Falcons have been released in the city from captive research stock. The first pair of these now-wild birds raised young that were placed on a shelf on a high-rise building in the downtown core in 1981. From mid-May to July, these birds may be observed at the nest by closed-circuit television in the main foyer of the Alberta Government Telephones Building.

Merlins raise young in old magpie nests throughout the city, in most of the larger developed and manicured parks, in the main cemeteries, and all along the river valley and ravines.

Great Horned Owl

Black-billed Magpie

American Kestrel nest at several sites in the city. Common Nighthawks nest on the roofs of downtown buildings and a few flat-topped suburban homes. A variety of land birds rear their young in the ravines and city parks. These include Belted Kingfisher, Pileated Woodpecker, Eastern Phoebe and Western Wood-Pewee. The Purple Martin is near the northern limits of its breeding range. Black-billed Magpie existed in small numbers until the late 1950s, when they started increasing. Today magpies are very common. Both White-breasted and Red-breasted Nuthatches nest in the city. The White-breasted first arrived from the southeast in the mid 1950s. Other birds to watch for as they raise nestlings are the Veery, Red-eyed and Warbling Vireos, Yellow-rumped and Mourning Warblers, and Ovenbird. The Western Tanager is easily found in Whitemud Ravine, together with the Rose-breasted Grosbeak and several sparrows, including Le Conte's, Vesper and Clay-colored, the latter bird being common.

From early August through October, many water birds are on the river. Both species of eagle move through going west along the valley. Huge flocks of Sandhill Cranes pass over in September. The movement of land birds, including some of the rarer warblers, is spectacular in August, particularly in Whitemud. Watch for Nashville, Blackburnian and Bay-breasted Warblers. In late September note the sparrows, including Harris'.

In winter, there are very few species of birds around Edmonton (36–38 on the Christmas bird-count). Mallard, Common Goldeneye and the occasional Common Merganser stay on the open water below the 105th Street Bridge and nearby Rossdale Power Plant. Merlins successfully pursue the thousands of Bohemian Waxwings. The occasional Northern Saw-whet and Snowy Owl enter the city. The Three-toed and, less commonly, the Black-backed Woodpecker, spend the winter in the ravines. Whitemud Park is one of the best places in Alberta to look for both in winter. Another good area lies north towards Bon Accord, alongside roads in "islands" of boreal forest among open fields. Boreal Chickadees move into the western ravines when the snow flies. The White-breasted and, less commonly, Red-breasted Nuthatches are at feeders. The Brown Creeper is around but uncommon. Golden-crowned Kinglets are often found on the university campus. Bohemian Waxwings' numbers have been over 16,000! Common and Hoary Redpolls are present, as are Evening and Pine Grosbeaks, and Red and White-winged Crossbills. Rarities, but still seen fairly regularly in winter, are Townsend's Solitaire, Varied Thrush, Rosy Finch and Steller's Jay.

Thousands of gulls are found from mid-April to the end of October at the Clover Bar disposal site. Ring-billed and California Gulls are the most numerous, with Herring and Franklin's present in smaller numbers. Early morning, before the garbage trucks arrive, is the best time. The site is located on the east side of the city, east of the Cloverbar bridge, north on 1st Street for about 3.2 km to the spot. Make sure to stop at the gate to ask permission to enter from the man in the booth. Iceland Gulls may be present, but you have to search for them.

TERRY THORMIN

Wagner Bog

Wagner Bog lies just west of Edmonton. Throughout the year, Pileated Woodpecker and Black-capped and Boreal Chickadees can be spotted. Both species of three-toed woodpeckers may be seen in winter. In late winter listen for owls calling. Spring and summer, numerous warblers are found nesting.

The property, originally private land, was well known to Edmonton naturalist and bird bander Edgar T. Jones. He arranged for the purchase and preservation of it by the provincial government, who gave it natural area status in 1971. The 259-ha block consists of Black Spruce–Sphagnum bog, with many calcareous ponds; half is in provincial hands, the rest is private property.

Drive west along the extension of Edmonton's 118th Avenue, to the corner where secondary road 794 proceeds north to Villeneuve. The bog lies to the southwest of this corner, with a very wet trail leading into the property at this point. Knee rubber boots should be worn when exploring the land.

Visitor accommodation and all services are in Edmonton.

Information on the area is best obtained from Terry Thormin or the John Janzen Nature Centre (see above).

To obtain bird and orchid lists and other information, contact the managing authority: Natural Areas Program, Land Management and Reservation Section, Public Lands Division, Alberta Government, 4th Floor, 9915 — 108 Street, Edmonton, Alberta T5K 2C9. In addition, there is a recent special issue of the *Edmonton Naturalist* devoted to this bog: *Edmonton Naturalist*, Special issue: the Wagner Bog, 1982, 10(2).

Birding Features

At any time, Pileated Woodpecker or at least its square chisellike holes at the base of trees will be seen. Black-capped and Boreal Chickadees and Great Horned Owl are usually present all year. By late February to early March, Northern Saw-whet, Boreal, Long-eared and Great Horned Owls are calling. They are best heard on clear, calm, moonlit nights on the trail into the bog. From mid-May to mid-July there are a broad variety of nesting birds at the bog. These include a few waterfowl, Red-tailed Hawk, Solitary Sandpiper, Lesser Yellowlegs, the owls heard in the late winter, Boreal and Black-capped Chickadees, Hermit and Swainson's Thrushes, Ruby-crowned Kinglet, Solitary, Red-eyed and Warbling Vireos, a variety of warblers, including the Cape May, and several sparrow species. From August through October, there is little activity except migrating Dark-eyed Junco and Tree Sparrow. From November to early April, both Black-backed and Three-toed Woodpeckers are found, as are the Golden-crowned Kinglet and sometimes winter finches.

TERRY THORMIN

Elk Island National Park

This island of boreal forest interspersed with aspen parkland and surrounded by farmland provides a variety of habitats for over 200 species of birds. The park is surrounded by a 2.4-m page wire fence and is the home of a large herd of Plains Bison, another of Wood Bison, and numerous Elk (Wapiti), White-tailed and Mule Deer, Moose and Coyote.

The park was established in 1899 when land was set aside as a federal timber reserve. In 1906, the northern part became an Elk preserve. Since then, the descendants of these original Elk have never been crossed with other subspecies. They are thus one of the few pure original herds of Elk in existence. This park also played a key role in preserving and housing the last herd of Plains Bison left in existence in those early years. In the mid-1960s one of the last of two remaining small herds of the largest North American mammal, the Wood Bison, was transferred to Elk Island.

The 194-km² park lies 35 km east of Edmonton on Highway 16. The Greyhound bus will stop at the south gate on the highway, if you ask. This company also runs a bus from Edmonton through Lamont, a town 5 km from the north gate. There is an extensive system of hiking trails through the rolling country in the northern two-thirds of the park. These trails and other amenities are illustrated on the park map-brochure, which is available from the information centre.

A campground is open in summer on a first-come basis. A more primitive group tenting area is provided for nonprofit organizations by reservation. Winter campers may use the boat launch area and the group tenting site. Commercial accommodation and other services may be obtained in Edmonton, 35 km west; Fort Saskatchewan, 25 km northwest; or Lamont, 5 km north.

Information on the park, including a bird checklist to be published shortly, is available from: The Superintendent, Elk Island National Park, Site 4, R.R. 1, Fort Saskatchewan, Alberta T8L 2N7, Telephone: (403) 998-3781. Park naturalists can assist you throughout the year at the main headquarters 16 km north of the main gate on Highway 16. There is also a book on nature in the park, *Island Forest Year: Elk Island National Park*, by D. E. Griffiths (Edmonton: U. of A. Press, 1979).

Birding Features

The park, surrounded by grain and cattle farms, contains a variety of habitats, some of which normally are found much further west and north. The interspersion of boreal forests and aspen parkland provides opportunities to bird-watch in White Spruce groves, Trembling Aspen clones, mixedwood forests, Black Spruce bogs, wetlands, eutrophic lakes and man-made grass meadows. During the breeding season observe Common Loon; four of the five Alberta grebe species (Western Grebe migrate through); the Black-crowned Night-Heron and Great Blue Heron; almost all the ducks on the prairies; possibly a Great Gray Owl; and both species of three-toed woodpeckers. Elk Island is one of the few places locally to find Mourning Dove, as this is near their northern limit.

During the fall and winter, look for Common Raven, Northern Goshawk, Spruce Grouse, Great Horned Owl, both Boreal and Northern Saw-whet Owls, Northern Hawk-Owl, both three-toed woodpeckers, possibly Brown Creeper and Golden-crowned Kinglet.

During spring (late April to early June) and fall (August and September) migration the numerous water bodies attract and hold a large number of water birds and some shorebirds. The mix of woodland types of habitat also makes the park an excellent source of land birds passing through. Look for American Tree and White-crowned Sparrows, particularly in the early spring.

The best water bird locality is the northwest end of Astotin Lake, accessible by trail and canoe. Astotin Lake is one of a very few areas outside of the mountains where Barrow's Goldeneye breed. This locality is closed to visitors during the breeding season. The interspersed spruce and aspen north and northeast of the recreation area are the best spots for land birds.

BILL FISHER AND STAFF OF ELK ISLAND NATIONAL PARK

Beaverhill Lake

Hosting huge concentrations of waterfowl and shorebirds each spring and fall, this large shallow body of water serves as a launching pad for arctic birds. Over 253 species have been reported. You can experience wave upon wave of Canada and Greater White-fronted Geese passing overhead, while nearby fields are covered with tens of thousands of these and Snow Geese. Of the 43 species of shorebirds noted for Alberta, all but three have been sighted at Beaverhill. Even Black-necked Stilts have been spotted on several occasions, including the first confirmed nesting record for Canada. Peregrine Falcons can be watched during migration, hunting shorebirds and waterfowl. Early spring and late fall bring tens of thousands of Tundra Swans. A winter trip to Beaverhill could result in sighting as many as twelve Snowy Owls from one location.

Beaverhill has fluctuated in water level from lows in the mid-1800s when buffalo walked across the dry bed, to highs in the early 1900s when cartloads of suckers and Pike were harvested. This perpetual interplay of water levels is the key to creating mudflats which provide vast food supplies for birdlife. Early ornithologists made major collections here, particularly in the 1920s.

With the constant changes of water level, local farmers pressed for drainage and/or damming. Finally, in 1972, a bay at the southeast corner was dammed off by Ducks Unlimited to create Robert Lister Lake. This small body of water now provides excellent breeding habitat.

The status of the crown land around the lake has changed from a Public Shooting Ground in 1925 to a National Nature Viewpoint declared by the Canadian Nature Federation in 1981.

The approximately 16-by-12-km lake lies about 65 km east of Edmonton on Highway 14. An access map is available from the John Janzen Nature Centre in Edmonton (see above). At Tofield turn north, and then sharply east just across the railway tracks and drive for from 4 to 8 km to side trails leading north about 1 km to the lake shore. In late spring, summer or fall you can drive along the south shore for about 4 km on a primitive trail to or from Robert Lister Lake and the dam. To reach the east shore, proceed east from Tofield for 6.4 km; south 1.6 km and east around the marsh for 4 km; north 1.6 km and then east 5.6 km; north 6.4 km and west to the end of the trail. Walk down to the shore. Another east access point lies 3.2 km north of the above west turn into the lake. The north end of the lake is reached from Highway 16, 20 km east of the main entrance to Elk Island National Park. To reach this north end, drive south from Highway 16, 3.2 km to the stone house and either hike or drive south on the primitive trail to the lake. The northwest end is reached 3.2 km west of the above stone house corner and 3.2 km south. This northwest side is the spot where we have watched wave after wave of geese leaving the lake to feed on nearby fields. The west side may be approached by driving 8 km north of Tofield and then east about 2 km to the end of the trail. All trails leading down and along the lake shore are usually not passable by car in early spring or after heavy rain.

The Greyhound bus goes through Tofield from Edmonton daily. A taxi may be rented in town to drive you out the 4 km to the south lake side.

Motel and hotel service are available in Tofield or Edmonton. Provincial roadside campsites are located on both Highway 14 to the south and Highway 16 to the north of the lake. Other services for vehicles and people are also available in Tofield.

Information on the natural history has been printed in several places, including a special issue of the *Edmonton Naturalist*, Vol. 5, No. 6, 1977, and an article by Dick Decker, "An Introduction to Beaverhill Lake," in *Alberta Naturalist*, March 1982. Much of the ornithological history of the lake has been documented in the book, *The Birds and Birders of Beaverhill Lakes*, by R. Lister (Edmonton: Edmonton Bird Club, 1979, 267 pp.). For additional assistance contact Terry Thormin. The John Janzen Nature Centre can provide a checklist for Beaverhill Lake, prepared by the Edmonton Bird Club.

Birding Features

The shallow lake, surrounded by grassy and often wooded shorelines, with a fluctuating water level, is a major feeding and staging area for waterfowl and shorebirds. Years of high water kill off the encroaching vegetation, widening the mudflats in late summer as the water drops. High water also inundates the colony of cormorants and pelicans. Upon the return of low water levels, these island nesters come back, as do other birds such as American Avocet, which feed and nest on the extensive mudflats during the summer.

Wind is also a major factor in the creation and maintenance of shorebird habitat. The prevailing winds from the northwest push the shallow waters up on the south end of the lake. This almost tidal action causes alternate flooding and drying of the shoreline, enhancing the mudflats.

The third factor important to the massive population of shorebirds is food — the immense numbers of midges hatching each year around mid-May. In calm periods these insects hang like low clouds, almost obstructing the view. When the wind picks up they seek shelter in the emergent and shoreline vegetation, and the shorebirds move in to feast. Dick Decker, in his article in *Alberta Naturalist*, mentions that in 1978 he estimated Pectoral Sandpipers in excess of 10,000 and 1500 Buff-breasted Sandpipers congregating in fields on the east side. Nearby pastures held 300 Black-bellied Plovers, 200 Red Knots and 150 Sanderlings. Several other species of shorebirds were also present in scattered flocks. If it is a late spring, with the midges hatching at the end of May, many sandpipers and plovers linger well into June.

The lake contains an intermittent colony of American White Pelicans and Double-crested Cormorants. This site is probably the best spot in Alberta to look for such rarities as Red-throated Loon, Great and Snowy Egrets, Brant, Wood Duck, Gyrfalcon (Peregrine Falcons are regular), Snowy Plover, Surfbird, Wandering Tattler, Black Turnstone, Western and Sharp-tailed Sandpipers, Black-necked Stilt, Red Phalarope, Parasitic and Long-tailed Jaegers, Glaucous, Thayer's, Mew and Sabine's Gulls, and Caspian Tern. Prairie birds spotted include Ferruginous Hawk, Prairie Falcon, Piping Plover, Long-billed Curlew, Sprague's Pipit (occasional breeder), Bobolink (occasional nester), Lark Bunting, Baird's Sparrow (occasional breeder), McCown's and Chestnut-collared Longspurs (occasional breeders). The lake, lying near both the Pacific and Central flyways, should attract other species.

If the season is early, the first Canada Goose appear in mid-March. They are followed by Greater White-fronted Goose and finally Tundra Swan. Early springs tend to hold birds at Beaverhill for a week or more, but in late years, these tens of thousands, often up to 100,000, move through very quickly. At the same time, ducks are building up in numbers. Rough-legged Hawks, eagles, Snowy Owls and Snow Buntings are going north. By early to mid-April the first shorebirds show up, usually the yellowlegs. The first large flocks of Lapland Longspur also appear. By the end of April all waterfowl, as well as grebes, cormorants and pelicans will be back. Most shorebirds will also have appeared. By this time Red-tailed and Swainson's Hawks and Northern Harriers occur regularly. There is a good possibility of spotting a Peregrine Falcon or even a Prairie Falcon. In April, check the grasslands on the south shore, about halfway along, for the dancing grounds of the Sharp-tailed Grouse. During the last few days of April or very early May, watch for masses of Sandhill Cranes going over in flock after flock, hour after hour. Late April and early May will often produce small numbers of Cinnamon Teals, Wood Ducks and Hooded Mergansers. By early May, many passerines are filtering through the nearby woods. May is the shorebird month. The best spots are along the south shore and the dam at Robert Lister Lake at the southeast corner. Before the lake is ice-free, check nearby flooded fields and wet meadows for yellowlegs, Pectoral Sandpipers, dowitchers and Hudsonian Godwits. If the spring is cold, the flocks go through in quick succession. In warm weather, with lots of food, their numbers are often large but spread out. The best seasons are those after a winter with little snow, followed by an early and warm spring. As the minimum meltwater pools in fields dry up, the birds congregate on the shore, where there is plenty of mudflat habitat. In early May, scan for groups of Hudsonian Godwits. Piping Plover and Long-billed Curlew occasionally straggle this far north. Large flocks of Red-necked Phalaropes can often be seen. In mid-May, inspect for the occasional flock of Ross' Geese or Smith's Longspurs. Check fields on the west side for these longspurs. The last three weeks of May will often produce small flocks of Lesser Golden-Plovers and Buff-breasted Sandpipers, especially in the fields just north of the north shore and occasionally in the fields along the east and west shores. This is midge time. The variety of shorebirds is surpassed only by their sheer numbers, with up to several thousand in the fields or along the shore. Examine each flock for Ruddy Turnstones, and Pectoral, Least, Semipalmated and Buff-breasted Sandpipers. The shorebird migration continues into June, gradually petering out by the middle or end of the month.

The nesters include Killdeer, Common Snipe, Willet, Marbled Godwit, American Avocet, a possible Black-necked Stilt and Wilson's Phalarope. These species continuously call, so the symphony remains until mid- to late July. Nesting waterfowl include the normal complement of prairie-pothole species. Eared and Western Grebes also raise young. The Great Blue Heron colony lies near the north end. Small rocky islands are home to American White Pelican and Double-crested Cormorant. Several colonies of California and Herring Gulls and Common Terns occur. Nesting marsh birds to ferret out include Pied-billed Grebe, Black-crowned Night-Heron, Marsh Wren, Yellow-headed and Red-winged Blackbirds and Le Conte's Sparrow. Yellow Rail, Sedge Wren and Sharp-tailed Sparrow are reported occasionally. Try Robert Lister Lake for these marsh species and waterfowl. Nearby open fields should be scanned for prairie birds, including Sprague's Pipit, Bobolink, Baird's Sparrow and Chestnut-collared Longspur.

The fall movement is considerably more prolonged than spring migration. By mid-July, the first shorebirds are back and by the end of the month most species are in. These early returnees consist of flocks of adult non- or unsuccessful breeders. Fall is also the best time for rarities and accidentals. By mid-August, the shorebird migration has swelled to a tide of hundreds to thousands of individuals including yellowlegs, Pectoral Sandpiper, dowitchers, Stilt Sandpiper and many others. Dowitchers are in the greatest numbers, but a good day can produce 15 to 20 species of waders. The numbers persist into September, and even early October some years, before a gradual decline occurs. The last shorebirds are gone by early November. Mid- to late August usually sees a buildup of geese and Sandhill Crane numbers. Predatory birds, too, return to harass the shorebirds. Look for Peregrine Falcon and Parasitic Jaeger and maybe even a Long-tailed Jaeger. By early to mid-September, Tundra Swans line the shores in thousands and remain numerous until late October before diminishing in November. September is the time to study each flock of waders carefully in search of one of Canada's rarest shorebirds — the Sharp-tailed Sandpiper. Recent records indicate that it is probably a regular visitor in numbers from one to six with most sightings just west of the dam at Robert Lister Lake. In October, check the fields for large flocks of longspurs and buntings. The south shore collects large numbers of ducks at this time, attracted by the feeding station lure programs. Scrutinize tall snags for Bald Eagles, which regularly pick off crippled ducks until after freeze-up. By early to mid-November the lake starts to freeze and most birds disappear.

In winter, try open fields and nearby woodlands. Snowy Owls can be very common, particularly in the northwest corner. A few Rough-legged Hawks are usually present, with the occasional Northern Shrike. Hoary Redpolls usually occur among the flocks of Common Redpolls. Snow Buntings may be common. By late February to early March, the first Great Horned Owl has started to nest and spring has returned.

TERRY THORMIN

Dinosaur Provincial Park

Dinosaur Provincial Park has the richest beds of dinosaur fossils in North America. More than 200 major finds of these prehistoric animals have been made within the park. These key collections may be seen in most major museums throughout the world. The park also contains some of the finest badland terrain in Canada. Of the 130 species of birds reported to date, 64 nest regularly in the park. Look for a great variety of prairie birds, two species of cactus, sagebrush and greasewood and dinosaur bones in place. Noteworthy mammals include White-tailed and Mule Deer, and Pronghorn (Antelope).

The park, established in 1955, became a world heritage site of UNESCO in 1979. Located 48 km north and east of Brooks, which in turn is 186 km south and east of Calgary on the Trans-Canada Highway, the park contains a major visitor complex. There is a looped road and a series of hiking trails that may be used to explore the northwestern part of the park. Access to the east and southeast section, a natural preserve, is allowed only if visitors are accompanied by a tour guide.

Visitor accommodation within the park includes two fully serviced campgrounds, one of which serves as an overflow and group site. Motels, hotels, groceries and gasoline are all available at Brooks. The article "The Birds of Dinosaur Provincial Park" in the *Blue Jay* of June 1978 has helpful information. Information on the park, including a bird checklist and a park brochure, is available from: Park Ranger, Dinosaur Provincial Park, Patricia, Alberta.

Birding Features

The first view of Dinosaur Provincial Park is dramatic, with gently rolling prairie suddenly dropping off into the Red Deer River valley of badlands, containing pinnacles, earth pillars, gorges and buttes. There are at least 14 types of habitat for birds within the park. About 15 per cent is prairie, 75 per cent badlands and 10 per cent river terraces. The riverine habitat supports the greatest variety of birds. Breeding birds in the park are mainly those with an eastern and southern affinity. Relatively few northern and western species occur. The mean annual rainfall is only 330 mm, of which 203 mm falls from May to September — a near desert!

The variety of microhabitats provides a visitor, during the breeding season from mid-April to July, with opportunities to see a Great Blue Heron colony on the island in the river near the western edge of the park; Canada Geese on nests on cliffs, or with young on the river; and a few ducks in the surrounding area, with minimal water. Several species of birds of prey nest within or come into the park to feed. Two pairs of Ferruginous Hawks breed in the park. Golden Eagle generally nests here. Prairie Falcons have at least four and possibly ten active eyries, and there are at least three active pairs of Merlins. American Kestrels and Sharp-tailed Grouse are present. Long-billed Curlews have nested on the prairie along the western boundary. Northern Saw-whet Owls have been heard calling in mid-May. Upland birds include Say's Phoebe in the badlands and Horned Lark on the prairie. Rock Wrens are abundant nesters in the badlands. Brown Thrashers occur in tall shrubs. The Mountain Bluebird, which has greatly declined in other areas, is still numerous. Common Yellowthroats are frequently seen in low shrubs along the river. Yellow-breasted Chats occur in thickets of thorny Buffalo Berry. Rufous-sided Towhees of the spotted race are found regularly in treed and shrub areas. Brewer's and Grasshopper Sparrows may be spotted in sagebrush flats. Vesper Sparrows are fairly numerous along escarpment edges. Lark Sparrows are among the most abundant and characteristic birds of the badlands and sage flats. Chestnut-collared Longspurs are typical of the prairies.

From early April to mid-June, and from mid-July to mid-September, there are opportunities to observe at least 43 other species passing through. The river and adjacent shrubs and trees provide excellent stopover sites for migrating passerines and shorebirds. Such species as Ruby-crowned Kinglet, Water Pipit, Black-and-white Warbler, Orange-crowned Warbler, American Redstart, White-crowned Sparrow and Lincoln's Sparrow have all been reported.

NORBERT KONDLA

Lake Newell and Kinbrook Island Provincial Park

Lake Newell, the largest body of water in southeastern Alberta, was man-made in 1912. The lake, its shore lined with poplar and willow, numerous nearby irrigation ditches and homesteads with abundant planted trees, and the surrounding short-grass prairie provide a major stopover area for thousands of migrating waterfowl and hundreds of upland birds. An added attraction is the goodly number of whitefish and Northern Pike which can be caught in spare moments away from bird watching.

The lake was created by the Canadian Pacific Railroad to attract settlers, who arrived between 1915 and 1919. By the early 1930s, these pioneers were in financial difficulties. In 1935, the entire area was transferred to a board of trustees, composed of local farmers, and it is now an Irrigation District.

The lake and small (38 ha) Kinbrook Island Provincial Park lie 16 km south of Brooks on Highway 1, 186 km southeast of Calgary. Greyhound buses from points east and west stop daily at Brooks.

Visitor services in Brooks include motels, a hotel, groceries and service stations. Camping is on a first-come basis at Kinbrook Island Provincial Park. Tillebrook Trans-Canada campsite lies 11 km southeast of Brooks. Information on Kinbrook Island Provincial Park can be obtained from: The Ranger, Kinbrook Island Provincial Park, Brooks, Alberta.

Birding Features
The lake, numerous smaller lakes and ponds, canals, ditches and extensive cat-tail marshes provide habitat for a great variety of birds not otherwise seen in the area. Many nearby farmsteads have native and imported trees and shrubs planted around the homes, attracting upland bird species usually absent from the prairies but now abundant both as migrants in spring and fall and as breeding birds.

The more interesting birds of the area include breeding Common Loons and Red-necked, Horned and Eared Grebes (Western pass through). American White Pelicans often feed on the lake. Double-crested Cormorants nest from mid-April until July in large numbers (over 500 nests) on an island at the south end of the lake. Tundra Swans often stop in large numbers during spring and fall. Canada Geese nest regularly. White-fronted Geese stop in large flocks on fall migration. Sage Grouse may be found at times in the area. Long-billed Curlew are quite common, as are Willet and Marbled Godwit. One island in the south end of the lake contains the second-largest colony of Ring-billed Gulls in the province, and California Gulls nest in large numbers (also over 500 nests) in the same area. The planting of trees around home-steads has attracted Mourning Dove, which nests. Burrowing Owl can be found throughout the area in small colonies. Horned Lark and Chestnut-collared Longspur are found on the open prairies.

NORBERT KONDLA

Cypress Hills Provincial Park

The Cypress Hills stand 600 m above the surrounding prairie. This oasis of forest capped with grass-covered plateau contains a combination of cli-matic, geologic and biological systems found nowhere else in the grasslands of western Canada. Among the 200 species of birds spotted here (98 confirmed as nesting) are Wild Turkey; the Mearn's (pink-sided) race of Dark-eyed Junco, the only place it can regularly be found in Canada; and in the Saskatchewan portion of the hills, Trumpeter Swan. Mountain plants and butterflies, Moose, Elk, White-tailed and Mule Deer are also present.

The Blackfeet discouraged white traders and trappers until the late 1860s, leaving this area the last refuge in southern Alberta for Wolf and Grizzly Bear. Fire destroyed most of the forest in 1886, and what remained was cut until the hills were made a dominion forest reserve in 1906, then a provincial park in 1945. Three major dams were built to provide water reservoirs for the herds of local cattlemen, and reforestation, regulated timber harvesting, fire protection, and regulated grazing and haying were practised.

This 210-km² park lies 20 km east of Medicine Hat on the Trans-Canada Highway, and 34 km south on Highway 41. Greyhound bus services Medicine Hat. Hiking trails and paved and gravelled roads within the park are shown on the brochure.

The park contains several campgrounds, some completely serviced. Amenities are available at Medicine Hat and at the town of Elkwater, within the park. For information contact: The Chief Ranger, Cypress Hills Provin-cial Park, Elkwater, Alberta.

Birding Features
The hills are significantly cooler and moister than the surrounding plains. Consequently, plants and animals have both prairie and cordilleran affini-ties. Some species are found nowhere else in Alberta; others are to be found no closer than 300 km to the west. The best birding sites occur around Spruce Coulee and Reesor Lake. The fire tower lookout west of the Elkwater townsite is another good spot. Descriptions below are based on an unpub-lished manuscript by C. A. Wallis and C. R. Wershler.

Fescue grasslands cover most of the upper plateau and much of the exposed slopes. Sharp-tailed Grouse are found in the low shrubbery coulees in the southern part and in the few remaining areas of lightly or ungrazed dense and tussocky grasslands. Watch for Upland Sandpiper in dense grass and shrub cover. Sprague's Pipit prefers the dense ungrazed grasslands and isolated clumps of ungrazed grasses within shrub clusters. Western Meadowlarks are found throughout the grasslands. Lush grass on the lower slopes, and locally on the plateau, are favoured sites for Baird's Sparrow. Vesper Sparrows prefer grazed areas and are most abundant on drier, more heavily grazed slopes below the plateau and in shrubbery on the plateau. Chestnut-collared Longspurs occur in heavily grazed grasslands at the edges of the park.

Look for a Song Sparrow in open willow shrubbery adjacent to Elkwater Lake and along the broader stream valleys. Redstarts occur in tall willows, often found in association with spruce and poplar. Mixed tangles of a variety of shrubs are favourite sites for Dusky Flycatcher and White-crowned Sparrow. Gray Catbird and Brown Thrasher are uncommon at lower altitudes near Elkwater Lake and in the Medicine Lodge Coulee area. Other birds found in shrubs at lower altitudes include Clay-colored Sparrow, Brewer's Blackbird and Rufous-sided Towhee. Both wet and dry shrublands attract MacGillivray's Warbler and Common Yellowthroat. Lazuli Buntings are seen occasionally in tall shrubs and along woodland edges on semi-open south-facing slopes. Look for these birds in the southwest corner and along Battle Creek near the Alberta-Saskatchewan border.

The areas with deciduous trees attract Veery and Red-eyed Vireo. Mixed woodlands are favoured by Cooper's and Broad-winged Hawks. In mature woods, look for Northern Saw-whet Owl, Hairy Woodpecker, Ovenbird and Orange-crowned Warbler. Ruffed Grouse, introduced to the area, are found throughout the mature forests. The workings of Pileated Woodpeckers are sometimes seen here. Red-headed Woodpeckers have been reported and Winter Wrens are rarely seen. The Common Poorwill appears sporadically in grassy forest openings along the edge of the plateau, but is more common in nearby Saskatchewan. Look for Audubon's race of the Yellow-rumped Warbler, pink-sided race of the Dark-eyed Junco, and White-winged and Red Crossbills in coniferous forests. Sight Western Tanager around beaver ponds.

Open water in the three main reservoirs attracts typical prairie waterfowl. There are plans to provide habitat for Trumpeter Swan, which once nested in the park. They still may be seen in the nearby Saskatchewan portion of the hills.

Townsend's Solitaire nests on exposed conglomerate cliffs at the northern edge of the escarpment.

Pakowki Lake

One of the largest bodies of water in southeastern Alberta, Pakowki Lake contains a wide variety of birds. The lake was established as a federal Migratory Bird Sanctuary in 1920, and to date, pressures to eliminate protection have been resisted. In drought years, most of the water dries up except in the northwestern area of the lake, the best birding spot. This site is 40 km southeast of Medicine Hat on Highway 3, and approximately 50 km south on secondary road 885. The nearest town with visitor services and a provincial campground is Foremost, 10 km north and 27 km west of the lake.

Birding Features
Because of its isolated location, there has been little work done on birds of the area. In years of no rain (up to 50 per cent of the time) small patches of water usually remain, producing one of the best marsh birding sites in southern Alberta. The north-central part of the lake has numerous islands ranging in size from a few acres to several square km. These islands make ideal nesting sites for colonial water birds. CAUTION: stay away from these islands during the nesting season to avoid disturbance and possible loss of young.

Rarities which have been seen here include Black-necked Stilt, Snowy Egret and Eurasian Wigeon. A regular visitor and probable nester is the White-faced Ibis, found nowhere else in Canada. The lake is the southern breeding limit in Alberta of Western and Pied-billed Grebes, Double-crested Cormorant, Redhead, Canvasback, Franklin's Gull and Marsh Wren. The lake contains one of the few known nesting colonies of Forster's Tern in Alberta and one of the largest Black-crowned Night-Heron colonies in the province.

Milk River Canyon and Vicinity

The Milk River Canyon and adjacent sites in extreme southeastern Alberta, and southwestern Saskatchewan, contain the only known breeding localities of Mountain Plover in Canada. Another bird of the American southwest, the Black-headed Grosbeak, also nests here. Birds more usual to the north and west, such as the Golden Eagle and Violet-green Swallow, have localized outposts of their breeding ranges. Plants such as Yucca, which normally don't reach north into Canada, occur here. Fish and other aquatic animals of the Mississippi-Missouri river systems reach northwest into this country, as the Milk River is the only Alberta river to flow south to the Gulf of Mexico.

The area is accessible from the west at Milk River on secondary and tertiary roads east from Highway 4; from the northwest off Highway 61, and from the north, south on Highway 48 through the Cypress Hills. The nearest commercial accommodation, groceries and gasoline is at Foremost to the northwest, Milk River to the west, and Medicine Hat, far to the north. All of these communities are over 100 km away. It is advisable when travelling in this country from mid-June to mid-September to take drinking water as the temperatures may reach very high levels.

Sage Grouse

Birding Features

There have been 157 bird species reported from the area, with at least 90 nesting. From late April to mid-July, the normal complement of prairie waterfowl may be found on the sloughs and rivers. Turkey Vultures have been seen. Numerous nests of Ferruginous Hawk are observed along the coulees, but active eyries are few. There are at least four active nests of Golden Eagle at this southeast outpost of their breeding range. Prairie Falcons are even more abundant with at least five active eyries located on ledges of sandstone outcrops or on cliffs. Sage Grouse are seen sporadically in the Lost River vicinity. They have a dancing ground north along Canal Creek.

This is the only area in Canada in which Mountain Plover have been found nesting. The nesting habitat is within 15 or 20 km of the Canada–U.S. border, between Onefour and Wildhorse in the southeast corner of Alberta. [See "Status and Breeding of Mountain Plovers *(Charadrius montanus)* in Canada," by C. A. Wallis and C. R. Wershler in *Canadian Field-Naturalist*, 1981, 95:2, pp. 133–6.] The best place to look for this plover is extensive unbroken grassland with very short native grasses. The birds arrive here about the second or third week of April and lay eggs about the second or third week of May.

Other summer nesting birds include Long-billed Curlew, which may be found in shorter grass, and Upland Sandpiper, found in thicker, taller grass. Willet and Marbled Godwit occur along slough edges and sometimes near the river. American Avocets are common along the edges of the larger sloughs, as are Wilson's Phalaropes. There are at least four pairs of Black-billed Cuckoos nesting along the lower Milk River. Burrowing Owls may be seen near the Milk River east of Comrey. Eastern and Western Kingbirds occur in wooded sites. Say's Phoebes nest commonly in badlands and coulees. Two different races of Horned Lark are present. The summer breeding race is the most common bird of the grassland. These birds move south for winter and are replaced by a more northern race that overwinters in the area. The Violet-green Swallow breeds throughout the badlands and riverine woods. This is an eastern outpost of the breeding range of this species. Other swallows that breed in the area include Bank along the Milk River; Northern Rough-winged along both the Milk River and Kennedy Creek; Barn around buildings; and Cliff with numerous colonies in coulees and the badlands. Interestingly coloured hybrids between the Bullock's and Baltimore races of Northern Oriole occur in most larger cottonwood stands. These stands are also home to Black-headed Grosbeaks, particularly along the lower Milk River. Lazuli Buntings nest in tall riverine shrubbery along the lower Milk River Valley. Rosy Finches have been observed going to roost in the evening within the urn-shaped mud nests of Cliff Swallows along the Milk River in February. The spotted (western) race of Rufous-sided Towhee is common in the woods along the river in summer. Lark Buntings are locally distributed in sagebrush country. Lark Sparrows are fairly common in the badlands and sagebrush flats and nearby woodlands. Both McCown's and Chestnut-collared Longspurs are fairly common in patches of shorter grass and near dried-up sloughs.

NORBERT KONDLA

Waterton Lakes National Park

The Rocky Mountains abut the prairies at Waterton, creating sharply differing habitats within a very few kilometres. Over 120 years of records exist on this fine birding site, with 228 confirmed species. Plan a trip to include mountains, different types of forests and the prairies, as many of these birds have specialized habitat preferences. An excellent bird list is available from the park office. The park also contains Grizzly Bear, Moose, Elk, Mule Deer and, in a paddock, Plains Bison.

The area was virtually unknown to whites until 1858, when the Palliser expedition named the lakes after eighteenth-century English naturalist Charles Waterton. Early settlers, including John Charlie "Kootenai" Brown, pressed the government to declare this unique area a forest reserve. It became a national park in 1911. Under the vision of "Kootenai" Brown and Albert "Death on the Trail" Reynolds, a ranger at Glacier National Park across the border in the U.S., and pressure from Rotary Clubs in Alberta and Montana, the two parks were united at the border in 1932, the world's first international peace park.

The 525-km^2 park lies 276 km south of Calgary via Highways 2 and 5. Commercial buses run from Calgary throughout the summer. Special tour buses can be taken to both the Canadian and American portions of the park. Consult a travel agent for details.

Good paved roads, back-country hiking trails, amenities and major interpretive features are all illustrated on the park map-brochure. Boats travel from the marina at Waterton to the far end of the lake in Glacier National Park, Montana, providing spectacular scenery and an excellent array of birds.

Motel accommodations should be booked ahead of time. Sites at the three major campgrounds, which accommodate every type of recreational vehicle and provide winter camping, are available on a first-come basis. Through July and August they are often full by midday.

Contact the staff naturalists at the townsite headquarters for information on finding the rarer species of birds. Two major reports on the birds of Waterton are available at headquarters. Further information may be obtained from: The Superintendent, Waterton Lakes National Park, Waterton Park, Alberta T0K 2M0, Telephone: (403) 859-2262.

Birding Features

Two major migration routes, Trans-mountain and Central, traverse the park. Several western species cross the adjacent low mountain pass to nest, or are blown over in severe storms. Other species reach their northern limit here.

The 13 habitat types within the park are: wetlands (98 bird species), poplar forests (75), coniferous forests (60), prairie and prairie shrubland (56), mixed forests (48), slope and limber pine shrubland (40), Krummholz (23), anthropogenic (20), conifer savannah (16), alpine and subalpine meadows (14), rock ledges (6) and cliffs (5).

Seven birding areas include most of these habitats. The Maskinonge Lake marsh, with thick deciduous woods, contains ducks and upland birds. The area near the buffalo paddock and the hiking trail proceeding north from the elbow of the Blakiston Valley Road offer prairie-grassland species. The Chief Mountain Highway, southeast from the park gate, also offers prairie-grassland species; the first 1.6 km contain deciduous woods and aspen parkland bird species. The Crandell Lake area contains Lodgepole Pine forest. At Cameron Lake, dense, humid, spruce-fir forests, more typical of B.C., host western species such as Lewis' Woodpecker. Hike from here into the Carthew Lakes, where alpine habitat, Bark Pine, and Alpine and Douglas Fir host their special species.

All five Alberta grebes may be observed. Tundra and Trumpeter Swans migrate through, as does the occasional Wood Duck. Barrow's and Common Goldeneyes are present, with Barrow's nesting. Harlequin Ducks nest along the rivers. Golden Eagles nest and Bald Eagles migrate through. Ospreys nest near the lakes. American Kestrel, Merlin, and Prairie and Peregrine Falcons occur, with all but the Peregrine seen regularly. All five grouse found are nesters: Sharp-tailed on the prairies, Ruffed in the parkland, Spruce and Blue in the forests, and White-tailed Ptarmigan in the mountain meadows. Of the 16 species of shorebirds occurring, most are spring and fall migrants. Spotted Sandpiper nests along streams, and Wilson's Phalarope near prairie potholes. Black-billed Cuckoos are rare summer visitors. Of the 6 owl species reported, the Great Horned and perhaps Great Gray nest. Of the 3 hummingbirds, only the Calliope is a confirmed nester. The 10 species of woodpeckers include: Northern Flicker, Yellow-bellied Sapsucker, Hairy, Downy, Three-toed and Black-backed, all nesting; Lewis' appears in the southwest corner of the park; even the Red-headed of eastern Canada has occurred. Eleven species of flycatcher are found, mainly those of parkland habitat. Swallows include Violet-green (mountain), Tree (parkland), Bank, Northern Rough-winged, Barn and Cliff. Steller's Jays nest.

Black-billed Magpie (parkland) can be found, as can Clark's Nutcracker (mountains) and chickadees including Black-capped, Mountain and Boreal. American Dipper is common along streams. A variety of thrushes and warblers appears in the woodlands. The prairies also host Western Meadowlark, Yellow-headed and Red-winged Blackbirds, and Indigo, Lazuli and Lark Buntings. Adjacent woodlands produce Black-headed Grosbeak, Rufous-sided Towhee and, higher up, Golden-crowned and White-crowned Sparrows.

K. E. SEEL

Calgary

Calgary, with foothills and mountains to the immediate west, prairies and irrigation lands to the east and south, and aspen parkland to the nearby north and west, offers a variety of habitats for over 300 bird species; of these, 182 nest within an 80-km radius of downtown.

The city began with the arrival of the North West Mounted Police in the mid-1870s. Before that, the Blackfoot Confederacy, a strong Indian alliance, controlled the area from present-day Red Deer south into the state of Montana. The railroad came in the mid-1880s, bringing a flood of settlers. Today Calgary has become the Canadian headquarters for major oil- and gas-related companies — a white-collared city with a variety of cultural assets. In addition, with the heritage of ranching from the surrounding grasslands, the "cowboy" element is still quite prominent.

The airport has direct links to many world cities. The east-west major passenger rail and bus lines, and the Trans-Canada Highway, provide ready access. A major motel village lies along 16th Avenue on Highway 1 on the north side of the city. Campgrounds are provided, particularly to the west and south, in the recently developed Kananaskis Country.

Information on natural areas in and around the city is available from the book *Calgary's Natural Areas: A Popular Guide*, edited by Peter Sherrington and published by the Calgary Field Naturalists' Society. The guide contains material on geology, flora and fauna, walking trips through twelve natural areas and six checklists. The list of birds gives those recorded for each area and when they can be seen. The society has also published a "Check List of the Birds of the Calgary Region." This list and other information are available from: Calgary Field Naturalists' Society, P.O. Box 981, Calgary, Alberta T2P 2R4. Information for the Calgary area has been gleaned from a draft of a booklet on bird finding in the region, soon to be published by the society.

Birding Features
Inglewood Bird Sanctuary. This sanctuary, with more than 216 recorded species, is located in the east centre of the city on the Bow River. A checklist is available at the office, the big house on site. Take 9th Avenue southeast from the city centre, pass the Gulf Oil Refinery, cross a railroad and take the first street to the south, or right. From this point, follow the signs to the

sanctuary parking lot. There are over 4 km of connecting trails through grasslands, shrub and riverine woods set on the banks of the Bow River. Washrooms, picnic tables, duck ponds and natural history displays all add to an enjoyable visit. The variety of birds is the consistent feature, plus migrants in April to May and August to October.

Shepard Sloughs. The drive through prairie, southeast of Calgary, provides a good cross-section of local birdlife. In winter Snowy Owls are usually present in several spots and raptors are common in spring and fall. A visit to the Shepard Sloughs at the height of migration can be accomplished in two to three hours.

Proceed south from Calgary on Highway 2; turn east on 22X, 1.6 km south of the city limits at the sign posted to Shepard. Travel east across the Bow River. Stop on the west side of the bridge and look for grebes and ducks. Inspect the poplars along the bank for a possible bird of prey. Continue east beyond the subdivision on the north side. Study the several sloughs, all of which are good for water birds and shorebirds.

At 11.3 km explore three small sloughs. Turn north for about 0.8 km where the road bends to the left, then straightens past another slough that has water during the spring. Farther along, beyond the next farmhouse, watch for Burrowing and Short-eared Owls in the pasture to the east. Turn right at the crossroads at 17.7 km, along the edge of Shepard, and proceed east. In spring scan the sloughs on the south. Turn north at 33.8 km. The paved road, Glenmore Trail, is at 37.0 km. Consult the bird-finding guide for Calgary, mentioned above, for details on further exploration.

Priddis and Radio Tower Sloughs. To see a cross-section of water birds and marsh species, drive south on Highway 2. Turn west onto 22X, just past the city limits, and proceed 0.8 km to Priddis Slough. Park on the available turnoffs, on either side. From mid-April to July, scan for a variety of water and shorebirds. A walk along the railroad track will sometimes produce warblers and sparrows. Water Pipits often occur here in the fall. Proceed west 0.4 km and turn north on the short road to the Radio Tower Slough. This marshy water body contains a selection of ducks, coots, Sora, and Yellow-headed and Red-winged Blackbirds.

Frank Lake. This "Beaverhill of southern Alberta" lies 41 km south of Calgary on Highway 2, and 6 km east on Highway 23. Access is from the northwest and south ends. A hike of from four to seven hours should suffice to circumnavigate the lake. April to May and September to October are the best times to spot up to 500,000 water birds, with the odd rarity a good possibility.

Kananaskis Country

Kananaskis Country is the official name of a major provincial recreation area southwest of Calgary. Over 245 species of birds have been reported there.

You can see Osprey and a possible Peregrine Falcon, the latter because of a special peregrine reintroduction project. In addition, White-tailed Ptarmigan, Blue and Spruce Grouse, and Calliope Hummingbird nest; Northern Pygmy and Boreal Owls are heard; and Three-toed Woodpeckers can be found.

The area has long been recognized for its scenic beauty, having been part of Rocky Mountain National Park from 1902 to 1911 and Banff National Park from 1917 to 1931. The land was then transferred to the province. The portion around the Kananaskis lakes was declared a provincial park in 1977. Bow Valley and Bragg Creek provincial parks are also part of Kananaskis Country.

The area totals 5200 km² and is bounded on the northwest by the Continental Divide and British Columbia, including B.C.'s Elk Lakes Provincial Park. Rangeland lies to the east and north. Kananaskis Country is composed of long valleys, foothills and mountains, forests, subalpine and alpine tundra. The various amenities, including trail layouts, are shown on the brochure entitled "This is Kananaskis Country," available from Travel Alberta offices or by writing: Kananaskis Country Office, Alberta Recreation and Parks, 412—1011 Glenmore Trail S.W., Calgary, Alberta T2V 4R6. Visitor accommodation and amenities are available in Calgary or at Canmore, at the north end of the complex. New facilities will soon be available in the valley.

For information on the natural and human history of the region, reports for reference and a bird checklist, contact: Interpretation Staff, Alberta Recreation and Parks, Kananaskis and Bow Valley Parks, Seebee, Alberta T0L 1X0.

There is a main road through the area and a driving loop that takes two days; a description covering this loop has been prepared by the Calgary Field Naturalists' Society (refer above). Much of the information used here has been taken from this guide.

Birding Features

Most of the montane birds of Alberta are represented here, together with the mountain specialties which can be found on short hikes from the road. Birds to see in this region include Lazuli Bunting in open areas and Mountain Bluebird at bird boxes on the east side of the region. At streams and rivers look for Harlequin Duck and American Dipper, with a Willow Flycatcher and Northern Waterthrush among shrubs. As you drive through the forests, stop and listen for the different thrushes, including Townsend's Solitaire on open ridges. Kinglets and Three-toed Woodpeckers are relatively common in these woods. Warblers abound in June. The open slopes have Blue and Spruce Grouse. At or near the Highwood Pass summit, get out and hike to see a White-tailed Ptarmigan, Rosy Finch, Clark's Nutcracker and Water Pipit. Check at the timberline for Hammond's Flycatcher and Brewer's and Fox Sparrows.

At Upper Kananaskis Lake scan for loons, grebes and ducks during migration. Hike the nearby trails for forest birds mentioned above. Look up — you may spot a Black Swift.

Drive to the administration area near Lower King Creek. Check out the large shrub meadow to the south. In fall you may find a Calliope Humming-bird and several warbler and sparrow species. Ask the resident naturalists for key spots.

At the research station, 9 km south of Highway 1, take the looped nature trail for a good variety of habitat and birds. You are welcome to examine the property around the buildings. You may spot a hummingbird. The Travel Alberta Information Centre, 8 km south of Highway 1, has had good luck with hummingbird feeders.

Banff National Park

Banff, the oldest national park in Canada and second oldest in the world, lies within the Canadian Rocky Mountains. Nearly 250 bird species have been reported in the park. Birds you have a good chance to spot, in season, include Harlequin Duck, White-tailed Ptarmigan, Northern Hawk-Owl, Black Swift, Three-toed Woodpecker, American Dipper, Varied Thrush, Townsend's Warbler and Rosy Finch. There are possibilities of sighting Northern Pygmy and Boreal Owls and Cassin's Finch. Banff contains populations of Elk (Wapiti), White-tailed and Mule Deer, Moose, Bighorn Sheep and Mountain Goat. Some, like the deer and sheep, may be seen very near town. Both Black and Grizzly Bears are common, so take appropriate precautions and don't leave food or garbage near your tent.

The discovery of the hot springs in 1883 led to the establishment of the 26-km^2 Hot Springs Reserve in 1885. This was the birth of the Canadian national parks system. Today the park has grown to 6641 km^2, composed of 65 per cent alpine habitat, 30 per cent subalpine forests and only 3 per cent montane lands.

The park lies 134 km west of Calgary. Highway 1 provides access to Banff townsite and Lake Louise for over a million visitors a year. Greyhound buses and VIA Rail run daily through the park between Calgary and Vancouver. Some of the Banff accommodation facilities provide regular pick-up service in Calgary. There are a series of roads and more than 1100 km of trails for hikers and cross-country skiers. The park brochures, available from headquarters, show these, other amenities, and special interpretive features. Commercial accommodation is in and around the town of Banff and at Lake Louise, 56 km north. Other cabins are available along this route. Gasoline and related services, including a great variety of tourist shops, are found in Banff and Lake Louise. Minimum services, including gasoline, are also available at Saskatchewan Crossing, where the David Thompson Highway 11 meets the Jasper-Banff road, 76 km north of Lake Louise. This David Thompson road links the Kootenay Plains (a prairie community of plants and birds occurring in the mountains) to Rocky Mountain House and Red Deer on Highway 2 — an alternative and lovely route into the national park. Contiguous to the west of Banff, Yoho National Park lies along Highway 1, and Kootenay National Park along Highway 93. Both routes cross over mountain passes, bringing you into subalpine country and the birds occurring in these highlands. There are ten serviced campgrounds within Banff

Park. Winter camping permits may be obtained from the park administration.

Information on natural and human history, and a seasonal bird checklist (the same as for Jasper) showing relative abundance and detailed descriptions, are included in "A Birder's Guide to Banff National Park," by G. L. Holroyd and K. Van Tighen in *Alberta Naturalist*, 1982, 12(1). For a copy, contact: The Superintendent, Banff National Park, P.O. Box 900, Banff, Alberta T0L 0C0, Telephone: (403) 762-3324. Most of the information for Banff has been taken from this bird guide.

There is also a special publication by the Bow Valley Naturalists: *Vermilion Lakes, Banff National Park, An Introductory Study*. This booklet may be obtained for $3.00 from: Bow Valley Naturalists, P.O. Box 1693, Banff, Alberta T0L 0C0.

Birding Features

Banff Park contains a wide variety of habitats from wooded valley lowlands and hot springs to alpine glaciers. Birdlife is most abundant in the lower Bow Valley near Banff. To the west is the Continental Divide, and beyond, the wet, heavily forested mountains of British Columbia. To the east lie the dry prairies of Alberta. The low mountain passes allow bird stragglers from B.C. to appear regularly at Banff. Similarly, the Banff lowlands are often visited by prairie species. Chinook winds from the west may bring in early spring birds. Banff often reports species as first arrivals for Alberta in this season of awakening. Birds may remain quite late into the fall before moving on.

Lake Minnewanka. The lake lies 6 km northeast of the Banff traffic circle. Continue on this road to check out Two Jack Lake. From early April to late May, scan both lakes for Common Loon and a variety of ducks including Ring-necked Duck and Barrow's Goldeneye. Mountain Bluebirds gather insects along the roadside. From May to August, Violet-green and other swallows feed over the water. Migrating waterfowl again become common in September and October. Check the lakeshores for warblers and sparrows.

Banff Townsite. Here you'll find a variety of birds in early spring. Migrants, including American Robin, Red-winged Blackbird and Song Sparrow appear in late March, particularly near the stables below the Cave and Basin Road. In late April, look for the first Violet-green and Tree Swallows over the town. By mid-May the Cliff Swallow has arrived to nest under the Banff Avenue bridge. Check the woods in the old residential area at the foot of Tunnel Mountain for a variety of passerines. A hike on the Tunnel Mountain trail could produce Clark's Nutcracker, Northern Pygmy-Owl or Cassin's Finch. In winter the town, with feeders behind many houses, has Clark's Nutcracker, all three species of chickadee, and the occasional White-breasted and Red-breasted Nuthatch. Check the powerlines for a Sharp-shinned Hawk or Northern Pygmy-Owl that may remain all winter. American Dippers winter at Bow Falls.

Cave and Basin Swamp. This swamp lies on the south side of the Bow

River, along Cave Avenue, 2 km west of Banff. Park at the Cave and Basin lot and take one of the several paths down through the trees to the marsh. This large wetland is fed by hot springs and remains partially open all winter. The tall willows growing in dense tangles throughout the marsh, together with the nearby spruce and pine forests, provide a variety of habitats well used by a mixture of birds. In late March to early May, look for such early species as a variety of ducks, Ruby-crowned Kinglet, Orange-crowned Warbler and Dark-eyed Junco. From late May to mid-July, look for ducks, including Barrow's Goldeneye and Cinnamon Teal; warblers such as Common Yellowthroat, Townsend's, Wilson's and American Redstart; and sparrows, including Savannah and Song. The swamp is a major staging area mid-August to November for several species of waterfowl, including Blue-winged and Green-winged Teal and Lesser Scaup. From October to April, the open water supports a large number of overwintering Mallards and Barrow's Goldeneyes, the odd Common Snipe and Killdeer. Stop and look in the water for the introduced tropical fish. The shoreline has garter snakes, the only place in the park where these animals are found regularly.

Fenland Nature Trail. The trail, 0.5 km from town adjacent to the Mount Norquay Road, is the perfect spot for the early riser. The trail begins with mature White Spruce and leads into a maze of willows and sedge marshes with a clear stream flowing through. Reconnoitre in late March to early May for Mountain and Boreal Chickadees, Brown Creeper, early flocks of Golden-crowned and Ruby-crowned Kinglets, Orange-crowned and Yellow-rumped Warblers. From the end of February through to April, at moonrise, listen for such owls as Great Horned, Northern Pygmy and Boreal. From mid-May to early July listen for a Varied Thrush and Townsend's Warbler. Other songs heard in June include those of Swainson's Thrush, Ruby-crowned Kinglet, Warbling Vireo, a variety of warblers (Orange-crowned, Yellow, Yellow-rumped, Common Yellowthroat and Wilson's), and sparrows such as Lincoln's and Song. From mid-August until early September, this is a good spot to locate mixed flocks of warblers and sparrows moving through the willows and spruce. In winter, you can almost always find the local common species.

Vermilion Lakes Drive. Begin just beyond the Fenland trail and drive west parallel to the Trans-Canada Highway for 4 km. These large shallow lakes are connected by several small channels through sedge and willow flats. From April to late May, this is probably the most important area in the park for migrating waterfowl. Open water appears in late April, and so do the water birds. These often include Tundra Swan and Cinnamon Teal, a variety of prairie ducks, and Hooded and Common Mergansers. Both the Bald Eagle and Osprey have nests beside the lakes. From late May to mid-July look for such rare park visitors as Red-necked and Pied-billed Grebes, Cinnamon Teal and Barred Owl. From late July on the duck numbers increase, to a peak in the last half of September. Winter brings Common Redpoll and Snow Bunting to the marshes. Check the small patches of open water at the warm springs on the third lake for American Dipper and a few ducks that stay all winter.

Muleshoe Picnic Area. This spot lies 11 km west of the intersection of Highway 1 and the road to Mt. Norquay ski hill. Park the car at the picnic area overlooking the Bow River. White Spruce, Balsam Poplar, willow and meadows are mixed with stands of Trembling Aspen and Lodgepole Pine, Douglas Fir and dry grassland. In April and May scan the adjacent oxbow lake and river for a variety of water birds, including Harlequin Duck and Common Merganser. Nearby woods contain Varied and Swainson's Thrushes and Townsend's Solitaire. Scrutinize the willows and open forest along the water for early migrants, including Ruby-crowned Kinglet, Orange-crowned Warbler and White-crowned Sparrow. Listen for Blue Grouse hooting on the slopes above the highway. In June to mid-July, go to the Douglas Fir and Lodgepole Pine forests on these slopes to locate Hammond's Flycatcher, Western Tanager and other breeding birds. At this season, see if you can spot five species of swallows (Violet-green, Tree, Bank, Northern Rough-winged and Cliff) hawking insects over the water. Common Yellowthroat and White-crowned Sparrow have their nests nearby. The aspen forests contain a wide variety of birds, including Pileated Woodpecker, Olive-sided Flycatcher and Orange-crowned Warbler. To the north of Muleshoe, the road crosses a wetland. Stop and ferret out a great number of species, including Green-winged Teal, Willow Flycatcher, Brewer's Blackbird, a variety of warblers and Lincoln's Sparrow.

Sunshine alpine meadows. Take the road by this name, 10 km west of the Norquay interchange on Highway 1. Park the car at the end of the Sunshine road and ride the gondola or hike up the ski-out trail. Pick up the topographic map sheet, Banff 820/4W, to keep from getting lost on these meadows. The rolling alpine heath, with herbs in the hollows and mats of Mountain Avens on the more exposed sites, is still mainly snow covered in June. The trip is worthwhile at that time, or later in early July when the snow is gone, because of the abundance of White-tailed Ptarmigan, Mountain Bluebird, Townsend's Solitaire, Ruby-crowned Kinglet, Water Pipit, Yellow-rumped Warbler, Rosy Finch, Dark-eyed Junco and Fox Sparrow. Skiers in the winter will be rewarded with the occasional White-tailed Ptarmigan, Common Raven, and Mountain and Boreal Chickadees.

Johnston Canyon. This spot lies on Highway 1A, 23 km west of Banff and just east of the Eisenhower junction. Leave the car at the parking lot and hike along the trail up the creek 3 km to the lower falls or 5 km to the upper falls. The canyon is narrow, shady and surrounded by mixed stands of spruce and Lodgepole Pine. At dusk or dawn, come here to watch the Black Swifts arrive or leave. This is one of only two known sites (the other is Maligne Canyon at Jasper) where these birds breed in Alberta. Their nests are difficult to spot. Look near the upper edges of the slimy canyon walls especially at the lower falls. American Dipper may be seen passing in and out of the water, as it too nests here. The forests have Winter Wren, and Townsend's and Yellow-rumped Warblers.

The willow swamp. This site, 1.6 km north of Johnston Canyon, should have Common Yellowthroat, Brewer's Blackbird and Lincoln's Sparrow from late May through early July. A hike into the swamp will flush a Willow Flycatcher and three species of sparrow — Savannah, Clay-colored and White-crowned.

The Vermilion Pass burn. The spot is reached by taking Highway 93 southwest for 6 km from the junction with Highway 1. This 1968 fire site extends 9 km farther on to Marble Canyon. Park at Boom Creek, the Continental Divide, or at the Stanley Glacier Trail head. In June and July, scan for nesting Northern Hawk-Owl. Blue Grouse are scarce, but also nest. Townsend's Solitaire and other more common species are found. The adjacent unburned woods are good sites to look for a Three-toed Woodpecker and Olive-sided Flycatcher. In winter watch for a White-tailed Ptarmigan, a possible Northern Hawk-Owl, Three-toed Woodpecker, Clark's Nutcracker and chickadees.

Moraine Lake road. On the 9-km road 1.6 km east of the lake, stop at the avalanche slopes in June and listen for an Olive-sided Flycatcher ("quick-three-beers") song, the flutelike notes of Hermit Thrush and call of Townsend's Solitaire. At Moraine Lake, park the car. In May the woods are echoing with the calls of Hermit, Swainson's and Varied Thrushes. From June to mid-July, look for a Harlequin Duck and American Dipper on the creek and lake. Check the meadows along the creek for Ruby-crowned Kinglet and White-crowned Sparrow. Take a walk in the forest above the road or towards Constellation Lake to find Winter Wren, Golden-crowned Kinglet and a variety of warblers, including Townsend's and Wilson's.

Bow Summit. This site lies along Highway 93, 20 km north of the junction with Highway 1. Take the 1.5-km trail to Peyto Lake viewpoint; from here proceed on the 1-km looped trail around the upper edge of the timberline. This trail passes through a variety of habitats, including subalpine fir and Engelmann Spruce at the parking lot, to stunted fir with heath and meadow vegetation higher up. From June to mid-July, an early-morning stroll should produce Clark's Nutcracker, Varied and Hermit Thrushes and Fox Sparrow. There may be a chance to view a White-tailed Ptarmigan, Water Pipit or Rosy Finch as they are all here above the treeline. Check the meadows south of the summit for Solitary Sandpiper, Mountain Bluebird, Water Pipit and Savannah Sparrow.

The avalanche slopes on the east side of the highway at Mount Wilson. This site lies 20 km north of the Visitor Services Centre at Saskatchewan River Crossing (junction of Highways 93 and 11). Park beside the highway at the old road. Hike along this trail to the base of the slope and bushwhack from here, looking for birds. The grassy meadows on the steep slope are separated by tangles of young aspen, alder, willow, rose and strips of more mature aspen forest. If Dusky Flycatcher is on your want list, here is the best spot in Banff Park to find this bird. You may also spot Golden Eagle, Rufous Hummingbird, Warbling Vireo and Orange-crowned and MacGillivray's Warblers.

Kootenay Plains. They lie just east of the park boundary and consist of flatlands from about 15 to 30 km east along the David Thompson Highway 11. On or near these plains you'll locate prairie birds, including several pairs of Western Meadowlarks. One year a pair of Black-headed Grosbeaks and another of Lark Buntings were spotted, the latter far west of their normal prairie range.

G. L. HOLROYD AND K. J. VAN TIGHEN OF CANADIAN WILDLIFE SERVICE
R. SEALE OF BANFF INTERPRETIVE SERVICE, PARKS CANADA

Jasper National Park

Jasper, the largest of the Canadian mountain parks, lies along the eastern edge of the Continental Divide. Over 250 species of birds have been reported. The park contains the southern breeding limits of the Willow Ptarmigan and one of only two known nesting sites of Black Swift in Alberta. There are large populations of Elk (Wapiti), some White-tailed and Mule Deer, Moose, Bighorn Sheep and Rocky Mountain Goat. A small herd of Mountain Caribou reside here at the southern limit of their range. Both Black and Grizzly Bears are present; Coyote and Timber Wolf are common.

Shortly after the transcontinental railroad went through the Yellowhead Pass to the West Coast, Jasper became a national park, in 1907. Today the Yellowhead Highway (16) bisects the park, providing access for the visitor to large tracts of wilderness, with over 1000 km of trails to explore. Highway 93 leaves the Yellowhead at Jasper townsite and connects this park to Banff National Park to the south.

The 10,800-km^2 park, with 800 km^2 of valley bottom land, lies 310 km west of Edmonton on Highway 16. The town of Jasper, with the park headquarters, is another 48 km southwest from the entrance gate. Greyhound buses between Edmonton and the West Coast run through the park daily.

A small, grass-covered airstrip sits in the valley. There are a series of short roads and numerous hiking trails. The park brochures show these and other amenities. The main commercial accommodation is near to and in the town. Other cabins and gasoline are available at Pocohontas and Miette Hotsprings near the east gate, at Sunwapta Falls, halfway to the Columbia Icefields and at the south end of the park. Gasoline, other services, shopping and groceries are available in the town. There are ten major campgrounds within the park. The main sites are south of town at Whistlers, Wapiti and Wabasso. Winter campers use special areas assigned by the park staff.

Information, including a bird checklist (the same as for Banff) and a detailed bird guide for the park, ''A Birder's Guide to Jasper National Park,'' by K. Van Tighen and G. Holroyd in *Alberta Naturalist*, 1981, 11: 134–40, are available from: The Superintendent, Jasper National Park, P.O. Box 10, Jasper, Alberta T0E 1E0, Telephone: (403) 852-4401. The interpretive service staff are found in the stone building in the center of Jasper townsite.

Birding Features

Habitats range from valley bottoms to alpine tundra. To the west of the Continental Divide lie the wet forests of British Columbia; to the east, the aspen parklands and prairies of Alberta. Rarities from both these areas are often found in the park. The Athabasca Valley is used as a migration route from the prairies to the West Coast.

Pocohontas Ponds. This area lies on the north side of Highway 16, 8.8 km west of the east park gate, and consists of sedge-bordered wetlands with nearby willows and White Spruce. Ospreys hunt here from early spring until fall. From mid-April to late May, look for Canada Goose, a variety of ducks, including Cinnamon Teal, and numerous migratory shorebirds. In June and July, passerines include Ovenbird, Magnolia and Orange-crowned Warblers, and Le Conte's Sparrow. From mid-July to September, the ponds are important staging areas for waterfowl and shorebirds. Up to ten Great Blue Herons may hunt here.

Talbot Lake. The lake lies on the southeast side of Highway 16, 18 to 24 km from the east park gate and 25 to 31 km from town. It is surrounded by a mixture of grasslands and spruce forest. The sedge bed complex at the north end is the most productive for the bird watcher. From mid-April to late May, Bald Eagles are seen and waterfowl congregate on the lake. Species include Red-necked and Horned Grebes, Canada Goose, White-winged and Surf Scoters, Common and Barrow's Goldeneyes, Oldsquaw and Hooded Merganser. From mid-May to mid-July look for a Marsh Wren and Le Conte's Sparrow at the north end of the lake. Common Loon and Canada Goose nest along the northern side. An active Osprey nest overlooks the lake across from the picnic site. From mid-July to late September, watch for large concentrations of waterfowl, including White-winged and Surf Scoters and Hooded Mergansers.

The Celestine Fire Road. The road meets Highway 16, on the northwest side, 40 km from the east gate and 9.5 km north of the town. This one-way fire road parallels the Athabasca River on its northwest side for 33 km to the Celestine Lakes parking lot. The road winds through Lodgepole Pine, White Spruce and Douglas Fir forests and dry grassy slopes. Late April and early May are good times to come at moonrise to listen for Northern Saw-whet and Northern Pygmy-Owls near the Snaring district warden station. Blue Grouse and Townsend's Solitaire can be heard and seen at the forest edges near open slopes. In June and early July, Lewis' Woodpecker, Say's Phoebe and Rock Wren occasionally are seen at the tight turn around the rock outcropping on the open slopes near Windy Point.

The Maligne Valley Road. This road stretches 48 km, from Highway 16, 1.5 km north of the town, to Maligne Lake. Maligne Canyon, with its several footbridges, is surrounded by pine forests. The water level of Medicine Lake is lowest during June but rises in July. Common Ravens nest in Maligne Canyon from April to early May. Townsend's Solitaires nest on the open slopes above the canyon and at Medicine Lake. Harlequin Ducks are best spotted at the outlet of Maligne Lake and on the Maligne River. In April and early May, listen for Boreal Owl at moonrise along the lower end of Medicine Lake. Winter Wren and Varied Thrush can be heard in the deep spruce woods at the lower end of Medicine Lake across from the outlet. Black Swifts are present in the canyon from late June to early September; this is one of their two known Alberta breeding sites (see Banff for other site). At dusk, go to the viewpoint 0.5 km south of the canyon to watch these birds return. In winter, patches of open water remain on the Maligne River, especially at the outlet from Maligne Lake. American Dippers can be seen here throughout the year if you wait and watch for them.

Jasper Townsite. From late May through to early July, look for a Rufous Hummingbird at feeders. In winter, the feeders attract Steller's Jay, and Northern Pygmy-Owls occasionally prey on House Sparrows. The owls often sit on telephone wires.

Cottonwood Slough. Visit these wetlands 2 km from town, on the left of the road to Pyramid Lake, if time is limited. The complex of sedge-filled wetlands, beaver ponds, grassy slopes, pine and aspen forests is home to a variety of birds. At moonrise, from March to early May, listen for Great Horned, Barred, Boreal and Northern Saw-whet Owls. Waterfowl, including Ring-necked Duck, are common from late April to late May, as are Pied-billed Grebe and Sora. In June and early July, watch for Rufous Humming-bird, Orange-crowned Warbler, Northern Waterthrush, Common Yellow-throat and Wilson's Warbler.

Athabasca River. This is the staging area for Harlequin Ducks. They sit on the tips of gravel bars and small islands near the town. American Dippers are seen on open river water throughout the winter.

The Whistlers' alpine meadows. Reach them by Sky Tram, which departs from near the parking lot. Before leaving town check hours of tram operation. These upper meadows and rubble slopes are the home base for White-tailed Ptarmigan, Horned Lark, Water Pipit, Rosy Finch, and Fox Sparrow from June to late August. At the timberline transition look for Brewer's and Golden-crowned Sparrows and the occasional Willow Ptarmigan. On the steep slopes at or below timberline, check for Townsend's Solitaire. In late August, look for Sharp-shinned Hawk, Northern Harrier and Prairie Falcon.

The Valley of Five Lakes. These small, clear ponds lie about 6 km southeast along the hiking trail from Old Fort Point. This route passes through Lodgepole Pine and Douglas Fir forests, willow stands and open grassy slopes. A much shorter route is off Highway 93, 9 km south of the junction of Highways 16 and 93. This 2-km hike is an easy one. From mid-May to mid-July in the wetlands, look for Northern Waterthrush, Common Yellow-throat and MacGillivray's Warbler. In Douglas Fir stands, note Hammond's Flycatcher and Western Tanager. The lakes are home to Common Loon and Barrow's Goldeneye. Aspen forests house Ruffed Grouse and Hermit Thrush.

Amethyst Lake. The spot consists of a moist upper subalpine valley with large lakes, extensive sedge and willow meadows, flanked by open spruce and fir forests, and expanses of open alpine meadows. The lakes are reached either on foot or horseback on an overnight trip. Proceed west from the Mt. Edith Cavell road near its terminus, or west from about three-quarters of the way up the Marmot ski road. The trip is about 15 km one way, or a 35-km loop. A primitive campsite at the lake and an outfitters' lodge both provide accommodation. Information on obtaining a booking for the lodge is available at the Jasper information office. This is a good spot to look for Willow Ptarmigan at their southern breeding limit. Gray-cheeked Thrushes have been noted singing here. Golden Eagles nest in the area. In the winter, this area is easily accessible on cross-country skis. Look for the tracks of flocks of Willow and White-tailed Ptarmigans that feed on the edges of the willow meadows. Once you find their tracks, follow them to the birds.

Throughout the park in winter, the hiker or cross-country skier should watch for roving bands of Black-capped, Mountain and Boreal Chickadees. Often they are accompanied by a few Red-breasted Nuthatches and Golden-crowned Kinglets. Ptarmigan watchers should take the cross-country ski trails along the open valley bottoms of Whistler's Creek near the Marmot ski area, Portal Creek, or the Maligne River upstream from Maligne Lake, to find these birds.

G. L. HOLROYD AND K. J. VAN TIGHEN, CANADIAN WILDLIFE SERVICE

J. PITCHER, INTERPRETIVE SERVICE, PARKS CANADA

Driving Loop: Edson/Cadomin/Hinton

The Edson loop includes foothill forests and mountain meadows. The trip provides an opportunity to explore Lodgepole Pine and Trembling Aspen–White Spruce forests, and Black Spruce–Tamarack bogs of the foothills. At higher elevations, you can find Engelmann Spruce forests and subalpine fir groves, together with two subalpine meadows higher yet.

Edson is 199 km west of Edmonton on paved Highway 16. The round trip through Edson-Hinton-Cadomin-Robb-Edson will take three days when paired with side trips to Silver Summit, north of Edson; to William A. Switzer Provincial Park, north of Hinton and south of Cadomin; to Prospect Mountain and Cardinal Divide. A quicker trip, to Cardinal Divide and Prospect Mountain only, can be undertaken from Edmonton in a two-day weekend. In one day, you can travel from Edmonton to Edson, up to Silver Summit and return to Edmonton.

Highway 16 is paved, but other roads have gravel, oil or dirt surfaces. They can be dusty in dry weather or muddy after a rain, particularly during spring breakup in April.

Accommodation is found at several highway campgrounds around the loop, including one just south of Cadomin, often used as the midpoint. There are several motels and hotels in both Edson and Hinton. Those in

Hinton fill up quickly from the Jasper Park overflow on busy weekends. Robb has one hotel. Restaurants and food stores are available in Hinton and Edson. Meals may be obtained in the Robb Hotel. Gas is available at all three places. Cadomin has a gas station and small grocery store, but both are closed on Sunday.

Birding Features

Begin at Edson. A variety of side roads from here provide good birding. The best and most easily accessible route is north from town to the Silver Summit Ski Hill on Highway 748. The trip is good at any time of the year. Watch for Gray and Blue Jays, Black-capped and Boreal Chickadees, Ruffed and Spruce Grouse, Common Raven, Downy and Hairy Woodpeckers. If you're lucky, you may sight Pileated, Three-toed and Black-backed Woodpeckers. During the summer, Black Spruce bogs are likely to have Yellow-rumped Warbler, Hermit Thrush, Golden-crowned and Ruby-crowned Kinglets and Yellow-bellied Flycatcher. In coniferous and mixed forests, look for a variety of warblers, including Magnolia, Northern Waterthrush, Bay-breasted and Blackpoll. Watch and listen for Solitary Vireo, Swainson's Thrush, Western Tanager, Olive-sided Flycatcher, White-throated Sparrow and Winter Wren. Deciduous forests will have Red-eyed and Warbling Vireos, Tennessee and Yellow Warblers, Least Flycatcher, Western Wood-Pewee and Yellow-bellied Flycatcher. Birds of the wet willow-alder areas include Common Yellowthroat, Orange-crowned Warbler, Alder Flycatcher and Lincoln's Sparrow.

From October through April look for Great Gray and Northern Hawk-Owls. This is one of the best areas in Alberta to locate a Great Gray Owl. Winter finches, such as Common and Hoary Redpolls, Red and White-winged Crossbills, and Pine and Evening Grosbeaks are also seen often.

The next leg proceeds west from Edson to Hinton, where the country becomes more rolling. Birds to look for are similar to those on the Silver Summit leg.

To continue the circle, turn south off Highway 16 about 3 km west of Hinton, onto Highway 40 south to Cadomin. The country and birdlife are similar to those along the Silver Summit road. The streams, rivers and logged-over patches provide habitat in spring and summer for Spotted Sandpiper, Barn and Tree Swallows, and Mountain Bluebird. When you reach the turnoff to Cadomin (48 km south of Highway 16), turn south for 1 km to Cadomin. Another 3 km past Cadomin the road crosses Whitehorse Creek. The campground is located at this crossing. Take a walk up and down the creek and look for an American Dipper. This bird usually nests under the waterfalls past the campground. The creek and adjacent woods often produce Harlequin Duck, Townsend's Solitaire, White-crowned and Chipping Sparrows, Dark-eyed Junco, and Boreal and Black-capped Chickadees. A stroll for a couple of km up the trail along the side creek may produce Western, Dusky and Olive-sided Flycatchers, Swainson's Thrush, Mountain Bluebird and Wilson's Warbler.

About 4 km past the campground the road crosses Prospect Creek. Just before the crossing, a side road leads west to Prospect Mountain, 5 km from this point to the top and its alpine meadows. This road is often very rough and may be impossible for low-slung cars with long wheelbases. If you can manage it, the trip is worthwhile, as birding is excellent at higher elevations. If your car can't make it, why not hike? Along the way watch for clouds of butterflies, especially in wet spots on sunny days in June and July. Birds to look for include Western and Dusky Flycatchers, Townsend's Solitaire and Mountain Bluebird. As you approach the tree line, watch and listen for White-crowned, Golden-crowned, Fox and Brewer's Sparrows. Above the trees in the alpine tundra, the most striking feature is the proliferation of flowers from mid-June and July to early August. Heathers and Mountain Avens form massive carpets. Dotted throughout are several species of saxifrage, Yellow Columbine, Moss Campion, louseworts and many others. Overhead in June, Horned Lark and Water Pipit perform their aerial song displays. Small flocks of Rosy Finches often drift by and can be seen foraging for food on the tundra. A careful search of these tussocks may turn up a family of White-tailed Ptarmigan. Occasionally a Prairie Falcon drifts over.

For the final leg of the trip, head northeast on Highway 40, then turn onto Highway 47 back to Edson. This road is often dusty or muddy, depending on the weather. The vegetation and birdlife are much the same as on other legs of the loop.

TERRY THORMIN

Grande Prairie: Peace River Country

The Peace River farming country consists of a relatively flat island of prairie and parkland surrounded by boreal forest. Trumpeter Swans nest in fair numbers west of the city of Grande Prairie. Their numbers had remained steady around 100 birds from 1946 to 1970, but have increased to about 250 birds at present. The numerous bodies of water provide migration staging sites for other waterfowl and shorebirds. Travellers driving to Alaska or north to Yellowknife should stop a day or two to explore the variety of habitats ranging from prairie to mountain. The city of Grande Prairie, with its 23,000 people, provides a good base.

Fur traders had arrived in this country by the late 1700s, using the Peace River as the main water route. The first settlement of any size began at Lake Saskatoon, just west of Grande Prairie, in 1881. Reports of fertile land to the north led to homesteaders walking in from Edson (over 300 km to the south) in the late 1800s and early 1900s. The first school opened in Grande Prairie in 1913. From the arrival of the settlers, the economic base of the region has been agriculture. The establishment of a plywood mill in 1953 began a new chapter in resource development — forestry. The discovery of one of Alberta's largest gas-oil fields in 1978 has brought in more money and people.

Grande Prairie lies 460 km northwest of Edmonton. The main road, Highway 43, is paved all the way northwest, passing through spruce forests for most of the route. Grande Prairie has a major airport, with three companies providing daily flights. Greyhound buses supply six daily runs to and from Edmonton. Cars can be rented at the airport or in town.

Good visitor services are offered in the city. Campgrounds are located at most of the provincial parks, highway sites and within the city. Gasoline and repair service is limited to the city and the few larger towns in the vicinity. Travellers going southwest into the hills or away from the settled community should carry their own gasoline supplies and repair kits. Traffic on these roads is light.

Specific information on the various sites can be obtained from the park rangers or attendants at each locality.

Birding Features

City of Grande Prairie (Trumpeter Swan Country). A visitor coming to the area with very limited time should hike the Bear Creek valley that runs through part of the city. The natural vegetation in the valley encourages a variety of birdlife to come into the city.

Bear Lake. A waterfowl feeding station, set on a few square metres of mudflat, is used each fall to draw ducks away from farmland crops. Birds returning to the spot in the spring, from late April to early June, make this an excellent site to check. Proceed west, 6 km on Highway 2, from Grande Prairie; north 5 km on a gravelled district road; west 3 km around the end of Hermit Lake, and 1 km north to the station.

The usual prairie slough ducks are found here, well north of their normal range. The area also attracts Trumpeter and Tundra Swans, Black-bellied Plovers and Golden-Plovers, and other shorebirds on migration. Several sparrow species are found in the adjacent woods. A pair of Trumpeter Swans nests on Hermit Lake, near the Bear Lake feeding station road.

Saskatoon Island Provincial Park. The island, bordered on both north and south by lakes but accessible by car, contains about 40 ha of developed land and 81 ha of natural woods with roads and trails. Aspen and willow, with scattered spruce, are interspersed with abundant Saskatoon bushes. Sedges and cat-tails spread along the shoreline. There is an excellent campground here. The village of Wembley, about 10 km south of the park, has groceries, a hotel and a service station.

The surrounding cleared farmlands make this park an island of native vegetation in a sea of crops. From late April to June, watch for five grebe species, Pied-billed, Horned, Eared, Western and Red-necked. Trumpeter Swans gather here before dispersing to their individual territories. Prairie slough ducks are found, including Canvasback and Redhead. Great Horned and occasionally Great Gray Owls are present. Yellow-headed, Red-winged and Brewer's Blackbirds may all be seen at this site. In the nesting season from late May through to mid-July, look for Sharp-shinned, Cooper's, Broad-winged and Swainson's Hawks, Merlin, American Kestrel, Sharp-tailed Grouse, Northern Hawk-Owl, Long-eared, Short-eared and Northern Saw-whet Owls, Rufous and Ruby-throated Hummingbirds, Hermit, Swainson's and Gray-cheeked Thrushes and a variety of warblers and sparrows. From the last week in May to the end of June, a pair of Trumpeter Swans nests on a muskrat house on the extreme east or extreme west end of Little Saskatoon Lake (the southern smaller lake).

In the fall, late August through October, Saskatoon Lake acts as a staging area for huge flocks of Tundra Swan, Canada Goose and Mallard. Smaller numbers of Trumpeter Swans and an occasional Snow and Greater White-fronted Goose are seen. Ducks are abundant. Bald and Golden Eagles hang around the water's edge and later on, in early November, they sit on ice around open patches of water to pick off the late-departing ducks. Large flocks of Lapland Longspur, Horned Lark, Water Pipit and numerous Rough-legged Hawks pass through, as do Sandhill Cranes.

The winter observer can see Northern Goshawk, Gyrfalcon at times, Ruffed and Sharp-tailed Grouse, Great and Horned, Snowy, the occasional Great Gray and Northern Saw-whet Owls.

For further help at Saskatoon Provincial Park, telephone the park office at (403) 766-2636 or the chief ranger's residence at (403) 766-2582.

Finding Trumpeter Swans

These, the heaviest North American bird, nest on Hermit Lake, near the Bear Lake feeding station (above) and on Little Saskatoon Lake (above). Another pair nests on Henderson Lake, 13 km north of Lake Saskatoon. Pairs of swans nest on each of Whitham, Martin, Updike, Albright, Ponita, Dickson, Sinclair, Preston and Chain lakes, all of which are located northwest of Hythe, which is 58 km west of Grande Prairie on Highway 2. The swans are flightless from early July to early September, when they begin taking short flights. They gather on Saskatoon and Bear lakes prior to migrating to a warmer climate. The last swans leave in October.

ELLEN AND GAVIN CRAIG

Saskatchewan

SASKATCHEWAN

1 Cypress Hills Provincial Park
2 Kindersley
3 Saskatoon
4 Finding Whooping
   Cranes in Saskatchewan
5 Batoche/Duck Lake/Carlton
6 Prince Albert National Park
7 Squaw Rapids
8 Last Mountain Lake
9 Regina
10 Qu'Appelle Basin Driving Route
11 Yorkton and Duck Mountain
   Provincial Park
12 Gainsborough, Saskatchewan,
   to Lyleton, Manitoba

0   100   200 km

Saskatchewan

Saskatchewan, from prairie sloughs to boreal forest, with its Whooping Crane stopovers, hawk and shorebird migrations and good roads, offers great birding for a minimum of effort.

The province of 570,271 km^2 contains nearly a million people. The population is concentrated in the southern half, over short-grass prairie and aspen parkland, now the centre of the wheat basket of North America. The northern half, underlain by rocks of the Precambrian Shield, consists of boreal forest and thousands of lakes. An outlier of mountain habitat, the Cypress Hills, lies in the southwest corner.

An experienced person can identify 100 species of birds easily within sight and earshot along 40 km of southern and central Saskatchewan roadways in late May and early June, the time when prairie birds nest. To spot Whooping Crane, Sandhill Crane and Ross' Goose, come in the fall; but check ahead, as the birds do not come or leave on fixed days. In late winter, in March, drop in to spot owls, including the Northern Hawk-Owl, Barred, Great Gray, Boreal and Northern Saw-whet. Four of these five, together with both species of three-toed woodpeckers, may be expected on a two-day trip out of Saskatchewan or Prince Albert. An additional 160-km drive north or east of Prince Albert could add coveys of Willow Ptarmigan.

The best birding spot is probably Last Mountain Lake, because of the hordes of Sandhill Cranes and geese. However, on a trip from Regina to the Cypress Hills you will no doubt add more species to your list. Kindersley, the third recommended site, should not be missed in spring or fall, because of the abundance of waterfowl, particularly geese. The Duck Mountains provide the southernmost readily accessible boreal forest habitat in the province, with hard-to-find birds. The fifth area is around Saskatoon in the fall, to tie in with the Whooping Crane migration.

With only a half day or a day available, a visitor is limited to those areas around Saskatoon and Duck Lake; or around Regina and the west end of the Qu'Appelle Valley. On a rushed trip, you could make Last Mountain Lake into one long day from either Saskatoon or Regina. It would be worth it. With two or three days available, you should best spend time out of Saskatoon: one day going north to hit Carlton and on to Prince Albert; the second day to Last Mountain Lake. The third day would be spent checking other sites recommended by local birders (see below). If you want to take three days out of Regina, you could cross the prairies and hit the Cypress Hills for prairie, parkland and mountain species.

Saskatchewan has an excellent bird-watching communications system headquartered in various communities:

Saskatoon: Chris Escott (306) 373-3522; Stan Shadick (306) 955-3242; Shirley and Jim Wedgwood (306) 374-3289; Pat and Jim O'Neil (306) 242-6335; Thelma and Jim Pepper (306) 653-3069; Betty Mundy (306) 664-2946; Mary and Stuart Houston (306) 244-0742; Mary Gilliland (306) 652-5907.

Regina: Chris Adam (306) 584-9564; Bob Kreba (306) 565-2807; Frank Brazier (306) 522-3306; Bob Luterbach (306) 522-3072 (home), (306) 565-5685 (office); Paule and Dale Hjertaas (306) 949-1672 (home), (306) 565-2888 (office).

Moose Jaw: Leith Knight (306) 692-4572 (home), (306) 692-2787 (office); Edith Kern (306) 692-2459.

Yorkton: Ben Kruser (306) 782-0164.

Good Spirit Lake: Joyce and Bill Anaka (306) 792-4780.

Raymore: Wayne Harris (306) 746-4544.

Fort Qu'Appelle: Manley Callin (306) 332-5947.

The natural history spirit is alive and well in Saskatchewan, which has had, and continues to have, a large number of very active people. Their mother organization is the Saskatchewan Natural History Society, Box 1784, Saskatoon, Saskatchewan S7K 3S1. If you plan a visit, write them for key contact people in the various communities.

A visitor to the province should obtain the provincial road map from: SaskTravel, Saskatchewan Department of Tourism, 3211 Albert Street, Regina, Sask. S4S 5W6. Topographical maps are available from the Department of Tourism and Renewable Resources in Regina, Saskatoon, Swift Current and elsewhere.

Providing information for this province has been a joint effort by C. Stuart Houston and J. Bernard Gollop.

C. STUART HOUSTON

Cypress Hills Provincial Park

In Saskatchewan, as in Alberta, the Cypress Hills form islands of forest, with an upper tableland of fescue grass surrounded by bald prairie. Portions of the hills were not covered by ice during the last glaciation, the only place in Saskatchewan that remained ice-free. Consequently, they became a refuge for several species of plants not normally found in the province. Similarly, Trumpeter Swan and mountain species such as Townsend's Solitaire and Rosy Finch are still here. Turkey Vulture and introduced Wild Turkey are also present.

The Cypress Hills have long served as retreats from the prairie for big game and man. The forested slopes offered shelter from winter blizzards and hot windy summers. Lodgepole Pine provided tepee poles for the nomadic plains people. The last major fire swept through in the late 1870s; consequently the evergreen trees are almost all about a hundred years old.

In Saskatchewan, the park comprises two blocks of land of about 78 km^2. An additional 130 km^2 of neighbouring, privately held prairie are usually considered part of the birding trip, since these lands occur between the two park sections.

Access to both parts is by paved roads from Maple Creek: 52 km northeast of the West Block on Highway 271 and 27 km north of the Centre Block on Highway 21. Maple Creek is 8 km south of the Trans-Canada Highway, in the southwest corner of Saskatchewan. The Gap Road, a rough dirt trail passable only in dry weather, connects the two blocks. Fort Walsh National Historic Park sits immediately south of the West Block. A dirt road from Fort Walsh connects to the Alberta portion of the park.

Cabins and "apartment" suites are available in the Centre Block. However, they are usually full; telephone for reservations one week in advance. Over 400 campsites in eight campgrounds fill up on the long weekends in spring and fall and during weekends in July and August. There is one primitive campsite in the West Block. Maple Creek has fine motel and hotel accommodation. Gasoline and a telephone are available in the Centre Block. The closest services are in Maple Creek, including a hospital and the RCMP.

Additional information is found in "Birds of the Cypress Hills and Flotten Lakes Regions, Saskatchewan," by W. Early Godfrey, Bulletin No. 120, National Museums of Canada, Ottawa; and "The Cypress Hills — A Natural History," available from the Saskatchewan Museum of Natural History, Wascana Park, Regina, Saskatchewan S4P 3V7.

The park has a resident staff, and a park naturalist is available from May through August. For further information write: The Superintendent, Cypress Hills Provincial Park, Box 850, Maple Creek, Saskatchewan S0N 1N0.

Birding Features

The hills, with their forested slopes of Lodgepole Pine (the only such forests in Saskatchewan) and White Spruce, are capped by a tableland of fescue prairie grasses. The habitat provides a unique opportunity to see several mountain bird species, including Dusky Flycatcher, Townsend's Solitaire, Audubon's race of the Yellow-rumped Warbler, MacGillivray's Warbler and Rosy Finch. Southern species may also be spotted, including the introduced Wild Turkey, Long-billed Curlew and Rock Wren. The best birding spot is along the Valley-of-the-Beavers Nature Trail.

From late May to late July is the best time for birding. Take Highway 21 south from Maple Creek and then the Park Road west to the administration area. The Valley-of-the-Beavers Nature Trail lies south of the administration building on the south side of Loch Lomond. On the trail, look for Dusky Flycatcher, Yellow-rumped (Audubon's) Warbler, MacGillivray's Warbler, Western Tanager and White-crowned Sparrow. On the northwest side of Loch Leven, adjacent to and west of the administration building, a short hiking trail leads to where Red Crossbills are often noted. Along the trail to Bald Butte, in the northwest corner of the Centre Block, look for Sprague's Pipit and Baird's Sparrow.

In dry weather, take the Gap Road towards the West Block. Watch for Long-billed Curlew, Upland Sandpiper, Sprague's Pipit, McCown's Longspur and Chestnut-collared Longspur. In the West Block, just before the ranger station, turn north and east to the Conglomerate Cliffs, Adams and Coulee lakes. In November and December, Townsend's Solitaire is found at springs along Adams Creek on the east side of the West Block or in ranch yards around the area. Around the cliff look for a MacGillivray's Warbler.

Adams and Coulee lakes are northeast of the cliffs. Nesting Trumpeter Swan and American Avocet can be found at these lakes. Drive back to the ranger station in the middle of the West Block. Proceed west beyond the station a short distance and then go north on the road. Look for Wild Turkey on the Lodgepole Pine slopes. Farther along this road in the forests near the edge of the park, watch for a Red-breasted Nuthatch and Red Crossbill.

Return to the ranger station. Take a short drive west toward the west boundary, then get out and hike in the woods adjacent to Battle Creek. Look for a Dusky Flycatcher.

Proceed east, back past the ranger station, to the road to Fort Walsh. Go there to see the reconstructed fort and whisky trader's cabin. They are very well done and there is an excellent interpretive program. Return north to just south of the Gap Road, where a ranch road takes off to the south. Follow it past the first ranch, immediately south of Fort Walsh, and continue on to the second ranch. On the south side of this second ranch, take the road west towards another ranch. Look for Rock Wren along this stretch. At the ranch and just to the west of it, check the brushy coulees and hillsides leading away from the hills for Lazuli Bunting and Lark Sparrow. Ranch stockyards are sometimes the place to spot a Rosy Finch from December to February.

WAYNE HARRIS

Kindersley

West of Kindersley, lands host a wide variety of prairie species in the summer. Fall brings migrating geese that stop over for several weeks. This is probably the best place in North America in the fall to see Ross' Geese by the thousands. Formerly short-grass prairie, the land today is either in crops or pasture. The latter provides excellent habitat for upland birds that were once common but now are limited to uncultivated lands.

Kindersley lies 206 km southwest of Saskatoon on Highway 7, or 193 km north of the Trans-Canada via Highway 21. Accommodation and services are excellent in Kindersley, which also has a campground.

Birding Features
Habitat west of Kindersley is worth a visit from late April to mid-July, and again in September. In summer, slow down on roads bordered by pastures. Watch for a Swainson's Hawk over these meadows. Keep a sharp eye out for the largest buteo in Saskatchewan, the Ferruginous Hawk. It can be either light or dark phase, with every eighth or tenth bird nearly black. The Northern Harrier is common, with the Richardson's race of Merlin a definite possibility. The larger shorebirds are active in these pastures. Watch for Long-billed Curlew, Willet and Marbled Godwit. There is also a good chance you'll spot a Burrowing Owl. Stop and listen for the ever-present descending trill of the Sprague's Pipit, giving its flight song almost out of sight overhead. Listen for the three chirps followed by a trill that identify Baird's Sparrow. McCown's Longspur is present, but less common and also hard to

see. You are certain to see the Chestnut-collared Longspur and hear its spectacular flight song.

If you have yet to see a Ferruginous Hawk, go west from Kindersley on Highway 7 for 21 km, to paved secondary road No. 307. Drive north for 16 km to where the road jogs west, 1.6 km south of Smiley. Turn east here for 1.6 km and then south for 2.4 km to the Kindersley-Elna PFRA pasture headquarters on the east side of the road. After obtaining permission to enter the pasture, continue south on the trail. Each shelterbelt of trees (representing shattered dreams of farming submarginal land) has a resident pair of buteos. The Ferruginous Hawk is more numerous than Swainson's on this prime pasture. Prior to the second week of July, please stay in your car and do not flush a hawk from its nest, as these birds readily abandon and then have no time left to try again. The first trail east beyond the Texas gate (cattle gate; drive slowly over the metal pipes) leads to Teo Lake, with American Avocets along the shore. These birds may also be seen at the south end of Teo Lake, where it crosses Highway 7, 12 km west of Kindersley. Waterfowl on the lake usually include numerous Gadwall. With luck, you may see a male Cinnamon Teal. By mid-September there may be 10,000 each of Ross', Greater White-fronted and Snow Geese based on Teo Lake.

In fall, Ross' Geese can usually be found at Buffalo Coulee Lake, a Ducks Unlimited project, 6.5 km north and 4.8 km west of Coleville. In an average year they pass close to the northwest and southeast corners of this lake. Another access point is the east-west road that crosses the north end of the lake. When these geese feed in fields, a car can approach slowly and gradually, 25 m at a time, until a superb view is gained.

About the beginning of October, the geese are best seen at Cutbank and Snipe lakes. Highway 21 comes close to the north end of Cutbank Lake, 11.2 km north of Glidden; Highway 44 touches the south end, 3.2 km east of Glidden. Snipe Lake Village lies 24 km east from the junction of Highways 44 and 21. Snipe Lake can be reached by driving from the village, 4.8 km north and 1.6 km east, then walking farther east to the shore. The sight of thousands of geese, including an occasional blue phase of the Snow Goose, is well worth the trip.

C. STUART HOUSTON

Saskatoon

Located in the aspen parkland, Saskatoon has boreal forest to the north and prairie grasslands to the south. Within 55 km of the city, 314 species of birds have been reported, of which 117 breed regularly. The city provides a base for locating Ross' Goose and Whooping Crane through September and October. Numerous water birds and upland species are readily found from late April to mid-July.

Daily planes and buses link the city with the rest of Canada. A wide variety of hotels and motels are available. However, some of the small neighbouring communities do not have visitor accommodation. There are

T.W.THORMIN / 83

Sharp-tailed Grouse

campgrounds available in the city and adjacent to it on the major highways, as well as at Pike Lake Provincial Park, 24 km southwest on Highways 7 and 60; at Blackstrap Lake Recreation Site, 35 km south on Highway 11; at Borden Bridge crossing of the North Saskatchewan River on Highway 16, 55 km northwest; and at Eagle Creek Regional Park, 22 km northwest of Asquith, 35 km west of the city on Highway 14.

Further information on the area may be obtained by contacting the Saskatchewan tourist office in Regina (see above). Bird-finding help, including where to obtain maps of Saskatoon and vicinity (topographic map sheets 1:250000, Saskatoon 73B and Rosetown 72/0 are a necessity here and elsewhere), together with a checklist showing seasonal abundance and dates, is available from the people listed above.

Each summer naturalists are stationed at Pike Lake Provincial Park, and at Beaver Creek Municipal Park, 13 km south of the city on the east bank of the South Saskatchewan River. Field trips are regularly sponsored by the Saskatoon Natural History Society. Contact the above people for dates and meeting places.

Birding Features

Within 55 km of Saskatoon, about 65 per cent of the land is sown to wheat, barley and oats, or remains in summer fallow; 25 per cent is in pasture and 10 per cent is woods, water or pavement. In wet years, literally thousands of sloughs appear in the spring. By fall they are often reduced to fewer than a hundred. There are eighteen named lakes and three reservoirs: Blackstrap Reservoir, 35 km south on Highway 11; Brightwater, 52 km south on Highway 11 and 8 km west; and the Bradwell Reservoir, 27 km southeast on Highway 14, about 6 km south to Bradwell and then 1.6 km south on the first road to the east side of Bradwell.

Original upland habitat consisted of interspersed prairie and aspen bluffs. Today the most extensive areas of prairie are on three government community pastures: west of Dundurn, 35 km south of the city on Highway 11; southwest of Pike Lake, 24 km south of the city on Highway 60; north of Asquith, 35 km west of Saskatoon on Highway 14. Smaller parcels include

Kernen's Prairie, 130 ha of native prairie about 8 km northeast of the city just off Highway 41. There are no forests, but aspen bluffs liberally dot the landscape. More extensive stands of aspen are found southwest of Dundurn and Pike Lake, northeast of Asquith, and near Borden.

The greatest diversity of bird species occurs between May 15 and 31, and August 24 to September 17. One-day counts in late May have produced 177 species and in late August, 145. However, fall migration in late September and October brings thousands of birds into the area. At Goose Lake, up to 12,000 Tundra Swans have been spotted, along with thousands of geese, Canvasbacks and other ducks and Sandhill Cranes. At Rice Lake, 30 km west of the city on Highway 14 and 5 km south, colonies of Eared Grebe, Franklin's Gull and Black Tern nest. Ross' Goose comes in to rest during migration. This is also a good place to start searching for a Whooping Crane through September and October.

In the breeding season, from mid-May through early July, Swainson's Hawk is common in the area; Sharp-tailed Grouse have several dancing grounds, occupied from March to late May, within 16 km of the city; Burrowing Owls are out on the prairie pastures; a Northern Saw-whet Owl may be seen in larger bluffs; the Yellow-breasted Chat appears regularly but sparsely, as do Sprague's Pipit and Loggerhead Shrike. Several sparrows occur, including Grasshopper, Le Conte's, Baird's, Clay-colored, Sharp-tailed, Vesper, Savannah and Chipping. In July and August, American White Pelican and Hudsonian Godwit appear regularly at the larger lakes.

Within the city limits, 262 species have been reported. The best spot is Cosmopolitan Park, with its treed path along the east bank of the South Saskatchewan River. Forestry Farm Park is another good site. In winter, the open water on the river may hold up to 400 Common Goldeneyes; the Snowy Owl hunts on and near the university campus; Bohemian Waxwing occurs regularly. Fifteen pairs of Merlins and five pairs of American Kestrels nested within the city in 1981, as did Black-billed Magpie, Purple Martin and Yellow Warbler.

J. BERNARD GOLLOP

Finding Whooping Cranes in Saskatchewan

Western Saskatchewan is on the principal migratory path of the Whooping Crane. Fall is the best season to see these birds, which often linger near one spot, from several days to a week or more, on their leisurely movement southward. These cranes pass through the province from late September through October. The birds may travel singly, in family groups of both parents and an immature, or in flocks of several individuals.

In spring, the birds move quickly through the province on their way north. They may be seen from late April to mid-May, depending on the weather.

Saskatchewan naturalists have set up a communications network to keep both themselves and other interested individuals informed of the

Whooping Cranes

whereabouts of the travelling cranes. The northern part of the province is coordinated by J. Bernard Gollop of the Canadian Wildlife Service in Saskatoon. Telephone him at (306) 665-4087 or (306) 665-4102, his office; or his home at (306) 343-1027. In the south, coordination is by Fred Lahrman of the Saskatchewan Natural History Museum in Regina, telephone (306) 527-6608. Both men have agreed to help you find cranes at the appropriate time.

The effectiveness of this network was shown by Dr. Roger Foxall of Ottawa, in 1980. With the help of the Houstons in Saskatoon, and other contacts, he spotted nineteen cranes in six and a quarter hours.

C. STUART HOUSTON

Batoche/Duck Lake/Carlton

Carlton has been renowned as a birder's paradise for 160 years, and is a great attraction for anyone with an interest in the history of ornithology. The first naturalist to visit Fort Carlton, then the pemmican provisioning centre for all of the Hudson's Bay Company Territory (i.e., western Canada), was Dr. John Richardson, surgeon and naturalist with the first Franklin arctic expedition in 1820. Richardson spent from May 10 to 26 at Carlton. He was so impressed that he returned there for the spring migration at the end of the second Franklin expedition in 1827. To do so, he travelled a thousand miles on foot from Great Slave Lake to Carlton, between Christmas Day of 1826 and February 12, 1827.

The area lies about 75 km north from Saskatoon or south 55 km from Prince Albert. The visitor can breathe in the history by visiting the old fort, whose palisades and buildings have been rebuilt just as they were in Richardson's time. Guides at the Fort Carlton Historic Park will show you around in season, and one can still see the furrows made by the Red River carts going up the hill behind the fort.

Visitor accommodation, services and car rentals are readily available at either Saskatoon or Prince Albert. Both cities have campgrounds. Saskatoon is served by three airlines on a daily basis, and Prince Albert by one line, in addition to bus service.

Since this is a major national historic site, much published tourist information is available from SaskTravel in Regina and Saskatoon. The National Historic Sites Information Service in Ottawa will, upon request, mail out an information package.

Birding Features

Carlton is on the scientific map as the type locality where the Swainson's Thrush, Rosy Finch, Clay-colored Sparrow and Smith's Longspur were first described. Further, Dr. Richardson and his assistant, Thomas Drummond, described subspecies of the Hairy Woodpecker, Loggerhead Shrike and Rufous-sided Towhee. They noticed differences in the pale form of the Merlin, and in the Boreal Owl, for over a century known as Richardson's Owl.

Carlton was next visited by Captain Thomas Blakiston, the magnetic observer and meteorologist with the Palliser expedition. Blakiston was at Carlton from October 23, 1857, until about June 10, 1858.

The detailed reports of Richardson, Drummond and Blakiston allow an opportunity unrivalled on this continent to know the condition of birdlife prior to agricultural settlement. Today the summer visitor will, without difficulty, see and hear from the road Rufous-sided Towhee, in the coulee leading down to the fort, and hear on all sides the buzzing song of the Clay-colored Sparrow. Imagine the excitement Richardson must have felt in discovering these new birds!

On the other hand, some of the larger birds that were common in Richardson's time, especially the Trumpeter Swan, Bald Eagle, Whooping Crane and Sandhill Crane, no longer breed in the area. The Passenger Pigeon, seen in small flocks by Richardson, has been gone for eighty years. Trumpeter Swan skins are no longer a major article of trade with the Hudson's Bay Company.

Now that wetlands are less numerous, there are fewer bitterns, ducks, Sora, Willet, Marbled Godwit and American Avocet than Richardson described. The scavenging Common Raven was once more numerous than the American Crow. The latter has thrived and increased greatly with settlement. Similarly, the Turkey Vulture is less likely to be seen, although with a little luck one may be spotted flying along the river. Hollow trees were more numerous in the wooded area, and Common Goldeneye, Bufflehead and Hooded Merganser more abundant. Today, at the little lakes between Carlton and MacDowall, particularly Roddick Lake, resident pairs of Common Goldeneye and Bufflehead may still be noted.

In the 1820s, Carlton marked a sharp boundary between treeless prairie, kept open by almost annual prairie fires from the south, and mixed forest of aspen and spruce of the north.

Much of the grassland has been plowed and converted to grainfields. Swainson's and Ferruginous Hawks and the Upland Sandpiper are no longer common. The Ferruginous Hawk is gone; a few Swainson's Hawks and Upland Sandpipers remain on the pastures.

Carlton is still at the boundary between birds of the prairies and those of the mixed forest. Brown Thrasher and an occasional Say's Phoebe represent the more southern species; Gray Jay, Blue Jay, White-throated Sparrow and an occasional Pileated Woodpecker of the north still nest here. Some warblers of the mixed forest, including the Connecticut, are heard singing throughout June. In the aspen parkland, Gray Catbird, Veery, Red-eyed Vireo, Warbling Vireo, Rose-breasted Grosbeak and American Goldfinch are readily heard singing in the wooded coulees. Spotted Sandpiper and Belted Kingfisher occur along the river bank.

With settlement came new birds, including the Mourning Dove, as well as the introduced species, House Sparrow, European Starling, Ring-necked Pheasant, Gray Partridge and Rock Dove. The Black-billed Magpie, gone with the buffalo for about thirty years, returned in the 1930s and has become common since the late 1950s. The Mountain Bluebird, because of bird boxes, is now more common than ever before.

The visitor in late June and July will also encounter flowers in profusion, especially the Prairie Red Lily, Saskatchewan's floral emblem.

For a circle tour from Saskatoon, follow Highway 12 north from the city for 37 km, branching right on Highway 312. About 10 km farther on, this highway turns west; take the secondary gravel grid highway, newly numbered as 6xx, north until you intersect paved Highway 212. Follow this west to the reconstructed fort. After studying the Carlton area, follow Highway 212 east on the return trip, across the Okemasis Indian Reserve into Duck Lake. Go into the museum to see some memorabilia of the Riel uprising. You can then take Highway 11 northeast through the Northern Forest Reserve to MacDowall. If you are planning a trip north, continue on to Prince Albert.

For a tour of mixed-forest lakes, on gravel or even mud roads from Duck Lake, I would especially recommend Adamson Lake, only 2 km off Highway 11, and Roddick Lake.

If a return to Saskatoon is planned, and you have a few hours, I recommend following signs to the St. Laurent Ferry. You can cross the South Saskatchewan River as it was done by horses and carts for more than a hundred years. Turn south for 5 km and join paved Highway 225 to continue south into Batoche, the site of the major battle in the Riel uprising. History buffs can visit the battlefield and another national historic site. Another 8 km south, turn right on Highway 312 across the bridge that replaced the ferry operated more than a century ago by Batoche Letendre. At Rosthern, turn south on Highway 11, back to Saskatoon. Historically minded readers should be sure to consult *The Birds of the Saskatchewan River, Carlton to Cumberland*, by C. S. Houston and M. G. Street, 1959, Saskatchewan Natural History Society Special Publication No. 2.

C. STUART HOUSTON

Prince Albert National Park

Prince Albert National Park preserves 2875 km^2 of fescue grasslands mixed with aspen parkland, which gives way to boreal forest in the northern half of the park. At least 227 bird species have been reported, including Great Gray and Boreal Owls, and a colony of 6000 to 7000 American White Pelicans. The park is home to numbers of Moose, Elk, Wolf, Lynx and Black Bear; it is, as well, the last home and resting place of Grey Owl, the author.

This block of wilderness lies 90 km north of Prince Albert, on Highway 2. The STC bus comes right to the town of Waskesiu, in the park, from June to September. At other times, the bus drops you off at the junction, about 15 km from the townsite. There are several hiking trails, with 100 km of cross-country ski trails through the rolling country. The park is a favourite of canoeists, who use the well mapped out routes, one of which leads to Grey Owl's cabin and grave.

Several motels and other privately operated accommodation units are available in the town. Reservations should be made well ahead for July and August. There are three major serviced campgrounds, plus primitive sites located on the canoe routes.

Information, including a park map showing trails and canoe routes, and a checklist, is available from: The Superintendent, Prince Albert National Park, Box 100, Waskesiu, Saskatchewan S0J 2Y0, Telephone: (306) 663-3511.

The naturalist-interpretive service operates all year. Drop them a note at the above address or contact them when you arrive.

Birding Features

The transition from aspen parkland to boreal forest makes this park a place to see a wide variety of bird species. Some, like the Veery and Sprague's Pipit, are near their northern limit, while others like the Wood Duck are at their western limit.

Perhaps the most frequently seen are boreal forest species. These include Great Gray and Boreal Owls, Black-backed Woodpecker, Gray Jay and Boreal Chickadee. Coniferous forest species easily spotted in the central and northern section of the park include Yellow-bellied and Olive-sided Flycatchers, and such warblers as Magnolia, Cape May, Black-throated Green, Blackburnian, Bay-breasted and Blackpoll. The northern bogs produce Nashville and Palm Warblers, Northern Waterthrush and Swamp Sparrow. Pine Siskin and White-winged Crossbill occur frequently. A great number of lakes, ponds and sloughs regularly provide habitat for most species of duck found in central Canada, as well as common Loon and Red-necked, Western and Horned Grebes.

The fourth-largest pelican colony in Canada is on Lavallee Lake in the northwest corner of the park. The nesting island also hosts colonies of Double-crested Cormorant and Great Blue Heron. This is the only completely protected spot for American White Pelicans in Saskatchewan. This Special Protection Area, National Park Zone 1, is off limits to all visitors except by special permission.

The interpretive service will assist you in locating excellent birding spots, including Trippes Beach, Spruce River Tower area and the Waskesiu River. If you are in search of warblers and sparrows from late May to early June, ask naturalists to show you where to find the Height of Land Tower area, Mud Creek, Boundary Bay and Narrows Peninsula trails. Take a canoe on the Bagwa Canoe route for a rewarding trip. From early May to early June and again in September, Namekus Lake and Shady Lake are excellent for viewing migratory species.

MERV SYROTEUK

Squaw Rapids

Good birding in the area east of Prince Albert, along the North Saskatchewan River, has been known since the fur trading days of the 1700s. Today a visitor can spot American White Pelican, Northern Goshawk and Gyrfalcon in late fall; or in summer, Barred Owl, Whip-poor-will, Chimney Swift and three-toed woodpeckers.

The Saskatchewan River was the main highway into western Canada and beyond in the fur trade days. After amalgamation of the Hudson's Bay Company and the Northwest Company in 1821, the river remained the main route until the railway arrived in the late 1800s. Saskatchewan's earliest settlement by white men, founded by Samuel Hearne in 1774, is just downriver from Squaw Rapids at Cumberland House. Be sure to visit this historic site. During the last half-century, the region has changed radically. Most of the big, mature White Spruce have been cut, with only a few stands left for use by the boreal birds. A large hydro-electric dam and reservoir was created in the 1960s, resulting in Tobin Lake above the dam, and open water, below it.

Squaw Rapids lies northeast of Saskatoon, about 170 km northeast of Prince Albert and straight west of The Pas in Manitoba. Several paved roads lead to the area, with Highway 123 the final route to the lake, dam and open water. Cumberland House is about 80 km farther east along this road. The nearest bus service stops at Carrot River, about 40 km southeast. For the adventuresome pilot, there is a small dirt airstrip near the generating station.

American White Pelican

Two provincial campgrounds are found in the area. The better one lies just up the hill from the generating station. The other is about 40 km northeast at a spot called the Dragline. Cabins may be rented at Squaw Rapids near the generating station and at Simpson's Sportsman's Lodge, 20 km northeast, from May to October. The nearest motel-hotels are at Nipawin and Carrot River, 40 to 50 km southwest. There is a small store at Squaw Rapids, and gasoline is available from May to October at both sets of cabins mentioned previously. Carrot River is the last gas outlet in winter. A telephone is available at Squaw River Cabins. Carrot River has the nearest hospital and RCMP office.

The cultivated land is held privately, and permission must be obtained to enter. However, most wooded land is still crown owned with free access. Some spots around the damsite and generating station are posted, prohibiting access. These areas should be avoided; in any case, they are not good birding spots. Several people make their living from trapping in the area. Avoid trap sets and keep away from their cabins, since these buildings often mean life or death to trappers in the cold of mid-winter.

There are no resident birders, but Wayne Harris has offered to advise anyone thinking of going in. Contact him at: Box 414, Raymore, Saskatchewan S0A 3J0, Telephone: (306) 746-4544.

Birding Features

The Squaw Rapids area is the western limit in Canada at which Whip-poor-will and Chimney Swift are found regularly. It is also one of the westernmost spots where the Barred Owl is common.

Tundra Swans occur in large numbers during spring and fall on Tobin Lake. Mergansers are also abundant in April. In late fall look for a Gyrfalcon along the shore.

Check the spruce muskeg just northeast of the turnoff to the dam. You should be able to spot Spruce Grouse and possibly a Great Gray Owl. Below the generating station look for American White Pelican from May to September; mergansers are here in September. There are large numbers of Bald Eagles along the river below the station in November and December. A variety of gulls, particularly Bonaparte's, are quite common below the generating station in August and September.

Continue on towards Cumberland House. Chimney Swifts are seen most commonly along the river just southeast of Simpson's Sportsman's Lodge early in the morning. Beyond the lodge, along Highway 123, watch for a Barred Owl and listen for a Whip-poor-will south of the campsite at Dragline.

Other birds to look for include the very common Northern Goshawk, with ten to sixteen seen on Christmas bird counts during the last three years. A Northern Saw-whet Owl may be heard in May. The Pileated Woodpecker is common year-round. Check the mature spruce stands and spruce muskegs for either of the three-toed woodpeckers. Winter Wrens are quite common in stands of large mature spruce. Interesting warblers to ferret out in the mature forests include Magnolia, Black-throated Green, Blackburnian, Chestnut-sided, Mourning and Canada.

WAYNE HARRIS

Last Mountain Lake

Large numbers of Sandhill Cranes and other water birds congregate each spring and fall on the wildlife management area north of Regina. The marsh/open water complex, surrounded by native grasslands, provides first-class habitat for nesting and migrating species. Whooping Cranes visit regularly.

The first Canadian federal bird sanctuary was established here in 1887. Created as the Last Mountain Lake Bird Sanctuary under the Migratory Birds Convention Act, lands set aside originally included the northern 17.6 km of lake. An additional 6100 ha of marginal farmland near the northern end of the lake was acquired in 1966 and 1967 to become the first federal-provincial wildlife area in Canada. In the following year, 1968, a further 3467 ha of provincial crown land was added, and the Last Mountain Wildlife Management Unit was born. Managed jointly by the Canadian Wildlife Service and the Saskatchewan Fisheries and Wildlife Branches, the unit illustrates how two governments can successfully work together for wildlife.

Roughly 19 km by 8 km, the 15,600-ha management unit is reached from Regina by driving 76 km northeast on Highway 11; then taking Highway 2 north for 71 km to a point 4 km south of Simpson. Drive 10 km east to the headquarters building and check in to find out about recent sightings. From Saskatoon, proceed south on Highway 11 for 80 km, then 56 km east on Highway 15 to Highway 2, south 9 km through Simpson, and east to the administration building. A regional park on the east side lies about 14 km west of Govan off Highway 20. Here you'll find some modern trailer sites with electricity. Hotel accommodation is available in the nearby towns of Imperial, Simpson, Nokomis and Govan. Hospitals and medical doctors are available in Nokomis and Imperial. Gasoline outlets are found in all villages except Stalwart, with Nokomis the best bet on Sundays. Retail outlets are closed on Monday. For further help contact Wayne Harris at Raymore (see above). For a detailed checklist of the unit, contact the area manager at the headquarters building or write him: Manager, Wildlife Management Unit, Canadian Wildlife Service, Box 280, Simpson, Saskatchewan S0G 4M0, Telephone: (306) 836-2022.

Birding Features

About 40 per cent of the unit is lake and marsh; the remainder is grasslands with a small amount seeded as lure crops, which draw cranes and waterfowl off adjacent privately owned cropland. Obtain the excellent map from headquarters (see above) to allow easy location of roads around the complex.

Starting at headquarters, ask if there are any special species, such as Whooping Crane. Sandhill Cranes come and go in great waves. They can best be observed from the road at headquarters as they go on their evening flight from fields to roost. Check the marshes beside the road just east of headquarters for Black-crowned Night-Heron. Swainson's Hawks are everywhere from May to September. Other raptors include eagles and Osprey, which are regulars from late April to mid-May and September to early

November. Check the shelterbelts, particularly around headquarters, for warblers during late August and early September. Le Conte's Sparrow is common in most grassy areas just east of headquarters.

Take the car and explore the rest of the unit. At every opportunity, scan the water for such species as Western Grebe, which occurs particularly in marshy bays. American White Pelicans fish in May and September. Good numbers of Tundra Swans occur in October and November. Shorebirds appear in huge waves in late May. Don't miss them! Loggerhead Shrikes are often present in shelterbelts along the west edge of the unit. At the northern end, Baird's Sparrow is common on native grasslands about 2 km west of the picnic site. At this spot cross the north arm of the lake and take the trail south into grassy uplands between the water bodies. Listen for Sprague's Pipit, and Le Conte's and Savannah Sparrows. Forster's Tern may be ferreted out in the marshes east of here, on the easternmost arm of the lake.

If you are here in late fall, scan carefully for a Snowy Owl, common in late November.

On your way in or out, stop at Sailor's Bay on the southwest corner of the unit and inspect the grazed pastures southeast of the bog bay for a Chestnut-collared Longspur.

WAYNE HARRIS

Regina

Formerly the site where Indians piled the discarded bones after major buffalo kills, Regina is located on the short-grass prairies. With the conversion of this area to cropland, few patches of native grasses remain. As they have for millennia, large flocks of migrating Tundra Swan, Canada, Greater White-fronted and Snow Geese and a variety of ducks all pass through, with longspurs also resting on the wet lowlands. Colonies of Burrowing Owl are an attraction for those who do not often see these birds.

The largest city in Saskatchewan, and the capital since the creation of the province in 1905, Regina contains the government offices. The city is dependent economically upon agriculture and government services. The railroad arrived in 1882 and settlers flooded in. Later, in the 1930s, as a job creation project, Wascana Creek was dammed and Wascana Lake and park were created. This man-made lake, adjacent marsh and parkland provide excellent habitat for a wide variety of water birds within the dry plains region.

The Trans-Canada Highway bisects Regina, providing easy access. VIA Rail passenger service, Greyhound and local provincial bus service, and Air Canada provide travel connections.

Visitor services are similar to those in all major cities. Campgrounds are available within the city, northwest on Highway 11 a few kilometres, and at McLean, about 50 km east on Highway 1. Additional visitor information on the area is available at the provincial tourist bureau, telephone (306) 565-2300. Those travelling outside the city should be aware that nearby centres have few to no services.

Birding contacts include those mentioned in the introduction.

Lorne Scott, the Saskatchewan bluebird man, is the Wascana Park naturalist. He bands many birds, including waterfowl. Contact him at the park.

For further help, a visit to the Saskatchewan Museum of Natural History at the corner of College Avenue and Albert Street is a must, with displays of Saskatchewan birds in their habitat. Numerous books on natural history, particularly about the prairie provinces, are available from the Blue Jay Bookshop at 2657 Cameron Street in Regina, or by writing Box 1121, Regina, Saskatchewan S4P 3B4. Detailed information on the birds of the area is also available in *Birds of Regina*, by M. Belcher, revised edition 1980, Special Publication No. 12, Saskatchewan Natural History Society, Regina.

Birding Features

Regina serves as a base for exploring the surrounding farmland in search of Burrowing Owl, migrating waterfowl in the spring, and numerous prairie species, such as the longspurs that pass in spring and fall.

In the winter there are fewer birds. Snowy Owls are usually present on the flat farmland southeast, south and southwest of the city, where the Snow Bunting is erratic. In the city, a Prairie Falcon and one or more Merlins overwinter. Look for them on the Legislative grounds. There are very few woodpeckers and chickadees; an occasional Red-breasted Nuthatch will winter at feeders, especially the one in the Regina cemetery. Sometimes a Townsend's Solitaire will stay; small numbers of Bohemian Waxwings are seen; grosbeaks are few and infrequent.

Spring migration begins in late March and lasts to early May. Numerous swans, geese and ducks stop on their way through, particularly in the low-lying lands along Wascana Creek south of Kronau, 25 km southeast of the city on Highway 33. Another good site to observe the hordes of spring migrants is Buck Lake, approximately 25 km south on Highway 6 and east about 10 km on a back road. The third spot, Condie Reservoir, lies 10 km northwest from Regina on the west side of Highway 11. Shorebirds in fair numbers and variety are also at these locations. Great flocks of Lapland Longspur, with the occasional Smith's Longspur, pass through these areas.

The nesting season runs from late May into July and provides opportunities to observe a variety of behavioural characteristics of the large flock of permanent resident Canada Geese of the giant race at the Wascana Water-fowl Park. At this location note the breeding Wilson's Phalarope, a few Common and Black Terns, some Marsh Wrens and sizeable colonies of Yellow-headed and Red-winged Blackbirds. In rural areas, watch for upland prairie species, including Baird's Sparrow and the occasional Grasshopper Sparrow, and McCown's and Chestnut-collared Longspurs.

During fall migration from September through October, some swans, geese and ducks stop at Buck Lake and Condie Reservoir. Within the last few years, Ross' Geese have sometimes stopped at Wascana Waterfowl Park and Wascana Lake within the city. Unusual ducks, including Surf and Black Scoters and Hooded Merganser show up in late October and November. Varied Thrush and Townsend's Solitaire also appear sometimes, as does the occasional warbler, including very rarely Golden-winged, Blue-winged,

Northern Parula and Black-throated Gray; an occasional Western Tanager, Black-headed Grosbeak, Indigo or Lazuli Bunting, Dickcissel, House Finch or Rosy Finch may be reported.

The Valeport Marshes at the south end of Last Mountain Lake provide an excellent site to see spring and fall migratory birds, including Tundra Swan, geese, ducks and numerous shorebirds. The best time and place is early morning on the east side. Proceed 26 km northwest from Regina on Highway 11 to Lumsden, then follow Highway 20 northeast for 8 km to Craven. Continue on 20 along the east side of the marsh. Bob Luterbach is the best contact for this site (see above).

MARGARET BELCHER

Qu'Appelle Basin Driving Route

Visitors travelling through southern Saskatchewan often complain of the long tedious ride. They may not realize that the railroads and later the highways were laid along the most level strips of land, to save construction costs. To relieve the monotony, why not depart from Highway 1 and sample the beautiful Qu'Appelle Valley that parallels this road for more than halfway across the province? To assist in this exploratory trip, order a copy of the 168-page booklet *Birds of the Qu'Appelle 1857–1969*, by E. Manley Callin, 1980, Special Publication 13, Saskatchewan Natural History Society, from the Blue Jay Bookshop (see above). This is one of the finest local publications available anywhere. Other information is available in *Bird Life in the Qu'Appelle Valley*, by D. R. M. Hatch and W. Harty, a 36-page booklet available from the Qu'Appelle Valley Management Board.

Birding Features
The route begins at Whitewood, 68 km west of the Manitoba-Saskatchewan border on Highway 1. Turn north on Highway 9. The road soon crosses a now invisible and unmarked oxcart trail between Lower Fort Garry (Winnipeg) and Fort Edmonton. This route carried trading goods and later the early settlers. They saw this land as a treeless plain set afire almost every year by lightning, or by Indians, to bring the buffalo north earlier in the spring. They observed Ferruginous and Swainson's Hawks as the common raptors. The Ferruginous has long ago disappeared and the Red-tailed Hawk is the most common raptor in the aspen bluffs. The once-common Upland Sandpiper, Long-billed Curlew, Baird's Sparrow and Sprague's Pipit are now found only on relict pastures.

Farther north, the Qu'Appelle Valley is breathtaking in its sudden appearance. The wide post-glacial valley, carved out by a river between 12,000 and 14,000 years ago, is completely out of proportion to the little river at its bottom. Stop at the parking area on the left, below the crest, and have a drink of cool, clear spring water. Climb the steep trail to the lookout spots above.

Across the valley, the north (south-facing) slope is covered mainly with short grass, brown in summer unless rainfall is above average, with only a few shrubs in the moister clefts of the hills. On the south side, below, note the dense tangle of aspen, birch, saskatoon, chokecherry and other shrubs; in places the bush is so impenetrable that the Turkey Vulture can nest on the ground without fear of discovery. Look for one soaring high overhead. Listen in May for the drumming of the Ruffed Grouse — like an old tractor starting up. Try to "whistle up" a Northern Saw-whet Owl; listen for the "wheep" of a Great Crested Flycatcher; catch a fleeting glimpse of a Cooper's or Sharp-shinned Hawk or a Long-eared Owl. In June and early July, the Red-eyed Vireo is everywhere. Listen for the three most characteristic valley songs — those of the Veery, the Rose-breasted Grosbeak and the Rufous-sided Towhee. Highway 9 is approximately the dividing line between two races of towhee, the Western and Eastern Wood-Pewee, the Lazuli and Indigo Bunting, as well as the western limit of the Bur Oak.

Note the buildings at the northeast corner of Round Lake. They mark the site of John MacDonald's XY Company fur trading post from 1810 to 1814, and the site of Hugh McKay's Presbyterian mission and school, established in 1884. A cairn north of Camp McKay explains the geology of the area, including the flat terrace on the south side of the valley.

At bridges across the Qu'Appelle there are hundreds of nesting Cliff Swallows. These crossings provide good viewpoints from which to see a Great Blue Heron or Black-crowned Night-Heron. On the dry slopes on the north side of the valley, watch carefully for the Lark Sparrow.

Turn west along Highway 247, which follows the north edge of Round Lake and later of Crooked Lake. Along the margins of both lakes are the Belted Kingfisher and Common Tern. On the lake, on sandspits or points, you will usually see groups of nonbreeding one- and two-year-old American White Pelicans, and perhaps a Double-crested Cormorant or two, though their nearest breeding colony is on islands in the Quill Lakes, about 100 miles to the northwest.

The marshes at the west end of each lake contain Virginia Rail and sometimes a colony of Western Grebe. At this point, in dry weather, there is a choice of continuing west along the valley to Lake Katepwa on a dirt valley road or returning to the Trans-Canada via Highway 47. At Indian Head, it is possible to tour the experimental farm founded in 1887 at the east edge of town, and the PFRA Tree Nursery Station south of town. Members of the Indian Head Natural History Society, especially Mary Skinner at (306) 695-3488 and Lorne and Joan Scott at (306) 695-2047, can provide details of recent local sightings.

Turn north at Indian Head on Highway 56. The Skinner Marsh is in the valley southeast of Katepwa Lake. It has been restored and is controlled by Ducks Unlimited (Canada), with the cooperation of the Saskatchewan government, as a Canada Goose breeding project. Further downriver are a few breeding pairs of Wood Duck, but these are likely to be seen only by a canoeist. Farther along Highway 56, you will see Katepwa Beach, once a superb swimming beach and one of Canada's smallest national parks. Now it is often covered by algae that bespeak excessive human and animal excreta upstream. At Lebret's Catholic mission, climb the stations of the cross. Farther along the road, stop and read the historic plaque that tells the tragic, romantic legend of how the valley got its name.

At Fort Qu'Appelle, contact Manley Callin at (306) 332-5947 for up-to-date bird information. This spot, situated between Mission and Echo lakes, was chosen as a North-West Mounted Police post in 1875 and later as a headquarters in 1880. At the end of Echo Lake, look for both Le Conte's and Sharp-tailed Sparrows, as well as the Marsh Wren and Common Yellow-throat.

At this point the rushed traveller can take Highway 10 as the quickest route to Regina and points west. Less hurried visitors may wish to follow major grid road 727 west along the north shore of Pasqua Lake and then out of the valley west for 20 km, jogging north 3.2 km on major grid 240, and then west on an unnumbered grid road with sheaf signs, another 22 km to Highway 6, which leads directly south into Regina. You now have an option of turning southwest on Highway 99, a final valley road that leads into Craven, past Kennell Church in its picturesque location on the south side of the river. Continue on Highway 20 to Lumsden, then take Highway 11 southeast to Regina, or northwest to Saskatoon. Large flocks of geese and waders are seen in the valley, especially in spring and fall migration.

C. STUART HOUSTON

Yorkton and Duck Mountain Provincial Park

Yorkton provides a base from which to explore east-central Saskatchewan. From here you can sample waterfowl, shorebird and aspen parkland habitats north and south of the town. Move northeast to the Duck Mountains and experience the southernmost boreal forest in the province. Everything from Black-crowned Night-Heron and American Avocet, through Piping Plover and Black-billed Cuckoo, to Common Loon and Boreal Chickadee is present.

The town has a variety of motels and other services. Campgrounds are nearby at York Lake, just south of town, and at Good Spirit Lake Provincial Park north 32 km and 17 km west. Yorkton is served by Greyhound and STC buses. Highway 10 from Regina intersects the Yellowhead Highway 16 at Yorkton.

Further information is available in "Birds of the Yorkton District, Saskatchewan," by C. S. Houston in *Canadian Field-Naturalist* 63, 1949, pp. 215–41; in the 12-page booklet "Exploring the Dunes," by R. J. Long, Saskatchewan Department of Tourism and Renewable Resources; and in "Birds of Madge Lake," by F. W. Lahrman in *Blue Jay* 14, pp. 53–4, 103.

Birding Features
The area is best visited from mid-May to early July when most breeding birds are on territory. The three best locations to see are York Lake Regional Park south of town; Good Spirit Lake Provincial Park north of Yorkton; and Duck Mountain Provincial Park to the northeast.

Begin at York Lake Regional Park. Take an evening stroll along the well-marked self-guiding nature trail that starts at the lake just west of the railroad track. Watch for a Black-crowned Night-Heron flying out to feed. A White-winged Scoter will be among the ducks on the lake. Listen for the Veery singing as though from the bottom of a rain barrel.

To the west 3.2 km is Rousay Lake, one of the best waterfowl marshes in western Canada, with numerous artificial nesting sites used by Canada Goose. South 6.4 km is Leech Lake, where the Sandhill Crane still nests successfully. These lakes are best explored by canoe, allowing a close look at Red-necked, Horned and Eared Grebes, Black-crowned Night-Heron and ten resident species of duck. You will hear and often see Virginia Rail and Sora. Wilson's Phalarope and Black Tern are numerous.

American Avocets feed along the mudflats. Apart from the first two weeks of July, many species of sandpiper come through at different times. The "slough-pump" noise of American Bitterns can be heard. Adjacent grasslands boast the Upland Sandpiper in addition to Willet, Marbled Godwit, Baird's and Le Conte's Sparrows, and Chestnut-collared Longspur. Warbling Vireo and Least Flycatcher sing from every small aspen bluff nearby. The Black-billed Cuckoo is heard mainly in years when tent caterpillars are numerous. The ubiquitous Black-billed Magpie, after a lapse of thirty or forty years from the buffalo's disappearance, came back in the 1930s and has been common since the 1950s.

If time permits, visit Good Spirit Lake Provincial Park. Follow Highway 9 north from Yorkton to Highway 229, then go west. At the park gate, ask for Joyce or Bill Anaka, keen local birders. Their residence phone is (306) 792-4780.

The lake was formed during a dry period centuries ago. Winds carved out an ever-deepening hole and deposited the sand as large dunes, especially near the southeast margin. Later, the hole became Good Spirit (or Kitchemanito, as the Cree called it) Lake. The beach is wide and remarkably level. Bathers must wade for hundreds of metres into the water before reaching swimming depth; hence it is one of the safest beaches to be found anywhere for children. Away from the swimming areas, Spotted Sandpiper have regularly spaced territories along the beach. A colony of Bank Swallows occurs along the sand dunes. Depending on water levels, Common Tern sometimes nest.

The beach dunes are constantly shifting. Behind them is a second sand ridge, where plants have largely stabilized the sandy soil. On the level land beyond the ridge, you'll find House Wren, Gray Catbird, Cedar Waxwing and Clay-colored Sparrow.

Duck Mountain Provincial Park is 104 km northeast of Yorkton via Highways 10, 8 and 57. The park contains beautiful Madge Lake, with its many points and islands within boreal forest. The Common Loon and Common Goldeneye are the most obvious water birds. Many pairs of Ring-necked Duck occur on surrounding sloughs. In the mixed forest, look for ferns up to 1.5 m high and several species of orchids. Listen for Hermit and Swainson's Thrushes each evening, interspersed with the clear notes of the White-throated Sparrow. Search for the Pileated Woodpecker, Boreal Chickadee and Swamp Sparrow. Try to sort out the songs of 14 species of warblers, including the Nashville, Connecticut and Blackburnian. In suitable habitat with tall, thin aspen, Philadelphia Vireo may be found. These

110

birds look like a yellow-tinged Warbling Vireo and sing like a Red-eyed Vireo, but higher and with a slower tempo. The world's first recorded nest of the Philadelphia Vireo was found on the edge of the Duck Mountains about 15 km south of the park gate. Ernest Thompson Seton located it while building a cabin on his homestead, 2 km southwest of the present Runnymede.

Solitary, Red-eyed and Warbling Vireos are also present. The Yellow-throated Vireo has been reported twice from Madge Lake.

C. STUART HOUSTON

Gainsborough, Saskatchewan, to Lyleton, Manitoba

This section of mixed-grass prairies and scattered woodlands lies in the extreme southeast corner of Saskatchewan and the southwest corner of Manitoba. At least 245 species of birds have been recorded in the area recently. An annual Christmas bird count at Lyleton has produced 41 species since 1971.

Prior to settlement the area was treeless grasslands with wooded river bottoms. Settlement began in the 1880s, and today only a few isolated pockets of original prairie remain. Over 70 per cent of the land is under intense cultivation, mainly for cash crops. With the planting of trees and shrubs around homesites and in towns, combined with trees and shrubs spreading to roadsides, railroad embankments and in upland pastures, there are now strips and islands of woodland that attract a wide variety of birds.

The area lies about 130 km southwest of Brandon, Manitoba, or about 250 km southeast of Regina. Greyhound services the major nearby towns of Melita and Pipestone in Manitoba and Carnduff in Saskatchewan. The railroad spur lines have been terminated. Hotels, gasoline and services are available in several communities.

Information on the area is well documented in an excellent report, *Birds of the Gainsborough-Lyleton Region*, by Richard W. Knapton, 1979, Saskatchewan Natural History Publication No. 10. It is available for $3.00 from the Blue Jay Bookshop (see above).

Material for this section was taken from this report, which includes a detailed description of all birds recently seen in the region.

Birding Features
The gently rolling country contains two small rivers, each running eastward: Gainsborough Creek in the north and Antler River to the south. Temporary and semipermanent sloughs are found in numerous small depressions. These are generally not saline, with the larger and deeper ones supporting stands of cat-tails, reed grass and bullrush. The shallow temporary sloughs are often overgown with sedges and grasses. The recent practice of increasing the amount of productive land by draining wetlands has reduced marshes and sloughs to less than one per cent of the total area in this corner of Manitoba. Shelterbelts around farmsites and windbreaks on

the edges of fields, combined with woodlands along roadsides, railroads and some pastureland, provide a break in the never-ending grainfields. This is a good region in which to find Burrowing Owl in pastures, Say's Phoebe, Loggerhead Shrike, Orchard Oriole, Dickcissel, Lark Bunting and Baird's Sparrow, all of which are rare or absent in other parts of Manitoba. The best season is from late May to mid-July.

Key spots to bird include the Gainsborough Dam on the creek of the same name, 9 km south of Gainsborough. Horned, Eared and Western Grebes breed here. The Black-crowned Night-Heron has a small colony at the dam and others on the creek. Other water birds use this water body for nesting and as a staging area on migration.

The Pierson Wildlife Management Area of bluffs, potholes and irregularly shaped fields lies 8 km southwest of Pierson. Several potholes have been blasted out, wildlife food plots cleared, and 10,000 trees and shrubs planted on this 194.3-ha block. A second unit within the same management area lies 14.5 km east of Pierson. This 64.8 ha of river bottom woodland, with grass-covered slopes, provides another birding spot worth visiting.

There are two larger bodies of water in the region: the dam on Ralph Wang's farm contains 1.5 ha of water surface and lies 10 km southwest of Pierson. This is private property, so ask for permission before entering. Mr. Wang came to this area as a boy in the 1940s and has carefully observed and recorded the wildlife for over twenty years. The other spot is the Ducks Unlimited (Canada) dam about 7 km west of Lyleton, with about 1.5 ha of water surface.

John Murray, a very keen birder from Lyleton, has kept almost daily records since 1968. He may know of other good spots worth visiting. He works as the customs officer at the border crossing into the U.S.A. on Highway 256.

The scattered sloughs in the area, together with the above-mentioned dams, attract the normal complement of water birds from late April to early October. The Northern Harrier is the most numerous and widespread nesting raptor and begins arriving in late March. Shorebirds are common migrants from mid-May to early June and in September. Watch for Lesser Golden- and Black-bellied Plovers. The Gainsborough Dam is a particularly good spot for these species. In winter look for Golden Eagle.

Mourning Dove is one of the most common and widespread species in this region. The doves begin arriving at the bluffs and shelterbelts in mid-April and are soon very abundant. The recent (1974) mass invasion of Orchard Orioles in this area now makes it possible to spot easily both this species and the Baltimore race of the Northern Oriole, sometimes in the same bluff. Other birds to watch for include Wild Turkey, Sprague's Pipit and Grasshopper Sparrow.

RUDOLF F. KOES

Manitoba

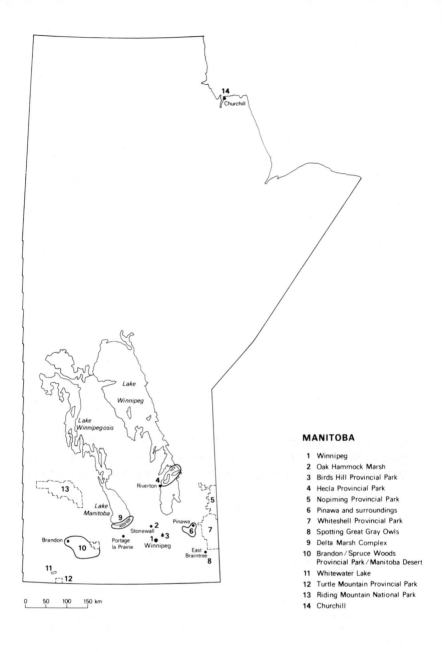

MANITOBA

1 Winnipeg
2 Oak Hammock Marsh
3 Birds Hill Provincial Park
4 Hecla Provincial Park
5 Nopiming Provincial Park
6 Pinawa and surroundings
7 Whiteshell Provincial Park
8 Spotting Great Gray Owls
9 Delta Marsh Complex
10 Brandon / Spruce Woods
   Provincial Park / Manitoba Desert
11 Whitewater Lake
12 Turtle Mountain Provincial Park
13 Riding Mountain National Park
14 Churchill

Manitoba

Manitoba's habitats range through prairie and parkland to hardwood and boreal forest to low arctic tundra. Most of these lie within a couple of hours' drive from Winnipeg (the tundra at Churchill is a short airplane flight away). Such variety hosts a truly phenomenal number of bird species. They come from the east, west, north and south of North America. Manitoba's birders hold the North American inland record for the months of May, June and August, while high counts in July and September probably constitute Canadian records. Southern Ontario is the only other place in Canada where you can approach this number of species.

The southern and western portions of Manitoba are part of the prairie pothole, or slough, basin of North America, most of which lies in Canada. An aerial survey of western Canada in 1955 found 1,335,000 potholes. By 1961 there were barely 49,000 left! Drought, combined with drainage for agriculture, took a heavy toll. These prairie sloughs are ten times more productive in waterfowl food than similar water bodies in the east; fifty to eighty per cent of all migratory ducks in North America breed on them. No wonder this region is sometimes called a "duck factory."

The province contains substantial populations of some of the "most wanted" species in North America, including Spruce Grouse, Yellow Rail, Ross' Gull at Churchill, Northern Hawk-Owl, Great Gray Owl, Three-toed Woodpecker, Sprague's Pipit, Connecticut Warbler, and Baird's and Le Conte's Sparrows. All except the gull are readily accessible in the southern section of the province along a good road system.

The population is spread in a thin strip along the far southern agricultural belt. Southern woodlands occur in a thin band north of that strip. Boreal forest covers the northern half of the province, and on the eastern edge penetrates far south. The arctic-subarctic region lies in a band on the north, with low arctic tundra at the far northeast, adjacent to Hudson Bay.

Early June is the best time to come. There are still a few migrants going north, but from late May to early July all local breeders are on territory. Waterfowl and birds of prey pass through in April and early May. Shorebirds and land birds come through in May in peak abundance. In August and early September shorebirds return, as do the northern land birds. Waterfowl stop here before the long flight south in September and October. November through March, search for the Northern Hawk-, Great Gray and Boreal Owls.

Selection of a few "hot spots" is always difficult. However, a few areas do stand out in order of preference: Churchill for the arctic tundra and ocean birds, the least remote, least expensive place to view them in North America. The only other fairly accessible comparable spot is the Dempster Highway in the Yukon; Oak Hammock Marsh for water birds; the Brandon area for Yellow Rail and prairie-slough water birds; Pinawa for boreal and hardwood forest birds, including Great Gray and Boreal Owls. The above four spots are musts for the serious birder. The Delta Marsh complex offers prairie marsh birds in abundance; Riding Mountain National Park has boreal and hardwood forest and numerous parkland and prairie birds, including all prairie pothole ducks, all five Canadian grebes, Northern Saw-whet and Barred Owls, Spruce Grouse, both three-toed woodpeckers, and a large number of warblers, including Golden-winged. A bonus is the resident naturalist who can help you find that elusive, hard-to-spot species.

A visitor with a half day to spare in Winnipeg, and no car, should go to Assiniboine Park; using a car, you can easily spend this time at Oak Hammock Marsh. A full day could begin early in the morning within the boreal forest at Pinawa and include an afternoon at Oak Hammock. A second day would allow a visit to the Brandon area. To see most species at Churchill requires at least two full days if you fly in, or a week if you travel by train.

Manitoba has an extremely active and friendly group, the Manitoba Rare Bird Alert. They have all offered to help and can refer you to other members if there is a need. Contact Norm Cleveland, Telephone: (204) 253-9622; Herb Copeland, Telephone: (204) 956-2830; Rudolf Koes, 135 Rossmere Crescent, Winnipeg, Manitoba R2K 0G1, Telephone: (204) 334-6617; or Ian Ward, Telephone: (204) 885-3104. The four active clubs in the province may be contacted through the Manitoba Naturalists' Society, 214 — 190 Rupert Avenue, Winnipeg, Manitoba R3B 0N2, Telephone: (204) 943-9029.

Rare Bird Alert members and others have prepared an excellent bird-finding guide to southeastern Manitoba: *Birder's Guide to Southeastern Manitoba*, by N. J. Cleveland, R. F. Koes, M. F. Murdoch, W. P. Neily and I. A. Ward, 1980, Eco Series No. 1, Manitoba Naturalists' Society. Copies of this 58-page guide can be obtained from the society for $4.95 plus postage and handling. Material from this publication has been used in this chapter. Write also for their "Field Checklist of the Birds of Southeastern Manitoba" (25 cents). Other material is available from the Museum of Man and Nature, 190 Rupert Avenue, Winnipeg, Manitoba R3B 0N2.

The Official Highway Map and a Manitoba Vacation Guide are available free from Travel Manitoba, Dept. 1001 — Legislative Building, Winnipeg, Manitoba R3C 0V8 (or as they advertise, "Telephone Collect (204) 944-3777").

Bird watchers wishing to consult additional literature on the birds of the province will find sources in *Manitoba Bird Studies/A Bibliography of Manitoba Ornithology*, by M. K. McNicholl (Winnipeg: Manitoba Dept. of Mines, Resources and Environment Management, 1975). A much-expanded edition is now nearly complete. Inquire locally as to its availability.

The compilation of this chapter was greatly assisted by notes, suggestions and other types of help from Gord Grieef, Wayne Neily, Robert Nero, Martin Siepman, Peter Taylor and Ian Ward.

RUDOLF F. KOES

Winnipeg

The oldest settlement in western Canada can boast that it is near the geographic centre of North America. Winnipeg began as a settlement in 1812. For almost half a century it was the headquarters of the mighty

Hudson's Bay Company. They owned and dominated most of western Canada and part of the northwestern United States. Today, Winnipeg, with a population of over 600,000, is the fourth-largest Canadian city.

Birding Features

Assiniboine Park. The park, set along the banks of the Assiniboine River, is noted for its passerine migration. Almost all warbler species found in Manitoba can be seen in the park during the latter half of May. This is also an excellent site to study the differences between Hermit, Swainson's and Gray-cheeked Thrushes during spring migration.

The 160-ha park is the largest and most popular outdoor facility in Winnipeg. It lies 6 km west of downtown, on the south bank of the Assiniboine River. By car, it is reached via Wellington Crescent or Corydon Avenue; or west via Portage Avenue to Overdale Street and a hike across the footbridge. The Portage or Charleswood city buses will bring you there.

The diverse habitat, including lawns, gardens, Bur Oak and river bottom forests, together with the adjacent river, attracts a great variety of species, especially during migration. Birding is best done along the south bank of the river east and west of the footbridge on the trails, and in the English garden immediately west of the bridge.

In the early spring, from April to early May, watch for over a dozen species of sparrow. In the second half of May, the warblers come in waves, with almost all species to be found in Manitoba passing through here.

Breeding birds include Wood Duck, Red-headed Woodpecker and Yellow-throated Vireo.

In the fall, beginning in early August and peaking in late August to mid-September, look for up to five species of vireo and over twenty different warblers. August also brings the Ruby-throated Hummingbird into the English garden.

In winter check for waxwings and finches.

La Barriere Park. Straddling the La Salle River, this park contains river bottom woods surrounded by open grassy spots. The area offers a good concentration of migrating smaller birds in both spring and fall.

The park is located 5.6 km south of Highway 100, at the south end of Winnipeg. Drive south from the city on Highway 75 to Highway 100 and then go west for 1 km, turn south at the first intersection. There are several good walking trails in the park on both sides of the river. Beware of poison ivy in season! For more information contact the Manitoba Naturalists' Society at the above address.

During the nesting season, from late May to mid-July, check for Broad-winged Hawk and Great Horned Owl in the dense woods. In addition, Red-headed Woodpecker, Yellow-throated Vireo, Orchard Oriole, Red-breasted Grosbeak and Lark Sparrow are present.

St. Adolphe Bridge. This is a spot to watch for raptors in the spring. Proceed south from Winnipeg on Highway 75; 11 km south of Highway 100 you will hit PR 429; proceed east on 429 about 1.6 km to the bridge, cross it and park on the wide shoulders off the road to watch migration.

The Red River Valley is a major funnel for migrating raptors. In late March and early April, look for the Red-tailed Hawk, which is the most common, Rough-legged Hawk, Golden and Bald Eagles, Marsh Hawk, Merlin and American Kestrel. The river and adjacent farmlands provide habitat for Canada Geese, ducks and other birds passing through.

BIRDER'S GUIDE TO SOUTHEASTERN MANITOBA

Brookside Cemetery and airport. The cemetery is an island of elm and other trees surrounded by encroaching residential developments and open prairie. The site is best reached on Notre Dame Avenue, which passes by the entrance gate. The Winnipeg Industrial Airport, just beyond the cemetery, and the western edge of the cemetery provide prairie habitat on the edge of the city.

Over 150 species have been observed in the cemetery, and several additional prairie birds have been spotted along the nearby airport. In winter the cemetery has little to offer, but it is one of the most reliable spots to look for Gray Partridge in Winnipeg. The airport should be seasonal for Snowy Owl and Snow Bunting. In spring and fall, most species of warbler and vireo found in southern Manitoba can be found in the cemetery, where particularly large concentrations of the yellow-shafted race of the Northern Flicker, myrtle race of the Yellow-rumped Warbler, and Palm Warbler have been observed. In summer the cemetery is the best spot in the Winnipeg area to look for nesting Mourning Dove. Gray Catbird and Brown Thrasher breed there. Fields around the airport runways are good spots to watch for Upland Sandpiper. A small marsh on the boundary of the airport is the closest place to central Winnipeg for locating breeding Black Tern, Yellow-headed Blackbird and Sora. Vast numbers of Lapland Longspurs can be seen along the airport runways in fall.

Kildonen Park. Like Assiniboine Park, this spot is well worth a visit, especially if your transportation is restricted to metro transit. The location on Main Street makes it readily accessible from downtown Winnipeg on the North Main bus.

Most of the warblers of southern Manitoba have been seen here at one time or another, although numbers do not usually reach those of Assiniboine Park or Brookside Cemetery. The open lawns with stately oaks constitute one of the most reliable spots in the Winnipeg area for Red-headed Woodpecker in the summer. Careful study of the Bank Swallow along the Red River should reveal a Northern Rough-winged or two.

MARTIN K. McNICHOLL

Oak Hammock Marsh

This major man-made development illustrates how a private organization and different levels of government can unite to develop a top birding area. Lying within a half-hour drive of Winnipeg, the diversity of habitats created has attracted 235 species since 1935.

This marsh and lake sit in a broad lowland known as St. Andrews Bog.

For years the remnant marsh attracted a variety of water birds. Restoration began in 1967 as a cooperative venture with Ducks Unlimited (Canada), and the federal and provincial governments. By the spring of 1974, they had produced 1418 ha of wetlands, including one large pond in the shape of a duck.

The present 3645-ha Oak Hammock Marsh Wildlife Management Area is about 24 km north of Winnipeg. Access is by either Highway 7 or 8. On Highway 7, proceed north to PR 223, east 8 km to PR 220 and then north on the gravel road for 4 km to the main parking lot. The Highway 8 access route is north from Winnipeg to PR 223, west 6.5 km to PR 220, and then north to the parking spot. Beware of this gravel road during spring break-up in April and after a heavy summer rain.

A detailed checklist of the birds of Oak Hammock Marsh is available from: Manitoba Department of Natural Resources, 1495 St. James Street, Winnipeg, Manitoba R3H 0W9. Write also for their 172-page study of the birds, *Birds of Oak Hammock Marsh Wildlife Management Area*, by R. Gardner (1981).

Birding Features

Agricultural lands surround the marsh. However, the management authority has included 1904 ha of upland habitat, providing sufficient variety of habitat to attract 105 species to breed. Dikes control the water levels and also provide access to three separate areas by foot. Five observation mounds give views of the whole complex.

The birds begin arriving at the start of the spring thaw in April. Waterfowl, including over 100,000 Snow Geese, come in until mid-May. Shorebirds arrive a little later. They come in May and early June, with almost all species found in North America having been recorded here. At times, one species such as Hudsonian Godwit or Northern Phalarope will dominate for a few days. Check the clumps of alders and willows near the main parking lot for the waves of warblers that pass through in May and late August. The birds that stay begin breeding in late May and continue into July. Watch for them as you hike along the dikes. The fall migration begins with shorebirds in mid-July and continues until late September. Waterfowl numbers reach a peak in late September to early October. At that time, look for Sandhill Cranes by the hundreds and Ross' Geese among the thousands of Snow Geese returning south.

This spot has become noted for sightings of such southern herons as Green-backed, Little Blue, Tricolored and Yellow-crowned Night-Heron. Rare egrets such as Cattle, Great and Snowy are also seen.

The large concentrations of birds of course attract the falcons, especially Prairie and Peregrine. Other raptors too may be seen on migration.

BIRDER'S GUIDE TO SOUTHEASTERN MANITOBA

Birds Hill Provincial Park

Birds Hill, with its Bur Oak, aspen, variety of conifers and deciduous shrubs, is a near-urban park with over 185 species of prairie, parkland and boreal forest birds reported. The park hosts a good-sized herd of White-tailed Deer, some Coyote, Red Fox and other small mammals.

Named after the Bird family, the first landowners in 1824, the area changed hands many times. The park was established in 1962, with the northern section formally declared a provincial park in 1964, and the remainder added later.

The highlands were built by a stream carrying sands and gravels to a delta in former Lake Agassiz. This all took place eight to ten thousand years ago.

The 3350-ha park is split: lands on the south for high-density recreation and the remainder left in a natural state. The lands lie adjacent to Highway 59, about 24 km northeast of Winnipeg. Bus service to the park from downtown Winnipeg runs a few times a day only in summer. One main driving loop circles the southern, active recreation area. A side road leads to park headquarters. A major horse-riding trail lies on the north side, as do several nature and hiking trails. Roads and trails are illustrated in the park material.

Visitor accommodation includes that at Winnipeg and nearby communities. Campers and trailer users have a major campground in the park, located off the south drive loop road.

Information on the park, including an excellent brochure and a comprehensive bird checklist, is available from: The Chief Ranger, Birds Hill Provincial Park, Department of Natural Resources, R.R. 2, Dugald, Manitoba R0E 0K0, Telephone: (204) 222-9151.

Birding Features

The main forests are aspen and Bur Oak communities separated by grasslands. There are further stands of White Spruce, plus Black Spruce bogs. A White Cedar bog and a man-made lake and lagoon add diversity. This variety of habitat provides opportunities to sight Pied-billed Grebe, Great Blue Heron and a variety of waterfowl. Northern Goshawk is most often seen in the fall. American Woodcock is found in low areas at dusk in the south end from mid-April to late May. Listen for a Northern Saw-whet Owl in the mixed and coniferous woods along the eastern and southern sections through April and May. Sprague's Pipit is rare but has been seen in meadows in the spring. Northern Shrike comes in late fall and winter. The mixed and coniferous woods provide a variety of warblers in June. Indigo Bunting is present in the open, drier sections in June and July. In winter, a variety of finches appear.

A drive around the loop road of the south should bring an Indigo Bunting and Rufous-sided Towhee. Look east of the west gate on the north side of the road, and also just east of the traffic circle. At the circle, turn right and proceed south and east. At the turn in the road, where it swings from south to east, check on the west side for an American Woodcock or Northern Saw-whet Owl. Continue on to the north leg of the loop. Just before meeting the road from the east gate, scan the east side for another Northern Saw-whet Owl, warblers and (in season) winter finches. Just beyond, as the road heads northeast, there is a side road heading north to the headquarters and the ranger station. Take this side trip to spot the occasional crossbill and warbler, west of the headquarters buildings. Return to the loop and continue west. Just beyond (west) of the parking lot, on the south side, carefully inspect fields for Sprague's Pipit, which sometimes appears.

For further specific locations check with park staff and the interpretive service at headquarters from early May to September.

RUDOLF F. KOES

Hecla Provincial Park

Superb boreal forest birding is available at and near Hecla Island. Northern Hawk-Owl and one of the three-toed woodpeckers are usually seen in winter, with numerous passerines found from late May to early July. Nearby Lake Winnipeg offers opportunities to view water birds. The big game enthusiast can see Moose on the island, and some deer, Timber Wolves and a few Red Foxes.

Settlers arrived in the area from Iceland in 1875–76 after the eruption of Mt. Hekla in their homeland destroyed their farms. In 1878 they formed the self-governing republic of New Iceland, with their own constitution and a provisional government that levied taxes and organized schools. In 1881 the boundaries of Manitoba were extended to include the republic. Today much of the cleared land has regrown and attracts a variety of birds and mammals.

The island, located about 145 km north of Winnipeg, may be reached by following PTH 8 or 9, then PR 234 and east on PR 233. The trip can be extended north to Matheson Island on PR 234. Greyhound bus travels part way up the road, but the best access is by car. The trip may be made in one long day; a more leisurely two-day trip will cover the return. There are a series of hiking, cross-country ski, and snowshoe trails in the park. No park map or brochure is yet available.

Commercial accommodation may be obtained in a luxury resort hotel at Gull Harbour, with more moderately priced cabins nearby at the north end of the island. Camping facilities occur at Gull Harbour and near Beaver Creek along PR 234, halfway to Matheson Island.

Birding Features
A visit can be made at any time of the year. Go in spring from mid-May to early July. A fall trip would be best in August and early September. November still has a goodly number of birds, especially a lingering Bald Eagle and waterfowl. After that it can be very cold and stormy, even into March.

The spring trip would begin on PTH 8 north to the Winnipeg Beach turnoff; take PR 229 east to PTH 9 and proceed north. Between Winnipeg and Winnipeg Beach, common roadside species include Horned Lark, Western Meadowlark, Brewer's Blackbird and Vesper Sparrow.

Proceed north to Gimli on 9; take PR 222 to Camp Morton, about 8 km north of Gimli, and enter Camp Morton Park. Scout out the area for migrant land and water birds as this site is a good birding area.

Yellow-headed Blackbird

Continue north on PR 222, then move to PTH 8 and on to Riverton. Travel east on PR 329 to the shores of Lake Winnipeg. The Riverton Marsh is known for its many water birds. Scan the water and marsh vegetation for a variety of waterfowl, rails, Marsh and Sedge Wrens, Yellow-headed Blackbird, and Le Conte's and Sharp-tailed Sparrows.

Reach Hecla Island via PR 234 and 233 east. Just over the causeway to the park, but before the entrance, take the gravel road parallel to the main road to the south. The gravel road terminates after 1 km, with a boardwalk leading to an observation platform in the marsh. Reconnoitre for waterfowl, rails, Alder Flycatcher and others.

Return to PR 233 and enter the park. About 200 m beyond the entrance there is a gravel road leading south. Park on the shoulder of the main road. Proceed beyond the barrier for a 1-km stroll, looking for a variety of passerines including Lincoln's Sparrow.

Continue the drive east on PR 233 for about 20 km, to the end. Birding is excellent along this stretch, with several stops a must. Sample both the coniferous and the mixed woods for a variety of birds, including Pileated Woodpecker, Gray Jay, Black-capped and Boreal Chickadees, Winter Wren, Swainson's Thrush, both kinglet species, numerous warblers and some crossbills. At Gull Harbour take a spotting scope and scan the water for American White Pelican, Double-crested Cormorant, diving ducks, gulls and terns. Check the sky for an occasional Osprey. The end of the road has some good walking trails on which to find warblers, etc.

To extend the visit, return to the junction of PR 233 and 234. Take 234 north to the end of Matheson Island. This is an 85-km road with no services. Fill up with gasoline before departing. The first stretch of road is generally open, but soon coniferous forests take over. Boreal species are common, with a Northern Hawk-Owl more often seen on this stretch than in most other places.

On the return to Winnipeg, you can either retrace your path or proceed straight south all the way on 8.

A fall visit may produce waves of migrating passerines, particularly at the far end of the island on PR 233. Hike the trails at this location and watch for these and the accompanying Sharp-shinned Hawk, Merlin and the occasional Peregrine Falcon.

In winter, the fields between Winnipeg and Winnipeg Beach often contain Sharp-tailed Grouse and flocks of Snow Bunting. At the north end of Hecla Island, at the termination of the road, look for Bald Eagle, either of the three-toed woodpeckers, Boreal Chickadee, Red-breasted Nuthatch, Northern Shrike, Evening Grosbeak, both redpoll species, both species of crossbill, and Pine Grosbeak. An occasional Northern Hawk-Owl or Spruce Grouse may show up. Watch for the impressive wing marks in the snow left by a Common Raven. These birds often carry on social behaviour and leave such signs as evidence. Going farther up to Matheson Island will likely, as in summer, result in a view of a Northern Hawk-Owl.

RUDOLF F. KOES

Nopiming Provincial Park

Some of the finest upland boreal forest birding in eastern Manitoba is found in the south end of Nopiming Provincial Park, along the Bird River Road. This route is particularly good for spring warblers.

The area has always been known for its fishing and trapping potential, but it came alive after gold was found in 1911. Claims were staked, and a major mine operated from 1926 to 1937 at the north end of the park.

Nopiming is located along the Manitoba-Ontario boundary, immediately north of Whiteshell Provincial Park, about 160 km by road northeast of Winnipeg. To reach the park, drive to Lac du Bonnet, the last source of gasoline and other services, and then take PR 313 and 315. An alternate route would be a driving loop of about 350 km (two or more days) north and east from Pine Falls on PR 304 and back south on 314 and 315. All of these roads are rough, especially during or after rain. When taking the loop, fill up your gas tanks at Lac du Bonnet, Pine Falls, Manigotagan and Bissett, the only services in the area.

The closest commercial accommodation is at Lac du Bonnet, with several motels and lodges. Campsites occur at Bird Lake in the south and others to the north.

Most of the birding information for this area has been taken from an unpublished manuscript by Peter Taylor, "The Birds of the Pinawa–Lac du Bonnet Area, Manitoba." If you require more information or help, contact him at P.O. Box 597, Pinawa, Manitoba R0E 1L0, Telephone: (204) 753-2977.

Birding Features
The Bird River Road (PR 315) from PR 313 to Bird Lake is excellent for boreal forest warblers from late May to early July. It is one of the few spots in Manitoba where the Northern Parula can be expected. In April, come here to

listen for owls, including Great Horned, Barred, Boreal and Northern Saw-whet. Later, in the peak breeding season, explore for Great Crested Fly-catcher, Yellow-bellied Flycatcher (at the edge of dense stands of young spruce), Eastern Wood-Pewee, Red-breasted Nuthatch, Brown Creeper and Winter Wren. There are small numbers of Hermit Thrushes, numerous Swainson's Thrushes, Veery and an abundance of warblers. These include Black-and-white, Nashville, Magnolia, and a small number of Black-throated Green, especially in the mature coniferous forest near Bird Lake. In addition, there are Blackburnian and Chestnut-sided Warblers, Ovenbird and Northern Waterthrush at several spots near the Bird River. The Mourning Warbler is present, and the Canada Warbler lurks where the understory is especially dense. Scarlet Tanager and Pine Siskin may be heard or seen. In some winters both PR 313 and 315 provide good prospects for sighting Northern Hawk-Owl and Great Gray Owl.

RUDOLF F. KOES, PETER TAYLOR

Pinawa and Surroundings

The Pinawa area contains a mixture of forest and spruce bogs with some cleared farmland. Over 150 species of birds may be seen here in a day during late May. This was part of the area in which 194 species were recorded in a single day on May 29, 1982. In winter, Northern Hawk-Owl, Great Gray Owl and both species of three-toed woodpeckers may be seen.

The Winnipeg River was an important fur trading route in the eighteenth century. Major settlement began in the late 1880s, with cutting and burning off the forest, as there was no native prairie. Clearing continues to this day. The forests have been almost completely logged over, with present growth mainly secondary. An extensive series of dams, with six hydro-electric plants, was built to harness the power of the Winnipeg River. The largest, at Seven Sisters Falls, offers tours.

The town of Pinawa, founded in 1963 in conjunction with the White-shell Nuclear Research Establishment, lies 112 km east and north of Winnipeg. There are numerous secondary roads which can keep a birder busy for two days in the late spring.

Accommodation in the town of Pinawa consists of one small motel, open year-round. There are two campgrounds 10 km west of town, one privately operated and serviced, the other a wayside primitive facility. The region is an active summer resort, with gasoline and other services available from at least May through September.

Come for birding in late spring from mid-May to early July. Bring insect repellent along! In winter, dress warmly and be prepared with emergency clothing and footwear, sleeping bag, candle, etc., as temperatures are known to fall very low.

A comprehensive unpublished paper has been prepared on the sur-rounding area by Peter Taylor. (See previous site for title and address to obtain a copy.)

Birding Features

Most of the country within 3 km of the Whitemouth River, and some land along the Lee and Winnipeg rivers, is cultivated. Marginal pastureland lies along the edges. The remainder of the country is forested with Trembling Aspen, the most abundant species, growing on well-drained sites. White Spruce, Balsam Fir, birch and Balsam Poplar are also present. Black Spruce and Tamarack are found in the wet areas, and Jack Pine grows on rock outcrops and sandy ridges. This diversity of habitat attracts a great variety of birdlife that breeds from late April to July.

The townsite of Pinawa is a small, recently created island of parklike habitat set in second growth boreal forest. Consequently, the birdlife within the town is unique for the area. Begin the exploration within the community by looking for Red-headed Woodpecker, Least Flycatcher, large numbers of Cliff Swallow and Purple Martin, House Wren, Brown Thrasher, Warbling Vireo and Northern Oriole. Now move to the forests at the edge of town to search for a variety of warblers.

Expand the range to the trails radiating out from the north end of the diversion dam at the head of the Pinawa Channel, located at the very end of PR 211. These hiking trails sometimes have ankle-high water in many places. Some are even impassable during wet weather. Before leaving the car, make sure you have a compass; stay on the well-defined trails. The bush trails are excellent for boreal birds from mid-May to early July. Begin the search for a Great Crested Flycatcher, Eastern Wood-Pewee, the odd Yellow-bellied Flycatcher, Brown Creeper, Winter Wren, Hermit Thrush and myriad warblers. They should include Nashville, Chestnut-sided and Ovenbird, all of which are common. The Northern Waterthrush will be near the channel. Listen for the Connecticut Warbler near clearings in the Black Spruce, together with abundant Mourning Warblers. A Scarlet Tanager should be seen.

Return to town, drive about 2 km west, then take the cemetery road north of PR 211. This north road is passable for about 3 km in dry weather, but stay off in wet seasons or when it looks like rain. A round trip of hiking and birding should take about five hours. Many warblers occur here in late spring. Search for Red-eyed Vireo, Great Crested Flycatcher, Veery, and Chestnut-sided and Mourning Warblers, all common to very common. The American Redstart has an unusually high concentration. Proceed for about 3 km, to where the road takes a sharp turn west and soon becomes impassable. At the west bend, take the 100-m trail north to where the Pinawa Channel widens into a large marsh. Stop and scan the water, or launch a canoe for a more detailed look. Least and American Bitterns, Mallard, Blue-winged Teal, Common Goldeneye, Sora, Virginia Rail and Marsh Wren all occur. Retrace your steps the 100 m and continue west and north on the trail. Inspect the mature conifers for a Winter Wren and a possible Black-throated Green Warbler. This road or trail ends in a Black Spruce bog, which should produce Boreal Chickadee, Golden-crowned and Ruby-crowned Kinglets, Yellow-rumped Warbler and abundant Connecticut Warbler.

Two other spots to check are the Winnipeg River in and near town, and the sewage lagoon, for a variety of waterfowl including Wood Duck and Hooded Merganser. The latter site is reached from a road that takes off south from PR 211, about 1 km west of the cemetery road. At the lagoon, moulting male Wood Ducks gather in summer; Virginia Rail and Sora are seen, and migrating flocks of various species pass through. Look for small numbers of Black Scoters, a rare Peregrine Falcon or a Yellow Rail. Return to PR 211 and continue west, looking for Indigo Bunting along the side of the road in June. At the Pinawa Fish and Game Association Waterfowl Sanctuary, check for about 100 male Wood Ducks moulting in July.

The Seven Sisters forebay, Natalie Lake, is located south of Pinawa and east of Highway 11, on PR 307. This body of water is often a good place to watch migrating waterfowl in early May. The top of the dam is the best vantage point. Scan for Common Loon, often large numbers of Red-necked and Horned Grebes, and smaller numbers of the other three grebe species. American White Pelican, Double-crested Cormorant and Tundra Swan come in mid-May. Greater Scaup often occurs in large concentrations with other ducks. White-winged Scoter appears most springs. Caspian Terns regularly pass through in late May, early June and September.

From Seven Sisters south to Whitemouth there is a network of farm roads from which to look for birds living in open country and forest. This strip is particularly good for raptors in spring and fall, including Red-tailed and Rough-legged Hawks, Northern Harrier, Northern Goshawk, Merlin and Short-eared Owl. In winter the Gyrfalcon is sometimes noted. Sharp-tailed Grouse are present all year and use several dancing grounds from March to May. Sandhill Cranes are seen from April to September and are most common during migration. A few Marbled Godwits probably breed south of River Hills. Passerines include Western Kingbird, Horned Lark, Black-billed Magpie and Brown Thrasher; the Eastern Meadowlark has been found, together with Vesper and Clay-colored Sparrows. The area is good from April to September but the best time is during spring migration in April and May. For a detailed side road description of a four- to six-hour trip through this strip, refer to Taylor's paper mentioned previously.

The Bog River extensive marsh complex lies east and north of White-mouth, north of Highway 44. The marsh is largely impenetrable, but is accessible from a gravel road that zigzags north and east from the junction of Highways 44 and 11, just east of Whitemouth. Along this road look for Eastern and Mountain Bluebirds. At the end of the road a powerline right-of-way runs northeast to cross the south end of the marsh. Try a canoe trip upstream from this right-of-way to PTH 44. This marsh and river is a good place to view Green-backed Heron, Least Bittern, Sandhill Crane, Virginia Rail, Sora and Yellow Rail.

Return to Highway 44 and proceed northwest. Reconnoitre for Ameri-can Woodcock along the way. Listen at dusk for it from mid-April to early June. The Pine Warbler occurs regularly in some mature Jack Pine stands along 44. In mixed stands of aspen, birch and Jack Pine stop and hunt for Scarlet Tanager. Listen for Indigo Bunting along the highway.

This whole region contains many Black Spruce bogs, but the finest accessible one is alongside PR 435 near Milner Ridge, about 3 km east of the junction with 214. The spot lies west of Pinawa, north from Highway 44. This is the locality to come to in June for Spruce Grouse; both species of three-toed woodpeckers nest in this bog; Boreal Chickadee, Gray Jay,

Hermit and Swainson's Thrushes, Solitary Vireo, Nashville and Yellow-rumped Warblers are all here; the Connecticut Warbler breeds in the more open stands, with up to four being heard at once; Golden-crowned and Ruby-crowned Kinglets, Yellow-bellied Flycatcher (rare), Alder and Olive-sided Flycatchers, and Lincoln's Sparrow are noted on any visit. If you enjoy flowers, a late June trip could produce a variety, including seven species of orchid. In winter this is the place to observe Spruce Grouse, Northern Goshawk, perhaps one of the two species of three-toed woodpeckers, Gray Jay, Brown Creeper and White-winged Crossbill.

PETER TAYLOR

Whiteshell Provincial Park

Whiteshell contains numerous lakes, trails, canoe routes and recreation spots. A wild goose sanctuary and game bird refuge provides other attractions.

The first recorded visit to the area was made by the La Verendrye expedition in the spring of 1733. The Winnipeg River, which flows through the north end of the park, then became an important fur trade route from Montreal. The last major use was in 1870, when Colonel Wolseley's troops used it on the way to Red River to fight the Metis. With the push to have a railroad linking Canada, construction began here in 1877, with the line opening in 1883. At the turn of the twentieth century, there was an unsuccessful attempt to farm the area. The soils were too poor. The first of many summer cottages to now dot the area was built in about 1920. The Manitoba government established the Whiteshell Forest Reserve in 1931. In 1939, Alfred Hole founded the goose sanctuary, beside the community of Rennie. In 1961 the whole area became a provincial park.

The park lies about 145 km east of Winnipeg via either Highway 1 or Highways 15 and 44. Greyhound bus services the park via the Trans-Canada Highway at least once a day on the way through. There is an extensive system of hiking and interpretive trails and canoe routes throughout the park. The routes are illustrated on the park map-brochure, which also shows the available campsites, interpretive features and interesting spots. The lengthy Mantario Hiking Trail, which passes through the area, has an excellent brochure.

Commercial visitor accommodation may be obtained at several places, including Falcon Lake and Rennie, plus lodges scattered throughout. Check the park brochure for these and the locations of seventeen campgrounds, some of which are serviced. Information and brochures on the park and other features are available from Travel Manitoba (see above).

Birding Features
The roads through the park, particularly PR 307, which loops through the north and west side, skirt several lakes. From April to September, a survey of these water bodies should produce Common Loon, Common Goldeneye,

Ring-necked Duck, Common and Hooded Mergansers, Spotted Sandpiper, Bald Eagle and likely an Osprey. The Herring Gull and Common Tern are also present. Raptors flying across the road include Broad-winged, Sharp-shinned and Cooper's Hawks. Watch for a Turkey Vulture, particularly in the Rennie River area. You may also spot Ruffed and Spruce Grouse, Barred and Great Gray Owls, Pileated, Hairy and both species of three-toed wood-peckers, Yellow-bellied and Olive-sided Flycatchers, and several species of vireos, warblers and sparrows.

A visit to the Alf Hole Wild Goose Sanctuary at Rennie will prove rewarding. Here you'll see Canada Goose, Wood Duck, Ring-necked Duck, scaup, Great Blue Heron and American Bittern. Go into the interpretive centre to see the displays on geese. Ask the staff about other local places to explore.

RUDOLF F. KOES

Spotting Great Gray Owls

Southeastern Manitoba is probably the best, easiest and most accessible area in North America to look for a Great Gray Owl. The birds live in remote northern coniferous forests. In recent years they have been found nesting in extreme southeastern Manitoba, in inaccessible boglands, on provincial forest land and adjacent areas. They may be spotted from Pine Falls, east of Lake Winnipeg, to near the U.S. border at Sprague.

The owls may be ferreted out from November to April, with the best times being January and February. These are the months when severe cold, deep snow and often low rodent populations force the birds out of the woods. Expect to sight them at all times during the day, but more likely just after dawn or near dusk. Drive slowly; look for telltale plunge spots where they have been hunting; examine the deciduous trees near spruce-tamarack forests for the characteristic dark, round-headed shape. If the grader gets through and ploughs out the side roads and forestry roads, try these trails as they usually are more productive.

Before departing make sure you have a full tank of gasoline, warm parka, mitts, tuque, warm boots, sleeping bag, candle and a shovel. Don't take any chances, as cars break down in cold weather.

There are several good spots to search, with the best roads as follows. Proceed north from Winnipeg on Highway 59 to PR 317; take it slowly eastward to Lac du Bonnet, and then carefully search PR 313 and 315, both good side roads, to find the birds. Return to Lac du Bonnet; go south 10 km on Highway 11, and then proceed east on PR 211, which is another good road, to Pinawa; travel south again on Highway 11 to the junction with PR 506; take 506, another key road, slowly down to Highway 1; swing east on 1 to PR 308 and follow it south to Sprague, near the border; take Highway 12 west to the junction with PR 210; follow 210, another good possibility, slowly to Marchand; move straight north on the side road to meet Highway 1; go east on 1 for 6 km to just across Brokenhead River and then take the side road, if it is open, north to Highway 15. Return west to Winnipeg on 15; or else continue searching and go east to Elma; then north to Highway 44 and follow it generally east to meet 1 near West Hawk Lake. Return west on Highway 1 to Winnipeg. To find out more about this large owl, read the award-winning book, *The Great Gray Owl (Phantom of the Northern Forest)*, by R.W. Nero (Washington: Smithsonian Institute Press, 1980).

ROBERT W. NERO

Delta Marsh Complex

One of the largest and most famous (for birding) fresh-water marshes in the world, the Delta Marsh, lies on the south shore of Lake Manitoba. The diverse habitat has produced 285 species of birds.

The Delta Waterfowl Research Station, a privately funded centre for research, was founded in 1938. With the success of the centre, the University of Manitoba also established a field station in 1970. Neither centre is public, and hence special permission is required before entering. Write: Delta Waterfowl Research Station, R.R. 1, Portage la Prairie, Manitoba R1N 3A1; and University Field Station (Delta Marsh), 230 Mackray Hall, University of Manitoba, Winnipeg, Manitoba R3T 2N2.

The Delta Marsh complex spans some 22,000 ha and lies 20 km north of Portage la Prairie. Highway 1 through Portage brings Greyhound bus service near the marsh. VIA Rail also passes through this city. The community contains a variety of motels and hotels. Campgrounds are located at St. Ambroise and Lynch's Point, on the east and west sides of the marsh, respectively.

There is a comprehensive bird checklist of the Delta Marsh area available from: Department of Mines, Natural Resources and Environment, Box 22, 1495 St. James Street, Winnipeg, Manitoba R3H 0W9. Peter Hachbaum has written a short book on the marsh in general.

Birding Features

The marsh complex consists of a treed beach ridge adjacent to the lake, behind which lie some of the largest stands of *Phragmites* in North America. There are open and closed marshes, some of which are linked to long narrow channels from the lake. A relict stand of hackberry trees, shrubs, sand beaches and sloughs add to the diversity, including 121 species of birds that have bred, or now breed, and 111 that migrate through regularly. Four search spots are recommended.

Lynch's Point on the west side is accessible by proceeding north on PR 242 from Highway 16. The stand of trees in and near the unserviced campground on the point is good for migrating passerines in May and August. Large concentrations of Snow Geese, with a few Greater White-fronted and Ross' among them, occur here from late April through early May and from late September through early October. The minimal beach area is not attractive to shorebirds.

Delta, in the middle, is reached via PR 240 north from Portage la Prairie. The nearby area is alive with birds from mid-April to early October. In the spring, look for grebes and ducks, including mergansers. American White Pelican and Double-crested Cormorant occur from spring to fall. Swallows, mainly Tree and Bank, cluster by the thousands on telephone wires and trees in late July and early August.

If you have permission to enter the Delta Waterfowl Research Station, it is reached by travelling to the end of PR 240 and turning east at the stop sign. Check for herons and shorebirds along the way.

The east Delta beach is reached via the road going north immediately east of the Delta channel. This beach usually has a variety of terns, including Forster's and Caspian. In spring scan for several ducks, including Greater Scaup, and shorebirds, including Red Knot (rarely) and Hudsonian Godwit.

The west Delta beach is reached by driving west 3 km from the end of PR 240 to the Assiniboine River diversion outlet. The nearby vegetation contains some of the highest nesting densities of Gray Catbird, Yellow Warbler and Northern Oriole in North America. Look for Orchard Oriole too. Check the diversion outlet into the lake for other species. Do not enter the University Field Station grounds without prior permission, as you may disrupt research.

St. Ambroise sits at the northeast side of the complex and can be reached via PR 430 north from Highway 1. The land around the unserviced campground provides opportunities for excellent birding, particularly in late May and early September. Scan the two small islands offshore for American White Pelican, Double-crested Cormorant and Caspian Tern. Use the observation tower at the end of the nature trail that leaves the parking lot. The beach is good for Piping Plover, with Sharp-tailed Sparrow nearby. See what else you can find.

Twin Lakes Beach occurs at the northeast edge of the marsh. It can be reached via Highway 6 and a short run to the lake. Hike the area west of the cottages and look for Piping Plover.

BIRDER'S GUIDE TO SOUTHEASTERN MANITOBA

Brandon/Spruce Woods Provincial Park/Manitoba Desert

A circular trip east and south of Brandon could turn up some of those "most wanted" birds on your list, such as Sharp-tailed Grouse, Yellow Rail and Baird's Sparrow. In this area, the late Jack Lane of Brandon began the first Bluebird Trail in western Canada. Because of him and his helpers, Mountain and Eastern Bluebirds are fairly common here.

The route passes through country ranging from completely cultivated fields to forests to sand hills and a sand "desert." The approximately 160-km trip should take a leisurely day or a very full morning.

The city of Brandon and town of Carberry contain a variety of motels, hotels and other services. Camping is available just west of Brandon and in Spruce Woods Provincial Park. VIA Rail stops at Brandon and Greyhound buses service the major communities. Winnipeg has the nearest major airlines stopover.

If you plan a visit to the sand dunes, obtain a copy of the booklet *The Sandhills of Carberry*, by John E. Dubois. Write to the Manitoba Museum of Man and Nature (see above) for a copy.

Birding Features

Late May to early July is the best time to come. Begin the tour in Brandon. Follow PR 457 east through Chater to the junction with PR 340. Between Chater and the junction, reconnoitre the pastures for Sprague's Pipit, Baird's Sparrow (look on the south side of the road), Chestnut-collared Longspur and other grassland birds.

To cut time and still see Yellow Rail, turn north on PR 340 and drive towards Douglas. Just south of town, the road runs straight through one of the best Yellow Rail marshes in Manitoba. Observers regularly report over fifteen here. In wet years rubber boots are needed. In dry times the rails are very scarce and hard to find. Bring a flashlight to spot them after dark. Check for other water birds, Sharp-tailed Grouse, and Le Conte's and Sharp-tailed Sparrows nearby. To return to Brandon, go north through Douglas and west on the Trans-Canada Highway.

To continue the trip, return to the junction of PR 457 and 340; take 340 southeast. About 2 to 3 km along this road, check the field on the west side for Sprague's Pipit. Further west, just over the ridge beyond, lies a field where Baird's Sparrow may be singing; walk over and check.

At Shilo the pavement turns to gravel and the road swings straight south through the National Armed Forces Gunnery Range. On this stretch, watch for Mountain Bluebird, Sprague's Pipit and Grasshopper Sparrow. At the Assiniboine River, cross on one of the few remaining ferries in the province. The ferry operates only during daylight hours from spring to fall. Explore the woods in the river bottom and around Treesbank to the south, looking for Yellow-throated Vireo and Indigo Bunting. Continue on PR 340 and turn east on PTH 2; at Glenboro, go north on PTH 5. Immediately before the Assiniboine River, a gravelled side road leads east into Spruce Woods Provincial Park. The woods along this road may provide good birding.

Return to PTH 5; drive north across the river. About 300 m beyond the bridge, turn west into the parking lot for the Spirit Hills Interpretive Trail. This is the trail for a unique walk into a "desert." The 3-km footpath covers deciduous and mixed woods, shifting and stabilized sand dunes, and the edge of the Assiniboine River Valley. This Manitoba desert contains dunes over 30 m high and sometimes 60 m thick. They are the deposits of a massive river that produced a major delta where it entered the former Lake Agassiz at the end of glaciation, 12,000 years ago. Although the sand dunes give the impression of a desert, rainfall here exceeds the limits of a true desert. Birds found here include Indigo Bunting and both species of crossbill.

As you continue north on PTH 5, inspect wires and fences along the roadside for Mountain and Eastern Bluebirds. At Carberry, either go east to the Delta Marsh (see above) or return west via PR 351. Along this short route to Highway 1, more bluebirds, Rufous-sided Towhee and Lark Sparrow may be seen.

RUDOLF F. KOES

Whitewater Lake

Whitewater Lake, a large shallow body of water, attracts numerous water birds during spring and fall migration. Geese and waders congregate here, and raptors accompany them, notably Prairie Falcon and Bald Eagle.

The lake lies about 25 km north of the Turtle Mountains, or just over 100 km south and a bit west of Brandon. Nearest services and accommodation are at Deloraine, about 15 km southwest of the water. The nearest campsite is at Turtle Mountain. Access into the lake is rather complex, with several possible routes (see below). Roads are set on "section" lines or the mile grid system.

Birding Features
A fairly extensive water surface, shallow depth and adjacent mudflats are fed by a number of small streams. The eastern end of the lake extends into a large marsh. Birders have not explored the area carefully in recent years, but visits have turned up many interesting species and some heavy concentrations. Bald Eagles begin gathering in late September and remain to freeze-up in late October to mid-November. In late October, large numbers of Tundra Swans gather here, one of the largest concentrations of these birds in Manitoba. Canada, White-fronted and Snow Geese, and a few Ross', show up every spring (mid-April to mid-May) and fall (mid-September to late-October). At these times, scan for grebes and many prairie ducks. Prairie Falcons remain as long as their prey does. Waders such as American Avocet also gather and remain into October. Check the nearby fields and shoreline vegetation for longspurs and other passerines.

There are numerous spots to watch and a variety of entry routes. Near Deloraine, at the junction of PTH 21 and 3, go north 1.6 km, east 3.2 km, north 3.2 km, and then east to the lake shore. After scanning the area, return west about 0.8 km; follow the road north for 3.2 km and turn east to the shore. Look over the flocks of Snow Geese for a Ross' Goose, and examine the lake and shoreline for other species. Proceed north 4.8 km, east about 6.5 km and south 4 km to the north shore. Depending on the water levels, a hike along the shoreline here could produce several species. Return to the car and drive back north for 4 km, then east for 7.3 km to another road leading south to the shore.

An alternative route enters from the east and begins at Boissevain. At the intersection of PTH 10 and PR 348, take 348 west and north for about 14 km. At this spot, leave 348 and take the road to the west for 2.4 km to one leading south to the lake, the same trail mentioned previously. On this leg, return via the route mentioned above.

For access to the south side of the lake, inquire locally as to the best routes.

Turtle Mountain Provincial Park

The Turtle Mountains comprise an island of deciduous forest rising out of the prairies in southwestern Manitoba. These hills are home to a variety of birdlife ranging from Common Loon, colonies of Great Blue Heron and Black-crowned Night-Heron, to such eastern species as Northern Cardinal and Northern Parula. Those interested in cultivated flower gardens can enjoy the International Peace Garden, sponsored and maintained by people from both sides of the border. Painted Turtles are common in the park, as are Beaver.

Since the end of glaciation 10,000 years ago, native people used the hills as shelter. Later the Metis hunters from Red River (Winnipeg) would sometimes overwinter in these hills to allow an early spring start to the buffalo hunt on the southern plains. During the 1860s and 1870s, the Sioux Wars in the U.S. drove "renegade" Indians north to seek safety from the U.S. Cavalry, which halted at the 49th parallel. The border came to be called the "Medicine Line" for this reason. Settlers flooded the plains in the late 1800s. Increased human activity finally resulted in two major fires, in 1897 and 1903. Only a few remnant stands of mature deciduous forest were left. The park became a timber reserve with a ranger headquarters built in 1911. These forest rangers cut fireguards and roadways, and encouraged grazing to get rid of the dry grasses and low bush. Even with these precautions, a fire swept in from North Dakota in 1921 and consumed a large section of the reserve. No more fires have occurred since then. The central part of the reserve became a park in 1961.

The park lies 100 km straight south of Brandon on PTH 10, or about 280 km southwest of Winnipeg via PTH 2 and 10. Greyhound buses service Boissevain, the nearest town, 21 km north of the park gate. VIA Rail service and car rentals are available in Brandon. Trails and roads, which are not all-weather, are liberally sprinkled throughout the very hilly country. These routes are well illustrated in the park brochure (see below).

Two campgrounds provide some services for the visitor. Commercial places to stay are found in surrounding towns or at Brandon. Gasoline, groceries and other necessities may be obtained at these communities.

Information on summer and winter opportunities, plus a park map and brochure, may be obtained from: Parks Division, Box 820, Boissevain, Manitoba R0K 0E0.

Naturalists are stationed at the park in summer to assist you in your visit. Contact them at the park office for recent sightings.

Birding Features
The rolling hills of the Turtle Mountains are covered with about two-thirds deciduous forest and one-third lakes and sloughs. Trembling Aspen is the

main tree species, with Black Poplar, White Birch, ash, Manitoba Maple, elm and Bur Oak interspersed throughout. The understory is rather dense in places. A visit from mid-May to mid-July will provide opportunities to spot a wide variety of water and land birds.

A number of species have been found breeding here, far to the west of their usual range. These include the Northern Cardinal, which often nests near the park office, and the Northern Parula, which is 300+ km west of its nearest usual breeding spot in Manitoba.

Other birds in the area include Common Loon, a good population of Red-necked Grebe, Double-crested Cormorant, a variety of dabbling and diving ducks, Willow Flycatcher (a suspected breeder), Marsh and Sedge Wrens, Eastern Bluebird, Yellow-throated Vireo, several warblers, Yellow-headed Blackbird and a possible Scarlet Tanager.

RUDOLF F. KOES

Riding Mountain National Park

Set on the Manitoba Escarpment, the sharply defined northern and eastern boundaries of Riding Mountain National Park are some 450 m above surrounding farmland. The park sits at the crossroads of three major vegetation zones: eastern deciduous forest, northern boreal forest and western grasslands. This mixed habitat results in almost 500 species of plants and attracts over 250 species of birds. Of these birds, 154 species are regular (fairly common to abundant) breeders, another 18 are rare breeders within the park but more abundant just outside, and 6 occur as summer visitors. The park is home to numerous Elk (Wapiti), Moose, deer, Beaver, Timber Wolf, Black Bear, Lynx, plus about 30 Plains Bison in an enclosure. It also sits on the line that seems to divide the range of the Satyrid Butterfly. These insects are observed east of the park only on even-numbered years and west in the odd-numbered.

In 1906 control of this area passed to the Forestry Branch of the federal government. Roads were poor and visitation was limited. Riding Mountain was declared a national park in 1930. This 2978-km² area lies north of Brandon on PTH 10. Greyhound buses service the park in the summer. There are over 160 km of hiking and horse trails through the forest and meadows and by the many lakes. These trails, amenities and major interpretive features are shown on the park brochure.

Accommodation includes over 300 units of motels, hotels and cottages in the village of Wasagaming. These are heavily booked in July and August. However, there are abundant campsites ranging from fully serviced trailer units to primitive camp spots. Two group camping locations are also available. Winter campers have a choice of two spots. The village contains all services needed for a comfortable stay in the summer. In winter, nearby towns have the required services.

Information on the park, including a comprehensive checklist of birds, is available from: The Superintendent, Riding Mountain National Park,

Wasagaming, Manitoba R0J 2H0. There are year-round interpreters stationed at Wasagaming. Call them at (204) 848-2811.

Birding Features

Riding Mountain, with its prairie, meadows, aspen groves, eastern and boreal forests, and numerous lakes, attracts a wide variety of birds. During the nesting season, from about the first of June to mid-July, the park is one of the most productive areas in North America for locating different species.

The several lakes and contiguous boreal forests are home to Common Loon, all five species of grebe found in Canada, American White Pelican, Double-crested Cormorant, and about ten colonies of Great Blue Heron; all the prairie ducks, and even Forster's Tern, are found nesting here; a Turkey Vulture, Northern Goshawk or Cooper's Hawk may be spotted. There are eight nest locations of Bald Eagle in the park. These kings of the air are most readily seen at several lakes, including Whirlpool, Audy and Moon. Osprey, Merlin and Spruce Grouse are regularly noted. Northern Saw-whet Owls are especially common around Clear Lake and can be heard late at night from mid-April to the latter part of May, together with Barred Owl. Both species of three-toed woodpecker, Gray Jay and Boreal Chickadee are common in this northern forest.

The deciduous forests are noted for the Great Crested Flycatcher, Eastern Wood-Pewee and Yellow-throated Vireo. The Golden-winged Warbler, a true eastern species, is common on the eastern and northern sides of the park. The Connecticut Warbler nests in aspen groves. These birds are easily found close to Wasagaming and elsewhere. Scarlet Tanager, Indigo Bunting and Rufous-sided Towhee can also be found in these deciduous forests. The park lies within the overlap zone of the Eastern and Western

Western Grebe

135

Kingbirds, Eastern and Western Wood-Pewees, Eastern and Mountain Bluebirds, and Indigo and (occasionally) Lazuli Buntings.

The grasslands are good sites for Sprague's Pipit, especially at the Audy
Prairie in the bison enclosure, northwest of Clear Lake. Sharp-tailed Grouse
and Western Meadowlark can be located in fields immediately adjacent to
the park on the south and southwest sides.

Some of the special spots to visit are noted below. Contact the interpreters for others.

Wasagaming, the village, is a good spot to look for a variety of warblers and
other boreal species. They can be spotted in the tall spruce.

Evergreen Trail begins at the north shore of Lake Katherine, 9.6 km east of
Wasagaming via Highway 19 and the Lake Katherine access road. A stroll
along this 1.6-km path could produce Connecticut and Mourning Warblers
as well as Le Conte's Sparrow, particularly along the first section.

Ma-ee-gun Trail provides access to boreal species. It is reached via Highway
10, 6.9 km northwest of the junction with Highway 19.

Highway 19 leads east from Wasagaming through boreal forest and is
recommended as a particularly good route. Stop several times and check the
woods for boreal species, particularly Spruce Grouse and Gray Jay.

Burls and Bittersweet Trail, on the east end of Highway 19, is good for most
species during migration. You'll also spot several of the eastern deciduous-
nesting species, many of which are rare to uncommon in Manitoba.

Highway 361, farther north on the east side, runs west from Highway 5 at
McCreary and takes you to the park's Mount Agassiz Ski Hill. This is a good
area for eastern species, particularly about 4.8 km within the park boundary.
Watch for Golden-winged Warbler, Indigo Bunting and Rufous-sided
Towhee, all of which are common here.

Canvasback

A winter trip to the park could produce a Northern Goshawk, both three-toed woodpeckers, and winter finches, including crossbills.

In the spring and early summer, check the sloughs around Minnedosa, south of the park on Highway 10, for a wide variety of waterfowl. Check the area also for Eared Grebe and Canvasback, Swainson's Hawk and Wilson's Phalarope.

A. ANGUS MacLEAN, RUDOLF F. KOES

Churchill

Churchill sits on the shore of Hudson Bay, in the taiga, the transition zone between the tundra and boreal forest. It is a paradise for birders wishing to see arctic flora and fauna within a short time and at a reasonable cost. To date, 176 bird species have been reported, including that rarity from the Arctic ice floes and Siberia, Ross' Gull. The only other comparable and reasonably accessible arctic site is the Dempster Highway in the Yukon.

The area has been inhabited since at least 950 B.C. A trading post was built in 1717. The first astronomical observations taken in Canada were done here in 1769. Samuel Hearne made his epic overland trip to the Arctic coast from here. Later, when western Canada needed a prairie port, one was built here and linked to the outside by rail in 1929. Naturalists now flock to the spot every year, swelling the resident 800 winter population to around 1500 in summer.

The port lies at the mouth of the Churchill River. It is accessible by rail and air from Thompson or Winnipeg. There are five hotels in the community, but accommodation may be hard to find from late May to the end of July. Arrangements should be made well in advance. Camping on the tundra is possible almost anyplace, but beware of Polar Bears. Follow all guidelines for bears, including no food or garbage within at least 100 m of the tent.

The best time to come is between late May and mid-July, with mid- to late June offering the greatest number of birds. At this time, however, there are hordes of insects — a mosquito head net and insect repellent are essential. Weather in this season is very unpredictable: it may rain, be very windy, cold, warm, foggy, all in one day. Bring rain gear, a down jacket or parka, a warm hat and mitts.

The services of commercial tour operators are available. One of the best is Mrs. Bonnie Chartier, of Churchill Wilderness Encounter, Box 85, Churchill, Manitoba R0B 0E0, Telephone: (204) 675-2729 office, and home (204) 675-2248; she is an experienced birder who is excellent in the field and can often provide useful information. To cover the area well, a car should be rented, if one is not willing to take a commercial tour. Rental cars are few in number, so book well in advance.

An absolute must is the book *Birds of the Churchill Region, Manitoba*, by Joseph R. Jehl, Jr., and Blanche A. Smith. This 87-page book is considered *the* standard reference for the area. It is available from The Manitoba Museum of Man and Nature (see above). *Birds of Churchill*, an informative brochure with a good map, should be obtained from: Manitoba Department of Mines and Natural Resources, P.O. Box 760, Churchill, Manitoba R0B 0E0, Telephone: (204) 675-8897. *Guide to Churchill*, a booklet containing information on local history, fishing spots and a list of all the commercial operators, is available from the Chamber of Commerce, Port Churchill, Manitoba. *Taiga, Tundra and Tidal* is a magazine-style booklet containing history, geography and some natural history. Write for it from: Northern Resource Development Centre, P.O. Box 760, Churchill, Manitoba R0B 0E0. "A Field Check-list of Birds — The Birds of Churchill" has recently been published. Like all new checklists, it requires a few corrections (spring occurs from mid-April to June; summer from mid-June onward) but is quite useful. To obtain it contact: Manitoba Department of Natural Resources, Box 22, 1495 St. James Street, Winnipeg, Manitoba R3H 0W9.

Don't forget to take a boat trip to observe Beluga Whales — an unforgettable experience! Information as to when and where the trips depart is available locally.

Birding Features

To cover the area thoroughly, a week in mid-June should be set aside. However, a long-weekend visit could be enough time for a keen person to observe at least the majority of the species. A birding day can begin at 3:00 A.M., at daylight, and last to 11:00 P.M., with some light past midnight in June.

"Churchill specialties" include Arctic Loon, Oldsquaw, Common and King Eiders, Willow Ptarmigan, Yellow Rail, Lesser Golden-Plover and many other shorebirds, Parasitic Jaeger, gulls including Thayer's, Sabine's, Ross' and Little, and Arctic Tern. The Ross' Gull has been seen since 1979 and bred in 1980, 1981 and 1982! Other species include Common and Hoary Redpolls and Smith's Longspur. This is one of the few readily accessible places in North America where Harris' Sparrow can be found nesting.

Reference to the map in the brochure *Birds of Churchill*, mentioned above, will show the best observation areas are:

Cape Merry, at the mouth of the Churchill River near the port facility. Scan for Arctic and Red-throated Loons, Common and King Eiders, Parasitic Jaeger, gulls mentioned above, and others including terns.

Akudlik, just west of the airport, where ducks, Yellow Rail and others can be ferreted out in the marshes and lakes.

Launch Road and Old Road to Fort Churchill. Scan the bay for both species of eiders and scoters. The west end beach near the point has shorebirds. Don't forget the garbage dump for gulls. East of the dump look for Lesser Golden-Plover, Whimbrel, Stilt Sandpiper, Short-billed Dowitcher and Hudsonian Godwit. Particularly survey Bird Cove on the bay for shorebirds. Take a short drive southwest of Bird Cove to explore for warblers and redpolls. West and south of the National Research Council launch site, at the east end of the road, check out the lakes for loons and Oldsquaw. Watch along Launch Road for Willow Ptarmigan, with Rock Ptarmigan seen here only in winter. Smith's Longspur also is noted on this road.

Landing or Farnworth Lake Road. This road south from the west side of the airport should produce Yellow Rail and numerous shorebirds as mentioned above.

Goose Creek Road south along the Churchill River provides easy access to some swans, geese, Tundra Swan, scoters and upland birds. Watch for a Bohemian Waxwing, and Common and Hoary Redpolls along here. About 4 km south on the road, watch for hawks and owls. Further south, about 8 km from the south turnoff, take the short road to the river for warblers and sparrows and scan the water for ducks. Near the end of the road make sure to scrutinize the far shore for a Bald Eagle or Osprey nesting in a tree or hunting over the water. When you come to the end, now called the Hydro road, check for swans, geese, ducks and shorebirds on the mudflats. Shorebirds are also found south of the road in the marsh. This is but a sampling of the richness of the avifauna. The ground and air appear alive with birdlife.

RUDOLF F. KOES, BONNIE CHARTIER

Ontario

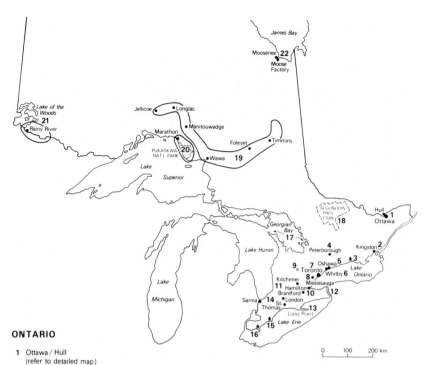

ONTARIO

1 Ottawa / Hull
  (refer to detailed map)
2 Kingston
3 Presqu'ile Provincial Park
4 Peterborough
5 Oshawa and nearby sites
6 Pickering, Ajax and Whitby
7 Toronto
8 Mississauga and Oakville
9 Luther Lake
10 Hamilton and Burlington
11 Kitchener, Waterloo, Brantford and Cambridge
12 Niagara River
13 Long Point
14 London, Sarnia and St. Thomas
15 Rondeau Provincial Park and nearby spots
16 Point Pelee National Park
17 Georgian Bay Islands National Park
18 Algonquin Provincial Park
19 Timmins to Jellicoe
20 Marathon: north shore Lake Superior
21 Rainy River / Lake of the Woods
22 South James Bay: Moosonee / Moose Factory / Shipsands Island

141

Ontario

Bird watchers arrive in Ontario to see land birds, especially warblers, and in particular those that occur in the Carolinean forests. The province's key habitats include these forests growing on the peninsulas which jut south into Lakes Erie and Ontario, plus the boreal forests of the north and west. Key bird species include Great Egret, Least Bittern, Oldsquaw, Harlequin Duck, Red-shouldered Hawk, Wild Turkey, Common Moorhen, Great Black-backed Gull, Yellow-billed Cuckoo, Barn Owl, Red-bellied Woodpecker, Chuck-will's-widow, Acadian Flycatcher, Tufted Titmouse, Carolina Wren, Northern Mockingbird, Blue-gray Gnatcatcher, White-eyed Vireo; warblers including Prothonotary, Worm-eating, Golden- and Blue-winged, Cerulean, Prairie, Pine, Louisiana Waterthrush, Kentucky, Northern Parula, Nashville, Black-throated Blue and Blackburnian; Eastern Meadowlark, Orchard Oriole, Scarlet Tanager, Northern Cardinal, Indigo Bunting, House Finch, and Henslow's and Field Sparrows.

Bordering four of the five Great Lakes, plus James Bay in the north, the province is second in size only to Quebec. From north to south at its deepest point, Ontario covers 1690 km and from east to west its greatest width stretches 1609 km, with an area of 891,198 km^2. The northern and western sections consist of forests and lakes set on Precambrian rock; the southeastern, better known area, shelters most of her industries and seven-eighths of the population. The south is mainly agriculture in crops with woodlots, but more and more land is being paved over with industry. Isolated stands of Carolinean forest remain, principally in parks. Roughly 250,000 lakes occur, with many in the north Precambrian region. These lands are covered with boreal forest and some deciduous stands. Arctic tundra lies around James Bay and farther north.

The best time to arrive would be May 7–14; the second weekend in May is called "Pelee Weekend." Migration there is at a peak. June provides nesting species in the Carolinean forests and farther north in the boreal habitats. The middle two weeks in September bring warblers and shorebirds on their way south. Gulls and winter specialties are at their prime the last week of November and the first week of December.

The most attractive spot for bird watching in the province is Point Pelee. This piece of land jutting into Lake Erie has been called the single best spot in North America in the month of May. Algonquin would provide a good alternate mix to Pelee if you have time only for two areas. These two sites are vastly different. Point Pelee has two factors to offer: the terminus of a trans–Lake Erie crossing and the Carolinean forest. The former element is probably what brings so many species together at once. When birds arrive, they are tired and will rest anywhere as long as it is above ground. The forest, however, does provide nesting habitat, attracting birds that are considered unusual for Canada. Algonquin contains boreal forest, the closest and most accessible habitat of this type for people from the south. Rondeau Provincial Park could be considered the third most attractive "hot spot." It contains the best representative stand of Carolinean forest left in Ontario. Not as many spring migrants arrive here as at Pelee but Rondeau hosts more nesting species. Ferret out the nest of a Chuck-will's-widow, Red-bellied Woodpecker, Acadian Flycatcher and Prothonotary Warbler, plus many others. Other areas worth searching include Long Point (also projecting into Lake Erie), and the many marshes around Pickering-Ajax-Whitby.

Upon arriving in Toronto with half a day to bird-watch, head east to the Pickering marshes. A person with no car should go to Toronto Island by ferry. A full day would easily cover both sites. A visitor with from two to seven days should begin at Point Pelee and then head east along the shores of Lake Erie. Don't forget Algonquin in your week. A late fall visit of one to two days should include a drive down to Niagara for water birds.

Toronto operates a Rare Bird Alert, with most of the other Ontario cities tied into this number. Telephone Harry Kerr at (416) 481-7948. For names and addresses of clubs across the province, contact the Federation of Ontario Naturalists, 355 Lesmill Rd., Don Mills, Ontario M3B 2W8, Telephone: (416) 444-8419.

An *Annotated checklist of the birds of Ontario*, by R.D. James, P.L. McLaren and J.C. Barlow (Toronto: Royal Ontario Museum, 1976), 75 pp., can be obtained from the museum bookstore and elsewhere. A new list is on press; ask for it at the museum. A new book with maps and details of specific sites is *A Bird-Finding Guide to Ontario*, by Clive E. Goodwin (Toronto: U. of T. Press, 1982). Obtain it from your local bookstore or by writing the Canadian Nature Federation (see Ottawa/Hull for address).

A new organization, the Ontario Field Ornithologists, has a journal, *Ontario Birds*, which covers topics such as field identification, specific distribution, status and site guides. Field trips occur all year, with a general meeting in autumn. Contact them at Box 1204, Postal Station B, Burlington, Ontario L7P 3T9.

Information on where to stay, general tourism material and maps may be obtained from: Ontario Travel, Hearst Block, 900 Bay Street, Toronto, Ontario M7A 1W3, Telephone collect: (416) 965-4008.

LINDA AND CHIP WESELOH

Ottawa/Hull

As the capital city of Canada, Ottawa is usually visited at least once by birders from across the country. Over 320 species of birds have been recorded within a radius of 50 km from the downtown Peace Tower. Between mid-May and mid-September, you can often check off more than 100 species in a day. On a really good day in spring or fall, it is possible to spot around 150.

The area was first settled in the early 1800s. Colonel John By began construction of the Rideau Canal in 1826 to allow English ships to avoid American cannons along the St. Lawrence. By 1832, when the canal was finished, a small lumber town called Bytown began to flourish. The name was changed in 1855 in a bid by the community to become the national capital. Queen Victoria made it her choice two years later. Construction began on the parliament buildings in 1859 and Ottawa's status was formalized by the British North America Act of 1867.

With a population in excess of 700,000, the Ottawa/Hull area is the fourth-largest urban region in Canada. The city is a two-hour drive from Montreal and five hours from Toronto. The Ottawa River runs across the region, separating the Province of Quebec on the north from Ontario. There are numerous hotels and motels, with even a hostel in the old city jail. All services are available.

The Ottawa Field-Naturalists' Club is a very active group; contact them at Box 3264, Postal Station C, Ottawa, Ontario K1Y 4J5, Telephone: (613) 722-3050. A comprehensive checklist is available from them for $1.00. The National Museum of Natural Sciences presents displays and interpretive programs at the Victoria Museum, located at the corner of Metcalfe and McLeod streets, Ottawa, Ontario K1A 0M8, Telephone: (613) 996-3102. The National Capital Commission operates several nature centres with interpretive programs. Phone (613) 232-1234 for further information. The Club des Ornithologues de l'Outaouais, 31 rue Bodeur, Hull, Quebec J8Y 2P7, also conducts field trips.

An excellent map of the city and vicinity is produced by the National Capital Commission and can be purchased at most local bookstores. It should be used in conjunction with topographic sheet 31 G/5 on a scale of 1:50,000, put out by the Department of Energy, Mines and Resources.

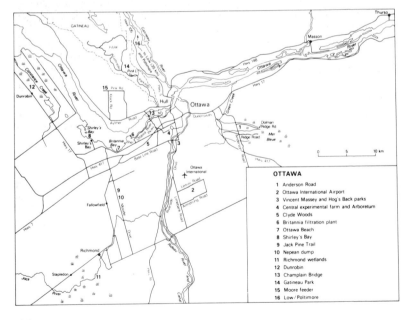

OTTAWA

1 Anderson Road
2 Ottawa International Airport
3 Vincent Massey and Hog's Back parks
4 Central experimental farm and Arboretum
5 Clyde Woods
6 Britannia filtration plant
7 Ottawa Beach
8 Shirley's Bay
9 Jack Pine Trail
10 Nepean dump
11 Richmond wetlands
12 Dunrobin
13 Champlain Bridge
14 Gatineau Park
15 Moore feeder
16 Low/Poltimore

Birding Features

Winters in the Ottawa/Hull area last from November to March. Temperatures range between $-10°$ and $-20°C$, with cold snaps down to $-40°C$ as well as warm spells. Most winters are snowy, with depths up to the thigh in non-windswept areas. At this time look for Snowy Owl, both three-toed woodpeckers, Gray Jay, Boreal Chickadee, Bohemian Waxwing and northern finches. The occasional Northern Hawk-Owl, Great Gray and Boreal Owls, or a Gyrfalcon comes in. Unfrozen water is at a premium at this time; check at Britannia and the Champlain Bridge.

Feeders are a mainstay of winter birding in the area. The Ottawa Field-Naturalists' Club maintains a good one at Jack Pine Trail; Moore's feeder is good too. (See below.)

Summer in Ottawa is often hot and humid. Temperatures range from $20°$ to $30°C$, with the occasional heat wave in excess of $30°C$. Biting insects can be a nuisance.

The more hardy species start breeding as early as February, while others are still incubating in August. May, June and July are the peak nesting months.

Spring and fall are the most pleasant periods, although weather conditions will vary. Bird watching at these times is usually the most productive. Spring migrants arrive in March and continue until mid-June. In early July, fall migrants appear and continue coming into December.

Anderson Road. From the south, take Highway 417 to the Anderson Road exit; turn left and travel north on Anderson. An alternate route begins on the Queensway to the Blair Road (south) exit. Travel to the T-junction at Innes Road, just past the bridge over Green Creek. Proceed east, swinging southeast after about 1.75 km. Anderson Road contains many habitats including marsh, deciduous woods, coniferous woods and open areas. Two side turns to the east (Ridge Road and Dolman Ridge Road) provide access to the major Mer Bleue Peat Bog. An interpretation centre is located on the Dolman Ridge Road. The major features of the Anderson Road are described below from south to north.

Ramsayville Marsh lies about 2 km north off Highway 417 on Anderson Road. From May through July this cat-tail marsh contains Pied-billed Grebe, Great Blue Heron, American Bittern, Least Bittern, puddle ducks, Northern Harrier, Virginia Rail, Sora, Common Moorhen, sometimes American Coot, Tree Swallow, Marsh Wren, Yellow Warbler, Common Yellowthroat and Swamp Sparrow. In August and September, huge flocks of Red-winged Blackbirds and European Starlings roost here.

End of Ridge Road. Proceed north on Anderson Road about another km from the marsh and turn east on Ridge Road. Park at the loop on the end and follow the trail along the southern end of the ridge. Great Blue Heron, Northern Harrier, migrating hawks, Mourning Dove, Belted Kingfisher, Hairy and Downy Woodpeckers, Northern Flicker, American Crow, Gray Catbird, American Robin, Hermit Thrush and other species are to be expected from May to September.

Between the Ridges. Go back to Anderson Road and proceed north for about 1 km on the east side. This small marsh is worth a stop. Check for Green-backed Heron, sometimes found in the trees on the west side of the road. Henslow's Sparrow and Sedge Wren can sometimes be heard singing from the fields a little north of the marsh.

Geomagnetic Trail. Continue north about another km and park in the lot opposite the entrance to the Energy, Mines and Resources Geomagnetic Lab. A stroll along the wide trails should yield many migrants in spring and fall and a good selection of breeders from May through mid-July.

Dolman Ridge Road. Go north a few hundred metres along Anderson and then east on Dolman Ridge Road to the end. This is an excellent route for exploring the Mer Bleue Peat Bog for spring flowers and birds. There are trails opposite the National Capital Commission interpretation centre.

Ottawa International Airport. The area of interest lies south of the actual airport, but still within its property. Birding is done along the perimeter roads. Proceed south on Bank Street for about 5 km south of the Rideau River, turn south on Albion Road for another 4.25 km to Leitrim and proceed west on it. The area enclosed by Leitrim on the north, Limebank on the west, Armstrong on the south and Pine on the east is good for birding at any season. You'll find open fields, planted conifers, some deciduous woods, a cedar wood and a damp site with cat-tails. From December to March look for Red-tailed and Rough-legged Hawks, American Kestrel, Snowy Owl and Northern Shrike. In migration, raptors can often be observed overhead. Grasshopper and Clay-colored Sparrows breed along Leitrim Road above the hill. Loggerhead Shrike occasionally nests in the area. In some years, Short-eared Owls can be found along Leitrim Road below the hill. Gray Partridge are also found here. Red-headed Woodpeckers nest on Armstrong Road.

Vincent Massey and Hog's Back Parks. These two adjoining parks are set on the east bank of the Rideau River, 5 km north of the airport. Both parks have parking lots: the one for Vincent Massey is off Heron Road; Hog's Back lies on the Hog's Back Road between Prince of Wales and Riverside drives. These parks contain some heavily disturbed areas, with deciduous habitat and some cedar. Both parks are heavily birded in spring and fall since they act as a trap for migrants, particularly warblers. Most people explore on foot, on the path along the Rideau River from the Hog's Back parking lot, north to the train crossing and back again.

Central Experimental Farm and Arboretum. Located on the west side of the Rideau River, this large block of land is operated by the federal government for experimental purposes in agriculture and horticulture. The cattle barn, flower gardens and arboretum are open to the public. The arboretum lies east of the junction of Island Park and Prince of Wales drives. The Ottawa/Carleton Transpo buses serve the area from downtown. Look for Bohemian Waxwing at the eastern side of the loop in winter. In April, look for owls in the conifers within the loop. In winter, scan the fields for Snowy Owls or Gray Partridge. From November to March the partridge tend to congregate on or near the manure piles near the beef showcase. In July, August and September you may find Lesser Golden- and Black-bellied Plovers and the occasional Buff-breasted Sandpiper in the fields.

Clyde Woods. Lying on the west side of the Central Experimental Farm, this cedar grove and deciduous wood is a good spot during migration and winter. Take the Queensway west to the Maitland Avenue interchange and drive south about 0.75 km. Turn east onto Glenmount and then left again onto Castle Hill Crescent and follow it to Clyde Avenue. Turn onto Clyde and park at the end of the road. A bus from OC Transpo will take you here, too. The area has houses on two sides, with a well-used bicycle path through the woods. Open fields lie to the south. The rock quarry, due north of the parking area, has numerous Rock Doves and European Starlings which often attract birds of prey in winter. At this season you will also find a Great Horned Owl, Hairy and Downy Woodpeckers, Black-capped Chickadee, White-breasted Nuthatch, Evening Grosbeak and other finches. In April look for Long-eared and Northern Saw-whet Owls. In May and June and again in August through October there are numerous birds passing through the woods.

Britannia Filtration Plant. For a rewarding birding trip, go to the block of land that juts out into the Ottawa River near the west end of the city. Take Richmond Road (17B); it parallels the Ottawa River to Poulin, just east of the intersection of Carling and Richmond. Take Poulin north to Britannia Road and turn right on it to the intersection with Cassels. Take a right onto Cassels, continue for a short distance and park where the woods meet the road. An OC Transpo bus services the site.

Britannia has been designated a "natural environment area" and can be birded all year. Take the path as far as the southwest corner of the pond to look for woodland species. From May to September you should find Belted Kingfisher, Common Flicker, Great Crested Flycatcher, Eastern Wood-Pewee, Brown Creeper, Gray Catbird, Cedar Waxwing, Red-eyed Vireo, Yellow Warbler, Common Yellowthroat and Rose-breasted Grosbeak. You may wish to circle the pond for a chance at others. In winter, look for Hairy and Downy Woodpeckers, an occasional three-toed woodpecker, Black-capped Chickadee, White and Red-breasted Nuthatches, Brown Creeper, a variety of finches and American Tree Sparrow. During migration, check out the ridge along the north side of Cassels. September is the month in which many Yellow-rumped Warblers can be spotted along here. Mud Lake should have a variety of water birds, including Mallard, Black Duck, Blue-winged and Green-winged Teals, Hooded Merganser and Wood Duck. Other species could include Pied-billed Grebe, Green-backed Heron, Common Moorhen and swallows. Go out to the point at the northeastern corner of the plant grounds for a good view of the river. In late May and early June, Arctic Terns appear on migration with the occasional Franklin's and Little Gulls and Double-crested Cormorant. Deschenes Rapids, immediately north of the point, is one of the few open-water sites on the river in winter and a variety of ducks are here.

Ottawa Beach. West of Britannia Filtration Plant on the south bank of the river, Ottawa Beach is one of the best birding spots in the region, with over 150 species recorded. On the east side is Britannia Pier, which juts out into the Ottawa River. To reach it take Pinecrest Road to its north end. The Ottawa Beach parking area is located in the middle off Carling Avenue (just east of Graham Creek). The entrance to Andrew Hayden Park, on the west side, is at the north end of Acres Road. The whole section is served by OC Transpo. Fall migration usually provides the greatest number and variety of species. At Britannia Pier check the river along the western side for ducks (and eastern side, too, after mid-September when the bathers have gone). Mudflats on Ottawa Beach host shorebirds and gulls. Andrew Hayden Park offers a good view of the open river for those birds that like deep water. The northeast corner is a good vantage point to check out the mudflats at Ottawa Beach.

Shirley's Bay is an Ontario Ministry of Natural Resources Crown Game Preserve. Although some birding can be done from the parking lot and nearby fields, the best spots are within the restricted zone of a federal rifle range. The Ottawa Field-Naturalists' Club has an access agreement. Visitors should contact the club for details. To reach this spot, go west from Ottawa Beach on Carling Avenue (17B) to Range Road and turn north to the parking lot. Look for the Connaught Rifle Range sign at the Range Road intersection with 17B. OC Transpo runs daily bus service to Shirley's Bay. The bay is fairly large and for the most part quite shallow, with an approximately 1-km dike across the mouth. This is another of Ottawa's prime birding spots. Over 100 breeding species have been recorded. More rarities for the Ottawa area have been spotted here than anywhere else. The openness of the bay precludes good winter birding.

To bird Shirley's Bay walk down the dirt road to the dike. The habitat along the first part of this road is fairly open. Typical birds to be expected from May to September include Eastern Kingbird, Gray Catbird, Yellow Warbler, American Goldfinch and Song Sparrow. The road then passes through damp woods. These trees can be alive with migrant vireos and warblers in May and early September, with fewer species in summer. At the dike, check the area on the left. Numerous puddle ducks can usually be found from April to November, with Mallard, Black Duck and the two teal species the most common. From July onwards the mudflat hosts migrating shorebirds, with up to 20 species present at a time. Occasionally all three species of phalarope can be observed together here. A Marsh Wren often can be heard calling from the cat-tails. Along the dike Great Blue Heron, Black Tern and swallows will be encountered. Scan the open water on the right during the spring and fall for loons, grebes, Brant, scoters and other waterfowl. During spring and fall, keep an eye open for migrating raptors overhead.

Jack Pine Trail. Go back south from Shirley's Bay to Carling (17B), then east to Moodie Drive. Take Moodie south, across Highway 417, the Queensway, and continue south through the town of Bells Corners, until you reach the junction with Knoxdale Road. Turn left onto Knoxdale, which then meets Moodie Drive again. Turn right onto Moodie and continue south for another 2 km. Watch for Jack Pine Trail on the left. The area consists of cedar and deciduous woods, open areas and a large beaver pond. There are several well-marked trails with boardwalks. These trails loop back to the parking lot. On a stroll along the trail you could encounter Red-tailed Hawk, Ruffed

Grouse, Great Horned Owl, Pileated Woodpecker, both three-toed wood-peckers, Blue Jay, Wood Thrush, Veery, vireos and warblers depending on the season. A winter feeder is a five- to ten-minute walk from the parking lot and usually attracts most winter species.

Nepean Dump. Continue south on Moodie Drive for 6 km from Jack Pine Trail, then turn left onto Cambrian Road. Almost immediately turn right onto Trail Drive. This dump, operated by the Regional Municipality of Ottawa-Carleton, is most frequently visited from October into December, when gulls are present. Check at the entrance station for permission to enter. On weekdays and Saturdays birds are more numerous because material is being delivered. Herring Gull is the most numerous, with lesser numbers of Great Black-backed and Ring-billed. Glaucous, Iceland and Thayer's Gulls are usually present; Lesser Black-backed Gulls are occasional. Gray Partridge can sometimes be found.

Richmond Wetlands. Fifteen km due south of the Nepean Dump, these wetlands lie southeast of the community of Richmond. Drive to the train tracks at the southeast edge of town and park. Walk south along the railway line for 5 km. Entering the fen can be difficult. Check with local birders for detailed instructions first. The wetlands have been designated a "natural environment area" and sections have been purchased by the regional authority. The sedge fen is the most interesting habitat. It is best birded at dusk or dawn in late May or early June. Birds include Great Blue Heron, a possible Least Bittern, American Bittern, a chance for a Yellow Rail, Virginia Rail, Sora, Common Moorhen, Whip-poor-will, all regular flycatchers, Marsh and Sedge Wrens, and a mixture of upland birds.

Dunrobin. From the Richmond Wetlands go back north to Highway 417 on the Queensway and head west. Take Eagleson Road north for 6 km. Turn right onto County Road 9, then right onto Riddell Drive, River Road or either of the next two rights. In April and early May or September and October, choose a spot on the road allowance overlooking Constance Creek and scan the skies for migrating raptors. A drive around the roads should yield Eastern Bluebird at the nest boxes and Loggerhead Shrike, which sometimes nest here. Check with local contacts for the location of nest sites. Typical birds to look for from May to September include Killdeer, Eastern Kingbird, Eastern Phoebe, American Crow, American Robin, Eastern Meadowlark, Bobolink and Savannah Sparrow.

Champlain Bridge. This bridge is reached from Island Park Drive. The Ottawa River Parkway runs along the river and provides a good access too. To the east, Nepean Bay may be scanned from near the eastern end of the parkway. The Remic Rapids, between the Lemieux Island and Champlain bridges, can be viewed from the overlook on the parkway. To reach Parc Brebeuf, cross the Champlain Bridge to the north side. Immediately turn east along the river, and then south at Begin Street in the residential area; go to the end of Begin Street and the parking lot. Water remains open all year in the rapids. Check the water for loons, grebes, waterfowl and gulls. Nepean

Bay occasionally has a Double-crested Cormorant, summering waterfowl and a large colony of Ring-billed Gulls. Check Parc Brebeuf in winter for Barrow's Goldeneye.

Gatineau Park. This park is located in Quebec, on the north side of the river. Access to it can be gained from many places; the most southerly and easiest access is along the Gatineau Parkway running right up the middle of the park. Habitat ranges from cultivated lawns to remote and wild spots. There are both deciduous and coniferous forests and also beaver ponds. The park is owned and operated by the National Capital Commission. Contact them for specific details and a bird checklist. Many species breed here, including several which are uncommon or absent elsewhere in the Ottawa/Hull area. Breeders to be encountered include Common Loon, Great Blue Heron, Yellow-bellied Sapsucker, Eastern Phoebe, Alder and Olive-sided Flycatchers, Red-breasted Nuthatch, House Wren, Brown Creeper, both kinglets and all the local vireos and warblers. In September and October, hawks and Turkey Vultures can be spotted from Champlain Lookout. A winter trip will produce woodpeckers, finches and other winter species.

Moore Feeder. This feeding station, sponsored by the local club, but on private property, is available to all birders. Please do not abuse the privilege. Be careful when parking in winter, as the ditch is often covered with snow. To reach it from the north end of the Champlain Bridge, take Chemain d'Aylmer (Highway 148) west for about 3.5 km to the Vanier junction and turn north on Vanier. Proceed about 5 km to Pink Road and drive west. After crossing Klock Road at about 4 km, look for a small sign marked "Moore" on the right hand side of the road. Park on the roadside and follow the trail to the feeding station. The trail starts at the gate and goes straight through a clearing. At about 100 m from the road another trail appears on the left. Take this trail into the cedars to the feeder. The feeder is active only in winter and attracts Hairy and Downy Woodpeckers, Gray Jay (irregular), Black-capped and Boreal Chickadees, White-breasted and Red-breasted

Common Loon

Nuthatches, Evening Grosbeak, American Tree Sparrow, northern finches and whatever else may be around.

Low/Poltimore. This area is the farthest out on the Quebec side. Take Highway 550 across the Gatineau River and immediately turn off onto No. 307, which proceeds in a northerly direction to Poltimore, and then head west to Low. An alternate route would be to take Highway 5 and then 105 north to Low, and then the gravel road east to Poltimore. The area is off the beaten track, so be sure to have a full tank of gasoline and dress warmly in winter. Take a detailed road map (see above) since it is easy to get lost. Birding is done along the road. You will pass through a mixture of deciduous and coniferous woods with some agriculture. The route is good year-round. However, Britannia and Vincent Massey are just as good if not better in spring and fall migration periods. Regular winter birds include Common Raven, Blue Jay, Black-capped Chickadee, White-breasted and Red-breasted Nuthatches, Hairy and Downy Woodpeckers, Evening Grosbeak and American Tree Sparrow. Less dependable species include Gray Jay, Boreal Chickadee and northern finches. You will find breeding birds here similar to those in Gatineau Park.

STEPHEN GAWN

Kingston

Situated on the northeast corner of Lake Ontario, at the start of the St. Lawrence River, Kingston is host to at least 333 bird species. Greater Scaups come in large numbers and the Ruddy Duck is now a regular visitor; the Wild Turkey is a regular; the Snowy Owl is often common in winter.

Founded in 1673 as a fur-trading post and strategic military stronghold, this city which was the capital of Canada in the 1840s contains many ancient fortifications and early Canadian landmarks. Old Fort Henry, originally built in 1812 and later rebuilt in 1832–36, has been completely restored as a museum of military history. Kingston is about 210 km east of Toronto via Highway 401. The city is serviced by Greyhound bus and has campgrounds, motels and hotels.

Bird watchers intending to visit the area frequently should obtain a copy of the 209-page book *History of the Birds of Kingston, Ontario*, 2nd ed., by H. R. Quilliam (Kingston: Kingston Field Naturalists, 1973). Information on this area has been drawn from Helen R. Quilliam's article "The Kingston Region: The Birds," in *Seasons* Vol. 22 No. 1, 1982.

Birding Features
Kingston sits at the northern limits of some bird species and the southern ranges of others. In spring, birds coming north across Lake Ontario often stop in great numbers to rest after a night flight, particularly if they meet a cold front. Under these conditions check city gardens, islands in the lake, or Prince Edward Point, 88 km west of the city by road or 43 km as the crow flies. In the fall, migrating birds often wait out bad weather on the north shore of the lake.

Kingston has gained some fame for the great influx of owls that feed on the hordes of meadow voles on Wolfe and Amherst islands. Their Christmas bird count has had more Snowy Owls than any place on the continent. In addition there are often large numbers of wintering Rough-legged Hawks feeding on these voles. Ten species of owl have been spotted in the area, including both Barn and Barred. In 1978–79 over thirty Great Gray Owls also feasted on these voles. Wolfe Island is also known as the spot to find a Gray Partridge. Amherst Island contains a variety of habitats, ranging through open fields, woodlots, marshes and sandy beaches. Shorebirds are usually quite numerous, particularly in migration. The Whimbrel can generally be counted on to stop around May 24. The Upland Sandpiper is fairly common. Check out the woodlots for late-migrating and nesting passerines. Short-eared Owl is regular, as are Northern Harrier and Red-tailed Hawk.

Moving northeast from the city about 40 km on 401, watch for the signs to the Ivy Lea Bridge. This is a good spot to look for enormous rafts of Greater Scaups in both spring and fall. Other ducks gather in huge flocks too. In winter, diving ducks appear in rafts where the current keeps the St. Lawrence open between the islands. Use the bridge to scan for a Bald Eagle attracted by the large supply of food. In spring, one can count 19 or 20 species of duck from the bridge. Look for Wild Turkey around the Canadian Customs office.

Spots within the Canadian Shield to search out include Canoe Lake Road, Otter Lake Sanctuary, the Rideau Trail near Gould Lake, and Frontenac Park. Check these sites for Golden-winged, Cerulean and Prairie Warblers, and the occasional Blue-winged Warbler. They have all become more numerous in recent years. Regular singers in June include Eastern Wood-Pewee, Yellow-throated Vireo, Red-eyed Vireo, Ovenbird, Rose-breasted Grosbeak and Indigo Bunting.

Prince Edward Point, projecting out from Quinte Peninsula, contains a national wildlife area. The point is well studied, with a regular bird-banding station in operation and many years of daily bird surveys to draw from. In late May, the trees are filled with flycatchers, vireos, warblers and grosbeaks, with the nearby ground full of thrushes and sparrows. Look for the Green-backed Heron that nests near the harbour. A Double-crested Cormorant is often spotted as you stand on the shore by the lighthouse. At this site, check for Bonaparte's Gull and Caspian Tern loafing on shore. Nearby, listen for Rufous-sided Towhee. In autumn, large numbers of Northern Saw-whet Owls pass through and are banded.

Presqu'ile Provincial Park

Located about 10 km south of Highway 401 near Brighton, about 110 km east of Toronto, this southern projection into Lake Ontario attracts about 225 species of birds annually. Nearly 300 have been spotted. At least 130 species are believed to nest in the park. The lighthouse functions as an interpretive centre and deals with natural history. The large sandy beach provides good swimming. Numerous motels are available along 401 and the campground in the park can be an overnight stop. It is a popular place in July and August, filling up early in the day.

Information on the park is available from the Ministry of Natural Resources and from Ontario Travel (see above). A new booklet has just been published by this ministry, *Birds of Presqu'ile Ontario*, by R. D. McRae. It costs $3.00 and is quite comprehensive, with detailed write-ups, map and index. Much of the material for this section was obtained from this booklet and later updated through correspondence with McRae. Write for it if you plan to visit.

Birding Features

The point contains marshes, woodlands and open fields. As you enter over the causeway, watch for Least Bittern, often seen flying across the road from May through July. In April and May and again in September and October, look for collections of Ring-necked Duck, Hooded Merganser, Common Moorhen, American Coot and other water birds. In winter, Swamp and Song Sparrows are sometimes spotted.

The Fingers Nature Trail, from mid-May to July, offers possibilities of Great Horned Owl, Pileated Woodpecker, Winter Wren and several warblers including Pine. Moving south, Owens Point at the southwest corner is the best site from spring to fall. In heavy rainstorms large numbers of shorebirds can be grounded here. During the fall migration the area sometimes churns with ducks, hawks, shorebirds, gulls and sparrows. Many unusual species are seen from this spot. Herons sometimes gather here in the evening to feed. In winter the odd Snowy Owl will appear.

Gull and High Bluff islands are off limits in the breeding season from March to September. However, with a good spotting scope you can observe close to 40,000 pairs of Ring-billed Gulls, and lesser numbers of Black-crowned Night-Heron, Herring Gull and Common Tern. The islands attract large numbers of ducks, with many nesting.

Take a spin along the south side of the point on Lakeshore Drive in April and May for warblers and sparrows. From September through May look for overwintering Common Goldeneye, Bufflehead and Oldsquaw. In October, the three scoters are present in rafts. In November, if you are lucky you may spot a King Eider at the west end of the road.

During a visit to the museum around migration time, scan the trees for the hundreds of warblers and sparrows on the site and along Paxton Drive. In mid-May you may see scores of Northern Orioles, Scarlet Tanagers and Rose-breasted Grosbeaks. One or two pairs of Blue-gray Gnatcatchers nest around here too. Ask at the museum for help in locating them. During March, April, October and November evenings, watch the ducks fly into Presqu'ile Bay for shelter.

If your visit is in April or October, take a walk along the cottage road on the north end of the tip. You'll spot juncos on the lawns, feeding. In winter this area attracts Northern Cardinal, Evening Grosbeak, Common Redpoll, Pine Siskin and Dark-eyed Junco.

A final site is Government Dock. From this location, during spring movements between February and April, watch tens of thousands of ducks.

You may spot Tundra Swans if they are around. In March, gulls cover Presqu'ile Bay in thousands. Look for Glaucous and Iceland among them.

If you are camping, scan the marsh near the campground office or hike along any of the other trails through the woods.

R. D. McRAE

Peterborough

Peterborough, northeast of Toronto, lies near a series of large lakes with nearby swamps and some mature northern forests. The region offers a birder opportunities to find Barred and Northern Saw-whet Owls, three-toed woodpeckers, crossbills and warblers, including Black-and-white.

Dating back to the early 1800s, the community still retains two fine residences of that period, one built in 1837 and the other in 1847. Greyhound buses service the city and there is ample accommodation available. A visitor from Toronto would drive east on Highway 401 to 35, then north to Highway 115. Take 115 into Peterborough.

Birding Features

The Cavan Swamp, as a remnant bog, exemplifies the type of habitat that once covered much of Peterborough County. Parts of the bog can be reached by driving west of the city on Country Road 10, and Cavan Twp. Roads 11 and 12. The north and south boundaries of the bog are approximately at these roads. Highway 7 and the Emily Park Road provide the east and west limits. Come to the bog to look for some northern species, including Northern Saw-whet Owl, flycatchers, Winter Wren, thrushes, Nashville and Black-and-white Warblers. A visit in June to mid-July could result in spotting many rare orchids, pitcher plants, Sundew and Labrador Tea. On a winter trip, look for owls, three-toed woodpeckers and finches.

Lakefield Marshes lie within the community of the same name. As you enter the town from the south on Highway 28, turn west at the first traffic light and drive to the end of the road. Take your canoe down the small stream for about 0.4 km to the marshes. These cat-tail marshes provide nesting habitat for a variety of birds, including Common Loon, Least and American Bitterns, ducks, Osprey, rails and Marsh Wren.

Proceed north from Lakefield, continuing on Highway 28, through Burleigh Falls and Woodview to Petroglyphs Provincial Park. Here you will be rewarded with Carolinean forest, Red and White Pine tracts, marshes and fast-flowing rivers. Take the 5-km self-guiding interpretive nature trail to a 27-m-high waterfall. The park holds the largest locally known collection of Indian stone carvings. These 900 or more petroglyphs date from about 1000 to 500 years ago. This park is an excellent spot throughout the year to locate resident northern species of birds, including both three-toed woodpeckers, Gray Jay, Common Raven, Boreal Chickadee and crossbills.

There is a series of sewage lagoons in the Peterborough area. The one at Omemee, west of Peterborough on Highway 7, is located north of Omemee on County Road 7. Turn west on the first concession road near Gliderport. The lagoons at Lindsay, west of Omemee on Highway 7, sit just off Highway 36 north of Lindsay, behind the landfill site. Now return to Peterborough and proceed east on Highway 7 to Havelock. The lagoons are off Highway 30 at the south end of town. Travel east on the Old Norwood Road to the first small gravel side road, which will lead you to these water bodies. These lagoons draw ducks, hawks, shorebirds and sparrows. Many birds nest very close to the water or in nearby vegetation. Several significant bird records are associated with these local lagoons, including those of Greater White-fronted Goose, Spotted Redshank, Red-necked and Wilson's Phalaropes, Little Gull, Franklin's Gull, Yellow-headed Blackbird and Blue Grosbeak.

A. GEOFFREY CARPENTIER

Oshawa and Nearby Sites

Oshawa, an industrial city, still possesses some excellent birding spots, especially in the wooded creek valleys running down into Lake Ontario. The waterfront often produces a great variety of birdlife, including a good sampling of gulls.

The city lies 40 km east of Toronto on Highway 401. Buses from Toronto service Oshawa regularly and all tourist amenities are available.

Birding Features
Oshawa's main claim to birding fame is the Oshawa Second Marsh. This 150-ha cat-tail marsh holds hundreds of ducks in migration. It was the site of the first known nesting of the Little Gull in North America in 1962. The marsh has also produced such rarities as Glossy Ibis, Bald Eagle, Ruff and Thick-billed Murre. Public access is at present restricted. If water levels are low in spring or fall, it may be worthwhile making the long trek out to the mudflats. Take the Harmony Road exit (Interchange 72) off Highway 401 and proceed 1 km south on Farewell Avenue to the Harmony Creek Water Pollution Control Plant. Park the car and walk along the south side of the fence. An alternate overlook into the marsh can be reached off Farewell Avenue, 0.8 km south of Highway 401. Turn east at this point onto Wentworth Street East, locally called the Ghost Road. Dense cedars and dogwood bushes on the south side of the road provide excellent owling in late fall. There is a good chance of ferreting out a Northern Saw-whet or Long-eared Owl.

Darlington Provincial Park lies just east of the above site. The Ghost Road ends at the west entrance to the park, with foot traffic the only way in. To reach the park by car, travel east on Highway 401 to Interchange 73, or Courtice Road. Follow the signs to the park. A nominal entrance fee is charged in summer, but there are both camping and picnic facilities. Check the wooded ravine; it is often full of warblers, Scarlet Tanager and Rose-breasted Grosbeak in May, especially in windy or rainy weather. The gravel spit running out into the bay is a gathering point for gulls and shorebirds. A Sharp-tailed Sparrow has been seen on the spit in the fall.

The Nonquon Sewage Lagoons are about 30 km north of Oshawa. To get there, leave Highway 401 at Durham Road 2, or Simcoe Street, and drive north through Oshawa and the hamlets of Columbus and Raglan to the town of Port Perry. Continue through Port Perry on Simcoe Street to the Eighth Concession Road, which is one concession north of the town limits. At this point turn west; the Nonquon River Water Pollution Control Plant is on the south side of the road at 0.5 km. One or two of the sewage ponds are usually only partly filled and attract large numbers and varieties of migrating shorebirds. Look for White-rumped and Baird's Sandpipers, Wilson's Phalarope and others. In June, the breeding birds should include American Black Duck and Blue-winged Teal on the ponds. In the surrounding birch and maple woods you should be able to spot American Woodcock, Great-crested Flycatcher, House Wren, Wood Thrush, Veery, Cedar Waxwing, Red-eyed Vireo, Northern Oriole and Rose-breasted Grosbeak.

On the way back south, sample different terrain by taking a short side trip along the crest of the Oak Ridges Moraine. Turn east off Simcoe Street 7 km south of Port Perry, onto the Tenth Concession Road. The rolling grasslands are inhabited by Upland Sandpiper, Horned Lark, Eastern Meadowlark, and Grasshopper and Vesper Sparrows. The adjacent woodlots contain Black-billed Cuckoo, Whip-poor-will, Scarlet Tanager and Indigo Bunting. The evergreens planted for sale at Christmas harbour Rufous-sided Towhee and Chipping, Clay-colored and Field Sparrows. Local people have an Eastern Bluebird nestbox project along the edges of the field.

MARG BAIN

Pickering, Ajax and Whitby

These three communities lie immediately east of Toronto. Their woodlots and wooded valleys, terminating in marshes and lakeshore at Lake Ontario, provide opportunities to view migrants and local breeders. There have been an impressive number of casuals reported, including Black-legged Kittiwake, Purple Sandpiper and Ivory Gull.

Highway 401, east from Toronto, provides the trunk route access. Accommodation and services are readily available throughout.

Birding Features
Pickering. The first community east along Highway 401 sits on the eastern side of the Rouge River Valley. This approximately 32-km strip of heavily treed forest ends in marshes at its mouth. Excellent birding can be had in the southern few km, especially during migration. The valley can be entered at several spots. To explore the south end, leave Highway 401 at Interchange 61 and take Meadowvale Road north to Sheppard Avenue. Turn east along Sheppard to Twin Rivers Drive and follow it down into the valley to the bridges over the Rouge River and Little Rouge Creek. Park along the roadside and explore the footpaths north and south along both streams. To sample the middle of the valley, continue along Twin Rivers Drive to the tableland on the east side. Turn south on Woodview Drive and follow it to

the end. Park at the entrance to the footpath. Walk down the slope into the valley and along the banks of the Little Rouge. To locate the mouth of the valley, proceed east on Highway 401 to the Port Union Road, Interchange 62. Take it south for 0.4 km to Island Drive. Proceed east to Rouge Hills Drive and then south to the lake. Rarities have included Great and Snowy Egrets and Harlequin Duck near the river mouth. Regular breeders include Least and American Bitterns, Wood Duck, Eastern Screech-Owl and Marsh Wren. Check the nearby woods for unusual warblers.

Claremont Conservation Area. Take Highway 401 to Interchange 64, Brock Road. Proceed north for about 13 km to the village of Brougham. Head east to Greenwood and turn north along Westney Road for about 1.6 km to the park gate. The area has large sections of land covered in mature forest. Common resident species include Ruffed Grouse, Eastern Screech-Owl, Pileated Woodpecker, large numbers of Red-breasted and White-breasted Nuthatches and Purple Finch. Summer breeders include Cooper's, Red-shouldered and Broad-winged Hawks, Whip-poor-will, seven species of flycatcher, Cedar Waxwing and a large and diverse collection of wood warblers. Winter brings Golden-crowned Kinglet, Bohemian Waxwing, Pine Siskin and a variety of "winter finches."

Ajax. This next community lies east of Pickering, near the shores of Lake Ontario. Birders know the area for its extensive cat-tail marshes, Corner Marsh and Shoal Point.

Corner Marsh is reached from Highway 401 at Interchange 65, Church Street. Take it south to Bayley Street. Continue west on Bayley to Station Road, south to Montgomery Park Road and finally east to the marsh. Rarities are showing up continually and range from Arctic Loon, Tricolored Heron and three species of jaeger to Dickcissel. In summer you can easily locate, among others, Mute Swan, Black Tern and Marsh Wren. In the fall, come to observe migrating raptors, including Sharp-shinned Hawk, Peregrine Falcon and Merlin. Check the woods for a large variety of passerines moving through in August and early September.

The Shoal Point marsh lies at the south end of Shoal Point Road, off Bayley St., east of Corner Marsh. Here the lower reaches of Carruthers Creek and its floodplain produce a small sedge grass–cat-tail marsh. Nearby there is a moderate-sized, wet, cedar-maple-ash woodlot. This area is presently privately owned but is open for foot traffic. Carruthers Creek lies along the lakefront several km east of the mouth of Duffins Creek. Local birders rank this as one of the best spots in the region. Several unexpected species have been spotted, including Black-legged Kittiwake, Snowy Egret, Purple Sand-piper, Blue Grosbeak, Little Gull and Worm-eating Warbler. A visit from early May to early July should produce the common nesters, including Wood Duck, Eastern Screech-Owl, four species of woodpecker, Willow and Alder Flycatchers, Veery, Yellow Warbler, Northern Waterthrush, Rose-breasted Grosbeak, and Swamp and Song Sparrows. Regular but uncommon breeders include Canada Goose, Common Moorhen, Barred Owl, Belted Kingfisher, Blue-gray Gnatcatcher, Black-and-white and Chestnut-sided Warblers and White-throated Sparrow.

Whitby. The town of Whitby, east of Ajax and west of Oshawa, is accessible off Highway 401 on Interchange 67, Brock Street. The region contains two conservation areas, several lakeshore woodlots, and extensive tracts of mature forest in local creek valleys and nearby tablelands. Lynde Shores Conservation Area, usually considered the best birding spot, can be reached by going south on Brock Street to Victoria Street and taking Victoria west for about 3 km. Look for the Lynde Shores Conservation Area entrance sign on the south side of the road. Parking is available in the adjacent lot. The site boasts a variety of habitats, including both cat-tail and Carr type marshes, wooded creek valley, mudflats on the floodplain, sand and gravel beach, and abandoned orchards and fields. No other spot in the entire region has produced such a variety of bird species. Visitors should expect anything, including such rarities as Red-throated Loon, Glossy Ibis, Yellow Rail, Black-legged Kittiwake and Sharp-tailed Sparrow. The lakeshore provides ideal viewing for migrant waterfowl, while nearby fields and woodlots host a diverse number of passerines that move through. Regular breeding species include Mute Swan, Gadwall, Northern Harrier, Virginia Rail, Sora, Black-billed Cuckoo, six species of flycatcher, Chestnut-sided Warbler, Common Yellowthroat, Rose-breasted Grosbeak, Indigo Bunting, and Swamp and Song Sparrows.

To get to the Thickson's Point area return to Victoria Street, drive east to Thickson's Road and take it to the foot at the lakeshore. An alternate route is off Highway 401 on Interchange 68 at Thickson's Road, straight south to the water. Park along the road. Local birders consider the Thickson's area one of the most significant sections of lakeshore, marsh and woodlot in the region. The woodlot, consisting of a mature stand of pine, maple and oak and bordered with a dense growth of shrubs, is owned by a local resident association. These people operate an assortment of active bird feeders around the edge of the woods, making the woods appear "alive" in winter. You reach the woods and part of the beach from the north side of the woods along an adjacent road. In spring (April, May and June) there is a wealth of migrant passerines in the woods. Unusual visitors have included Carolina Wren, Yellow-billed Cuckoo, Prothonotary, Kentucky and Hooded Warblers and Lark Bunting. Watch here and in the shelterbelt down at the water for the Long-eared, Short-eared and Northern Saw-whet Owls that occasionally show up. Regular common breeders include a host of species such as Least Flycatcher, Gray Catbird, Red-eyed Vireo, Common Yellowthroat, Northern Cardinal and Swamp Sparrow. The adjacent marsh and wooded barrier beach provide shelter for a variety of migrant waterfowl, shorebirds and smaller passerines. Great Egret, Peregrine Falcon and American Avocet have all appeared. Common breeders include Mallard and Spotted Sandpiper. The foot of Thickson's Road also provides an excellent vantage point to scan the lake for flocks of migrant cormorants, swans, geese, ducks, shorebirds, gulls and terns.

Heber Down Conservation Area. To reach this inland area, leave Highway 401 at Interchange 67 on Brock Street and drive north through the town of Whitby for about 3 km to Taunton Road. Drive west for 1.6 km and north on Country Lane to the park. The site occupies an ancient lakeshore and glacial

TJ THORMIN /82

Hooded Warbler

embayment, providing an interesting blend of biogeographical features. Much of the valley is covered by a mature growth of White Cedar, maple, hemlock, pine and oak. Numerous nature trails provide access to nearly all the unique spots. The site is particularly alive in May and September. Resident species include Ruffed Grouse, Great Horned Owl, Pileated Wood-pecker, White and Red-breasted Nuthatches and Purple Finch. Summer breeders from May to early July include Red-shouldered Hawk, American Kestrel, Black-billed Cuckoo, Eastern Screech-Owl, Whip-poor-will, several species of flycatcher, Wood Thrush, Veery, Ovenbird, Mourning Warbler, Rose-breasted Grosbeak, Rufous-sided Towhee and White-throated Spar-row. A winter visit could provide the above-mentioned resident birds together with Evening and Pine Grosbeaks, Common Redpoll, Pine Siskin and both species of crossbill.

J. ROBERT NISBET

Toronto

Toronto, the linchpin of Upper Canada, contains a host of attractions, including the biggest zoo in the country, a variety of galleries and museums, and over 200 parks — something for everyone. Over 305 species of birds have been listed within a radius of 48 km of the Royal Ontario Museum at Bloor Street and Avenue Road.

The region was mentioned by Etienne Brule during his explorations with the Huron Indians in 1615. More than a century later fur traders from New France built Fort Rouille on the shores of the island-girded bay. They burned and abandoned this post by the time the British visited in 1759, when it was renamed York. During the War of 1812, the Americans captured and burned the community. The British retaliated by burning Washington, singeing the home of President Madison; from its new coat of paint rose the nickname "The White House." As Toronto grew and prospered, it remained a centre of conservatism. With the influx of thousands of Europeans in this century, the city expanded its cultural elements by encouraging the development of an ethnic mosaic.

For information on the parks contact: Tourist Marketing Branch, Ministry of Industry and Tourism, Hearst Block, Queen's Park, Toronto, Ontario M7A 2E5. The Toronto Transit Commission, telephone (416) 484-4544, will provide information on how to travel to any point in the city.

One of the local naturalist groups has published an excellent book, *A Bird Finding Guide to the Toronto Region*, by Clive E. Goodwin. It is available for $2.00 plus $1.00 postage from: Civic Garden Centre, 777 Lawrence Avenue E., Don Mills, Ontario. If you plan a visit you should obtain a copy. Much of the material in this section has been obtained from this guide. Further information is available from the Federation of Ontario Naturalists' office (see above).

The Toronto Rare Bird Alert number is (416) 481-7948; also check with Dave Fidler at (416) 833-6369 and Ron Scovell at (416) 745-9111.

Birding Features

The shoreline of Lake Ontario and the river valleys into the lake, combined with the Niagara Escarpment, provide some excellent birding opportunities year-round. From November through March, diving ducks and winter gulls reach their largest numbers. By March, the earliest migrants appear. Northbound birds peak in numbers in the third week of May. The woodlands are superb at this time, with some birds in full breeding activity and others such as warblers moving through en masse. The lakefront hosts flocks of Ruddy Turnstone, Red Knot, Whimbrel and Dunlin. June can be very hot, as are July and August. Shorebirds begin passing south in July and large flocks of swallows appear by early August. By the end of the month flycatchers and warblers are moving steadily, and shorebird movement becomes heavy. In September, look for the huge flocks of Blue Jays and clouds of Monarch Butterflies along the lake. At this time check the lakeshore and inland for hawks high in the sky; the mudflats and wet fields and shoreline for a variety of shorebirds, including Pectoral and Semipalmated Sandpipers, Black-bellied Plover and Lesser Golden-Plover; the marshes for herons and dabbling ducks. Offshore boat trips are sometimes organized to spot pelagic birds like scoters, Parasitic and Pomarine Jaegers and maybe a rare Sabine's Gull. By late October most birds are gone and you must await the winter influx.

Specific sites include:

Toronto Island Park. Perhaps the best single bird-watching area in the city is Toronto Island, a group of thirteen islands located in the harbour. Ferry service departs from the foot of Bay St. at the waterfront. Ferries go to Ward's Island, Centre Island and Hanlan's Point. Ward's Island and Hanlan's Pt. are best. If going to the latter, hike the west shore for shorebirds and water birds, and the small weedy areas back from the shore for sparrows, Rufous-sided Towhee and other thicket-loving birds. These areas are best during the May and September-October migration periods. Follow the west shore around to the south where there are extensive stands of low willows, good for warblers. From here you may want to take the sidewalk as you walk eastward. You will encounter the Island Nature School and the Filtration Plant. Just east of the plant, a roadway leads to the left to the Nature Sanctuary. There is good birding here at all seasons as the underbrush has not been cleared; in the winter, the three feeders are a major attraction for all birds. As you hike eastward you will enter an area of grass, picnic tables and flower beds. There is a good viewing point for Lake Ontario off to your right. Continue east parallel to the shore; you will eventually reach Ward's Island. Ward's Island is a cottage/residential area and in summer you may find orioles, vireos, wrens and other woodland songbirds. In winter there will be chickadees, nuthatches, woodpeckers, creepers, cardinals and others at the feeders. If you have watched the time, you can take the ferry back to the mainland from here rather than walking all the way back to Hanlan's Pt. In the many ponds that you will have passed, watch for Canada Goose, Mallard and Wood Duck, all year. In winter there will be scaup, Oldsquaw, mergansers and other diving ducks. This area is also good for raptors in September.

Eastern Headland (Leslie St. Spit). This relatively new birding area in Toronto is a dry rubble landfill operation and as such is open to the public only on weekends (foot or bicycle traffic). The spit is a 4.8-km-long peninsula made up of several bays and small peninsulas. It is host to the largest Ring-billed Gull colony in the world (approximately 80,000 pairs in 1982) as well as to nesting Herring Gulls, Common and Caspian Terns, Black-crowned Night-Herons and at least one pair of Great Black-backed Gulls. It is an extremely good area for shorebirds during migration; Whimbrel are seen regularly on the May 24th weekend and Brant may also be present then. Turnstones, Red Knots, Sanderling and "peeps," including White-rumped and Baird's Sandpipers, are seen every year. Most of the Toronto-facing shore is sand, while the open lake shore is concrete and rubble; hence the former is better for shorebirds. In winter, Great Horned, Snowy, Saw-whet and Short-eared Owls can be seen. The spit is not a superb area for land birds yet, as the forest cover is not very mature or well developed; sparrows can be good at times. Open-field birds, longspurs, larks and Snow Buntings are often present at the far end of the roadway near the lighthouse. It is a long walk to the end and the air temperature on the spit is often several degrees colder than away from the lake. During summer and fall there is bus service to the end of the spit; call the Toronto Transit Commission (see above).

Lambton Woods. Located in the community of Islington in the Borough of Etobicoke, Lambton Woods has been described as the best example of eastern hardwood forest in west Toronto. To reach this forest, go west on Edenbridge Dr. off Scarlett Rd. or east on Edenbridge Dr. off Royal York Rd. James Gardens, on Edenbridge, is at the entrance to Lambton Woods. As might be expected, the speciality of Lambton Woods is land birds and the area is good at all times. During migration, spring and fall, warblers, vireos, sparrows, flycatchers and thrushes are common. Watch for accipiters as well. In winter the various feeders supplement the natural food crops. Watch for a Blue Jay, Northern Cardinal, flickers, Downy and Hairy Woodpeckers, Great Horned Owl and even a Northern Goshawk! Pileated Woodpecker, a late Yellow-rumped Warbler, Purple Finch, goldfinches and redpolls are common winter birds.

Sunnybrook Park. Toronto has many good ravines for birding, and Sunnybrook Park, adjacent to the West Branch of the Don River, is one of the best. Watch for a Red-headed Woodpecker, Blue-gray Gnatcatcher and Eastern Screech-Owl in summer. The latter species is best seen or heard at dusk in late winter in response to a tape or whistle.

Other areas in Toronto that are good for land birds include the Metro Zoo, Cedarvale Ravine, High Park, Sherwood Park, Morningside Park. For water birds, the keen birder might try East and West Humber Bay parks, Grenadier Pond in High Park, Sunnyside on Lakeshore Blvd. from the Humber River to Ontario Place, and Ashbridge's Bay Park. See Goodwin's guide (refer above) for directions.

LINDA AND CHIP WESELOH

Mississauga and Oakville

The region immediately west and northwest of Toronto, including Mississauga, Oakville and the counties of Peel and Halton, has always been a high quality bird-watching locale. Unfortunately, over the last fifteen or twenty years urban sprawl has left but small pockets of refuge behind. GO TRANSIT lines and related bus service provide access to some sites. Check with their office for schedules.

Birding Features
The Lake Ontario waterfront still retains highlight spots. To discover them, drive Lakeshore Road from east to west, stopping periodically at roads terminating at the water to scan the shoreline. Ducks and geese are most numerous from September to March. Favourite locations include: Marie Curtis Park, opposite the Long Branch GO TRANSIT station on Lakeshore Road at Etobicoke Creek; Albert E. Crookes Memorial Park, found along Goodwin Road south of Lakeshore Road; the St. Lawrence Starch Plant, at Port Credit Harbour via Stevebank Road south of Lakeshore or via Port Street; Jack Darling Memorial Park and Rattray's Marsh, located 1.6 km east of Meadowwood Road, west of the Lorne Park traffic light; Lakeside Park, reached via Winston Churchill Blvd., or south on Southdown Road; Oakville Harbour, via Mary Street; and Bronte Harbour, found by driving south on Bronte Road or by the Queen Elizabeth Way and Lakeshore Road.

A trip to the shoreline is always worthwhile, even to watch the big ships; you may spot a variety of ducks such as Redhead, Greater and Lesser Scaups, Common Goldeneye, Common Eider, Common and White-winged Scoters, and maybe even a Barrow's Goldeneye or Harlequin Duck. Shorebirds arrive in April and May and again in September and October. They include Ruddy Turnstone, Red Knot, Dunlin, Sanderling and even Purple Sandpiper. Watch for the occasional Great Black-backed Gull.

The river valleys are, as in most Canadian cities, among the last refuges for wildlife. Take a walk in any of the four leading to Lake Ontario: the Port Credit River and Etobicoke, Sixteen Mile and Bronte creeks. A wide mix of plants, birds and mammals can be spotted in summer and winter. These valleys can be entered at the numerous east-west road crossings except for the Queen Elizabeth Way and Highway 401.

The Niagara Escarpment stands out as a ridge from the Niagara Peninsula in the south to Tobermory, northwest of Toronto at the tip of the Bruce Peninsula. Much of its length is rocky and inaccessible with extensive wooded tracts. Often these are the only native woods left and hence are considered some of the finest accessible birding areas in Ontario. To gain access to some of the spots, drive north to Campbellville, at Interchange 38 west of Toronto on Highway 401, and take the first road to the right, or east (the fourth line). Within the first 3.2 km, the Mahon, Turner and Robertson tracts are indicated by signs. Two others, the Britton and Cox tracts, may be reached from the sixth line. These sites, with rocks and trees providing shelter and secluded nesting locations, are great for birding from April to July. However, look out for the hordes of mosquitoes! Common bird species include Turkey Vulture, Northern Goshawk, Cooper's Hawk, both species of cuckoo, Yellow-bellied Sapsucker, Brown Thrasher, Wood Thrush and Blue-gray Gnatcatcher. Vireos and warblers abound, particularly in late May and June. A sampling of warblers include Golden-winged, Blue-winged, Yellow, Cerulean, Chestnut-sided, Mourning, Hooded and American Redstart to name a few. Look for a Rose-breasted Grosbeak.

During the harsh winter months, the few birds that do occur on the escarpment include Ruffed Grouse, Hairy and Downy Woodpeckers, the occasional Three-toed Woodpecker, White-breasted and Red-breasted Nuthatches, Northern Shrike and the "winter finches."

Northern Cardinal

163

There are several conservation areas in the region. Mountsberg, with its nature interpretation centre, nature trails and observation tower, is worth a visit for fall and spring migrating water birds. Also check the Palgrave and Clairville conservation areas (refer to a Metro Toronto map for directions).

BARRY RANFORD, LINDA CRAIG

Luther Lake

Luther Lake, about 38 km straight north of Guelph or about 75 km west-northwest of Toronto, has three attractions: the lake, with its large variety of water birds including 15 species of ducks which have nested, many of them every year; the northern woods, with both southern Ontario species and northern birds such as Ruby-crowned Kinglet; and Wylde Lake, an unusual raised boreal bog in which Lincoln's Sparrow nest, one of the southernmost points for this species.

The complex comprises some 6500 ha, with about 2025 in open water. The marsh was established when the headwaters of the Grand River were dammed in 1952. A permit is required to put any boat, including a canoe, on the main lake prior to July 31. Permits may be obtained from the superintendent's house at the dam. Outboard motors are not allowed.

Access to the area is best gained by car. Nearby Arthur (about 10 km southwest) and Orangeville (about 24 km east) are served by Gray Coach (bus); taxis may be hired at either place. Commercial accommodation is available at both towns. Camping is not permitted in the Luther complex, but there are several public campgrounds within a few kilometres.

The eastern end of the lake and dam. From the intersection of Highways 9 and 10, just east of Orangeville, take Highway 9 west for 22.9 km, or 3.7 km past the turnoff to Grand Valley. Turn north onto an unmarked dirt road (the next north turnoff, 1.6 km farther west, has a microwave tower about 200 m west of it). Drive 8.2 km north; turn west onto an unmarked dirt road; proceed 3.7 km to a sharp right-angle bend in the road and proceed north 3.2 km to the dam and parking lot on the west side of the road. Hike the road that parallels the north shore for about 2.4 km to a lookout tower, which provides excellent viewing of the lake. If you are coming from Arthur, the unmarked dirt road turnoff north from Highway 9 lies 14.7 km east of the intersection of Highways 9 and 6.

Wylde Lake. This raised bog may be reached from Orangeville by driving west 26.2 km on Highway 9 to an unmarked dirt road. This is the boundary between Wellington and Dufferin counties. Look for the sign. Drive north for 5.3 km to the point where the road takes a sharp left hand turn. Park on the shoulder and walk eastward for about 1.5 km to the lake. Carry a compass when hiking in this area. On a dull day it is very easy to get lost in the Wylde Lake region of several square kilometres. From Arthur, the unmarked dirt road lies 11 km east on Highway 9.

Northern woods. These woods are reached from the dam site parking lot. From the dam, an internal road not open to vehicles curves through the northern part of the area, roughly parallelling the shore for 6.4 to 8 km. This road provides access to the large block of woodland on the north shore of the lake. The far end of this road can also be reached via Concession 8/9 off West Luther Township. From the dam about 2.4 km along the trail, a lookout tower provides a good overview of the lake. Continue to hike for 5.6 km from the dam, to a trail signposted "Esker Trail" which leads, in 0.8 km, to a second observation tower. This trail provides good views of a willow swamp.

Further information, together with details on permits mentioned above, may be obtained from: Grande River Conservation Authority, 400 Clyde Road, Cambridge, Ontario, Telephone: (519) 621-2761.

Birding Features
Main Lake. Good overviews of the main lake may be had from the dam and especially the observation tower 1.6 km south of the dam. The latter tower is reached from an internal road, open to private vehicles, that leaves the parking lot at the dam. Exploration by canoe is helpful, but stay near shore as sudden squalls are common.

Waterfowl that breed, in approximate order of abundance, are Mallard, Gadwall, American Wigeon, Blue-winged Teal, Lesser Scaup, Redhead, Ring-necked Duck, American Black Duck, Green-winged Teal, Northern Pintail, Wood Duck, Hooded Merganser, Canvasback and Northern Shoveler. Not all of these species breed every year. Also look for Common Loon, Red-necked and Pied-billed Grebes, Great Blue and Green-backed Herons, Black-crowned Night-Heron, a rare Least Bittern, American Bittern, Virginia Rail, Sora, Common Moorhen, American Coot, Northern Harrier, Osprey, Wilson's Phalarope on the islands, Black Tern especially at the North Bog, Marsh Wren and Swamp Sparrow.

In the fall, as the lake is drawn down, large areas of mudflats are exposed on the semi-floating bogs scattered through the lake and around the edges. These floating bogs are essentially bottomless; avoid walking on them.

Wylde Lake. This lake contains one of the southernmost breeding locations of Lincoln's Sparrow. Search and listen for them at the sharp bend in the road where you leave the car.

Northern woods. Look here for the usual woodland species of southern Ontario. A bonus includes a number of rather boreal species, such as Winter Wren, Ruby-crowned Kinglet and Nashville Warbler. At the dam parking lot, a Purple Martin colony is active in season.

DAVID BREWER

Hamilton and Burlington

Hamilton, locked between Lake Ontario and the Niagara Escarpment, offers a wealth of cosmopolitan attractions combined with some fine bird-watching spots. The city, with a population of 306,500, is home to Canada's two major steel-producing firms and contains the largest open air food market in our country. Nearby Burlington, to the north, houses the Joseph Brant Museum of Indian relics.

The two cities lie southwest of, and adjacent to, Metropolitan Toronto, on the southwest end of Lake Ontario. Access and accommodation are both easy to find.

Birding Features

Dundas Marsh. This site, often called Cootes Paradise, lies within the grounds of the Royal Botanical Gardens, west of the harbour and Highway 403. The marsh is considered to be the best all-round bird-finding spot in the district. To find the area take King Street west onto Marion Crescent. Park in the lot adjacent to the Children's Garden House. Spencer Creek flows into the western end of the marsh at the Dundas Hydro Pond and the Old Dejardins Canal. The creek may be reached on King Street by proceeding west past McMaster University and turning right on Cootes Drive. Cross the creek and park on the shoulder. Walk north to both the pond and canal; a path follows the canal east to the center of the marsh. At the end of the "willows" in the marsh, if the water is low, a mudflat appears, attracting shorebirds, gulls and terns. Westdale Ravine, on the south shore of the marsh, is a prime spot for viewing spring migration.

Hamilton Harbour. The east end of the harbour contains a landfill site. Here, in water kept open by the actions of the steel mills, you'll spot 10–15 species of overwintering waterfowl. Specialties such as Barrow's Goldeneye and Tufted Duck have been recorded in recent years.

Grimsby Peak. This is the best place for hawk watching. The area lies 19.2 km east of Hamilton, off the Queen Elizabeth Way. Exit at Christie Road, follow it south through town and up the very steep hill. Turn right (west) at the top of the hill and continue for about 1.6 km to signs for the Beamer Conservation Area.

Beverly Swamp. The swamp plays host to a horde of nesting land birds. From the junction of Highways 5 and 6 (Clappisons Corners), drive north on Highway 6 to West Flamboro Concession No. 8. Turn left and proceed 6.4 km to the swamp. Several km of poorly drained woodlands attract a variety of nesting birds. From May to July, survey for Yellow-bellied Sapsucker, Acadian and Willow Flycatcher, Winter Wren and White-throated Sparrow.

JOHN OLMSTED

Kitchener, Waterloo, Brantford and Cambridge

These communities occur at the boundary between the Great Lakes–St. Lawrence forests of Sugar Maple and American Beech to the north, and

Carolinean forests of oaks and hickories to the south. Birds of both forest types regularly breed here.

Kitchener was founded in 1799 by Mennonites from Pennsylvania. German settlers came in 1833 and called the village Berlin. The name was changed at the height of World War I.

These cities lie about 60 km southwest of Toronto, with Highway 401 the main route for vehicular traffic, including regular bus service. A variety of accommodation services and recreational opportunities are available. Before you visit, order the 1:50,000 topographic map 40 P/8 Cambridge from the Map Distribution Office in Ottawa.

Birding Features

The Grand River Valley, running south through Kitchener and Brantford to Lake Erie, represents the southern forest type of the area. Portions of the valley bottom contain virtually unbroken forest for long distances. Parks Canada has recognized the entire area between Cambridge and Paris as a National Site of Canadian Significance.

An auto tour of the western portion of the valley begins in Cambridge. Drive south along West River Road. This road begins just east of the intersection of Highways 97 and 24A on the west side of the Grand River, in the old town of Galt. Proceed south and note the forested ridge to the west. The Galt Ridge, a terminal moraine, was left when the last glacier from the east was stalled for a time before melting back. The road lies between the river (on the east) and the forested ridge (on the west), providing access to an excellent natural area. These lands extend from the river west over the ridge along a small river valley to Beake Pond, locally called Taylor's Lake, near Highway 24A. All of the land is privately held, but permission to enter is usually allowed if you ask. Habitats include upland deciduous forest, mixed and coniferous swamp, and old fields. Birds to look for in May to mid-July include Green-backed Heron, Blue-winged Teal, Turkey Vulture, Ruffed Grouse, Eastern Screech-Owl, Ruby-throated Hummingbird, Downy Woodpecker, Eastern Kingbird, Brown Thrasher, Cedar Waxwing, Common Yellowthroat, Bobolink, Eastern Meadowlark and Rufous-sided Towhee. A pair of Red-shouldered Hawks has bred in these woods for many years — the last pair remaining in local counties.

Both Golden-winged and Blue-winged Warblers breed in the forests surrounding Taylor's Lake. Nashville and Chestnut-sided Warblers are found in the swamps and upland forests, respectively. American Bittern and Sora have been heard frequently in the marsh at Taylor's Lake. White-throated and Swamp Sparrows, as well as Least Flycatcher, breed in the excellent bog 1 km south of Taylor's Lake. Both Upland Sandpiper and Clay-colored Sparrow have been found in the central fields north of the powerline.

As you continue to travel south on West River Road, notice the bridge crossing the Grand on your left. A large colony of Cliff Swallows nests on the concrete bridge supports. This is also an excellent spot to view waterfowl on the river in the winter. Continue south and you soon start to travel upwards as the road leaves the valley floor. Turn right onto the first road and head west. Cottrell Lake, on the right, causes the road to make a curving detour. Continue west, straight through the next intersection, and you soon enter the large Sudden Tract Forest. Park at the small parking lot provided on your right.

Sudden Tract is owned by the Region of Waterloo and is open for recreation, with several well-developed trails. The woods contain nesting Red-bellied Woodpecker. In 1981, Acadian Flycatcher moved into the woods beside a small pond north of the parking lot. Look for Louisiana Waterthrush, which has been reported at times.

When you leave the Sudden Tract, head east, back the way you came. This time turn right, south, at the first road 1 km from the parking lot. Drive south to the next road and turn left. You are now travelling east on the Brant/Waterloo County Line. Turn south, at the first road, and head down the hill into the valley again. The forest along these slopes is northern in character, with Alder Flycatcher, Brown Creeper, Winter Wren, Black-and-white Warbler, Chestnut-sided Warbler, Northern Waterthrush and White-throated Sparrow, all breeding west of the road. To the east, the drier forested slopes contain Yellow-throated Vireo and Blue-winged Warbler. The vireo is usually found in the drier mature forests of the valley. Both Red-eyed and Warbling Vireos are quite common, while Philadelphia and Solitary Vireos come as migrants only.

Travel south until you meet the pavement of the Glen Morris Road. Turn west and proceed away from Glen Morris for 2 km or until a gravel road appears on your left. Take it and head for the forested ridge in the distance. Go through the turns and stop just as the road crests and leaves the forest. You will find a gravel trail to hike on the east, heading down into the valley. You are now in the Pinehurst Lake–Spottiswood forest complex. It is an area full of rare southern plants and birds. After walking for 100 m down the trail, you will see a small path heading off to the left. Follow it to the Indian Lookout to obtain a view of the Grand River Valley. When you resume your walk down the gravel road, towards the skeet club in the valley, listen carefully. These forests contain breeding Acadian Flycatcher, Blue-Gray Gnatcatcher, Yellow-throated Vireo, Cerulean Warbler, Chestnut-sided Warbler and American Redstart. Yellow-billed Cuckoo and Yellow-breasted Chat have also been found along the continuation of this forest west of the township road. Pied-billed Grebe and Wood Duck are on the lakes along the ridge west of the road. Northern Bobwhite and Gray Partridge are sometimes found in nearby fields.

To return to Cambridge, either retrace your route or take a longer circle route. The directions for the latter are as follows. Continue south on the road you are now on until it stops at Highway 24A on the edge of Paris. Turn left onto 24A; travel down into the town centre. Turn left at the main intersection and cross the bridge over the Grand River. Turn left again at the first street and follow this road along the east side of the river all the way back into Cambridge.

The Crieff Bog — Puslinch Wetland is a rich and diverse swamp complex with a decidedly northern flavour. The coniferous swamp and other wetland types, marsh sedge meadow, spring and river, serve as the headwaters of the Fletcher Creek.

Scarlet Tanager

Drive south from 401 along Highway 6, 2 km from Morriston to the first road to the west. Take it and drive west to the first road; turn left onto this gravel road and head down towards the swamp. Turn left again into the conservation area parking lot at the edge of the forest. In 1981, 70 species of breeding birds were found in the immediate vicinity. North of the parking site, an old gravel pit has been set up as a long-term natural regeneration research project. North and east of the pit, many sparsely vegetated old fields contain large numbers of Grasshopper Sparrow. In addition, Savannah, Vesper, Chipping, Field and Song Sparrows are all found commonly. Upland Sandpiper occurs here and in the fields south of the railroad tracks. Watch for several pairs of Indigo Buntings that live along the hedgerows.

Immediately south of the parking lot, in various portions of the swamp, breeding birds to be found include Sharp-shinned and Broad-winged Hawks, Long-eared Owl, Brown Creeper, Alder Flycatcher, Black-and-white, Nashville and Mourning Warblers, Northern Waterthrush, White-throated Sparrow and Swamp Sparrow. In the deep swamp south of the YMCA camp, south of the county line on the next road south, Swainson's Thrush and Canada Warbler have been seen.

The wetlands are best known for their rare plants, including Showy Lady Slipper (hundreds), Yellow Lady Slipper, Bog Candle Orchid, Calopogon, Loesel's Twayblade, Round-leaved Sundew and Pink Pyrola.

East of the parking lot, a fine upland wood is easily reached by a well-marked walking trail. Birds of mature forest occur, such as Great Horned Owl, Hairy Woodpecker, Great Crested Flycatcher, Eastern Wood-Pewee, Blue Jay, Red-eyed Vireo, Wood Thrush, Ovenbird, Scarlet Tanager and Rose-breasted Grosbeak. In some years, Pine Warbler has been heard singing in the tallest White Pines.

In 1976 Ontario Hydro constructed the large powerline through the swamp, west of the road. Both Blue-winged and Golden-winged Warblers breed in the shrubbery under the powerline south of the railroad tracks. Veeries also sing in this area.

Walk the railroad tracks immediately south of the swamp to find the sedge meadow and marsh complex. This is a nesting area of Virginia Rail, American Woodcock and Common Snipe. In some years Sedge Wren have appeared in late June and stayed to breed. It is also the best area to see and hear Swamp Sparrow. Black-billed Cuckoos are frequent in the drier spots.

Purple Finch has occurred in the swamp forest south of the tracks and Eastern Phoebe has nested in the culvert under the tracks.

PAUL F. J. EAGLES

Niagara River

The Niagara River connects Lakes Erie and Ontario. At the world-renowned Niagara Falls, the river drops 54 m on the Canadian side and 56 m on the American, creating one of the outstanding spectacles on the continent. The Niagara River, which can be covered in one long day from Toronto, is a must for fall bird watchers. The principal attraction is the water birds which congregate from mid-October until late December. It is possible to observe almost all of the waterfowl species of eastern North America along with late-migrating shorebirds, loons and grebes. The chief item however is the gulls — up to twelve species have been recorded in a single day. The most abundant are the Glaucous, Iceland, Great Black-backed, Herring, Ring-billed and Bonaparte's. A very careful scan should produce Little, Franklin's and Thayer's Gulls. The keen-eyed birder can occasionally spot one of the rarer species: Lesser Black-backed Gull, Black-headed Gull, Black-legged Kittiwake and Sabine's Gull.

Birding Features

Begin the trip at Niagara-on-the-Lake, reached via Highway 55 leaving the Queen Elizabeth Way east of St. Catharines. As you enter Niagara-on-the-Lake, 55 turns into Mississauga Street and ends at Queen Street. Turn left here and continue along the lakeshore (Queen Street turns into Niagara Blvd.) until you reach Wilberforce Drive. The feeders along this street (especially at 8 Wilberforce) are excellent sites for Tufted Titmouse, Carolina Wren and the usual nuthatches, siskins, redpolls, goldfinches and woodpeckers. Return towards Niagara-on-the-Lake via Niagara Blvd. and Queen Street. On the way, go towards the lakeshore at every opportunity; you will eventually reach Front St. At the end of Front, a park overlooks the mouth of the Niagara River. This is the best place to check for ducks, including scoters, Oldsquaw and eiders. The one or two streets inland from Front St. are sure places to locate Northern Mockingbirds, House Finches, robins, redpolls, siskins and the occasional crossbill and Bohemian Waxwing. Return to Front St. and follow it to the east where it undergoes a name change or two. Turn to the left on any of several sidestreets and go to the river for further chances at scoters and eiders. In less than a kilometre you'll pass through Fort George and join up with Niagara Parkway. As you drive between Niagara-on-the-Lake and Queenston, stop occasionally and check the gulls that are feeding on the river.

Follow the sign pointing to "Village of Queenston" and leave the parkway. Drive along Queenston St. until you can turn left on Dumfries St., which changes into a gravel road as it approaches the river. At the small parking area, leave the car and follow the old roadway which makes its way along the edge of the gorge (upriver). The path will eventually lead to the outflows for the Sir Adam Beck Power Plants. Along the way check the smaller gulls for a Little, Franklin's or Black-headed Gull.

Back on the parkway, which can be reached by continuing through Queenston and turning right, the next stop is upstream, beyond and on the south side of the Sir Adam Beck Power Plants. A small parking area is provided on the left. Check the gulls that are feeding below for Glaucous, Iceland, Thayer's, Lesser Black-backed and others.

Continuing along the river, the next stop is the Niagara Parks Commission School of Horticulture. Parking is available across the road from the school and visitors are welcome to walk on the grounds and check the feeders.

The next stop is at the falls. Plenty of parking is available, along with several restaurants and washrooms. The area below the falls can be viewed from the walkway along the top of the gorge and from the dock of the *Maid-of-the-Mist*. This latter location is accessible by a roadway (marked private but used by many birders) behind the Princess Elizabeth building. The gulls in this section should be checked for Glaucous, Iceland, Lesser Black-backed and Thayer's, as well as Black-legged Kittiwake. Watch for loons and grebes, scoters, eiders and Barrow's Goldeneye on the river.

The area above the falls is accessible from a walkway along the river and a parking lot beside the Electrical Development Co. of Ontario building. This parking lot is directly across from some small wooded islands and a large stranded barge only 200 to 300 m above the lip of the falls. The parking lot adjacent to the building on the downstream side provides the best location for viewing the rocky ledges in the river. These resting places are often covered with gulls. Check them carefully for the rarer species. The gulls in the air should be studied especially for Little Gull. Sabine's Gull has also been seen from here. The shallows around the ledges are inhabited by numbers of dabblers of many species, including Gadwall, American Wigeon and a few Hooded Mergansers. The rocks in the middle immediately above the islands may also contain a Purple Sandpiper or other late-migrating shorebird.

Continuing upstream along the parkway, you arrive at the diversion dam (International Control Structure). Parking is available. Check the rafts of ducks on the river for scoters, Canvasback, Redhead and Ruddy Duck.

From this point, it is a pleasant trip along the parkway to Fort Erie. There are no exceptional stops, but birds are present throughout. You will pass rafts of waterfowl, and the edge of the river may host a Great Blue Heron or Belted Kingfisher. At Chippawa, where the Welland River flows into the Niagara River, scrutinize for Purple Sandpipers and other shorebirds. In late fall at Fort Erie, check the centre of the river below the Peace Bridge (between Fort Erie and Buffalo, N.Y.) for phalaropes.

Spend some time along the stretch of parkland where Lake Erie enters the Niagara River, inspecting the flocks of ducks and gulls; watch particularly for Sabine's Gull. Scoters should be present too.

MARTIN PARKER, CHIP WESELOH

Long Point

One of Ontario's most outstanding staging areas for migrating waterfowl, Long Point, is a 32-km sandspit jutting east into Lake Erie. The point lies about 80 km southwest of Hamilton or 120 km southwest of Toronto. Around 300 species of birds have been recorded. Waterfowl of all types, including thousands of Tundra Swan and Canvasback, pass through in spring. The rare Prothonotary Warbler nests here too. Bald Eagle and Piping Plover probably still breed here, one of the last spots where they do so in heavily industrialized southern Ontario. Over 440 species of plants have been reported, including some found nowhere else in Canada. Thirty-one species of mammal occur, including a large herd of White-tailed Deer. Turtles and snakes are abundant, with 5 species listed as threatened in Canada.

The barren point, formed over 4000 years ago, was a land largely avoided by the native peoples. Long Point was mentioned by missionaries wintering nearby in 1669–70. For the next hundred years the point lay across the path of trappers and traders. The first settler arrived in 1790. With the decimation of waterfowl in the early and mid-1800s, a group of concerned businessmen got together to preserve some habitat and hunting areas. They purchased 6000 ha on May 4, 1866 and by August had incorporated the Long Point Company.

The company preserved this land of sand dunes, meadows, ponds, marshes and forest for over a century. They recently donated most of their holdings to the federal government, to be managed by the Canadian Wildlife Service (cws). These areas are now protected as the Long Point National Wildlife Area. Two sections of wetlands at the base of the point had previously been purchased by the cws from other landowners and are now the Big Creek National Wildlife Area. The Ontario Ministry of Natural Resources manages Long Point Provincial Park, Lee Brown Waterfowl Management Area and the Crown Marsh.

Several nearby communities have commercial accommodation, including Simcoe and Port Dover to the northeast about a half hour away. Most visitors to Long Point prefer to camp in the provincial park, the Backus Conservation Area, or Turkey Point Provincial Park, all within fifteen minutes of the birding areas.

Detailed information is available from the Long Point Bird Observatory's headquarters in the Backus Conservation Area, located about 4 km north of Port Rowan. Inquiries should be directed to: Long Point Bird Observatory, P.O. Box 160, Port Rowan, Ontario N0E 1M0, Telephone: (519) 586-2909. Additional information is available in a report: *Breeding Birds of Long Point, Lake Erie*, by J. D. McCracken, M. S. W. Bradstreet and G. L. Holroyd, Canadian Wildlife Service Report, Series No. 44, 1981, 74 pp.

Birding Features

The point is still forming through processes of erosion and deposition of sand in an eastward direction. It consists of a series of ridges separated by swales and ponds, with extensive marshes in the lee of the spit. Succession from the lake inward begins with a sand beach and foredune which became colonized by grasses and cottonwoods. A marshy area and pond lie between the foredune and the next landward area. Juniper and cottonwoods come next, followed by White Cedar, Tamarack and White Pine. Succession culminates in an oak-maple climax forest on the oldest ridges. The point is the last remaining "wild" area in the heartland of southern Ontario industry.

Begin your trip in Port Rowan. Tundra Swan can sometimes be found at the dock from mid-March to mid-April. Ducks can often be spotted at the sewage lagoons. To reach them, drive west through Port Rowan; turn right on Mill Road (the first one after passing the water tower), drive 0.6 km and park at the gate to the fenced lagoons to your right.

Drive on to the Lee Brown Sanctuary with its numerous ducks and geese. Proceed west through Port Rowan; cross Highway 59 and continue west for 4.2 km on Regional Road 42 to the sanctuary on your left. Other spots good for water birds include the marshes adjacent to the Highway 59 causeway which links the town of Long Point Beach to the mainland south of Port Rowan. Check the ponds and marshes at the end of Hastings Drive as well. Proceed south on the causeway and turn west on the first road. While you are there, the pine plantation should be surveyed for other spring migrants. Beginning about the middle of June, the adjacent beach provides nesting habitat for spectacular numbers of turtles.

Areas in and around the provincial park at the end of Highway 59 often support large numbers of migrants. Go to the small pine plantation along Lighthouse Crescent, the last road on your left before the provincial park. Warblers of all types occur here, together with a large assortment of other birds. On suitable days in the fall, the provincial park provides good opportunities to view migrating hawks, particularly Sharp-shinned Hawk and Northern Harrier.

Although Long Point is best known for its concentrations of migrants, it supports many breeding species, some of which are rare, threatened, or endangered in Ontario. Look for nesting Bald Eagle and Piping Plover. The marshes support Ontario's largest breeding population of Forster's Tern, as well as King Rail and probably Little Gull.

At the base of the point, the Hahn Woods host Canada's second-largest breeding population of Prothonotary Warbler, as well as nesting geese, ducks, Red-headed Woodpecker, gnatcatchers and vireos. This wooded swamp is owned by the Canadian Wildlife Service and can be checked by driving 7 km west from Highway 59 along Regional Road 42 past Port Royal. Park at the roadside and enter the swamp along the border of one of the gullies. Don't cut across the farmer's field! Come equipped with chest-waders and mosquito repellent.

If time permits, it is always rewarding to take a walk in the Backus Woods, a Carolinean forest, where you may find nesting Pileated Wood-pecker and Cerulean and Pine Warblers. Drive 8 km north along Highway 59 from Port Rowan; turn east along Highway 24 for 1.7 km and exit into a well-hidden parking lot in the woods on your right. Follow any of the hiking trails; bring your rubber boots.

Your final stop should be a drive (or walk) through the St. Williams Forestry Station. From the Backus Woods, drive east for 2 km along

Highway 24 and turn left at the South Walsingham east 1/4 line. Follow this road for 1.4 km and turn right down a sandy trail until you find one of the many interesting Jeep paths cut through the pine plantations. It might be best to walk in as driving conditions are poor. Look for nesting Broad-winged Hawk, Red-breasted Nuthatch, Hermit Thrush, Pine Warbler, Prairie Warbler and Grasshopper Sparrow. In spring, just after dusk, listen for Whip-poor-will and Chuck-will's-widow.

JON D. McCRACKEN

London, Sarnia and St. Thomas

London, lying 150 km southwest of Toronto, is the centre of a rich farming area, at the more northerly limit of the Carolina forest. The Thames River and deciduous forests attract a wide variety of birdlife. South, on Lake Erie, Hawk Cliff witnesses thousands of raptors every year. An extensive series of walking trails leads through the parklands along the river. For more information, contact Pete Read at (519) 472-2887.

Birding Features
Walking Trails. These trails along the river contain typical birds of the forest and floodplain of southern Ontario. Bridges that give access to the trails include Adelaide Street, Highbury North, Richmond North, Guy Lombardo and Oxford.

Gibbons, Springbank and Greenway Parks. These parks are worth visiting for woodland birds. The Greenway Pollution Treatment Plant lies near Greenway Park; it keeps the river open for much of the winter. Ducks, gulls, other late-season migrants, and sometimes swallows and warblers, are noted near the plant in winter. Consult your city map for specific access.

Walker or Westminster Ponds. The water occurs on the east side of Wellington Road South, just north of Southdale Road, behind the tourist information booth. Scan for House Wren, Gray Catbird, thrushes and warblers.

Byron Bog. The site lies off Oxford Street just west of Hyde Park Road. The bog is fenced off, with access through a locked gate. Telephone the London Parks Department at (519) 473-2500 for permission. In spring and summer look for woodpeckers and a variety of warblers. In winter the Three-toed Woodpecker and winter finches are sometimes here.

Komoka. The area lies about 8 km west of London on Middlesex County Road 14. Camp KeeMoke lies about 2 km west of Komoka. The camp, with Oak-Pine woods and a spring-fed stream, has two entrances: about 2 km west of Komoka on County Road 14, or at the Wonnacott farm 0.5 km further west on No. 14, at the southwest corner of the woods. Obtain permission here from the owner or farm resident. Permission to enter may be obtained from H. Wales, at (519) 471-4277, or P. Read, at (519) 472-2887. Check for Red-bellied Woodpecker, Northern Mockingbird, Yellow-throated Vireo and Louisiana Waterthrush.

Komoka Swamp, with its special variety of birdlife, may be found by driving about 3 km west of Komoka on No. 14 to the Oriole Park Road, Caradoc/Lobo Townline; travel north just beyond the Oriole Park Camp-grounds. The bush lies on either side of the road. Look and listen for Willow Flycatcher, Gray Catbird, Blue-winged Warbler and Yellow-breasted Chat.

Strathroy Sewage Lagoons. Go west from London on Middlesex County Road 14, Commissioners Road west to Mt. Bridge, for about 14 km. Turn right at the lights on Highway 81 and travel about 15 km to Strathroy. Turn left onto Middlesex County Road 39, which is Metcalfe at the lights but changes into Albert as you go west. Continue west on No. 39 to the town limits and turn left onto the first road past the Strathmere Lodge complex. Continue along the road; cross over the tracks to the second gate on the left. You may scan the lagoons from the car or stop and look them over from the viewing stand. Particularly watch for phalarope, Stilt Sandpiper, yellowlegs and peeps during migration when the water is low.

Dougal Murray's Woods. Access is gained from Highway 2 west of London. At about 5 km west of Melbourne, take the 8th sideroad (Ekfrid) south for 6.5 km. The woods are at the end of the road, just past Dougal Murray's home. Contact him at (519) 289-5856, or his son, David, at R.R. 1 Melbourne, for permission. While on the 8th sideroad, at the second concession road south watch and listen for Northern Bobwhite and Upland Sandpiper. At the woods look for Pileated, Red-bellied and Red-headed Woodpeckers.

Sarnia Lighthouse. The site occurs in Sarnia, west about 85 km from London. On Highway 402 drive to the last turnoff at Bridge Street. Follow it to St. Clare and continue north across Michigan Avenue to Victoria Street. Turn left onto Victoria to Fort Street, where you turn right. Proceed north to the water's edge. This spot is good for observing loons, geese, gulls and jaegers during the fall, especially in October and November with north winds.

Hawk Cliff. This spot is reached by driving south of London on Highway 4 through St. Thomas to Union (about 25+ km from London). At Union take Elgin County Road 27 east to County Road 22, the first crossroads. Take 22 south to Elgin 24; straight ahead, the unpaved road leads to the parking area overlooking Lake Erie. The Ministry of Natural Resources operates a hawk-viewing weekend in late September. The best times are between September 15 and 20. You should be able to spot falcons, accipiters, buteos and eagles in large numbers. In early October, Blue Jays may pass at the rate of 500 per minute. The nearby woods usually abound in migrating jays and warblers.

PETE READ

Rondeau Provincial Park and Nearby Spots

Rondeau, a projection of land into Lake Erie, contains the largest stand of southern hardwood left in Ontario. Some 324 species of birds have been recorded here, with 128 found breeding. Come here to find an Acadian Flycatcher and a Prothonotary Warbler plus numerous land and water birds. Look for thousands of Broad-winged Hawks on migration and other birds of prey, plus an excellent potpourri of warblers, including Worm-eating, Northern Parula, Cerulean, Kentucky and Hooded. Unique plants are also an attraction, with almost 800 species recorded.

The 4816-ha park lies southeast of Windsor-Detroit, 12 km off Highway 401 on Interchange 12. There are opportunities to boat, canoe, fish, camp, hike and cycle; there are also 8 km of bathing beach. Commercial accommodation may be found in nearby Chatham, Blenheim and other summer resorts.

The park has a major interpretation program and a variety of natural history displays. Write: Park Naturalist, Rondeau Provincial Park, R.R. 1, Morpeth, Ontario N0P 1X0, Telephone: (519) 674-5405 or (519) 674-3169.

Birding Features

The southern hardwood forest, extensive marsh and shallow harbour make Rondeau a must for active birders, both during migration in April-May, September-October and the nesting season of late May and June.

Bates Marsh, with water and marsh on both sides of the road, lies 4 km south of Highway 3 on Highway 51. Stop and scan the wet areas for water birds, especially Mallard, teal and herons. At low water levels, shorebirds use the mudflats on migration. Look for Killdeer, yellowlegs, Dunlin and dowitcher. Continue another km to the park.

About 1 km inside the park, look for the picnic ground. The Marsh Trail entrance sits just off the main road on the right. This 7-km biking/hiking trail begins by winding through the edge of an oak forest bordering on the marsh. During migration, numerous warbler species are spotted. The marsh, at this point, is usually not frozen in early spring and thus attracts various species of waterfowl and shorebirds. The southern half of the trail provides excellent chances to spot Great Blue and Green-backed Herons, Black-crowned Night-Herons, Least and American Bitterns, the park's resident Bald Eagle, Virginia Rail, Sora, Forster's, Common and Black Tern and Marsh Wren.

To reach the Rondeau walking trail, go back to the main road and south for another 1.4 km. This trail takes you through a beech-maple forest, with spicebush understory. Warblers and other woodland birds are common in spring. Reconnoitre for nesting Wood Duck, Black-billed Cuckoo, Red-headed Woodpecker nesting along the western side of the trail, Red-eyed and Yellow-throated Vireos, Common Yellowthroat and Northern Cardinal.

The Tulip Tree Trail begins beside the interpretive centre. Continue south on the main road for 2.3 km to the gravel road and follow it to the centre. The trail penetrates a pine-oak forest and then a beech-maple stand. In addition, there are several sloughs that are crossed via boardwalks. Check out the trees for Tulip, Sassafras, Shagbark, Hickory and Black Walnut. Nesting birds include Wood Duck, Hooded Merganser, Yellow-billed and Black-billed Cuckoos, and Great Crested Flycatcher; Winter Wren have nested; Prothonotary Warblers nest in the adjacent sloughs. A Pileated Woodpecker is often seen or heard.

Around the interpretive centre look and listen for American Woodcock, Whip-poor-will and Chuck-will's-widow. In winter check the feeders for various woodpeckers, including Red-bellied, and for nuthatches, sparrows and winter finches.

Take the lakeshore road from the interpretive centre south to the entrance of the South Point Trail. The hike leads you through an open Black Oak forest, to the shore of Lake Erie and then north through a beech-maple forest. Watch for an Eastern Phoebe nesting on the buildings near the trail entrance. In mid-May watch for rare southern migrant warblers, including Worm-eating, Northern Parula, Yellow-throated, Cerulean, Kentucky, Connecticut and Hooded. Birds that nest include Great Horned Owl and Eastern Screech-Owl, which resides permanently; an Acadian Flycatcher is most often found along this trail and makes Rondeau one of its Canadian strongholds; Brown Creeper, Blue-gray Gnatcatcher and Wood Thrush are typical along the trail; warblers include Prothonotary, Cerulean and Yellow-breasted Chat; Indigo Bunting are also present; open grassy areas and edges often have sparrows, including Henslow's, Field and Lincoln's, with wet areas containing Swamp Sparrow.

The South Point Trail serves as access to the South Park beach. Here you may find thousands of migrating waterfowl. Shorebirds and gulls are also numerous. Look for Herring, Ring-billed and Bonaparte's Gulls. Rare species such as Common Black-headed, Franklin's and Little Gulls frequently appear.

The Morpeth Cliffs are great to view waterfowl and migrating hawks in the fall. To reach these cliffs, return to the park gate on Highway 51 and go straight onto County Road 17 for 5.5 km. Park along the road at the point where it turns north to Morpeth.

P. ALLEN WOODCLIFFE

Point Pelee National Park

Two major migration flyways intersect at Point Pelee, making spring and fall migration spectacular. Of the over 360 species noted, about 90 stay to nest. On a good day in spring, at the peak of migration, you may spot 25 to 30 different wood warblers and 6 species of vireos. In autumn, thousands of Monarch Butterflies pause here on their way south. Come here to observe a spectacular succession of abundant wildflowers, including Canada's only wild hibiscus, the Pink-flowered Swamp Rose Mallow, Prickly Pear Cactus and such shrubs as Hop and Spicebush.

This southernmost extension of mainland Canada comprises 1566 ha of national park, with most of the point farther south than the northern boundary of California. Windsor and Detroit, with all transportation links and visitor amenities, are about 50 km to the northwest on Highway 3. No individual campsites are available within the park, but several commercial campgrounds operate in the area. Two group campsites are available for booking within the park. Motels are found at Leamington and other nearby communities.

An active naturalist program is provided at the visitor/interpretive centre. Current listings of unusual sightings are posted there. Write: The Chief Park Naturalist, Point Pelee National Park, R.R. 1, Leamington, Ontario N8H 3V4, Telephone: (519) 326-3204.

Birding Features

The moderating effect of Lake Erie provides the point with a climate that is representative of areas farther south than its latitude suggests. The considerable diverse habitats, including woodlands, 1000 ha of marshlands, and open meadows, attract 60 per cent of the bird species found in Canada. The visitor centre is the point of origin for the Nature Trail, the trail through Tilden's Woods and out to the East Beach, and for the train to the tip. Be there at the crack of dawn for the best birding. Watch the spectacular spring aggregations of Red-breasted Mergansers in their tens of thousands. Various plovers and peeps, together with Ruddy Turnstone, Spotted Sandpiper and Sanderling can be seen here too.

In the fall, the tip is the launching pad for migrating accipiters, Peregrine Falcon, American Kestrel and other diurnal raptors. You may spot a Parasitic Jaeger, particularly when there are northwest winds.

The woodlands between the tip and the visitor centre are the most productive spots for passerines on migration. Blue-gray Gnatcatcher and Orchard Oriole are common in the hardwoods near the tip. Many warblers and vireos are present in spring. The Hackberry-dominated woods in the vicinity of the concession stand near the tip are particularly productive.

The Nature Trail provides access to the maple swamps and Red Cedar groves in the south-central portion of the park. Carolina Wren, Prothonotary Warbler and Louisiana Waterthrush occur in the wetland forests; the Red Cedar savannah and scrub support Chipping Sparrow, Prairie Warbler and Yellow-breasted Chat. Worm-eating, Kentucky, Hooded and Cerulean Warblers are found regularly in the strip of forest between the savannah and the West Beach in the spring. Concentrations of Northern Oriole and Scarlet Tanager are regular along the trail in May. In early winter, Hermit Thrush and Yellow-rumped Warbler find shelter in the Red Cedar savannahs.

Tilden's Woods provide similar birding to that along the Nature Trail. In addition, Buttonbush sloughs contain Green-backed Heron, rails, Marsh Wren and Common Yellowthroat.

North of the visitor centre, Ander's Field and DeLaurier Parking Area provide excellent habitat for sparrows and other grassland birds. Sedge Wren and Grasshopper and Henslow's Sparrows are regular. Common breeding birds here include Bobolink, Eastern Meadowlark, Red-winged Blackbird, American Goldfinch, and Savannah, Field and Song Sparrows.

Continuing north, the Marsh Boardwalk offers access to the extensive Pelee marshes. In the spring and summer, Least and American Bitterns are

T.W.THORMIN/82

Bobolink

common, as are Virginia Rail, Sora and Common Moorhen. The early morning and dusk periods are best for visiting the marsh.

Particularly during the spring, it is worthwhile to stop at some of the picnic areas along the west beach, especially those just south of the park gate. The woods here are narrow, forming a bottleneck for northbound warblers and other passerines, and such rarities as Bewick's Wren, Summer Tanager and Blue Grosbeak.

Immediately north of Point Pelee's park gate, a network of roads traverses the reclaimed agricultural land north and east of the park. When damp, these fields, known as the Onion Fields, provide good habitat for shorebirds; gulls roost here. The Onion Fields are the most reliable areas for Buff-breasted Sandpiper in late August and September; Lesser Golden-Plovers are regular visitors too.

Approximately 5 km northeast of the park boundary is Hillman (Stein's)

Marsh, an excellent area for waders and waterfowl. Great Egret, Least Bittern, King Rail and Forster's Tern are regular summer birds. A wet woodland along the concession road at the north end of the marsh has had a pair of Prothonotary Warblers in recent years.

About 3 km north of Hillman Marsh along the lake, Wheatley Harbour is a good place to look for gulls and waterfowl. Laughing Gull has been found here among aggregations of Bonaparte's Gulls. Across the road from the harbour, a channel and adjacent woodlot serve as a gathering spot for Black-crowned Night-Heron; Yellow-crowned Night-Heron has also been found here. The Great Egret is common. On a good day in the fall, thousands of migrating Blue Jays follow the lakeshore.

WILLIAM J. CRINS

Georgian Bay Islands National Park

The islands in Georgian Bay, with temperatures buffered by surrounding waters of Lake Huron, lie in the transition between northern Canadian Shield and southern deciduous forest. Over 200 species of birds have been recorded with 75 to 100 nesting.

Georgian Bay Islands National Park is one of the more recently established havens in our country. Thirty-five species of amphibians and reptiles provide the natural history highlight for the islands. Otter, an occasional Fisher, Marten, Black Bear and Moose add to the experience.

The sixty-seven islands making up the park are split into two segments. The east group lies over 100 km north of Toronto off Highways 400 and 69 and Muskoka County Road 5. The western group of islands is situated off the north end of the Bruce Peninsula, with access from Tobermory at the end of Highway 6. In summer, a water taxi or private boat is the only means of entry. In winter, cross-country skis, snowshoes or snowmobiles are used to cross the frozen bay. Sixteen different campsites are provided on the islands. Commercial accommodation may be obtained on the mainland. An interpretive program is offered. Write: The Interpretive Service, Georgian Bay Islands National Park, Box 28, Honey Harbour, Ontario P0E 1E0, Telephone: (705) 756-2415.

Wye Marsh. On your way to the park stop in at the nearby Canadian Wildlife Service interpretive centre at Wye Marsh near Midland. Naturalists are there to help you.

Bruce Peninsula. Straight west from Midland across Nottawasaga Bay, the Bruce Peninsula should be visited as part of your trip to the western group of islands in the national park. The "Bruce," with its rugged northern cliffs on the east side and coniferous forests adjacent to a gently sloping west shoreline, provides habitat for a wide selection of birds. It contains one of North America's finest displays of rare wildflowers, ferns and orchids.

Birding Features

Beausoleil Island, the largest of the group and the centre for interpretive activities, lies just off Honey Harbour. The island's west side contains a very complex mixed forest of ash, aspen, hemlock, cedar and fir. The most common nesting birds include Barred Owl, Red-breasted Nuthatch and Winter Wren. Twelve species of warbler have been recorded as nesting, including Magnolia, Black-throated Green and Canada.

The central southern section of Beausoleil Island includes a dense, closed canopy hardwood forest. At least 5 species of woodpecker nest, including Pileated, Red-bellied and Red-headed. Six species of flycatcher are found regularly, including the Acadian Flycatcher, which has extended its range considerably north to this spot. Over 12 species of warbler are present, including the Cerulean. Three vireos are here too, including the Yellow-throated.

The north end of the island consists of rugged Canadian Shield habitat with scrubby vegetation such as White Pine, White Oak and ground juniper. In spring and early summer, common sounds of a Brown Thrasher, Yellow-rumped and Prairie Warblers, and White-throated and Song Sparrows are everywhere. Thermal air currents along the bay area are used by Red-tailed, Red-shouldered and Broad-winged Hawks, as well as by Turkey Vultures.

The waters and shoreline around and between the islands regularly host Great Blue Heron, Mallard, mergansers, Osprey, Spotted Sandpiper, Herring and Ring-billed Gulls, Common and Caspian Terns and Belted Kingfisher. An occasional Double-crested Cormorant, Green-backed Heron and Black-crowned Night-Heron is also noted.

LESLIE JOYNT

Algonquin Provincial Park

One of the largest (754,312 ha) provincial parks in Canada, Algonquin lies in the transition zone between coniferous forests of the north and broad-leafed trees of south central Ontario. Spruce Grouse, Gray Jay and Boreal Chickadee cohabit with Brown Thrasher, Wood Thrush, Northern Oriole, Scarlet Tanager and Indigo Bunting. Indeed, there are 237 species on the park's checklist, with 128 known to have lived in the park and 89 species considered common. In some sites, more than 100 species nest within a 10-km^2 block. Moose, White-tailed Deer, Black Bear, Wolf, Beaver and Otter occur.

Indians roamed this area for at least some four thousand years. Loggers arrived in the 1840s, drawn by the magnificent stands of Red and White Pine. During the felling of trees, they left debris that fed massive forest fires. The park was established in 1893, after decades of this devastation. Logging continues today with some 550,000 trees felled annually, with forest management to insure regeneration.

The park lies 193 km north of Toronto via Highway 11 to Huntsville, then Highway 60 east for 43 km to the west gate. The east gate lies 5 km from Whitney and is reached by travelling north on Highway 127 from Bancroft or west along Highway 60 from Barry's Bay.

A variety of campgrounds and some private lodges occur within the park. Pick up guidebooks on special themes, maps and brochures at either gate. You may also obtain them, and an excellent publication, *Birds of Algonquin Provincial Park* (not free), which includes an annotated check-list, by writing: Ministry of Natural Resources, Algonquin Provincial Park, Box 219, Whitney, Ontario K0J 2M0, Telephone: (705) 633-5572.

Birding Features

Almost all of the species of birds recorded for Algonquin can be found along the 56-km Highway 60 corridor between the west and east gates. There are ten nature trails along the route.

Begin at the west gate. Proceed for 3 km to the Oxtongue River Picnic Grounds. Gray Jay and Common Raven can be seen here, as well as Red-eyed Vireo, Chestnut-sided Warbler and White-throated Sparrow. The Whiskey Rapids Trail occurs at Km 7.2. The Belted Kingfisher is regular, as are Least Flycatcher, Ruby-crowned Kinglet, and several warblers including Black-and-white, Nashville, Magnolia and American Redstart. On the Hardwood Lookout Trail at Km 13.8 search for Eastern Wood-Pewee, Red-eyed Vireo, Black-throated Blue Warbler and Ovenbird.

Check your gas tank at the Portage Store at Km 14.1, to fill up if necessary.

Continue to the Hardwood Hill Picnic Grounds at Km 16.7. Directly across the highway, a logging road which heads north is open to the public. The road passes by Source Lake, swings west along an abandoned rail line and eventually joins the road to Arrowhon Pines Lodge. Park the car; a hike along this road for about 2 km should produce Black-billed Cuckoo, Eastern Wood-Pewee, Winter Wren, and several species of vireos and warblers, including Mourning. Upon reaching the railway bed, follow it along the edge of a couple of marshes, West Rose Lake and Wolf Howl Pond. You could locate Wood and Ring-necked Ducks, Hooded Merganser, Spruce Grouse, Black-backed Woodpecker, Alder and Olive-sided Flycatchers, Red-breasted Nuthatch, Brown Creeper, Swainson's Thrush, Cape May Warbler, Rusty Blackbird and Lincoln's Sparrow. On a night walk in early spring you may hear Great Horned, Barred and Northern Saw-whet Owls calling.

Stop at the museum at Km 20 to check out the exhibits and talk to the naturalist. Chimney Swift, Common Flicker, Pileated Woodpecker, Yellow-bellied Sapsucker, Eastern Phoebe, Eastern Wood-Pewee, Northern Parula, Scarlet Tanager and Indigo Bunting can be found near the buildings.

A very good spot, the Mew Lake Campground area, is at Km 30.6. Watch as you drive by the old airfield at Lake of Two Rivers on the way to the campground. At the airfield, American Woodcock, Common Snipe and Common Nighthawk are frequently heard and seen in spring. Early to mid-May, search for the relatively common Sharp-shinned and Broad-winged Hawks, with the occasional Northern Goshawk, Northern Harrier and Osprey. In both spring and fall, Horned Lark, Water Pipit and Lapland

Longspur stop here on migration. During the nesting season from May to early July, breeding birds on the airstrip include Killdeer, Bobolink and Savannah and Vesper Sparrows. A hike around the edge of the strip should flush Ruffed Grouse, Eastern Kingbird, Gray Catbird and Brown Thrasher.

The trailer sanitation station at Km 35.6 should produce Chestnut-sided, Mourning and Canada Warblers, Rose-breasted Grosbeak and Chipping Sparrow close to the station. At the next trail, at Km 39.7, listen for thrushes. Wood Thrush and Veery are heard near the start, with American Robin and Hermit Thrush by the lookout.

The Spruce Bog Boardwalk at Km 42.5 is one of the most reliable sites for Spruce Grouse, particularly in April and May. Look for Gray Jay, Black-capped and Boreal Chickadees, Red-breasted Nuthatch, Hermit Thrush, Golden-crowned and Ruby-crowned Kinglets, and Nashville and Magnolia Warblers. The Sunday Creek Bog could produce American Bittern, American Black and Ring-necked Ducks, Common Merganser, Belted Kingfisher, Black-backed Woodpecker, Yellow-bellied Flycatcher, Cape May Warbler, Common Yellowthroat and Lincoln's and Swamp Sparrows.

At Km 46.3 take the road to Opeongo Lake through spruce bogs and marshes. You might spot Great Blue Heron, American Bittern, Wood Duck, Olive-sided and Alder Flycatchers, Swainson's Thrush, Rusty Blackbird, Purple Finch and Lincoln's Sparrow.

The same trip in winter can be very productive for Evening and Pine Grosbeaks, Common Redpoll, Pine Siskin and American Goldfinch. In some winters both Red-winged and White-winged Crossbills are present.

RICHARD KNAPTON, RON TOZER

Timmins to Jellicoe

Northern Ontario is famous for its mining communities, friendly people and good representation of northern birds, such as Great Gray Owl, three-toed woodpeckers and numerous warblers. With two main highways looping through the country, a visitor can spend an enjoyable week in late June viewing birds, spectacular floral displays and Moose.

These lands were roamed by Indians for thousands of years. The rivers and lakes were the routes for them and for the fur traders travelling west. The railway was built after the discovery of minerals in the very early 1900s. Roads followed in the 1960s.

Timmins is an easy two-day drive north of Toronto by Highways 11 and 101, through North Bay. The good birding season of June also is the time for mosquitoes and blackflies. Commercial accommodation is available in various communities. Camping sites are fairly numerous at provincial parks and several private resorts. Stock up on food and other supplies at Timmins. Gas stations are few, located only at the major communities. Carry a spare gas can, extra supplies and a warm sleeping bag.

There is very little literature available on the area. Write: Timmins District Office, Ministry of Natural Resources, 896 Riverside Drive, Timmins, Ontario P4N 3W2. Ask them to refer your letter to other district offices if the information you request is not in their jurisdiction.

Birding Features

The Ramada Inn at Timmins makes a good base from which to survey the surroundings. Northern Harrier, Common Snipe and Alder Flycatcher fly over the fields behind the parking lot; Lincoln's Sparrow sing nearby. To explore, begin at or before dawn at Kamiskotia Lake, on the west side of Timmins, about 15 km northwest of the inn on Highway 576. The dump, 1 km north of the lake, should have a serenading Hermit Thrush, Mourning Warbler and Dark-eyed Junco. A Common Loon may call. While Yellow-bellied Sapsucker drums, Winter Wren sings its silvery cascade and Northern Waterthrush calls from the burn at the turn in the road. South of the lake, a few Hermit Thrushes, numerous Swainson's Thrushes and a Veery will sing. A dozen different warbler species twitter along the route, with Tennessee, Nashville, Magnolia, Ovenbird and Mourning being the most common.

Slip up to Cochrane, north about 80 km on Highway 11. Ask the local people for directions to Lillabelle Lake, which lies 5 km north and east of town. In 1957 the following birds were reported: Common Loon, Red-necked Grebe, American Bittern, Mallard, American Black Duck, Blue-winged Teal, Ring-necked Duck, Lesser Scaup, Ruddy Duck, Osprey and Solitary Sandpiper.

Highway 101 will take you west to Foleyet. About halfway along this road from Timmins watch for Half-way Restaurant. A short distance farther west, look for the bog where dead trees stand across the road from a big sand bank. A Black-backed Woodpecker nested here. About 16 km east of Foleyet you'll see the Mooseland Resort, with a few rooms and meal service. Accommodation is limited, so book ahead.

Continue west and stop regularly to listen for from 15 to 17 warbler species. Rarities include Northern Parula and Wilson's Warbler. Listen for Olive-sided Flycatcher, Red-breasted Nuthatch, Ruby-crowned Kinglet, Evening Grosbeak and Lincoln's Sparrow.

Continue west on Highway 101 beyond Foleyet for about 10 km, watching for Merlin. At the large burn area with skeletons of tall birch reaching above the new growth of cherries and birch, locate the bridge across the narrows of Burntwood Lake. You should be able to spot Common Loon families; listen to the Hermit Thrush; list the different warblers and Lincoln's Sparrow. Farther west, you'll pass The Shoals Provincial Park and across the Prairie Bee River, where the variety of marsh life is unequalled in this part of Ontario.

Approaching Wawa, watch for the spectacular canyon that contains an outlier population of Indigo Buntings, together with Winter Wren, Ruby-crowned Kinglet and Northern Waterthrush. Stop at the Husky gas station and restaurant about 10 km north of Wawa on Highway 17; listen and scan for birds.

At White River there are several motels along Highway 17. Those on the south side of the road have marshes with Blue-winged Teal; perhaps Ring-necked Duck; Common Snipe displaying; and Lincoln's Sparrow singing. The Shell restaurant overlooks a small lake with a variety of waterfowl and

Cliff Swallows for you to watch while breakfasting. A small colony of Bobolink adds to the effect.

Between White Lake Provincial Park and Highway 614 you will find Gloria's Motel, a bit quieter than those at White River. The forest around Gloria's and the lake across the highway south of the motel make for good birding. Turn north onto 614 and continue towards Manitouwadge.

Manitouwadge contains one motel of the same name. Reserve in advance. A Barred Owl has been spotted across the lake north of town; about 10 km north of town by the side of the Industrial Road, check for a Great Gray Owl, usually in young growth following a burn or clear cut.

This is the road for woodpeckers. Watch for Common Flicker, Pileated Woodpecker, Yellow-bellied Sapsucker, or Hairy Woodpecker, all drumming and nesting. A nesting pair of Black-backed Woodpeckers has been noted at the marsh with dead firs, about 20 km north of the town along the Industrial Road. At this spot also search for Ring-necked Duck, Hooded Merganser, Rusty Blackbird and Olive-sided Flycatcher.

Turn west onto Highway 11 to Longlac. There are several good motels both here and farther on at Geraldton. Longlac, at the north end of the very long Long Lake, sits by an extensive marsh on the north side of the highway. At this point a bridge spans a narrow neck of water. Stop for American Bittern, Black Tern and other marsh birds. Late May is the time for shorebirds on the beach on the south side of the highway. Try driving north on the side road about 3 km east of Longlac off Highway 11. You may spot a Great Gray Owl from 5 to 10 km north on this road. Hermit and Swainson's Thrushes are common along this road.

Go back to Highway 11 and drive east to Klotz Lake Provincial Park, about 20 km east of Longlac. There are good camping facilities here. This is about the wildest section along Highway 11, a "hot" area with good chances for Spruce Grouse, a scolding Solitary Sandpiper, Bonaparte's Gull, Black-backed Woodpecker, Yellow-bellied Flycatcher, Bohemian Waxwing, Bay-breasted Warbler, Wilson's Warbler, Rusty Blackbird, Evening Grosbeak, Purple Finch and Pine Siskin.

Now proceed west towards Geraldton. Beyond Suckle Lake, a few km west of Longlac, look along the north side of the road for the small clearing and longhouse by the lake and an extensive alder swamp. Cliff Swallows nest under the eaves of the house; listen for a Yellow-bellied Flycatcher and Connecticut Warbler near the alders.

The Park Bay View Motel, a few km east of Geraldton, lies across a small lake from a good camping area. Nearby lakes boast a good variety of waterfowl and the wet spots approaching Geraldton are good for shorebirds in season.

Farther on at Jellicoe, stay at the Cedar Shores Motel, which is quiet between arrival and departure of aircraft. The nearby lakes contain a variety of waterfowl, including Common Goldeneye. Mourning Warblers are common along the highway. There are northern outliers of populations of Scarlet Tanager and Rose-breasted Grosbeak.

DR. J. MURRAY SPEIRS

Marathon: North Shore Lake Superior

Lake Superior's north shore, at Marathon, offers opportunities to spot both species of three-toed woodpecker as well as large numbers of Rough-legged Hawks and a wide diversity of shorebirds on migration. In June a vast collection of orchids is waiting to be found.

Marathon lies 302 km east of Thunder Bay on the Trans-Canada Highway 17. Pukaskwa National Park sits to the southeast and Neys Provincial Park to the west. Both parks harbour remnant herds of Woodland Caribou. Several campgrounds are available along the highway. A variety of motels occur in town and along the highway. All services are available, as many hunters and fishermen use the area regularly. Topographic maps are available in Marathon. Ask for map 42 D/gw Marathon and 42 D/15 Coldwell.

Birding Features

The most productive area in town lies on either side of the CPR line, southward for about 3.2 km to Escott Ridge. These grassy meadows, birch, willow and poplar stands are bounded on the west by the lake shore and on the east by a high glacial ridge. Survey carefully in fall for a mix of passerine species and such rarities as Townsend's Solitaire, Blue-winged Warbler and Cassin's Sparrow. The Peninsula Golf Course and high school playing fields are particularly good for shorebirds such as Buff-breasted Sandpiper.

The 60-m-high Escott Ridge is a good place to spot migrating birds in fall. Access to the top lies along the trail just west of the scree slope in an adjacent forest area. The commanding view provides an excellent opportunity to watch tens of thousands of winter finches on their way west and numbers of hawks, including hundreds of Rough-legged.

Day tripping out of Marathon is suggested. The two largest stretches of continuous sand beach on the Canadian north shore of Lake Superior are accessible from here: the Pic River mouth and Neys Provincial Park. Both areas also provide habitat for resident Spruce Grouse, Northern Goshawk, both three-toed woodpeckers, Gray Jay and Boreal Chickadee. The beaches host migrating shorebirds.

To reach the mouth of the Pic River, go 6.4 km south of Marathon to Highway 617 (Heron Bay Road); continue south 10.4 km through part of the Heron Bay Indian Reserve to the mouth of the river. The bridge over the Pic River, connecting Heron Bay Road to the north end of Pukaskwa National Park, lies 1.6 km north of the mouth of the river. The actual river mouth is partly owned by the American Can Company but access is not restricted. However, please respect private property.

Neys Provincial Park lies about 24 km west from Marathon on Highway 17. Here you should search for resident Spruce Grouse, Northern Goshawk, both species of three-toed woodpecker, Gray Jay and Boreal Chickadee. In late-May and June the woods are full of thrushes, vireos and warblers. Fall migration may bring such rarities as Summer Tanager and Western Kingbird.

The two abandoned fishing communities of Jackfish and Coldwell act as bird oases, with unique habitats foreign to most of the typical Superior shoreline. These include sand beach with adjacent long-grass meadows and open scrub deciduous growth. These sites provide excellent foraging and staging opportunities for migrating sparrows. Many stray species, including Northern Wheatear, have also stopped here on their travels.

To reach Coldwell, drive on Highway 17 about 4 km east of the Neys Provincial Park gate, to the east side of the Coldwell peninsula. To reach Jackfish, drive west along 17, watching for the Prairie and Steel rivers. About 3 km west of the Steel River bridge, look for a road leading southwest to the CPR line and the timber loading yard. Leave the car in the yard and walk about 1.2 km west along the tracks to the site of Jackfish.

J. ROBERT NESBIT

Rainy River/Lake of the Woods

The Rainy River/Lake of the Woods region is an area unique to birding in Ontario. This small parcel of cultivated land, sandwiched between the boreal forests of Manitoba, Minnesota and Ontario, attracts western birds in numbers and variety found nowhere else in the province. Black-billed Magpie, Sharp-tailed Grouse, Western Meadowlark and Brewer's Blackbird can be found in the scrubby pastures. Le Conte's Sparrow, Sedge Wren, Sandhill Crane and Yellow Rail frequent the large marshes. American White Pelican and Double-crested Cormorant nest on isolated islands on Lake of the Woods, as have Piping Plover and even American Avocet.

To reach the area, drive west from Ft. Frances on Highway 11 or south from Kenora on Highway 71, which meets 11 east of Rainy River. Topographic maps Rainy River 52D/15 and 52D/10 Scale 1:50,000 will help. Gas stations are few and far between and most of the roads are gravel.

Accommodations are available at the CN Hotel or the Beaver Motel in Rainy River. Light-housekeeping cabins may be rented at Oak Grove Camp and Windy Bay Lodge. Lake of the Woods provincial campground has campsites.

Birding Features

Begin at the Rainy River sewage lagoons. Turn north off Highway 11 on the side road just east of the railway station. After crossing the railway tracks you'll see a dirt road to the left. The lagoons are a few hundred metres down this road. Shorebirds and ducks are present in migration, and in late May up to 1000 Wilson's Phalaropes have been counted.

Return to the side road and turn left (north); drive to the first crossroads (1.3 km); turn left again and travel 1.5 km, to where there is an aspen woodlot on your left and open fields to your right. These fields produced two singing Sprague's Pipits in June of 1980. The woodlot holds Connecticut Warbler and Eastern Bluebird in breeding season.

Another 0.5 km to the west, you'll come to Highway 600, the main north-south road of the region. Turn north and drive slowly, watching the fields and fence rows for open-country species such as Western Kingbird and Western Meadowlark. In breeding season it is a good idea to stop often and listen. Upland Sandpipers are heard more often than seen; Sprague's Pipits were discovered in this fashion.

Drive north on Highway 600 for 3.2 km, to River Road; turn west, and after 1.6 km you'll pass an ill-defined crossroad. The grassy track to the north leads into willow and alder thickets which should yield a Golden-winged Warbler in late May and June.

Approximately 6 km to the west of Highway 600, you'll reach the Rainy River. River Road follows the river north from here for a short distance. The oak woods along the bank are a favourite with Red-headed Woodpeckers.

Going north from the river, you'll pass through extensively cultivated fields which hold large flocks of longspurs in early spring. These should be scanned carefully for rare species.

Approximately 4 km after leaving the river, turn left to cross Wilson Creek, then almost immediately turn north again. North of Wilson Creek 1.8 km, a road runs west to Oak Grove Camp, which lies on the bank of the Rainy River. A trail leading south from the camp, through the woods along the river, provides an enjoyable walk. Look for Hill's Oak, a species rare in Ontario.

Back out on River Road and 2 km north of the Oak Grove Road, a dirt track to the left leads down to a gas dock on the river. The marsh here is favoured by Yellow-headed Blackbirds. In April, open water harbours large concentrations of ducks, cormorants and pelicans.

A few hundred metres to the north of this track, the River Road turns east for 2 km, then north for 0.8 km and then finally east again. At this second right turn, the fields on either side of the road usually contain feeding flocks of blackbirds, including Brewer's and Yellow-headed. Sand-hill Cranes are often heard or seen flying to the north at this point.

Drive east 6 km; you'll rejoin Highway 600 at the point where the highway makes a 1.6-km jog to the east before the road turns north again. Two km north of this left turn in the highway, you'll see a grassy clearing on the left (west) which often contains Sharp-tailed Grouse. A further 6 km north, you'll come to a side road leading to the west. This dirt road runs 5 km to the lake, where you'll have an excellent view of Sable Island just across the inside channel. The extensive sedge marshes to the south have had Yellow Rail, Le Conte's Sparrow and Sandhill Crane.

Returning to Highway 600, continue north for 1.6 km. The highway turns east here but you'll want to continue north on the road which leads to the lake and the government wharves. Scan the lake for American White Pelican.

Back at the stop sign at Highway 600 where it goes east, turn right on the gravel road heading west. Travel as far west (2.6 km) as you can before turning north to the lake (another 1 km). The road eventually ends at a rocky hill. Park and walk over the hill to a windswept view of the Lake of the Woods. The forest here is known as Budreau's Woods and produces a variety of migrants in the spring and fall. In the spring when conditions are right, hawks migrate overhead as they follow the shore of the lake north. A path through the woods leads to Budreau's Beach, which runs off in a crescent to the southwest. The beach is often good for shorebirds in migration. Around a rocky point, visible at the far end of the beach, you'll have a fine view of the north end of Sable Island. The land here is privately held. Please obtain permission before crossing. This is another spot for waterfowl concentrations in the spring.

In May and June, scan the beaches of the island for shorebirds. Piping Plovers are usually present though somewhat difficult to see, and rare species such as Marbled Godwit, American Avocet and even Black-necked Stilt have been found. Later in July thousands of Franklin's Gulls loaf on the beaches of the island. It's best to allow a good deal of time to cover this spot as it's one of the best sites in the region.

Return to Highway 600 and take it east for 11.6 km to Highway 621. Lake of the Woods Provincial Park is located 5 km to the north on Highway 621. Campsites are available there. Highway 621, to the south of its junction with Highway 600, runs through several kilometres of boreal forest offering such northern species as Common Raven, Gray Jay, Boreal Chickadee and three-toed woodpeckers.

You'll eventually return to Highway 11 by travelling straight down Highway 621. Here you turn west (right) to return to Rainy River. All of the side roads between Highways 621 and 600 can prove fruitful. Continually scan the woodlots and fields for Black-billed Magpies. They have nested along Worthington Road 3, which is three side roads east of Rainy River.

Another important spot worth checking is the Highway 600 marsh, which borders Highway 600 for 2 or 3 km. The best access point is 13.5 km north of Highway 11. The marsh has been more or less dry for three or four years but still produces Sharp-tailed Grouse, Le Conte's Sparrow and Sedge Wren in late May and June. To the east lies a large tamarack bog. Sandhill Cranes have been heard calling from the bog and may nest here. As well, in April of 1982, two Great Gray Owls were heard calling at this spot.

RON RIDOUT

South James Bay: Moosonee/Moose Factory/Shipsands Island

The "true north" for the Ontario birder, Moosonee lies about 18 km upstream from the mouth of the Moose River on James Bay. Northern birds abound in the tidal marshes of lower James Bay and the adjacent complex of fen-bog muskeg.

Indians have been here for centuries, utilizing the game. The Hudson's Bay Company established a post on Moose Factory Island in 1673 which became a major fur rendezvous centre. There was a succession of intense struggles between rival fur companies at this site. Nothing remains of the original structures today except a blacksmith shop and powder magazine of the early 1800s.

No roads lead into the area. Access in summer is by train, a four-and-a-half-hour excursion from Cochrane. The train leaves Cochrane at 8:30 A.M. Saturday to Thursday and departs Moosonee at 5:15 P.M. June 27 to September 7. Telephone (705) 472-4500 for reservations. Cochrane sits on

Highway 11, north of North Bay and Timmins. Air flights from Timmins are daily, except Sunday.

Visitors will find accommodation at three lodges in Moosonee. Contact the Ministry of Industry and Tourism (see above) for names and addresses. Camp at Tidewater Provincial Park. Water taxis or freighter canoes will take you to both Moose Factory Island and the park.

Information and bird checklists are available from: Moosonee District Office, Ontario Ministry of Natural Resources, Box 190, Moosonee, Ontario P0L 1Y0.

Birding Features

The two villages, the tracts of boreal forest and the variety of extensive fen habitats provide fine northern birding opportunities. During migration in late April and May and again in August and September, the townsite contains hordes of Horned Larks, White-crowned Sparrows, Lapland Longspurs and Snow Buntings; an occasional Northern Wheatear is often seen. From May through October, regularly encountered birds include Merlin, Osprey, Spruce, Ruffed and Sharp-tailed Grouse, Black-backed and Three-toed Woodpeckers, Gray Jay, Common Raven, Boreal Chickadee, Winter Wren, Swainson's Thrush, Ruby-crowned Kinglet, Philadelphia Vireo, Black-and-white, Tennessee, Orange-crowned, Yellow, Magnolia, Yellow-rumped, Palm and Wilson's Warblers, Northern Waterthrush, American Redstart, Evening and Pine Grosbeaks, Purple Finch, White-winged Crossbill, and White-throated, Fox and Lincoln's Sparrows.

In winter look for the three grouse species, both three-toed woodpeckers, Northern Hawk-Owl, Great Gray and Boreal Owls, Common Raven, Northern Shrike, Pine Grosbeak, both redpolls and White-winged Crossbill. Willow Ptarmigan are present along the coast and at some inland locations in variable numbers.

During spring migration, water birds include Common Loon, Brant (Atlantic race), Snow Goose (including blue phase), Canada Goose, Old-squaw, all three scoters, several species of duck, jaegers, Bonaparte's Gull, and Common and Arctic Terns. In the fall, the area hosts one of the world's most extraordinary goose hunts. Along the tidal flats of James Bay, hundreds of thousands of geese stop to feed on the way from the far northern breeding grounds. Hunters fly in (in numbers nearly as great as the geese) to harvest their quotas.

A trip to the river mouth, 19 km away, and the Shipsands Island migratory bird sanctuary can be made via motorized canoe. You can also see the adjacent coastal marsh areas of the James Bay shoreline by canoe. In summer this marsh and adjacent willow-alder complex will produce a variety of ducks, Merlin, Sandhill Crane, Yellow Rail, Common Snipe, Greater and Lesser Yellowlegs, Marbled Godwit, Wilson's Phalarope, Bonaparte's Gull, Philadelphia Vireo and Le Conte's, Sharp-tailed and Savannah Sparrows.

The coastal marshes host vast flocks of Snow Geese and an occasional Ross' Goose during migration. Several species of duck are common, including Mallard, American Black, Green-winged and Blue-winged Teals, Northern Pintail, Northern Shoveler, American Wigeon and Lesser Scaup.

Spectacular shorebird concentrations occur during spring and fall passage. Common species include Semipalmated and Black-bellied Plovers, Lesser Golden-Plover, Ruddy Turnstone, Whimbrel, both yellowlegs, Red Knot, White-rumped, Least and Semipalmated Sandpipers, Dunlin, Short-billed Dowitcher, Sanderling, Marbled and Hudsonian Godwits and Wilson's Phalarope. Never common, but fairly regular during migration, are Red-necked Grebe, Northern Goshawk, Golden and Bald Eagles, Gyrfalcon, Peregrine Falcon, Stilt and Buff-breasted (fall) Sandpipers, Red-necked and Red Phalaropes, all three jaegers, Little Gull and Black Guillemot.

PAUL PREVETT

Quebec

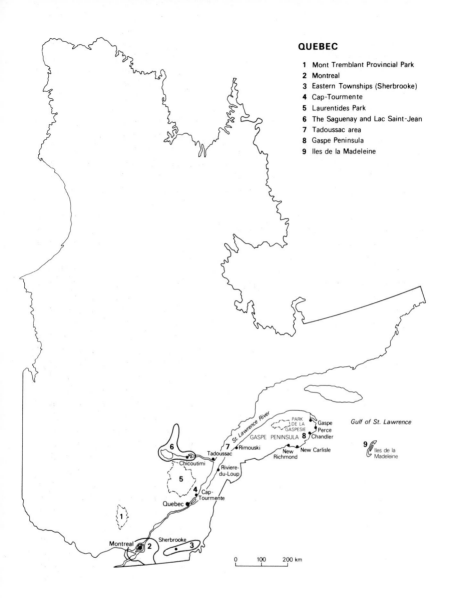

QUEBEC

1 Mont Tremblant Provincial Park
2 Montreal
3 Eastern Townships (Sherbrooke)
4 Cap-Tourmente
5 Laurentides Park
6 The Saguenay and Lac Saint-Jean
7 Tadoussac area
8 Gaspe Peninsula
9 Iles de la Madeleine

St. Lawrence River

Gulf of St. Lawrence

PARK
DE LA
GASPESIE

GASPE PENINSULA

Gaspe
Perce
Chandler
New Carlisle
New
Richmond

Rimouski

Tadoussac

Chicoutimi

Riviere-
du-Loup

Cap-
Tourmente

Quebec

Montreal

Sherbrooke

9 Iles de la
Madeleine

0   100   200 km

Quebec

Quebec, with major international air, sea and land connections, is among the most easily reached places where marine and boreal hard-to-locate species can be found. Those of particular interest that can be ferreted out quickly include Northern Gannet, Razorbill, Common Murre, Black Guillemot and Atlantic Puffin, all at Bonaventure Island. Both three-toed woodpeckers and the Boreal Chickadee may be spotted frequently in several places near major centres.

The province has three distinct regions. The farmlands of the St. Lawrence Lowlands lie adjacent to the St. Lawrence River, which cuts southwest-northeast through the province. The Appalachian Uplands are part of a chain that extends from the Gaspe Peninsula into the eastern United States as far as Alabama. These uplands include the Eastern Townships (east of and adjacent to Montreal), with peaks as high as 1268 m at Mont Jacques-Cartier in the Chic-Chocs in the Gaspe. This high country hosts mountain birds and even caribou. The third area, the Laurentian Plateau, covers four-fifths of the province and lies north of the St. Lawrence and Ottawa rivers. Characterized by rounded rocky elevations and many lakes, these lands are covered with boreal forests in the south, grading to tundra in the north.

Quebec has a multitude of islands, including an archipelago, Iles de la Madeleine, in the Gulf of St. Lawrence. This group of islands offers a unique opportunity to observe sea and land birds in a beautiful setting.

Quebec is Canada's largest province, covering 1,356,797 km². The north boundary is Hudson Strait and Ungava Bay; James and Hudson bays are on the west; the Gulf of St. Lawrence lies on the southeast. The offshore waters make seabird watching very attractive. Inland, the lowlands of the St. Lawrence Valley grade upward into the Appalachians of the Gaspe, and the rolling boreal hills and flatlands north of the St. Lawrence provide a wide selection of habitats in which birds may be sought.

May is the month of migration. Coming to visit at that time, you can see birds moving toward the Arctic while local species are setting up breeding territories. Make your visit for marine species from June 24 through July. Winter birds move south into the settled country, so come then for the boreal hard-to-find species.

The top birding area in the province is the Gaspe Peninsula, where both boreal and sea birds are found easily. The many ferries that ply the St. Lawrence River provide a visitor with both fresh-water and marine species. If you come from May through mid-July, stop at Westmount Summit in Montreal to look for easily accessible and abundant species. Mont-Tremblant Park, north of Montreal, is an excellent spot to look for the many eastern warblers during the nesting season. The largest concentration in the world of the greater subspecies of Snow Goose is found at Cap-Tourmente, east of Quebec City, in spring and fall.

In a half day in Montreal you can easily get up to Westmount. If you have a full day, then go north to Mont-Tremblant Park for those warblers. You can do Cap-Tourmente in a half day out of Quebec City. The Gaspe needs at least three full days once you arrive there since the best birding is at the far eastern end. You may have to wait in Perce three or four days before you can get over to Bonaventure because of bad weather and/or rough seas. Similarly, it takes three days for Iles de la Madeleine, plus two days' travel time each way from Montreal.

There are many helpful people in Quebec. The language problem for anglophones is not too much of a handicap, if you try. Those offering to assist include:

Montreal area: Marika Ainley, 4828 Wilson Ave., Montreal, P.Q. H3X 3P2, Telephone: (514) 481-9927; Felix Hilton, 336 Brookhaven Ave., Dorval, P.Q. H9S 2N7, Telephone: (514) 631-3437; Mabel McIntosh, 136 Millhaven Ave., Pointe Claire, P.Q. H9R 3V8, Telephone: (514) 695-5576.

Sherbrooke/Eastern Townships: Paul Boily, 5311 Ch. Ste. Catherine, Rock Forest, P.Q. J0B 2J0.

Quebec City: Jean Hardy, 134½ — 25e Ave., Quebec, P.Q. G1V 1V5, Telephone: (418) 525-5766.

Lake St. Jean and Montreal area: Richard Yank, 566 Chester Rd., Beaconsfield, P.Q. H9W 3K1, Telephone: (514) 697-1997.

As in all provinces, birders have developed their own local clubs. For assistance in a particular area, drop a note to: Province of Quebec Society for the Protection of Birds, Box 43, Station B, Montreal, P.Q. H3B 3J5.

The Canadian Motor Association provides a good map of Quebec in English. Transports Quebec puts out an even better map entirely in French. The latter is available by writing: Le Ministere des Transports du Quebec, Quebec, P.Q., Telephone: (418) 643-6864.

MABEL McINTOSH

Snow Geese

Mont-Tremblant Provincial Park

Set in the Laurentian Mountains, Mont-Tremblant is an excellent place to locate many of the eastern warblers and such boreal species as Black-backed Woodpecker, Gray Jay and Boreal Chickadee.

The 3200-km^2 park lies about 145 km north of Montreal. Take the Laurentian Autoroute No. 15 (toll) to St.-Faustin and watch for signs to the park as you drive north through the community of Lac Superieur. There are several campgrounds in the park, with motel accommodation in adjacent communities. Massive hills, deep valleys, waterfalls and lakes and streams make this a popular vacation site. A variety of hiking, skiing and snowmobile trails provide easy access to the woods.

Birding Features

In summer, when the woods of Montreal are quiet, come up here to look for many eastern warblers. Once inside the park, drive north along the main road for a few kilometres before stopping to listen and search. About 27 km north of the gate, look for the path to Lac Tador to locate Spruce Grouse, Yellow-bellied Flycatcher and Rusty Blackbird. If you don't find Spruce Grouse, continue on to Lac Savane where they are best found in August. At various spots, stop and ferret out Black-backed Woodpecker, Gray Jay, Boreal Chickadee, Olive-sided Flycatcher and various nesting warblers. The Golden-winged Warbler has been present at Ruisseau des Pruches three years in a row. The Red and White-winged Crossbills have been infrequent visitors in summer.

MABEL McINTOSH

Montreal

Montreal, Canada's largest city, lies on the St. Lawrence River, along which a great variety of birds pass on migration. Ducks and geese are plentiful from early April to late May and again in September and October. Waves of passerines also come through. Summer visitors would be advised to spend a day in the Laurentian Mountains to the north for boreal species and eastern warblers.

The Montreal area was first explored by Jacques Cartier in 1535; a fur trading post was established by Samuel de Champlain in 1611; a settlement was founded in 1642. It remained under France's rule until 1760, when the British took possession.

Montreal is second in size only to Paris, among French-speaking cities of the world. It lies immediately east of the northeast corner of Ontario. Major road arteries enter the city from all compass points. Bus connections are possible from throughout Canada and the U.S.A. VIA Rail provides connections from east and west and from the U.S.A. Two major airports handle all traffic. Mirabel, 55 km north, looks after international flights; Dorval, 16 km west, handles domestic and U.S.A. flights. Countless large sea-going vessels enter the Montreal docks. The Metro, the subway and bus system, provides an excellent way to get around. Telephone (514) 288-6287 and 842-2281 for routing information. Buses run frequently and maps are readily available in any of the Metro stations. Maps of the city and province may be obtained from the Quebec Tourist Office in Place Ville Marie or in summer at Dominion Square. A directory of hotels, motels and campsites is available from the Canadian Automobile Association office at McGill College or at the Quebec Tourist Office.

Birding Features
Spring and fall are the best birding seasons for Montreal. Migrants begin coming around the end of March and finish about early June. They return around mid-July and terminate in October. People from the west looking for warblers, or those from the south interested in such boreal species as Spruce Grouse, Gray Jay and Boreal Chickadee, should go north to the Laurentians.

Mount Royal Park and Protestant Cemetery. The 200-ha park crests the top of the mountain in the middle of the city. Mount Royal Protestant Cemetery lies on the north slope. A wide road leaves Pine Avenue and winds up the hill to the lookout and cross at the summit. Numerous footpaths cut through the deciduous and coniferous woods. Just west of the lookout, a pond and nearby wet area draw more birds. Bus access is easy by No. 62, 65 or 165 up Cote-des-Neiges and a transfer to No. 11, which runs over the mountain on Camillien Houde Dr. Cars should take Cote-des-Neiges, turn right on Camillien Houde and park at the second parking lot. Get out and walk from here. To reach the cemetery, pass the parking lots and bear left to cross Camillien Houde. Car traffic is allowed in the cemetery from 8:00 A.M. to 4:30 P.M. except Sundays. You can walk in anytime.

This mountain, in the middle of an urban centre, attracts many species on migration and in winter. The cemetery is particularly rich in birds. Warblers coming through in May include Golden-winged, Cerulean, Prairie and Kentucky. Common nesting species include Great Crested Flycatcher, Eastern Wood-Pewee, American Redstart, Northern Oriole, Rose-breasted Grosbeak and Indigo Bunting. In spring and fall, most species of eastern hawks fly over and both eagles have been reported occasionally. In fall, winter and spring, seek out the owls in the evergreens within the cemetery. Look for Northern Saw-whet, Boreal, Long-eared and Great Horned Owls. Northern Goshawk is a year-round resident.

Westmount Summit Park. Adjacent to Westmount lookout, at the top of a low mountain, this preserve attracts many bird species. Take a bus (62, 65 or 165) along Cote-des-Neiges. Walk up Belvedere Avenue or drive up and park on Summit Circle. To drive from Westmount Blvd., take Victoria north and turn right on Sunnyside Avenue, then left on Upper Bellevue, which leads to Summit Circle and the lookout.

This is a good spot for spring migrants from mid-April to mid-June. The woods are often alive with Blue Jay, Brown Thrasher, and Hermit and Swainson's Thrushes. The Gray-cheeked Thrush is a specialty in May.

197

Search for Golden-crowned and Ruby-crowned Kinglets and most of the eastern warblers, including such rarities as Prothonotary, Worm-eating, Golden-winged, possibly Blue-winged, Cerulean, Prairie, Kentucky and Hooded. Other birds that come through in numbers include Scarlet Tanager, Rose-breasted Grosbeak, Dark-eyed Junco and Fox Sparrow. The best time to look for warblers is from May 15 to 25.

Driving Loop: Nun's Island, La Prairie, Cote Ste. Catherine to La Salle.
Driving distance about 48 km. Allow six to eight hours for the trip, depending on the season and activity of birds. Begin in downtown Montreal at the corner of University and Dorchester. Take University south onto the Bonaventure Autoroute (10). After about 4 km, take the Nun's Island (Ile des Soeurs) exit and drive onto the island (Blvd. Ile des Soeurs). Drive to the south end of the boulevard and park. Check out the woods opposite for owls, both three-toed woodpeckers and Northern Shrike in winter. Continue through the woods or follow a trail skirting the south end of the forest to the western section of the island. At present this wasteland is being turned into a golf course. Here, in season, you'll spot Gray Partridge, Snowy and Short-eared Owls and winter finches. Ducks are scattered along the river.

Return to the car and drive back along Blvd. Ile des Soeurs to Champlain Motors, a large dealership immediately next to the Champlain Road Bridge. Park at the entrance and hike to the river's edge behind the buildings. Scan for water birds including Common and Red-throated Loons, Red-necked, Horned and Pied-billed Grebes, and Canada Geese. In May search for Brant, Eurasian Wigeon, scoters and Red-necked Phalarope. From September to November check for Red and Red-necked Phalaropes and Little and Sabine's Gulls.

Drive under the Champlain Bridge. Follow along the bridge ramp on your left. Look to the right in winter for a Snowy Owl. Follow the road to the right, circling under the Bonaventure Autoroute, and follow the signs for the Champlain Bridge. Cross the bridge (a small toll is charged) and take the first exit to the right, which is signposted to Sorel and New York State. The road then splits. Follow the signs for New York State and/or Highway 132 west. Once on Highway 132 look for the second Brossard exit. Take this exit onto the riverside road called Marie Victorin Drive, to just beyond the Seaway Authority, or drive on to the wasteland adjacent and beyond the building. Scan the La Prairie Basin for Red-throated Loon, Oldsquaw, Ruddy Duck and Red-breasted Merganser. Shorebirds are few, but often some uncommon species appear, including Whimbrel, Willet, Purple Sandpiper, Long-billed Dowitcher and Hudsonian Godwit. Franklin's Gull and Caspian Tern are spotted often. During migration a Peregrine Falcon often appears here.

Drive back onto Highway 132 and take the next exit onto a boat ramp. Scrutinize the shoreline, weed patches and nearby land for shorebirds, and the river for waterfowl and other water birds. Continue driving west along 132 and again take the next exit onto Marie Victorin (turn right at the lights). Travel west along this route, stopping wherever possible to scan the basin for ducks. In winter check the power poles opposite on the seaway wall for a Snowy Owl. After driving about 4 km look for a brown provincial park sign for Parc Cote Ste. Catherine on the right. Drive up the ramp and over the seaway lock bridge. Continue along the road to the right or left of the bridge and park. The fast water in this section keeps the river open all winter, attracting a few Eurasian Wigeons, large flocks of Common Goldeneye with the odd Barrow's, Harlequin Duck and/or King Eider. In winter and early spring a Bald Eagle and Snowy Owl are often sitting on the ice. Look for Glaucous and Iceland Gulls, and the rarer Laughing, Franklin's and Lesser Black-backed Gulls. Sometimes such rarities as Leach's and Wilson's Storm-Petrels are noted. Check for Purple and Western Sandpipers on migration. There is an active heronry on Heron Island opposite. Go into the park and check the swimming pool in fall for shorebirds. Drive 1.6 km west along the road (left from the bridge) to reach woods, which should be examined in late fall, winter (in shallow snow) and early spring for owls, particularly Northern Saw-whet, and both three-toed woodpeckers.

Retrace your route to the bridge and return to Marie Victorin. Turn right onto it and drive about 1.5 km to Highway 132; turn right at the lights onto Highway 132 west and drive to, and over, the Mercier Bridge; take the second exit onto Clement, after leaving the bridge; turn left at the lights onto Clement and follow it to St. Patrick; turn left onto St. Patrick, which follows the old Lachine Canal, and drive through several stop signs to the end at the fence and gate. If this gate is open, drive directly into the Lachine landfill site. If it is locked, then park and walk around the fence to your left. Explore the peninsula for shorebirds, including Baird's Sandpiper, which appear in small numbers every fall and remain for several weeks. Check the gulls for rarities. Jaegers pass through from May to July and from September to November. Examine the waterfowl on the river for that rare species needed for your list.

Return to the car and go back to St. Patrick. Turn right on this one-way street and stop at the Lachine Museum parking lot on the left, about 100 m along the street. Walk across to the riverside park and scan the river back towards the Mercier bridge. Keep an eye open for a Little Gull, Arctic Tern or jaegers in May and June.

Return to the car and continue east along La Salle Blvd. Again stop at any convenient spot and scan the river. After about 7 km, look for a park on the right extending out into the Lachine Rapids. This spot is at the junction of Bishop Power Blvd. and La Salle Blvd. Park where you can and walk out onto this landfill park. Look for gulls and ducks, including Harlequin. In spring and fall an Osprey may appear, and a Snowy Owl may be found in winter.

Return to the car and drive 0.8 km east along La Salle Blvd. to Lacharite Ave. at the first lights. Park on Lacharite and cross La Salle Blvd. to the river edge. Scan the exposed rocks at the bottom of the rapids for gulls and shorebirds. In May through July you may spot a Little Gull or Caspian Tern. Inspect to the right for ducks among the flooded trees and marsh. Return to the car and go back to Montreal via La Salle Blvd., Wellington Street and the Bonaventure Autoroute.

La Salle Waterfront. This area can be explored as part of the driving loop described above or by taking a bus and doing it as a single trip. Take Metro to

Angrignon Park. Go to the river and walk east to Lacharite St. Opposite this point the rocks in the river attract such wandering species as Great Cormorant, Laughing, Franklin's and Little Gulls, and Arctic and Caspian Terns. If the water is low, shorebirds are present in spring and fall. In winter and early spring, at the dam, Eurasian Wigeon, Barrow's Goldeneye and Harlequin Duck have been spotted. A walk beyond the Lachine Rapids in early summer or early fall may produce any of the species of jaegers.

Montreal Harbour. The best spot to locate waterfowl from November to February is at St. Helen's Island in the harbour. From downtown take Sherbrooke St. east to Papineau Avenue; turn right on Papineau and continue to Jacques Cartier Bridge; turn off onto St. Helen's Island. Park on the north side facing Montreal. Walk to the east along the river, checking for unusual birds such as Red-throated Loon, grebes, scoters and Glaucous and Iceland Gulls. Such rarities as Razorbill have been spotted here. To search for a Gyrfalcon in winter, go south on University Street. Follow the blue signs to Man and His World, pass Cite de Havre and park near the entrance to the Concordia Bridge. Note the thousands of Rock Doves that feed on spilled grain. They will suddenly flush, signalling a Peregrine or Gyrfalcon on the hunt. Both white and grey phases of Gyrfalcons have been seen here.

Beauharnois Power Station. This is a good site for gull, tern and jaeger watching, with up to 25,000 gulls congregating from late October to December. From Montreal take Highway 20, then 138 and turn southwest onto 132; continue for about 19 km on 132 through the community of Beauharnois, and another 2 km over the bridge in front of the power station; turn right and park beside the main lawn. The Montreal Provincial bus goes to Valleyfield once every hour; ask the driver to drop you off at the St. Lawrence Seaway locks. Here you may see Lesser Black-backed, Common Black-headed, California, Mew and Sabine's Gulls. In late summer and early fall the Little Gull is a regular. If the weather closes in, look for Arctic Tern in May and June. Jaegers are regular in spring and fall, as are Purple, Baird's and Buff-breasted Sandpipers. Large concentrations of ducks build up in the fall. These include mainly scaup, with a few scoters, Ring-necked Duck, Bufflehead, Oldsquaw and Ruddy Duck. In winter you may spot a Gyrfalcon or Snowy Owl. Note — from late October to March a visitor should wear warm windproof clothing and footwear.

Richelieu River Driving Loop. Along this loop in spring and fall up to 30,000 Canada and up to 500 Snow Geese, plus up to 20 species of duck are spotted regularly. The river acts as a natural funnel out of Lake Champlain to the south. The geese arrive in late March and stay to early May, when the shorebirds are most numerous. You should be able to spot a dozen or more species of shorebirds on the loop. The trip is about 210 km long and should take about six hours. The best areas are between St. Jean and Noyan. To reach the river, take the Champlain Bridge and Sherbrooke Autoroute No. 10; leave on Highway 35 after the first toll booth; cross the Richelieu and take Highway 133 for 5 or 6 km, taking various side roads to and from the river to check for birds. Turn right onto Highway 225 at Sabrevois and continue south. Turn east to Henryville. Swing south, on the west side of Henryville at the first road to South River. Drive south a few km across the river to check out the large concentrations of geese often found here. Return north to Highway 133 and immediately turn right at La Pointe and head south again. Stop and check the flooded fields for Greater White-fronted Geese among the Canadas. Look for Willet, Ruff and Marbled Godwit with the shorebirds. Follow the signs to the village of Venise-en-Quebec and Highway 227.

Continue on 227 south along the Baie du Venise to Highway 202 west, after checking this bay for ducks. Continue west on 202 to Clarenceville and turn north to the edge of the river at Highway 225. Check here for ducks. At this point go straight west on 225, scanning on both sides of the road for shorebirds and herons in the flooded fields. Herons along this loop include Great Blue, Green-backed and Black-crowned Night-Herons, all of which are common in wet fields along the route. Southern species regularly come up the river each spring. Look for Cattle and Snowy Egrets and Glossy Ibis, together with the more rare species like Little Blue, Tricolored and Yellow-crowned. Turn south along 225 and then west on 220 at Noyan; cross the Noyan bridge over the Richelieu River and take the first right onto Highway 223. Reconnoitre the side roads down to the river. Particular spots to check include the marina and jetty in the village of Ile-aux-Noix. Take the road just past the jetty and marina and drive right along the river for approximately 2 km before turning sharp left inland to Highway 223. At the sharp left turn, park and walk into the marshy area ahead of you. Short-eared Owl and the rarer herons and egrets mentioned above have been seen here. Return to Highway 223 and turn right. At approximately 2 km north, look for a large barn with a sign informing you they have antiques for sale. Park and go to the farm opposite the barn for permission to walk across the fields to the shore. Once permission is received, hike down and scrutinize for swans and geese, including Greater White-fronted Geese of the Greenland race. Ducks abound as do shorebirds on the mudflats in spring. Return to 223 and every few km drive down a side road to the river for a scan. Continue north to Highway 35 and thence to Montreal. An alternative is to go back to Highway 133 and on to the Philipsburg Sanctuary (see below). On the way check fields on the right which border the Pike River. You may spot some of the above herons, particularly Glossy Ibis.

Philipsburg Sanctuary. Most birds seen in northern New England and Quebec can be found at the sanctuary. You can drive directly here or visit at the tail end of the Richelieu River loop (see above). To come directly, leave Montreal over the Champlain Bridge and Sherbrooke Autoroute No. 10. Turn right immediately after the first toll booth onto Highway 35 and cross the Richelieu River; continue on Highway 133 beyond the community of Philipsburg to within 0.8 km of the Vermont border; turn left and park at the Gaie Blue Motel. The trail begins at the end of the motel property. George Montgomery lives in Philipsburg on weekends and can be reached by telephone at (514) 248-2863, or on weekdays at 4689 Westmount Avenue, Westmount, Montreal, P.Q., Telephone (514) 486-3531. He will assist you if possible. The motel is open from May to mid-October. The sanctuary is owned and operated by the Province of Quebec Society for the Protection of Birds. It contains about 485 ha and lies on the north end of Lake Champlain. At this point the foothills of the Green Mountains meet the St. Lawrence Valley plain, resulting in a wide diversity of habitat. Come and spot birds not normally seen in Quebec, but that regularly breed at the sanctuary. These include Northern Rough-winged Swallow, Yellow-throated Vireo and Field Sparrow. Other uncommon species include Wood Duck, Virginia Rail, Sora, Pileated Woodpecker and Common Raven. The Golden-winged Warbler has nested here and a Cerulean Warbler may be found. This is the only place near Montreal where a Turkey Vulture is spotted regularly in summer. In addition, you have a good chance of sighting any one of the warblers of the east and south.

Morgan Arboretum. The arboretum, north of Ste.-Anne-de-Bellevue, west of Montreal, hosts Gray Jay and Boreal Chickadee some winters. It can be visited as the first part of the driving loop to Ile Perrot (see below) or as a shorter trip. To come directly, take Highway 40 west from Montreal; take the Ste.-Anne-de-Bellevue exit and turn north to the arboretum. The parking lot near the wolf pen has jays and chickadees in winter, with people feeding them. At this time, look for winter finches and check the larger elm trees for both three-toed woodpeckers. During migration, the hill overlooking Ste.-Anne-de-Bellevue to the south is good for hawks from September to November, with sightings of up to 2000 birds. Around noon is the best time to scan the skies. In April and May, the woods abound with waves of migrating passerines, particularly in wet weather. Winter Wrens are very common in spring and summer.

Driving Loop: Ile Perrot, Hudson, Rigaud Mountain. Driving time a full day of 120 to 280 km. On this trip you can ferret out winter birds including owls, both three-toed woodpeckers, Boreal Chickadee and finches; in spring and fall, the passerines are numerous in many spots. Leave from the corner of University and Dorchester Avenue; take Dorchester west to Fort and follow the signs to Highway 2-20; follow 2-20 west about 35 km to Ste.-Anne-de-Bellevue; cross the bridge onto Ile Perrot and turn left at the second set of lights onto Don Quichotte Boulevard. Continue southeast through one stop sign and up a steep hill. At the crest of the hill, park and hike into the woods on the right. Check for Great Horned and Barred Owls and a Northern Goshawk all year. Woodpeckers are here too.

Continue along Don Quichotte, examining the fields on both sides of the boulevard for hawks, a Short-eared Owl in summer, and Snowy Owl or a possible Northern Hawk-Owl in winter. Migrating hawks are here in April and September. About 2 km beyond the Wentworth Golf Course clubhouse, explore the bushes on the left for migrating warblers and sparrows. The woodlot next to this bushy area often has an Eastern Screech-Owl. Continue along Don Quichotte to Windmill Point Park on the left. Leave the car and scan the open water for loons, grebes, geese and ducks. Hooded Mergansers are often here in spring. The bushy area regularly contains a Northern Cardinal and migrating warblers and sparrows. Return along Don Quichotte to the four-way junction with Ile Perrot Boulevard and turn left on it.

Inspect the edge of the river as you drive and stop where you can. Continue on to St. Joseph Blvd. and turn right just beyond Village-sur-le-Lac. About 2 km farther north from the corner, look for the large spruce plantation in an open field on the left. Park the car and ferret out a variety of boreal species in winter among the spruce, including Long-eared Owl, Gray Jay, Boreal Chickadee, Red-breasted Nuthatch and winter finches. Continue along St. Joseph, crossing Don Quichotte Blvd. to rejoin Ile Perrot Blvd.; turn right onto Ile Perrot and after about 0.8 km look on the right for the small parking area which backs into a large woodlot. Leave the car here or at any one of the streets to the left. Walk about 100 m to the start of a ski trail into the woods. The woods contain boreal species, including Boreal Chickadee and crossbills in winter. A Great Horned Owl is resident and an occasional Barred Owl appears. Long-eared and Northern Saw-whet Owls sometimes roost in the smaller hemlocks at the edge. Retrace your route to St. Joseph Blvd., then to Don Quichotte Blvd., and to Highway 2-20; turn right across the bridge back to Ste.-Anne-de-Bellevue; take the first exit to St. Pierre Ave. and turn left on it, continuing to Highway 401, the Trans-Canada.

At this point you have a choice of continuing north to the Morgan Arboretum (see above) or west on Highway 40.

Continuing on Highway 40 west, once across the main Ile aux Tourtes Bridge over the southern end of the Lake of Two Mountains, start looking for a Rough-legged Hawk or Snowy Owl on both sides of the highway in winter. Occasionally at this season a Short-eared Owl will appear during the day. Follow the highway for about 5 km and take the exit to Highway 342 and Hudson. This whole area is excellent for winter finches, owls, migrants and breeding birds. Turn right on Cameron Avenue, which is signposted to Hudson. Drive down a steep hill and then inspect the streets to the left of Cameron for bird feeders in winter. There have been an ever-increasing number of Northern Cardinals, Bohemian Waxwings and winter finches here. All the streets eventually lead to the lakeshore road; just keep progressing northward. At the lakeshore, turn left on Main Road and drive along the shore of the Ottawa River. Stop where you can. The best site is Thomson Park. Scan for loons, grebes and geese in spring and fall.

In late spring and summer Aird's marsh is a good spot. It is about 3 to 4 km west of Hudson, on Main Road. Look for Finnegan's Market on the left. Turn in and park near the road. This private property is available to birders, but be respectful. Check the pond a few metres south and then continue hiking to the railroad track. Turn west to the second pond. Little Blue Heron, Great Egret and Tricolored Heron have been spotted here. Least Bittern, Sora and Virginia Rail nest in this area. At Highway 201, turn left (signposted to St. Clet) and drive south. At the junction with Highway 342, look for the ever-present Upland Sandpiper in the fields near the restaurant in spring and summer. Continue south to Highway 40.

At this point you may go under the highway and continue south or, alternatively, go west for a stretch and explore the Ottawa River in the spring and fall. There are a number of ferries that cross the Ottawa River going west. Take any of the exits off Highway 40 to survey both sides of the river for loons, geese and ducks during migration. The last ferry before the Ontario border crosses at Pointe Fortune village. Cross here and turn left into Dollard des Ormeaux Park and proceed above the dam. Check for waterfowl. In the channel wall below the dam, Northern Rough-winged Swallows have nested for years.

Now going back to the intersection of Highways 342 and 40, drive under 40 and continue south on the east side of Rigaud Mountain. The mountain can be explored along three roads: one on the north, Mountain Ranches; St. Georges across the middle; and St. Henri on the south side. Search for such goodies as Yellow-billed Cuckoo, Blue-gray Gnatcatcher, Yellow-throated Vireo and Cerulean Warbler. Barred and Great Horned Owls are resident. Hawk flights can be watched in the fall and spring. Check carefully for Turkey Vulture, Golden or Bald Eagle. Take the first road on the right, Mountain Ranches, just south of Highway 40, and drive west along it for about 4 km and then return to Highway 201.

Continue south to St. Georges road to the right. Drive west along it for about 7 km, checking for the same species mentioned above. Go to the T-junction and then retrace your route back to 201. Continue south, now looking for an Eastern Bluebird. Again swing west on St. Henri. About 100 m after the turn west from 201, look for Northern Rough-winged Swallow. Continue west for about 3.2 km, searching for a pasture on the left just beyond a farm. Climb over the fence and walk the field in search of Grasshopper and Vesper Sparrows and an Eastern Bluebird. Return to Highway 201 and continue south. Drive up a short hill looking for the St. Angelique road on the left, signposted to St. Lazare. After 2.5 km look for Poirier road going south and take it for about 1.5 km to a large pine plantation. There are two main trails leading into these pine woods on the right. Walk into either one looking for boreal winter birds. You'll probably find a Northern Goshawk, Gray Jay, Boreal Chickadee, Golden-crowned Kinglet and many winter finches. Return to the car and continue south on Poirier, which joins St. Emmanuel. Drive south on it to Cite des Jeunes or Highway 340 heading east. You now can take any of the side roads around here and to the west. They are all productive year-round.

This is an excellent area for an Upland Sandpiper in summer; for Lesser Golden-Plover and Black-bellied Plover on the turf farms in the fall along St. Emmanuel towards St. Dominique, about 5 km south of Highway 340; also look for these plovers on the turf farms just north of the Coteau Station, north of Highway 20. In winter the area is great for a Rough-legged Hawk and/or Snowy Owl.

Drive west of St. Clet from Highway 201, crisscrossing these side roads using a good topographical map. A Short-eared Owl is often seen, with a chance for a Northern Hawk-Owl in late October. Northern Shrike is a regular winter visitor, while a Loggerhead can be expected in March and April. Both three-toed woodpeckers, Gray Jay and Boreal Chickadee are sometimes in the woods in winter. Return to Montreal along any of the east roads, or south on 201 to Highway 20, then east to the city.

Valleyfield and St. Anicet. Valleyfield lies about 80 km west of Montreal, along the St. Lawrence River. Take Highway 132 west to the first St. Lawrence Seaway lift bridge, just west of the town. Stand on the western end of the seaway road to watch for hawks in spring; a light southwest wind is the most favourable. This is probably the best hawk-watching site in the Montreal area in spring. Try and come between April 15 and May 15. The seaway and edge of Lake St. Francis is good for scoters and other diving ducks. The Dundee Marsh lies at the western end of this lake. Rails are found in the marsh, as are abundant Marsh Wrens. Stray western birds are often noted too.

Mont-St. Bruno. The mountain is a few km east of Montreal. This high area is rich in birds, particularly in spring. The top, a provincial park, is easily reached. Leave Highway 20 just beyond the city, on Highway 30 south, and watch for signs to the park. Here you will see all the birds found on Mt. Royal plus hawks and owls. Eastern Screech-Owl, Great Horned and Barred Owls are present all year. Some Northern Saw-whet Owls nest here and others pass through on migration. Check the golf course evergreens for a roosting Short-eared Owl. Breeding birds include Common Merganser and Pied-billed Grebe, at times Yellow-billed Cuckoo, Blue-gray Gnatcatcher, Yellow-throated Vireo and Cerulean Warbler. In addition, all breeding birds from the area have been seen here and at Mont-St. Hilaire (see below) sometime during the nesting season, with the exception of Golden-winged Warbler and Grasshopper and Henslow's Sparrows. In August and September come here to view Broad-winged and Red-tailed Hawks. The Red-shouldered Hawk nests on the mountain; a Rough-legged Hawk cruises the nearby fields in late fall and early winter. The Pileated Woodpecker is present all year. Both three-toed woodpeckers come in winter. Warblers are numerous on migration, with some staying to nest. The mountain is always a good spot to look for winter finches and sparrows.

Mont-St. Hilaire. The mountain lies just east of the Richelieu River, south of Highway 20. This peak has been a federal bird sanctuary for many years. Many trails lead up from a central point located on the south side. Ask for directions to the Gault Estate. The nature centre is operated by McGill University. The woods are largely deciduous and hence have fewer species than Mont-St. Bruno. Great Horned and Barred Owls are common. Warblers are numerous on migration. Yellow-throated Vireo and Cerulean Warbler can generally be found on the north side of Lake Hertel.

Ile du Moine. This is the best place near Montreal to turn up unusual shorebirds and water birds. This island in the St. Lawrence is about 9.5 km long and lies 10 km east of Sorel. Take Highway 132 from the Champlain Bridge, then Route 20 for a few km to Highway 30; take 30 to the point where it joins 132; turn left at the traffic light and drive about 2 blocks; turn right at the sign for Ste.-Anne-de-Sorel. Drive through the village and park at the bus stop just beyond the restaurant Chez Bedette. Arrangements must be made ahead of time with the boatman, Jean Rousseau, who speaks *only* French. He is available only on weekends, except when he is on vacation. He lives beside the parking lot at 3706 Chenail du Moine, Ste.-Anne-de-Sorel, Telephone (514) 743-3025. He knows very little about the birds of the area. The island is used for grazing cattle and sheep which are ferried across to the island each May and taken off in November.

The best time to visit is from June to the first week in September. After that a visit is too dangerous because of hunters. Take a looped walking tour around the northeast end. The northwestern shore is the best spot for shorebirds.

The number of migrating waders is never large in August and early September, but the diversity is worth the trip. In August the Lesser Golden-Plover can be seen from the road if you scan the south side of the island, with Stilt Sandpiper and perhaps a Ruff on the beach on the north side. In early September, look for godwits, Whimbrel, Baird's and Buff-breasted Sandpipers. Red Knot also arrives at that time. Check the gulls and terns on the point of land on the adjoining island northwest from the north beach. Look especially for Laughing, Franklin's, Little and Sabine's Gulls. In spring, summer and fall watch for Forster's and Caspian Terns. The grasses have recently grown to six feet tall. Consequently, a Sharp-tailed Sparrow first appeared at the northeast side in 1979. Five singing males were present in 1981. The marshes host a few herons. Look for Little Blue, Tricolored and Yellow-crowned Night-Herons.

MABEL McINTOSH, BOB BARNHURST

Eastern Townships (Sherbrooke)

The mixed hilly, forested and agricultural lands east of the Appalachian Mountain foothills, centred on Sherbrooke, contain 228 species of birds that are reported regularly. In addition, nearly 60 accidental and stray species have been noted. Look for a variety of waterfowl plus upland boreal species including Black-backed Woodpecker.

Settlers arrived here in the late 1700s, at what had been the hunting and fishing grounds of the Abenaki Indians. A mill was built at the junction of the Magog and St. Francois rivers in 1796 to serve the increasing number of people. The community of Sherbrooke was born. The approximately 15,000-km² block of land lies some 150 km east of Montreal and 240 km south of the city of Quebec.

Sherbrooke has a variety of commercial accommodation. Campsites occur at Mont Orford Provincial Park, about 25 km west of the city.

An active group of birders in Sherbrooke has offered to assist. They may be contacted by writing: Paul Boily, Societe de L'oisir Ornithologique de l'Estrie, St-Francis Valley Naturalists' Club, 5311 Ch. Ste. Catherine, Rock Forest, P.Q. J0B 2J0; or by telephoning: Paul Boily (819) 864-4540; Andre Cyr (819) 842-4394; Arthur Langford (819) 562-3171; Julien Ruest (819) 567-3485.

To explore the complex road system in this area, topographic maps should be acquired. They are available on 1:50,000 at Skinner and Nadeau, on Wellington North Street in Sherbrooke.

Birding Features

The Eastern Townships have produced 151 species confirmed as nesters

Red-shouldered Hawk

and at least 15 probables. Some of these include Common Loon, Pied-billed Grebe, Great Blue and Green-backed Herons, Hooded and Common Mergansers, several hawks including Red-shouldered, both Bald and Golden Eagles, Spruce and Ruffed Grouse, Common Moorhen, Yellow-billed and Black-billed Cuckoos, Barred, Long-eared and Short-eared Owls, Black-backed Woodpecker, Boreal Chickadee, and many warblers, including Northern Parula, Black-throated Blue and Black-throated Green. There are several birding spots to choose from. The best sites include:

Lake Boivin Nature Centre. It is located at Granby, 71 km west of Sherbrooke on Highway 10 and north on Highway 139; drive east through Granby to the lake and centre. This is *the* site for fall concentrations of waterfowl. Come in late October for hundreds of geese, Mallards, American Black Ducks, and mergansers which gather here because of the hunting ban at the lake. Least Bittern, Black Tern and Common Moorhen nest in small numbers. Cattle Egret, Tundra Swan, Little Gull and Tufted Titmouse have been locally reported in recent years. Obtain topographic map GRANBY 31 H/7 for a reconnaissance of the surroundings in a search for other species.

Mont Orford Provincial Park. The park lies west of Sherbrooke, about 22 km on Highway 10 and then north on 141 for a couple of km. This is the locale for a variety of easily accessible woodland habitats where a mixed collection of songbirds can be seen, including warblers moving north in the second week of May. Rarities include Worm-eating and Golden-winged Warblers. Hawk flights of medium numbers come in the first part of September, including the occasional Turkey Vulture. Uncommon nesters include the Eastern Screech-Owl, Pileated Woodpecker and Yellow-throated Vireo. Trails to hike and other nearby spots are best found on topographic map ORFORD 31 H/8.

Lake Magog. Access to this lake is easily obtained at Deauville, from Highway 10 at Interchange 41. Concentrations of loons and grebes have been observed recently on the lake, along with numerous species of water-fowl, including the Eurasian Wigeon and the occasional Barrow's Golden-eye. In the fall, the most obvious collections of birds are the thousands of Ring-billed and Herring Gulls. Look for possible Franklin's, Little and Ivory Gulls, or a Forster's Tern. Local nesters include Least Bittern, Common Moorhen, Purple Martin and Marsh Wren. Migration has brought in other species, including Little Blue Heron, Yellow Rail, Purple Sandpiper, Willow Flycatcher and Sharp-tailed Sparrow. Topographic map ORFORD 31 H/8 will help you locate spots.

Megantic Mountain near Val-Racine and Notre-Dame-des-Bois. Lying east of Sherbrooke about 65 km and approximately 15 km straight north of the intersection of the borders of Maine, New Hampshire and Quebec, this mountain is the second-highest hill in extreme southern Quebec. Northern forests grow at the top, attracting nesters such as Black-backed Wood-pecker, Gray Jay, Boreal Chickadee, Gray-cheeked Thrush and Blackpoll Warbler. Recent summers have seen Golden Eagle stay and probably nest. Hawks fly around the mountain in their southern movement in the fall. To explore this high country, take the side roads shown on topographic map LA PATRIE 21 E/6.

PAUL BOILY

Cap-Tourmente

The sedges along the mudflats of Cap-Tourmente bring in 200,000 Snow Geese each spring and fall. This national wildlife area attracts other marsh species on their way through, together with local nesting birds.

One of the areas set aside and protected by the Canadian Wildlife Service, Cap-Tourmente lies about 50 km east of Quebec City off Highway 138, on the north side of the St. Lawrence River. Head east along the river at Beaupre. Make sure to visit the shrine at Ste. Anne-de-Beaupre. Avoid the week preceding July 26 because of the huge crowds of people coming to celebrate the feast day of Sainte Anne. Accommodation at other times is readily available.

Information on the wildlife area and the interpretive centre may be obtained by writing: The Interpretive Service, Canadian Wildlife Service,

Cap-Tourmente, St. Joachim, Comte Charlevoix, P.Q. G0A 3X0, Telephone: (418) 827-3776.

Birding Features

The federal government felt so strongly about interpreting this amazing spot that they constructed the second major Canadian Wildlife Service interpretive centre here (the first appeared at Wye Marsh, in Midland, Ontario). For centuries, the largest known concentration of the greater subspecies of Snow Goose has gathered here on the mudflats to build up reserves before either heading south to winter in Virginia and South Carolina, or north to nest in the Dewey Soper Bird Sanctuary on Baffin Island (refer to Bird Sanctuaries in the NWT). The sedges and their roots are the attraction. The Yellow Rail is often ferreted out here too.

An easily hiked trail leads to the cliff, where you can scan the flats with your scope. Make sure to visit the interpretive centre to get both human and natural history background.

BASED ON CAP-TOURMENTE BROCHURE

Laurentides Park

One of the largest parks in Quebec, Laurentides is covered in boreal forest. Come here to spot both species of three-toed woodpeckers in winter. A Gray-cheeked Thrush has recently been sighted here on territory. Parts of the interior of the park have yet to be explored. New species are expected. On a trip watch for Moose, Beaver and Black Bear, numerous River Otter, Mink, Fisher and Marten.

With an area of 10,360 km², the park contains more than 1500 lakes, many streams and rivers. To reach the west side, take Highway 155 north and then attempt to find a logging road heading east. The easiest way to explore the park is to drive 40 km north of Quebec City along Highway 175, and through the middle of Laurentides. Take the loop road 175 north, and then 170 west and back south on Highway 169. The east side, where the Laurentians are the highest, is best explored on Highway 381.

The central portion is the most developed, with three campgrounds along Highway 175, a hotel, restaurant and several service stations near the mid-point. One campground is available at each of the eastern and western edges. In the northwest corner along Highway 169, a lovely campground on Lac-de-la-Belle-Riviere is worth considering for an overnight stay.

Numerous logging roads crisscross the park, but access on them is heavily restricted and only by a special permit. Camping is allowed only within the designated campgrounds. Camp Mercier, near the southern end of Highway 175, is open to the public, with several trails through thick boreal forest. In winter, only the main highways are cleared of snow, limiting exploration on back trails to snowshoes and cross-country skis.

There are two canoeing circuits open to the more adventurous. Check with park officials for maps, etc. For assistance contact: Department of

Recreation, Fish and Game, 1550 Ouest Boulevard, St. Cyrille, P.Q. G1R 4Y3, Telephone: (418) 643-5349.

Birding Features

The hilly, rugged terrain is full of lakes and rivers flowing either south to the St. Lawrence or north to the Saguenay and Lac Saint Jean. The southern and central portions are covered by spruce and Balsam Fir with limited areas of Tamarack, aspen and White Birch. The northern section slopes to the Saguenay–Lac Saint Jean lowlands, with boreal forests slowly giving way to deciduous groves.

Birds of the boreal forest, regularly observed all year, include Gray Jay, Common Raven and Boreal Chickadee. Common nesters are Winter Wren, Swainson's Thrush, Ruby-crowned Kinglet, Philadelphia Vireo as the most common vireo, and several warblers, including Nashville, Magnolia and Blackpoll.

In spring and early summer, groups of Evening Grosbeak, Purple Finch and Pine Siskin are common along the roads. White-winged Crossbill may be seen all year. The abundant water bodies provide ideal habitat for numerous nesting Common Loon, scattered Great Blue Heron, abundant American Black Duck, Green-winged Teal and Common Goldeneye. Less numerous are Ring-necked Duck and Common Merganser. The Osprey is the most common bird of prey during the summer. Next in abundance is Broad-winged Hawk. A few Northern Goshawks are always present. Both Spruce and Ruffed Grouse are common residents. Look for Spruce Grouse in stands of Balsam Fir near mileage marker 68 on Highway 175. The Black-backed Woodpecker nests in the park and the Three-toed is seen every winter. Search the higher hills in the northern section for Gray-cheeked Thrush singing on territory in late June.

RICHARD YANK

The Saguenay and Lac Saint Jean

This land of boreal forest is bisected by southern deciduous stands that follow along the Saguenay River. Such habitat variation results in a mix of southern and northern bird species, with over 270 recorded. This is the one area in Quebec where a Yellow Rail can be found easily. It is also the northern limit for at least 20 species, including Black-crowned Night-Heron, Virginia Rail, Mourning Dove and Indigo Bunting. Several northern species come this far south, including Willow Ptarmigan.

The almost circular Lac Saint Jean was once a glacial trough and an arm of the sea. Missionaries, the first white men to come north, arrived here in 1647. A fur-trade post was constructed in 1676. Settlers finally arrived in the late 1840s. Many of their homes and churches remain today — the result of true craftsmanship.

Lac Saint Jean, over 30 km in diameter, sits about 400 km northeast of Montreal or approximately 200 km north of Quebec City. Highways 40 and

155 will bring you in from Montreal; Route 175 takes you up from Quebec City. Several other routes are available; check a road map for details. Quebec Air has several flights daily from both Montreal and Quebec City into Bagotville Airport, a ten- to fifteen-minute drive from Chicoutimi, the main city in the region. Limousine, taxi and car rentals are all available at the airport. Air Alma offers two flights daily from Montreal to Roberval and Alma, on Lac Saint Jean. VIA Rail provides one train daily from Montreal to Chicoutimi and the south shore of the lake. Voyageur Bus Lines offer several express trips daily from both Montreal and Quebec City into the area.

The region is a popular recreation centre, with scenery, sand beaches and a variety of local festivals. A good number of hotels, motels, campgrounds, restaurants, service stations and other tourist amenities are present. Reservations are recommended for the peak season in July and August.

For information on the Saguenay area, call Noel Breton at (418) 548-3022; on the Lac Saint Jean area, call Michel Savard at (418) 662-3158. A good reference is "Status of Birds, Lake Saint John Region, Quebec," by P. Browne in *Canadian Field-Naturalist* 81(1), 1967, pp. 50–62.

Birding Features

Highland vegetation on the lands overlooking the Saguenay River and gorge, together with that surrounding Lac Saint Jean, is typical boreal type of the Laurentian Plateau. The lowland cover around the lake and down the valley to Chicoutimi consists of deciduous forests of the Great Lakes. Because of the isolation of the area, knowledge of its birds is very recent. This is an area for the real explorer-birder to establish range extensions of more species. Peak times to visit include: April 15 to May 20 and September 1 to November 1 for waterfowl; May 1 to June 1 and August 5 to October 20 for shorebirds; May 20 to June 10 and August 5 to September 20 for land birds. Several species mentioned above are at their northern limits. Others, like the Common Moorhen, Eastern Screech-Owl and Field Sparrow, are found both here and in southern Quebec.

The Willow Ptarmigan generally reaches the northern extremities of this area in small numbers each winter. In peak years they are abundant as far as the lake. To find this bird in winter, take the logging road north from Ste. Monique, near Pointe Taillon on the north shore of the lake; north through St. Ludger-de-Milot for 150 km to Chute-des-Passes. There are no services beyond Milot so be sure you have spare car parts, warm clothing, emergency rations and lots of gasoline.

The Saguenay Valley is part of the migration corridor between James Bay, to the northwest, and the St. Lawrence River. Several western stragglers get caught up on this route and regularly return.

St. Fulgence is located 16 km east of Chicoutimi along Highway 172. Just south of town, a 3-km-long, 0.5-km-wide strip of shoreline provides one of the few suitable stopovers for waterfowl, and particularly shorebirds, passing through the valley. The area has produced over 200 species, including the Yellow Rail. This is the most reliable spot to find this bird in Quebec. Look for Yellow Rail calling from the sedge marsh on the south side of the road just west of Anse-aux-Foins. They are heard in early July, with up to eight individuals noted in 1980. The same area has produced the only regional records of the Sharp-tailed Sparrow.

RICHARD YANK

Tadoussac Area

The north shore of the St. Lawrence River at the mouth of the Saguenay River is best known for Beluga Whale watching. The shallow waters at the junction of these two rivers produce abundant shrimp and capelin, attracting scores of the large mammals. Shorebirds arrive on their way to and from the north, together with hawks and the Common Nighthawk.

Jacques Cartier visited in 1535 during his exploration of the St. Lawrence. Pierre Chauvin built Canada's first trading post here in 1600 as the headquarters for his fur trading monopoly. The oldest wooden chapel left standing in North America, built in 1747, contains the bell from a Jesuit church that first sat on this site in 1641. This north shore remained a quiet area of fishing villages for three hundred years, until exploitation of the vast forest and water power resources began in 1930. Now good rail and roadway systems link the communities to the rest of Canada.

You reach the area along Highway 20 on the south shore of the St. Lawrence to Riviere-du-Loup, and then cross the river by ferry (four to six times a day in summer and less frequently in winter) to Highway 138 and on to Tadoussac. The provincial bus services the community. Two motels and two hotels are available in town and there is a campground at the top of the hill by the cross. A youth hostel (Auberge du Jeunesse) is available near the ferry wharf. The people at the hostel are, of course, French-speaking and very friendly.

A telephone booth may be found near the post office on the main road. The service station opposite (the only one in town) provides good service. A drugstore and hospital are at Les-Escoumins, 30 km farther northeast on Highway 138. The two ferries (Riviere-du-Loup to St. Simeon, and Trois-Pistoles north to Les-Escoumins) take seventy-five minutes and run on a schedule tied into the tides. Reservations are needed, as the trips are very popular in summer.

Birding Features

A driving loop is the way to explore the North Shore. Come in the spring (late April to early June) or fall (August to early September) for abundant shorebirds. Begin by taking the ferry for Riviere-du-Loup across to St. Simeon. As you cross, scan for water birds. Upon landing, drive to Les Palisades, a park 27 km northwest on Highway 170. Check out the good birding habitat here. Return southeast to Highway 138 and proceed north on it to Baie-Ste.-Catherine. At half to high tide, survey the water's edge for shorebirds that feed and roost regularly. Continue on over the Saguenay River on a five-minute ride to Tadoussac. This is a good overnight spot. Take a cruise to whale-watch in season. Also check out the small chapel and cross. Continue on 138 to Grandes-Bergeronnes. The wharf and mouth of the river, which empties into the St. Lawrence, should produce Great Blue Heron and Black-crowned Night-Heron, ducks of numerous species and shorebirds. Just beyond the community, watch for Parc Bon Desire; here you will find a variety of species, including water birds, hawks (especially Northern Harrier), shorebirds, warblers and finches. Continuing north, stop at the harbour at Les-Escoumins to see the Osprey that often fish here at half tide, and the gulls, including Bonaparte's. Proceed to Pointe Romaine, about 10 km farther. Scrutinize the birds on the mudflats at half and full tide for something you've missed. At the next three communities, Sault-au-Mouton, St. Paul-du-Nord and Riviere-Portneuf, take time to reconnoitre the salt marshes, mudflats, sandy areas and flats during half and high tide. Now return to Les-Escoumins, take the ferry across to Trois-Pistoles and continue your trip. This ferry ride, or the one from Matane to Godbout, farther east, provides chances from late October to mid-November to spot Dovekie, Thick-billed Murre, Greater Shearwater and Northern Fulmar.

MARGARET ELLIOT

Gaspe Peninsula

Set at the northeastern end of the Appalachian Mountains, which extend down into the southeastern United States, the Gaspe is surrounded by water on three sides. This thumb of land into the Atlantic Ocean provides opportunities to ferret out everything from Woodland Caribou on and near the tundra in the highlands, to warblers and finches in the boreal forests. At the east end, hundreds of thousands of seabirds nest in huge colonies. More than 150 species of birds nest on the Gaspe Peninsula, with 290 species having been recorded.

Off the mainland, near Perce Rock on the eastern tip, Jacques Cartier arrived with his three ships on July 24, 1534, to claim the region for France, and so began Canada. Long before Cartier landed, fishermen had been harvesting the abundance of fish found in the nearby sea. They later established clusters of homes around the perimeter of the Gaspe. Shipwrecked sailors and United Empire Loyalists in the 1700s added to the mix of peoples. Communities remained isolated, with the sea the only access, until the highway (now 132) was completed in 1929. Today many of the people, whose families have been here for up to three hundred years, still split cod, salt and dry it on wooden racks along the beach.

Accommodation, including hotels, motels and campgrounds, is plentiful, particularly at the east end. July is a busy month, so contact your local travel agent for reservations.

There is one main bird-watchers' club for the whole of Gaspe, Club des Ornithologues de la Gaspesie. Contact them at Box 245, Perce, P.Q. G0C 2L0. There are several parks, with visitor and interpretive centres. For information, contact: Perce Wildlife Interpretation Centre, Perce and Ile Bonaventure Migratory Bird Sanctuaries, Canadian Wildlife Service, Box 190, Perce, P.Q. G0C 2L0, Telephone: (418) 782-2240.

Birding Features

The one road around the perimeter, Highway 132, allows a visitor to make a leisurely or quick trip, sampling different habitats along the way. A five-day trip is the minimum time recommended for birders touring the Gaspe.

Pointe-au-Pere. Check out the marsh, about 5 km northeast of Rimouski on Highway 132, between the St. Lawrence River and the highway. Inspect it for herons, waterfowl and shorebirds especially in the spring and fall. Contact the Club des Ornithologues de la Gaspesie for specific times for certain key species.

Gaspe Provincial Park (Parc de la Gaspesie). This rugged region lies in the Chic-Choc Mountains. One of the few herds of Woodland Caribou in the east reside on the slopes of 1268-m Mt. Jacques Cartier, the highest peak in these mountains. Moose, White-tailed Deer and Black Bear are also plentiful. As many as 150 species of alpine flowers abound on the 30-km² summit of Mount Albert. The fisherman may angle for salmon and trout in the rivers. There are more than 240 km of hiking trails to explore. Naturalists provide information and guided walks to the top of Mt. Albert and Mt. Jacques Cartier. The boreal forest and alpine tundra attract over 240 species of birds, including Water Pipit and Common Redpoll. To reach the park, take Highway 132 along the south shore of the St. Lawrence River to Ste. Anne-des-Monts and then drive south on Route 299 into the park. There are campgrounds and other amenities for the visitor.

Forillon National Park. At the eastern tip of the Gaspe, on Highway 132, the park appears as a massive, tilted block emerging from the sea. Nearly 230 species of birds have been reported, with 49 confirmed nesters. The 200-m-high cliffs of Ordovician and Devonian rocks abut the gulf waters; pebbled beaches and small coves of the Bay of Gaspe indent the southern side. Telescopes mounted on headlands assist the visitor in spotting Pilot Whales, seals in good numbers, and hosts of seabirds on the cliffs. White-tailed Deer and Moose abound. The cliffs also contain species of alpine plants that inexplicably occur here. Naturalists are available to provide guided walks and programs. Three regular campgrounds plus a winterized one await the visitor. Nearby villages offer a variety of accommodation outlets.

This 240-km² park is home to large colonies of Double-crested Cormorant, Herring Gull and Black-legged Kittiwake. Ducks, birds of prey, warblers and finches are numerous during spring and fall migration. They are best observed in the valley of L'Anse-au-Griffon and the salt marsh of Penouille at this time.

Barachois Salt Marsh and Pointe-St. Pierre. Continuing along Route 132, stop at Gaspe and see the fish hatchery which produces a million salmon and trout fry a year for Quebec's lakes and rivers. A visit to the Gaspe Regional

Museum is essential to learn of the history of the peninsula. They have a variety of temporary displays that change through the year. Admission is free. Telephone (418) 368-5710.

Drive on south to Pointe-St. Pierre, just beyond St. Georges-de-Malbaie. The exposed cape provides excellent viewing of seabirds. Watch for all species of falcons too. In front of the cape, scan the small rocky island used by Common Eider for nesting and Great Cormorant, to rest. These birds, plus Oldsquaw and mergansers, are recorded regularly in spring and fall. Carefully study any gathering for Harlequin Duck, Purple Sandpiper and Dovekie, all commonly reported. In winter thousands of Oldsquaws remain.

The Barachois of Malbaie, 5 km farther west, contains the mouths of four rivers emptying into the sea. The resultant huge salt marsh is sheltered from heavy seas by an 8-km sandbar. Birds are everywhere. The new Highway 132 and the old road provide access to wet meadows, marsh and the open sea. The staff at Perce Wildlife Interpretation Centre, 11 km farther south at Perce, will assist with more information. The marsh provides food and a resting stop for migrating geese, ducks and sandpipers each spring and fall. From mid-April to mid-June, water birds are plentiful. Such rarities as Little Blue Heron, Glossy Ibis, Greater White-fronted Goose, Eurasian Wigeon, Redhead, Ruddy Duck, Sandhill Crane, Willet and Wilson's Phalarope have been spotted in spring and early summer. Just offshore and in bays, scan for rafts of Brant, scoters and mergansers. In summer, cormorants and gulls rest on dry land. Many waterfowl nest, including a variety of ducks, and sometimes such rarities as Yellow Rail and Sharp-tailed Sparrow. The surrounding fields and forests shelter a variety of land birds. By mid-July, the shorebirds begin arriving and some are seen as late as November. The hunting season opens the third week of September. Stay away for at least the first weekend.

Behind Barachois the roads go inland. Take one early in the morning. A good hike could begin along the gravel road commencing at Route 132, between Portage River and Murphy Creek. The walk terminates in 3 km at a gravel pit. From early June to early July, the morning hiker can spot 15 species of warbler plus numerous other land birds.

Perce and Perce Wildlife Interpretation Centre. The great shiplike block of limestone rising 86 m from the sea is the landmark of Perce. The community was once the largest fishing port on the Gaspe. Today it is a resort town. The centre contains exhibits and films on the natural history of the wildlife of the Atlantic Coast. The Northern Gannet film is worth the trip. Discover seaweed, shellfish and other creatures in tide pools. The self-guiding nature trail, walking trails, naturalist-led walks and bookstore add to the visit. The centre and scheduled activities are available to the public from June 24 to September 1; the rest of the year, reservations are required. At low tide you can walk across to Perce Rock, sculpted by the Atlantic for millions of years. Watch for nesting Great and Double-crested Cormorants, Herring Gull, Common Murre and Black Guillemot on the rock. Don't forget to arrange for your trip to Ile Bonaventure Park.

Behind the town, Mont Ste.-Anne and Mont Blanc provide excellent

Northern Gannet

views. Take one of the trails, such as the Crevasse or the Grotto, and check out the plants as you climb. On the way up, ferret out Common Raven, Boreal Chickadee, Gray-cheeked Thrush, Pine Grosbeak, White-winged Crossbill and Fox Sparrow.

Ile Bonaventure Park. The provincially operated island park, just off Gaspe, is also a migratory bird sanctuary under the auspices of the Canadian Wildlife Service. Today some 100,000 birds, including the world's second-largest Northern Gannet colony, provide a spectacular sight in June, July and early August. More than 150 species of birds have been recorded in the immediate area. The naturalists at Perce Wildlife Interpretation Centre lead free guided walks along the main trail. None of the four trails crossing the island is more than 3 km long. No admission is charged to enter the park, but a fee of $7.00 per person (1982) is levied as a ferry charge.

The boat circles the island and then deposits its visitors. The last boat departs from the island at 5:00 P.M. Overnight stops are not allowed. For ferry reservations telephone (418) 782-2974. In summer, a small snack bar operates.

The 4.16-km² island, 3.5 km offshore, was used by French fishermen as a summer base, probably before Jacques Cartier arrived in 1534. In 1690 the English drove some French settlers off the island. By 1831 there were thirty-five families located here. As fishing declined, most people left, with a few staying to till the land. By 1963 all permanent residents had gone. A few buildings still stand as a monument to their courage to live on such a barren land. For a glimpse into the past, step into some of the buildings and talk with the historical interpreters. The eastern and northern cliffs were declared a sanctuary in 1919. Since 1971 the island has been owned by Quebec Tourism, Fish and Game Department, and in 1974 the whole island was

T.W.Thornin/82   *Red-headed Woodpecker*

declared a migratory bird sanctuary. Whales and Seals are a common sight off the island and more than 450 species of plants have been identified, not including the mushrooms, mosses and lichens, yet to be studied.

The seabirds draw the visitor. Nesting species include Leach's Storm-Petrel, Northern Gannet, Herring Gull, Black-legged Kittiwake, Razorbill, Common Murre, Black Guillemot and a few Atlantic Puffins. Other interesting species include the odd Greater Shearwater in summer, Harlequin Duck year-round, the odd Purple Sandpiper in spring, Red-necked Phalarope in fall, a few jaegers also in fall, and an occasional Thick-billed Murre in summer. The surrounding shallow, rich seas provide food. Come in late June or July since the kittiwake, murres and Razorbill begin departing near the first week in August. Numerous land birds nest on Bonaventure.

Warblers are common. It is quite easy to spot a Pine Grosbeak or Fox Sparrow. At the end of August or early September, come for erratic species passing through, including Red-headed Woodpecker, Great Crested Flycatcher, Yellow-breasted Chat, Dickcissel and Lark Sparrow.

Cap-d'Espoir. This spot, 16 km west of Perce on Highway 132, overlooks Double-crested Cormorant colonies. Other seabirds are regular too.

Other spots. Excellent birding is found at several sites along the Gaspe south coast adjacent to the Baie des Chaleurs. Stop at the mouths of rivers and marshes. Most locations are along Highway 132. Recommended spots include Chandler, 30 km southwest of Cap-d'Espoir; Port Daniel, another 35 km, where you should not only check the coastline, but drive north into the deep forests of Reserve Port Daniel for warblers and other upland birds; Paspebiac, a further 37 km; Bonaventure, around the bend another 22 km, contains a museum housed in a 200-year-old building, among the first built by the Acadian settlers. St. Simeon, 7 km farther, is another site to check out. Move on to New Richmond, 32 km up the bay. North of New Richmond 15 km, near St. Edgar, there is a forest interpretive centre open in summer. Nature tails occur along the Petite Cascapedia River. Guided walks are provided for visitors. The centre and programs are free. Then proceed to Carleton. Here you can bird-watch and drive to the top of the 580-m Mount Saint Joseph to obtain an exceptional view of the Gaspe coast and the north shore of New Brunswick. Proceed south, off the highway, to the end of the point at Miguasha. The Miguasha Fossiliferous Site lies 6 km southwest of Nouvelle on the road leading to the Miguasha-Dalhousie ferry. The site contains a museum and laboratory open to the public in summer. Tours are given around the property. You can learn more about fish and watch an Osprey.

REAL BISSON

Iles de la Madeleine

Lying 250 km southeast off the Gaspe Peninsula, the archipelago of Iles de la Madeleine is a unique spot for birders. With over 250 species reported, including thousands of water birds, masses of shorebirds on migration, and northern species in the upland Black Spruce forests, a visitor can spend a minimum of two full days exploring lagoons, mudflats, high cliffs and forests.

The islands were first visited by Jacques Cartier in 1534, but not settled until 1755 when the Acadians were expelled from Nova Scotia. Today the 14,000 people who live here earn a living from tourism and fishing. French is the predominant language; English is spoken by the approximately 2000 people inhabiting Grosse Ile to the north and the fifty families on Ile de la Grande Entree beside Grosse Ile. Ile Brion, 19 km north of Grosse Ile, is uninhabited.

The archipelago consists of nine islands and a few islets. The six larger islands are linked by 51 km of sand dunes. The islands can be reached in a five-hour ferry ride from Souris, P.E.I.; there are two runs per day. Fifty vehicles can be carried, with food trucks given priority. A weekly ferry ship, operated by the Cooperative de Transport Maritime et Aerien, runs between Montreal and the islands. Cabins are available and cars are taken on deck. Places on either ship should be reserved ahead, since travel in July and August is heavy. Eastern Provincial Airways and Quebec Air both service the islands from Montreal, Quebec, Mont-Joli, Sept-Iles, Gaspe, Charlottetown and Halifax. Avis and Budget have cars for rent at the airport on Havre aux Maisons. Excellent roads provide easy access to all birding sites.

Approximately a dozen motels and hotels offer a range of accommodation on the islands. Six campgrounds are available, including ones at the south side of Havre-Aubert, at Gros Cap on the south end of Cap-aux-Meules, near Fatima on the north side of the same island, and one in the middle of Grande Entree. The one hospital is at Cap-aux-Meules.

For additional assistance, or to forward a list of birds you noted on a visit, contact: Yves Aubrey, 925 Quinn, Longueuil, Quebec, J4H 2N7.

Birding Features

The red sandstone islands contain two large and several small tidal lagoons. Elevations range up to 168 m on the highest hills of Havre-Aubert and Cap-aux-Meules. The dunes are covered by Beachgrass, with the uplands containing stunted Black Spruce and Jack Pine. Extensive forests are separated by pastures and abandoned land invaded by alders.

The outstanding nearby birding sites of Great and Little Bird Rocks are accessible only during totally windless days (maximum of ten days per year). The water surrounding these rocks is so shallow, especially at low tide, that an approaching boat may strike the rocky bottom if there is even a minimum swell. On perfect days, a fisherman from Grosse Ile can be hired to take you out. On the oval rock, thousands of Northern Gannets, Black-legged Kittiwakes and hundreds of Common and Thick-billed Murres, Razorbills and Atlantic Puffins nest. The Little Rocks, about 1 km away, are entirely occupied by Northern Gannets.

On the ferry out to the Iles de la Madeleine, look for pelagic birds. If you leave from Souris, P.E.I., the last three hours of the five-hour trip are usually quite rewarding. Greater Shearwater and Leach's Storm-Petrel are common. Sooty and Manx Shearwaters, Wilson's Storm-Petrel, Sabine's Gull, and Red and Red-necked Phalaropes are only occasional. If luck is with you, you may spot a Northern Fulmar. Northern Gannet are numerous as you approach the archipelago, and alcids are commonly observed.

The best time to come to the archipelago is from mid-May to early July. Migrants include Canada Goose, which comes in from mid-May to mid-June. Common Goldeneye pass through in spring and reside here in winter. The Oldsquaw outnumbers every other duck in spring, fall and winter. Common and Red-breasted Mergansers are common migrants. Glaucous and Iceland Gulls are numerous spring migrants; some winter here.

Breeding birds are numerous. A small local population of Horned Grebes nests on the relatively inaccessible ponds of Pointe de l'Est Sanctuary (see below) and on the northern part of Havre-aux-Basques. American

Black Duck, Northern Pintail and Green-winged Teal are the most common nesting ducks. Mallard, Blue-winged Teal, American Wigeon and Ring-necked Duck are less numerous breeders. A small population of Greater Scaup nests at the same sites as the Horned Grebe mentioned above. Common Eider have nested for the past ten years on Brion Island. Red-breasted Merganser nest in fair numbers on Pointe de l'Est ponds. Great Blue Heron feed all over the archipelago but nest only on Grosse Ile. American Bittern is common on every pond. Virginia Rail is rare, but Sora is very common on every wet field and marshy spot. American Coot has recently nested at Fatima on Cap Vert Lake. Semipalmated Plover and Least Sandpiper nest in Havre-aux-Basques and around Grosse Ile. Piping Plover is scattered on all beaches but difficult to locate. Killdeer have recently begun nesting. Every alcid found in the east, except the Dovekie, nests on the archipelago. A good spot to find alcids is the Bird Rocks (see above). Alternatively, look for these species on Brion Island.

Brion Island can be reached from Grosse Ile using a local fisherman as a guide. These men can be hired for a reasonable fee to go directly to the island, or even circle it, before landing you. A walking trail circles the island. Atlantic Puffins are common on the northwestern and southern (below the lighthouse) sides on the southeast end, where you will also spot numerous Great Cormorants. At the far eastern end, check the seals basking on the cliffs. A few murres occur in the summer. A colony of more than 2000 Black-legged Kittiwakes is located on the northeastern side, along with numerous Razorbills, Great Cormorants and Atlantic Puffins.

Black Guillemot is a common nester in the red sandstone cliffs all around the archipelago. A good spot is under the Etang-du-Nord lighthouse. Great Black-backed and Herring Gulls are the most common gulls and are year-round residents. They nest on Seal and Range islands inside the lagoon on Grosse Ile, and on Brion Island. Black-legged Kittiwakes are abundant breeders, with colonies on the north and northeast sides of Entree Island, Brion Island and the northeast side of Bird Rocks. Terns nest in large colonies in Havre-aux-Basques; on the three small islands at Havre-aux-Maisons; near the harbour between Pointe-aux-Loups and Detroit Bridge; on the ponds at Pointe de l'Est; and on Brion Island. The Arctic Tern makes up 5 to 10 per cent of the population. The Northern Harrier is the most abundant bird of prey and is well distributed over the islands. The Osprey is a rare nester. Merlin is a common breeder in the stunted Black Spruce woods. The Mourning Dove is a scarce breeder found in small numbers. The Boreal Owl nests around Solitary Lake on Havre-Aubert; near the Gros Cap trailer park on Cap-aux-Meules; and at the Pointe-de-Fort face of Cap de l'Est on Grosse Ile.

Northern Flicker is the only common woodpecker; others are scarce to rare. The Yellow-bellied Flycatcher is the only common member of its group. It is found breeding in the Black Spruce forest. The Horned Lark, an abundant breeder, remains all year but is rare in winter. The Bank Swallow is probably the most common breeding land bird on the archipelago and occurs on all the sandstone cliffs. Tree, Bank and Barn Swallows are regular breeders. The Common Raven is a common nester on the cliffs. Many pairs may be found on Cap de l'Est on Grosse Ile in May and June. The American

Crow is numerous year-round and flocks can be observed congregating at dusk to roost.

The Black Spruce forest draws several species to breed, including Boreal Chickadee, American Robin, Hermit and Swainson's Thrushes, Veery, Golden-crowned and Ruby-crowned Kinglets, Tennessee, Yellow-rumped and Blackpoll Warblers, White-throated and Fox Sparrows. Gray-cheeked Thrush may be spotted at the top of the highest wooded summits on Havre-Aubert and Cap-aux-Meules islands. In the alder groves watch for Yellow, Chestnut-sided and Mourning Warblers, Common Yellowthroat and a few Song Sparrows. When you locate an area of woods and swamps, survey for Red-winged and Rusty Blackbirds, Palm and Wilson's Warblers, Lincoln and Swamp Sparrows.

The spectacular fall migration of thousands of shorebirds (mid-July to October) is worth coming to see. They feed intensely on mudflats and fields before heading south. Almost every shorebird from the east has been reported. Lesser Golden-Plover and Black-billed Plover are numerous, with the latter more common. Ruddy Turnstone, Greater and Lesser Yellowlegs, Red Knot, White-rumped, Least and Semipalmated Sandpipers, Dunlin, dowitchers and Sanderling are common and can be found everywhere in season. Look for Whimbrel in small flocks on beaches, marshes, wet fields, and fields with wild berries in July and August. Common Snipe and Pectoral Sandpiper are common in marshes and wet fields. Hudsonian Godwit may be spotted in flocks, with up to 400 birds in Havre-aux-Basques, where they gather before their departure south. Red and Red-necked Phalaropes are rare but may be encountered out at sea.

Other fall migrants include occasional Red-necked and Horned Grebes. The three scoter species are common in the fall and are often seen in summer. Oldsquaws outnumber every other duck in fall and winter and are regular in November, with flocks of 500 or more. Harlequin Duck is scarce and unpredictable, but regular around Old Harry Head on Ile de l'Est late in the fall. Flocks of a few hundred Common Eiders are around in late fall. The Dovekie is a late fall visitor. Some years it is more abundant than others. Glaucous, Iceland and Ring-billed Gulls are common fall migrants, with Glaucous and Iceland being common winter residents too. The Bonaparte Gull is a common migrant. The Common Black-headed gull is a regular from August to December, with flocks of up to 30 birds. Check at Havre-aux-Basques and just west of the Gros Camp trailer park on Cap-aux-Meules, where they have been spotted in recent years. Caspian Tern is reported every year from various spots in August and September. Northern Goshawk, and Rough-legged and Sharp-shinned Hawks are regular fall migrants. The Peregrine Falcon has been recorded in the fall at Havre-aux-Basques, feeding on the numerous shorebirds and ducks. The Snowy Owl is a regular winter resident. Regularly one or two will remain over summer near Pointe-aux-Loups on the sand dunes and at Brion Island, feeding on the introduced rabbits.

The good road system allows a visitor to explore the island thoroughly. Two driving loops have been set up, each requiring a leisurely day.

South Driving Loop. Begin at sunrise at tiny Lake Solitaire, just south of the junction of Lapriere and Alpide roads on Havre-Aubert. This is one of the few fresh-water bodies on the islands. By starting here before dawn, you may even hear a Boreal Owl. At dawn you could hear a Gray-cheeked Thrush in a walk around the lake. Also look for warblers. Take Lapriere Road south to the main road and turn west towards Etang-des-Caps. Stop at several viewing spots, including the small side road on the left, Etang-des-Caps. Continue on the main road and swing east on Montagne Road. Turn south on Pointe-des-Canots Road if it is dry and drive to the end. As you walk down to the water at the southern end of Havre-aux-Basques, listen for songbirds. Here, gulls and terns often rest. Check them out for the Common Black-headed Gull and other rarities. Piping Plover occur here with other shorebirds. A hike of less than a kilometre to the west at the end of this road brings you to Etang-des-Caps Lake to spot ducks and listen for American Bittern and rails.

Return to Montagne Road and continue east to Highway 199, where you will swing north towards Cap-aux-Meules. Stop a few times along Havre-aux-Basques to scan the water. At one or two sites hike through the wet grass on the west side of the road. Carefully scrutinize the shorebirds that are feeding heavily. You may locate a Willet, Stilt or Buff-breasted Sandpiper, Marbled Godwit or a Ruff, or maybe even a phalarope. At the northern end of this arm, just before Cap-aux-Meules, look for the tern colonies and study the birds for a good comparison between Common and Arctic. You may also see Horned Grebe and a variety of other water birds with young, in season.

Turn west at the first road, Chiasson, and drive to Etang-du-Nord. On the beaches around the little lake, south of the harbor, explore for shore-birds and gulls. South of this lake, on Goelands Island, Great and Double-crested Cormorants are spotted sunbathing and preening. Scan the sea for birdlife. Continue northeast beyond Fatima and turn north off the main road, onto Poirier Road. Stop near Cap Vert Lake on the west side. You should observe grebes, ducks and American Coot. Take a stroll on the nearby marshy fields on the north side of the lake and listen for Sora and Sharp-tailed Sparrow. Carefully check for shorebirds, particularly Lesser Golden-Plover, Buff-breasted Sandpiper and Godwit. At the far end of Poirier Road, scan to the north to the long dune where gulls are numerous. At low tide the mudflats are used by shorebirds and gulls. This should complete the day. If you have more energy left, go owling at night. Try every wooded lot, open field or marsh for Great Horned, Long-eared or Boreal. The latter were recently reported near the Gros-Cap Provincial Trailer Park on the south end of Cap-aux-Meules and at Solitaire Lake.

North Driving Loop. Begin at sunrise on the highest summit of Cap-aux-Meules Island, near the junction of Patton and de l'Englise. Climb the hill to the radio antenna and listen carefully. You may hear Yellow-bellied Fly-catcher, Hermit, Gray-cheeked and Swainson's Thrushes, warblers and sparrows. Proceed to Highway 199 going north towards the community of Havre-aux-Maisons. Stop before the iron bridge; inspect the point to the west and the lagoon for ducks, shorebirds and gulls, with Caspian Tern a good possibility. Beyond the bridge survey the mudflats for shorebirds.

Continue on 199 to the windmills near the north end of Havre-aux-Maisons and take the gravel road, de la Cormorandiere, to its end. This puts you on Dune de Sud. Piping Plover should be running along the dunes. Take your telescope and look out east about 2 km to Shag Island, aptly named for the colony of Great Cormorants that nest on it. Take a walk in early summer along the dunes and you'll spot these birds flying overhead with their white flank patches clearly visible.

Return to 199; near the Detroit Bridge, three small islands in the lagoon host a mixed colony of Common and Arctic Terns. A few pauses as you drive along the beaches and lagoon shore, from the bridge to the salt mine on Grosse Ile, provide opportunities to scan for shorebirds. Particularly check the small ponds between Pointe-aux-Loups and Grosse Ile. The Grosse Ile bay seems to draw rare shorebirds, including Willet, Stilt Sandpiper, Ruff and Hudsonian Godwit. The Sharp-tailed Sparrow is said to nest on the north side of the bay across the road from the wharf. Continue on 199 to Pointe de l'Est National Refuge. In summer, staff provide guided tours. The schedule is displayed in all post offices.

Turn east on Old Harry Head Road. Drive to the end and climb to the cliff top to scan for seabirds. In fall, this is one of the best sites for alcids. Following a summer windstorm, alcids, shearwaters, petrels, jaegers and fulmars may be expected.

At Grande-Entree Harbour, the final stop, check both inside and outside of the lagoon. On the inside, at low tide scan for possible rarities among the shorebirds and gulls. Near the end of summer, on the outside, thousands of cormorants, gulls and kittiwakes congregate to feed on the small fish that utilize this area. Late in the fall, from the end of October onward, the Dovekie is fairly abundant in the lagoon and at Old Harry Head.

If there is still light, return on 199 to Gros Cap on Cap-aux-Meules. The small pond just west of the campground and south of the road often has rare species.

YVES AUBREY

New Brunswick

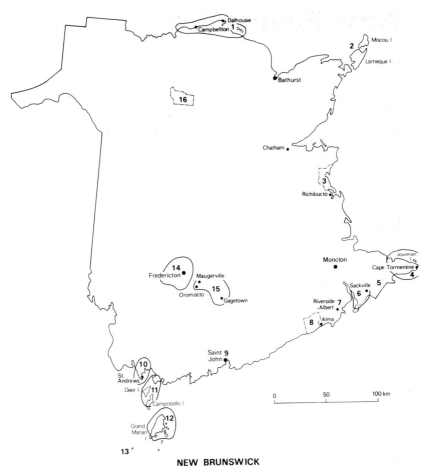

NEW BRUNSWICK

1 Campbellton to Dalhousie
2 Miscou Island and Lameque Island
3 Kouchibouguac National Park
4 Cape Jourimain National Wildlife Area
and Cape Tormentine
5 Tantramar Marshes
and Tintamarre National Wildlife Area
6 Driving Loop: Dorchester, Upper Rockport, Sackville
7 Albert County Coast/Shepody National Wildlife Area

8 Fundy National Park
9 Saint John
10 St. Andrews
11 Deer Island and Campobello Island
12 Grand Manan Archipelago
13 Machias Seal Island Migratory Bird Sanctuary
14 Fredericton
15 Driving Loop: Maugerville to Gagetown
16 Mount Carleton Provincial Park

225

New Brunswick

Most people interested in avifauna come to this province for marine species, including pelagic birds in the outer Bay of Fundy. The variety of warblers and other species that nest in the Acadian forests are an additional pleasure. Birds of boreal distribution, especially in the highland areas of the province, are of particular interest to birders from warmer climates.

Land birds frequently sought by visitors include Spruce Grouse and Black-backed Woodpecker. Chances are good of seeing the woodpecker, but finding the grouse often takes a lot of effort, or some luck. Yellow Rail is a possibility in the Tantramar area. Breeding Common Eider and Black Guillemot, shorebird concentrations on the upper Bay of Fundy, and phalaropes and gulls from the ferries south of St. Andrews are all spectacular at certain seasons. This variety of birds, combined with the colony of Atlantic Puffin and Razorbill at Machias Seal Island, could make your stay in New Brunswick a visit to remember!

The province stretches about 400 km in length and width and is 90 per cent forested. Much of the present forest originated following fire, lumbering or other disturbance during the past 200 years. Deciduous woods of Sugar Maple, Beech and Yellow Birch are found on well-drained hilltops and slopes of White Elm, with Balsam Poplar or Silver Maple on river floodplains. Widespread breeding species include Yellow-bellied Sapsucker, Red-eyed Vireo, Ovenbird, Black-throated Blue Warbler and Rose-breasted Grosbeak. Characteristic of floodplains are Veery, Warbling Vireo (somewhat local), Yellow Warbler, Northern Waterthrush and Northern Oriole. Mixed forests prominent in much of the province include Red and White Spruce, Balsam Fir, White and Yellow Birch, Red Maple, White Pine, Hemlock, Tamarack and aspens. This mixed vegetation attracts a large variety of birds. Ruffed Grouse, Hermit Thrush, and Nashville, Northern Parula and Blackburnian Warblers are usually conspicuous breeding species. Spruce-fir coniferous forest occurs mainly in the northern areas and close to the foggy Fundy coast. Red, Black or White Spruce and Balsam Fir are the principal trees. Breeding birds include Spruce Grouse in unsettled areas, Black-backed Woodpecker, especially where there are dying or recently dead trees, Yellow-bellied Flycatcher, Boreal Chickadee, Winter Wren, a wide variety of warblers, including Magnolia, Cape May and Bay-breasted, and Pine Siskin. Confined mainly to the northern highland areas are Three-toed Woodpecker, Gray-cheeked Thrush, Blackpoll Warbler, Pine Grosbeak and Fox Sparrow. Black Spruce–Jack Pine coniferous forests occur on poor soils such as glacial sand plains. This habitat has a relatively small variety of birds but may be the best place in which to find Spruce Grouse. By contrast, rich wet sites, often dominated by White Cedar, usually are nesting habitat for numerous species, including Canada Warbler and Brown Creeper.

Nonforested habitats are less common but often are interesting. Fields can attract Northern Harrier, American Kestrel, Bobolink and Savannah

Sparrow, among others. Open bogs have few birds, mainly Common Yellowthroat and Savannah Sparrow, with Lincoln's Sparrow and Palm Warbler in the scrub around the edges. Fresh-water marshes occur mainly along the lower Saint John Valley and in lowlands near the coast. Impoundment areas attract a wide diversity of water birds, including American Bittern, Pied-billed Grebe, American Black Duck, Blue-winged Teal, Sora and Common Snipe. The numerous ponds, lakes and rivers have a variety of birds, including Common Loon, Common Goldeneye, Common Merganser, Spotted Sandpiper and Belted Kingfisher.

Tidal marshes are scattered, mainly near river mouths, especially at the head of the Bay of Fundy and along the eastern coast. Sharp-tailed Sparrow is the characteristic nesting species but a variety of herons, ducks and other birds frequent these areas. Salt-water lagoons and sandy beaches are found mainly along the eastern coast. There you should find Piping Plover nesting, and numerous Great Blue Herons, Red-breasted Mergansers, Ospreys and Common Terns. The lagoons host an abundance of shorebirds and water birds during fall migration.

Island seabird colonies are most numerous in the western Bay of Fundy, with a few in Miramichi Bay and Baie des Chaleurs. You'll commonly find Double-crested Cormorant, Common Eider, Great Black-backed and Herring Gulls, Common Tern and Black Guillemot. Leach's Storm-Petrel, Razorbill, Atlantic Puffin and most of the Arctic Terns are confined to the area near Grand Manan.

In deeper waters offshore, local breeders are joined in summer by Southern Hemisphere seabirds, including Greater and Sooty Shearwaters and Wilson's Storm-Petrels spending their winters in the north. Small numbers of Northern Gannets, Manx Shearwaters and Northern Fulmars may be seen in summer near the mouth of the Bay of Fundy.

The best time to come is from late May to mid-July for breeding species, the last week in July to mid-September for shorebird migration, and late August to mid-October for land bird movement. In December and January look for wintering ducks and seabirds in the outer Bay of Fundy. Most of the northern and eastern coast is frozen by early January. Late winter is often of little interest unless there is an incursion of northern finches or birds of prey. In late April and throughout May you can encounter the best of spring migration.

Key spots to visit include: Grand Manan, for everything; the Passamaquoddy Passages, for inshore marine birds and phalarope and gull concentrations; the Fundy National Park and Marys Point areas, for birds of shore, forest and marsh; the Tantramar Marshes; Miscou Island, for breeding Piping Plover and Sharp-tailed Sparrow, and for fall migration; the wetlands of the Jemseg area, for ducks and marsh birds.

Any of these sites can be visited in a half day, except Grand Manan and neighbouring Machias Seal Island, which require a minimum of three days to cover both islands. Fundy and Kouchibouguac national parks can also be sampled in half a day.

You may wish to obtain a copy of *The Birds of New Brunswick*, by W.A. Squires (2nd ed., Saint John: New Brunswick Museum, 1976).

There is no formal bird alert telephone number in New Brunswick, but there is a grapevine system. Call at least one of the following offices for advice or news:

Saint John: Natural Science Dept., New Brunswick Museum, (506) 693-1196
Fredericton: Canadian Wildlife Service, (506) 452-3086
Sackville: Canadian Wildlife Service, (506) 536-3025
St. Andrews: Sunbury Shores Arts and Nature Centre, (506) 529-3386

For assistance and the names of clubs in various localities, contact the main organization: New Brunswick Federation of Naturalists, 277 Douglas Avenue, Saint John, N.B. E2K 1E5.

People who have provided information and have offered to help you include:

Albert: David Christie, Mary Majka or Mike Majka, R.R. 2, Albert, N.B. E0A 1A0, Tel.: (506) 842-2100

Fredericton: Peter A. Pearce, P.O. Box 400, Fredericton, N.B. E3B 4Z9, Tel.: (506) 452-3086 office; Owen Washburn, R.R. 8, Lower St. Marys, Fredericton, N.B. E3B 5W5, Tel.: (506) 472-3842 home or 454-0213 office

Hampton: Richard Blacquiere, R.R. 2, Hampton, N.B.

Hartland: Don Kimball, R.R. 5, Hartland, N.B. E0J 1N0, Tel.: (506) 375-8589

Lameque: Hilaire Chiasson, C.P. 421, Lameque, N.B. E0B 1V0, Tel.: (506) 344-2286

Lower Dover: Louis Lapierre, Lower Dover, N.B., Tel.: (506) 854-1552

Moncton: Brian Dalzell, 87 Allison Dr., Moncton, N.B. E1E 2T7, Tel.: (506) 855-3276 home or 855-2745 office or 662-8670 Grand Manan

Newcastle: Harry Walker, 276 Heath Court, Newcastle, N.B. E1V 2Y5 Tel.: (506) 622-2108

Plaster Rock: Erwin Landauer, R.R. 2, Plaster Rock, N.B. E0J 1W0, Tel.: (506) 356-8670; Wilma and Bill Miller, R.R. 1 Nictou, Plaster Rock, N.B. E0J 1W0, Tel.: (506) 356-2409; R.P. Richter, R.R. 1, Plaster Rock, N.B. E0J 1W0, Tel.: (506) 356-2496

Rothesay: James G. Wilson, 2 Weck Rd., Quispamsis/Rothesay, N.B. E0G 2W0, Tel.: (506) 847-4506 home or 657-7820 office

Sackville: Canadian Wildlife Service, Box 1590, West Main St., Sackville, N.B. E0A 3C0, Tel.: (506) 536-3025, Peter Barkhouse, Peter W. Hicklin, Al Smith (536-0164 home) or Stuart Tingley (536-2862 home)

St. Andrews: David J. Clark, P.O. Box 232, St. Andrews, N.B. E0G 2X0, Tel.: (506) 529-3727 home or 529-8891 office

Saint John: Cecil L. Johnston, 29 Coronation Centre, Saint John, N.B., Tel.: (506) 672-3344; David Smith, 149 Douglas Ave., Saint John, N.B. E2K 1E5, Tel.: (506) 652-2872

St. Stephen: Daryl Linton, R.R. 1, 172 Church St., St. Stephen, N.B. E3L 2X8, Tel.: (506) 466-3487

Shediac: Leo Martin, C.P. 159, Shediac, N.B., Tel.: (506) 532-3405

Tidehead: Alan Madden, P.O. Box 77, Tidehead, N.B. E0K 1K0, Tel.: (506) 759-9779

To obtain a good road map and other material useful to a visitor, contact: Tourism New Brunswick, P.O. Box 12345, Fredericton, N.B. E3B 5C3, Telephone toll free in Canada 1-800-561-0123, Telephone from outside Canada (506) 453-2377.

Campbellton to Dalhousie

The western end of Baie des Chaleurs attracts well over 200 species, with 102 known as nesting. Habitat diversity and a waterfowl staging area make the area quite productive. Access is via Highway 17 from the west and Highway 11 from the east, VIA Rail and the Charlo Airport. Contact Alan Madden, in Tidehead, for help (see above).

Birding Features
Tidal flats and fresh-water marsh, hardwood, softwood and mixed woods, meadows with hedgerows and rocky coastline are all represented. Route 11 serves the area as the main highway. However, the best birding is along Route 134. Begin at the west end, at Tidehead:

Atholville–Tidehead Boom. Turn north off Highway 134, onto Boom Road at the Tidehead-Atholville boundary. Proceed 300 m to view the marsh. Continue 1000 m and stop at several spots. In spring the marsh is often flooded and covered by high tides. Waterfowl are best from mid- to late May and mid-August to November; waders from late July to October.

Sugarloaf Provincial Park lies at the western edge of Campbellton on Route 11. At dawn ferret out flycatchers, warblers and other forest species from mid-May to mid-September.

Restigouche Estuary has several thousand scoters between Campbellton and Dalhousie in late April and May.

Bon Ami Point and Rocks. In Dalhousie, proceed east on Main Street, then when Route 134 turns right, continue straight about 1.5 km to Bon Ami Point. This is a spring and fall stopover area for waterfowl. In early May you'll see scoters; November and December are good for both species of goldeneye. Over 100 Barrow's Goldeneyes have been observed here.

Eel River Lagoon and Head Pond. Take Route 134 about 5 km southeast from Dalhousie to where it crosses the sand bar at Eel River. Park by the road on the south side of the lagoon. The mudflats and water of the tidal lagoon are interesting for herons, ducks, shorebirds and gulls. Rarities have been discovered here during migration. Upstream, the cat-tail head pond is of exceptional interest for northern New Brunswick. Here you may spot Pied-billed Grebe, Green-backed Heron, Hooded Merganser and Marsh Wren. Walk to the marsh along the lagoon. It can also be scanned from three sites in the village of Eel River Crossing: at the steel bridge crossing the river, at the wooden bridge, or from the main street at the north end of the village. A canoe gives best access. Water birds are most numerous during May and September. Shorebirds are best in May and late July to October.

ALAN MADDEN

Miscou Island and Lameque Island

Set at the "Land's End" of New Brunswick, these two islands, particularly Miscou, have changed little since they were settled over two centuries ago. They are good spots in spring or fall for passing water birds. The historical richness of the area is best portrayed at the nearby Acadian Historical Village, about 40 km west of the islands on Route 11, just west of Caraquet. The two islands lie in the northeastern corner of the province, off Highway 11, on Route 113. Some commercial accommodation and camping is available on the islands and at the town of Lameque. For help contact Hilaire Chiasson (see above).

Birding Features

The area offers bogs, long beaches and wind-swept low forests. For migrants, come in April and May, and again during August to mid-October. In June and July, check the woodland for songbirds and watch for breeding Piping Plovers on the beaches.

On your way out to the islands, stop at Shippegan to check the harbour on both sides of the bridge for gulls and shorebirds. Shippegan and Lameque are important fishing centres. The spring passage of water birds, particularly eiders and scoters, is readily visible from the eastern shore of Lameque Island. In seasons other than spring, hurry on to Miscou Island.

On arrival at Miscou Harbour, at the southern end of the island, look for a gull and tern roost, and in late summer for shorebirds such as Hudsonian Godwit and yellowlegs. Proceeding north on Route 113, turn east on the Wilson Point (Pte. Noire) Road, which runs first through woods where there are numerous passerines in summer. Moving on to the peatlands, you can expect to see Northern Harrier, Savannah Sparrow and, in late summer and early fall, Whimbrel. At the T-junction turn north, drive to the end of the road and park. You are now at the southern end of Mal Bay South, a shallow lagoon that is good for herons, ducks, geese and shorebirds. Walk north along the marshy shore about 1.5 km to the lagoon outlet and then return along the beach. Check Mal Bay for shore and water birds, the beach for shorebirds and the sea for Northern Gannet, cormorants, ducks and gulls. Now head back to Route 113 and turn north.

A side road marked Plage de l'Ouest (West Beach) leads to the beach and dunes on the Baie des Chaleurs. Route 113 crosses a fair amount of bog on the way to the northern end of the island, Miscou Point. At the lighthouse you will often find a small number, but good variety, of migrant shorebirds on the beach. Offshore there are likely to be loons, Northern Gannet, cormorants and sea ducks. You can walk southeast along the beach to reach

Mal Bay North, an area similar to Mal Bay South. It's about 3 km to the northern part of the lagoon, 5 km to the outlet.

HILAIRE CHIASSON

Kouchibouguac National Park

The diversity of easily accessible habitat enables birders to visit sites ranging from a barrier island system to bogs, and to see numerous bird species in a short time. At Kouchibouguac (pronounced koo-she-boo-GWAK), birders have reported 217 species, with 90 confirmed nesters. Waterfowl are particularly abundant on migration. Don't miss the herd of Gray and Harbour Seals at the mouth of the St. Louis River.

The park, a 238-km^2 segment of maritime coastal plain, is located on the shore of Northumberland Strait about 100 km north of Moncton and 45 km south of Chatham along Highway 11. The SMT bus service passes the park every day. The nearest VIA Rail station is at Rogersville, 35 km west of the park entrance. An extensive system of hiking and bicycle trails and 50 km of roads are open for your use.

Accommodation is available along Route 11 in nearby communities such as St.-Louis-de-Kent. The park has a major campground, group tenting and wilderness camp areas. Commercial camping is available along the highway.

The park has a detailed bird checklist and brochure showing the roads and trails. For more information check with the park library; they have a major unpublished avifaunal survey of the park. Write or telephone: Interpretive Service, Kouchibouguac National Park, Kouchibouguac, N.B. E0A 2A0, Telephone: (506) 876-2443 or 876-2444.

Birding Features

Forests, constituting 52 per cent of the park, are dominated by conifers and mixed stands. Bogs cover 21 per cent of the land area. Estuaries and lagoons make up 18 per cent; open fields, 4 per cent; salt marshes cover 3 per cent. The barrier island system is only 2 per cent, and ponds and brooks less than 1 per cent of the area. The seacoast is the major feature on the east side.

Spring migration from mid-April to mid-May brings in water birds, birds of prey, blackbirds and sparrows. From late May to early June, waves of shorebirds, flycatchers, warblers and swallows arrive. Nesting occurs from late May to July. Fall migration begins in late July; the best time is August for shorebirds and some water birds such as Northern Gannet and cormorants. September brings masses of songbirds and waterfowl. In October and November, Canada Geese pass through. The best times for the largest number of species are late May and mid-September.

Each nature trail covers a different habitat type and offers good birding. Kelly's Beach and Callander's Beach are fine vantage points from which to overlook large areas of the lagoon systems. A good telescope is useful. The barrier island system is another good area. From late spring to early fall, a walk from Kelly's Beach, on the boardwalk across the dunes to the ocean, should prove very satisfying. You should see Northern Gannet, cormorant, waterfowl and Osprey, shorebirds (notably nesting Piping Plover), gulls, terns and Sharp-tailed Sparrow. During breeding season, Tern Island supports a colony of several thousand Common Terns.

St.-Louis Cape is probably the best location in the park to observe Brown Thrasher and hear Whip-poor-will.

To best observe the eider and scoter migration along the shore in spring, go to the community of Point Sapin, just north of the park. From there you can continue north on Route 117 to Escuminac, explore along the shore of Miramichi Bay towards Chatham, and return to the park on Route 11. The shallow inshore waters of Miramichi Bay are bordered by sandy beaches, salt marshes and small, sheltered estuaries, worth checking from April through October. Contact Harry Walker (in Newcastle, see above) for help.

ROBERT LeBLANC*, HARRY WALKER

*Park Warden Robert LeBlanc was fatally injured in the line of duty in the spring of 1982.

Cape Jourimain National Wildlife Area and Cape Tormentine

These marshes on the southeast tip of New Brunswick have produced over 200 species of birds. The average person should easily locate 40 to 50 during a four-hour visit in spring or fall. A few small mammals and maybe a Red Fox can be seen.

The land has been farmed for over 150 years. The settlers diked it for hayland and later abandoned it when the seas broke down their dikes. Prominent road- and railway beds were built across the marshes in the 1960s as part of a proposed causeway to Prince Edward Island. Brackish ponds formed on one side of the road and salt marshes remained on the other. The area was set aside as a national wildlife area (NWA) in 1979.

To reach the 640-ha site, drive east on Route 16 to Cape Tormentine, at the CN Marine Ferry Terminal. To reach the wildlife area, go northwest on Highway 955 through Bayfield for 5 km, turn off at the overpass and travel north on the abandoned causeway approach.

There are three small motels at Cape Tormentine and one major campground 16 km north. Other services are available nearby. Two helpful brochures, a map with a description of the area, and a checklist of the birds that gives abundance and season of occurrence are available from the CWS in Sackville. Contact Al Smith and Stuart Tingley (in Sackville, see above) for more information.

Birding Features

Cape Jourimain NWA is made up of a complex association of salt and brackish marshes, barrier beach, sand dunes and uplands, with the old roadbed down the middle. Most of the upland is covered with grasses, shrubs and stands of young evergreen and deciduous trees. To explore, use a vehicle along the abandoned causeway or go by foot along the railroad bed and the several walking routes shown on the above-mentioned map.

The best times to visit are mid-March to mid-May for migrant water birds; mid-May to early June and August through September for migrant passerines; June and July for nesting Osprey, Common Tern, Willet, warblers and Sharp-tailed Sparrow; in early July plan on spending a minimum of four hours to cover the wetlands, higher areas and seacoast adequately.

Waterfowl and shorebirds are the most abundant and conspicuous birds on the cape. Waterfowl are present year-round, except when the marshes are frozen in mid-winter. Dabbling ducks occur in the marsh, and sea ducks, in the coastal waters.

Some 20 species of shorebirds are regulars and 30 species have been observed in recent years. Some stop over in the spring, but July to September is the best time to watch for waders. You can spot Semipalmated and Black-bellied Plovers, Willet, both yellowlegs, Red Knot, Hudsonian Godwit, Least and Semipalmated Sandpipers, and others. Occasionally a Ruff from Europe is noted.

Look for the common Great Blue Heron and occasionally such other heron species as Little Blue Heron, Great and Snowy Egrets and Glossy Ibis. The lighthouse is used by a large colony of Cliff Swallows. Osprey cruise the marshes, with Northern Harrier on the uplands all summer and fall. Winter brings Rough-legged Hawk and an occasional Snowy Owl.

The ferry terminal at Cape Tormentine is best for observing migrating loons, grebes, cormorants and sea ducks from late summer through to November. Come here from late October to mid-May for Glaucous and Iceland Gulls.

STUART TINGLEY, AL SMITH, PETER BARKHOUSE

Tantramar Marshes and Tintamarre National Wildlife Area

These formerly tidal marshes derive their name from the French term "tintamarre," applied to the "grand bruit, accompagné de désordre" of the many waterfowl that inhabited the wetlands. The Canadian Wildlife Service (CWS) keeps close tabs on this area and has reported over 200 species. Several birds are probably more numerous here than anywhere else in the Maritimes, including American Bittern, Northern Harrier, Virginia Rail, Short-eared Owl and Marsh Wren. The Yellow Rail is a rare but probably regular summer resident.

The marshlands were protected from the sea with dikes built by the Acadians and other settlers, creating 207 km^2 of fertile lands. Recently, parts of the upper reaches have been impounded as waterfowl management areas by the CWS and Ducks Unlimited (Canada).

The Trans-Canada Highway, Route 2, crosses the lower Tantramar in the southeastern corner of New Brunswick. Regular services and accommodation are available in Sackville. The Owens Art Gallery, at Mount Allison

University in Sackville, has a fine collection, including works by the Group of Seven. The town also has the last harness shop still producing handmade horse collars in eastern Canada.

The CWS, located next to the post office on Main Street, has a comprehensive bird list giving both the status of, and dates to see, specific species. Write for a copy (see above for address). They also have a map of the area.

Birding Features

The variety of habitats include tidal marsh, impounded and natural freshwater marsh, lakes, diked hayfield and pasture, bog and swamp, and mixed and coniferous forest. A number of marsh dwellers rare in the Maritimes, such as Wilson's Phalarope and Sedge Wren, probably breed in the area of impoundments 2 and 3 and are seen regularly. The best times to visit include late May to early July for breeding marsh birds, and November to the end of January for wintering Rough-legged Hawks, Snowy Owls and Snow Buntings.

The following is one suggested route for birding the Tantramar. On a return trip from Sackville, you will log about 65 km by car and from 1 to 15 on foot. During spring, some of the dirt roads are muddy.

Both diked and tidal marshland can be visited near Fort Beausejour National Historic Park not far off the Trans-Canada Highway. Take the Fort Beausejour exit from Route 2, just east of the junction of Routes 2 and 16 at Aulac. The old fort site offers a good view of the upper part of Cumberland Basin and the surrounding marsh and upland. To get to the marsh, continue past the fort parking lot and across the CNR main line. Park and walk west along the dike towards the mouth of the river. Sharp-tailed Sparrows are in taller wild grasses here and are often seen perched on fence lines.

You approach the main impoundments from Route 16. Driving towards P.E.I., about 12 km from Route 2, turn left onto a side road to Jolicure. About 0.8 km from the highway you will come to the crossroads at Jolicure. Two of the Jolicure lakes, visible from the road 1.5 and 2.7 km straight ahead, may have Common Loon, Ring-necked Duck and other water birds. After checking the lakes, return to the crossroads and turn southwest.

Two km from the crossroads, turn right on Hay Road, a narrow, sometimes rather rough track into the area. You may be able to drive 2 km to the impoundments, but usually the road is bad and you will have to walk or else consider entering from Goose Lake Road, described later. Early morning and evening, when the marsh birds are most vocal and active, are the best times. Observe from the elevated dikes. You can easily spend several hours watching the ducks, rails, bitterns, snipe, etc., here but mosquitoes are sometimes a problem, so have some repellent handy. When you've finished, go back to the gravel road from which you came and turn right.

This route takes you southwest along the High Marsh Road, which swings northwest through drained hay- and pastureland, an area full of grassland and open-country birds, with a chance of water birds flying up from the creeks and ditches. In the twilight hours, look for a Short-eared Owl.

Continue on the High Marsh Road, through the covered bridge over the Tantramar River, to Route 940. Turn right towards Midgic. About 3 km to the north, just beyond the Tantramar River and the railway, part of the wildlife area lies on the east side of the road.

Three km beyond the railway, turn right at the T-junction in Midgic and drive 2.6 km to the dike of impoundment 6. From here (Goose Lake Road) you can walk the dike eastward to the Paunchy Pond impoundments (about 3 km). From this point you will have to turn back to Midgic and turn left on 940 to Sackville.

DAVID CHRISTIE, STU TINGLEY, AL SMITH

Driving Loop: Dorchester, Upper Rockport, Sackville

To see 50,000 Semipalmated Sandpipers in one flock is a thrill never to be forgotten. This is the area to do it, on a 45-km round trip from Sackville. From Dorchester, on Route 6, halfway between Moncton and Sackville, turn southwest on Route 935 to Johnsons Mills and Upper Rockport, where you turn east to Sackville. You can go the reverse way around the loop, but this puts you on the opposite side of the road from the shore, and it is more difficult to spot the birds. The town of Sackville contains all services and an office of the Canadian Wildlife Service, on Main Street.

Birding Features
The Rockport–Dorchester Cape area is unique for its road access near extensive intertidal areas with shorebird roosting sites. The pebble beaches and intertidal mudflats provide habitat for large numbers of shorebirds to roost during high tide and to feed during low tide. Roosts of Semipalmated Sandpipers reaching upwards of 50,000 can be approached to within 15 m by car.

The best time to come is from mid-July to mid-September. The truly peak numbers occur within a very short period of time and can easily be missed. White-rumped Sandpiper, Dunlin and Sanderling are generally seen later in late September and October. Time your visit to the Dorchester to Upper Rockport leg for between two hours before and two hours after high tide. At that time the birds roost near or on the road. Approach these gatherings by vehicle rather than on foot, since a human figure flushes them more easily than a vehicle.

About 8 km south of Dorchester on Route 935, you will reach the shore of Shepody Bay at a broad cove known as Grande Anse. This is the site of the first large shorebird roost. The second roost lies about 2.5 km south. The third spot is about another kilometre.

Other birds to watch for at this season include a few hundred Semipalmated and Black-bellied Plovers, a few Ruddy Turnstones, several Red Knots, a couple of hundred White-rumped and Least Sandpipers, Dunlins, Sanderlings and Short-billed Dowitchers. A few Hudsonian Godwits should be there too. Watch for Great Black-backed, Herring and Ring-billed Gulls. Black Scoters swim offshore.

After another 3 km, the road crosses the peninsula to Upper Rockport on Cumberland Basin. On the far side, turn left and drive towards Sackville until you reach an area of Black Spruce with some Jack Pine on the left. Stop here to look for Palm Warbler and Spruce Grouse. Pine Grosbeak may also be spotted. You'll have to hike around to find the grouse.

PETER W. HICKLIN, REID McMANUS, STUART TINGLEY

Albert County Coast/ Shepody National Wildlife Area

Visit one of the major staging areas for migrant shorebirds on the Atlantic coast. You could spot 100,000 Semipalmated Sandpipers at Marys Point.

This area lies along Routes 114 and 915 just east of Fundy National Park. Bus service from Moncton to Alma, a village adjacent to the park, is once daily on weekdays. The park and Alma contain most of the accommodations, but there are also some at Hopewell Hill and Hopewell Cape to the east.

For more information, refer to contacts in Albert (see above) and the interpreters at Fundy National Park (see below). The CWS plans a detailed checklist for the birds of Shepody NWA, including abundance and seasonal occurrence.

Birding Features

The area encompasses a great variety of habitat, including spruce-fir forests, turbid coastal waters, brushy upland fields, dikelands used for pasture and hay, mixed forest, tidal marsh, intertidal mudflats, rocky shore, impounded fresh-water marshes, streams, lakes and villages.

In addition to the shorebird migration from late July to mid-September, look for marsh birds in summer; geese from mid-March to early May; eiders and scoters from April to early May; hawks in late April and passerines coming through in April and May. Rarities occur mainly in the fall.

Take the driving loop from Alma east to Albert and return (about 75 km). Heading east on Route 114, about 1 km from the centre of Alma, bear right onto Route 915 towards New Horton and Harvey. There are some steep grades and curves unsuitable if one is towing a large trailer.

Waterside Marsh, 11.5 km from Alma, is a tidal marsh with numerous ponds, fronted by a long gravel beach. It attracts herons, geese, ducks, shorebirds (mainly at high tide) and gulls. In spring watch for rafts of sea ducks on the bay offshore. Semipalmated Plovers nest along the marsh edge of the beach, Sharp-tailed Sparrows in the taller marsh grasses.

Back on 915, drive 11.7 km east of Cape Enrage Rd. and turn right onto Marys Point Rd. During the fall migration, visit the shorebird roost at Marys Point. The birding is usually good from about two hours before high tide to two hours after high tide. To reach the roost, park near a private drive 3.1 km from the end of Marys Point Rd. and walk down that drive (200 m) to the beach. About 100,000 Semipalmated Sandpipers rest here at peak season, around the beginning of August. Hundreds to a few thousands of Semipalmated and Black-bellied Plovers, Red Knots, White-rumped and Least Sandpipers, Dunlins, Short-billed Dowitchers and Sanderlings may be seen at the peaks of their migration. The birds rest here between periods of intense feeding on the mudflats. Do not approach the roost closely or otherwise frighten the birds. Patient observers have ample opportunity to see the birds in flight as the flocks adjust their position on the beach in response to the rising or falling tide.

About 2.5 km farther along Marys Point Road, there is a "tidal dam" and dike system at Harvey which prevents the sea from flooding the Shepody River and adjacent former marshland now used for agriculture. Interesting birds occupy the pastures and hayfields: Canada Geese in spring; Northern Harrier and Short-eared Owl during summer; Rough-legged Hawk in winter. Most can be seen from the road between Harvey and Albert. For the owls, however, drive the agricultural road that crosses the dam from Harvey to Hopewell Hill, a distance of about 4.7 km. Chances are good of seeing one or more Short-eared Owls at dusk.

About 1.5 km from the dam, Marys Point Road rejoins Route 915 at Harvey Corner. Turn right towards Albert, 3.7 km away, then left towards Alma on Route 114 and drive 3.8 km to a gravel road on the left. At 0.9 km from 114, stop just south of the creek. Between here and another road 7 km to the west is the 560-ha Germantown section of Shepody NWA. Seven large impoundments have good numbers of breeding marsh birds.

Bird these impoundments by walking west along the dikes. Early morning and evening are the best times. To return to your car, either double back or cross one of the dikes between impoundments to reach a trail just within the edge of the woods and follow it back to the road. To return to Fundy Park, go back to 114 and turn left towards Alma (21.5 km).

DAVID CHRISTIE, MARY MAJKA, MIECZYSLAW MAJKA

Fundy National Park

Facing the sea along a line of cliffs, the rolling plateau lands of Fundy National Park average about 300 m above the sea. Over 200 species of birds have been recorded, with at least 96 species as fairly regular nesters. The Black-backed Woodpecker is found often.

Settled about 1820, the land was used for agriculture and lumbering. Since the park was established in 1948, the remaining fields have been reverting to forest. Defoliation by Spruce Budworm killed much of the fir and spruce during the 1970s. Today most of the forest is in a period of rapid successional change.

The 207-km^2 park lies 80 km west from Moncton and 60 km east of Sussex, on Route 114. The Fundy Coach Line bus service runs Monday to Friday, leaving Moncton in the afternoon and the other end, Alma, in the morning. The park contains 70 km of roads and 100 km of trails. There is a

TWTHORN/82

Black-backed Woodpecker

variety of accommodation and campgrounds, including a winter campsite, at the park and adjacent Alma.

A comprehensive report on the birds at Fundy is available at certain libraries. For local help, contact: The Superintendent, Fundy National Park, Alma, N.B. E0A 1B0, Telephone: (506) 887-2000.

Birding Features

Mixed forest dominates the park, followed by spruce-fir and deciduous forest; turbid coastal waters lie along a 22.5-km coastline; the remainder (5 per cent) of the land is old fields and human-dominated sites, wetland thickets, meadows and bog, intertidal rock, gravel and mud, lakes, and swift, rocky rivers.

During spring and fall migration, birding can be interesting all along the coast, particularly near headquarters and at Herring Cove, Matthews Head and Point Wolfe. Watch for small birds in the bushes and at the edge of the woods. At and just after dawn, large flocks may pass low overhead.

In April and early May, loons and sea ducks can be watched from Matthews Head and at the far end of the Coppermine Trail. Take your spotting scope. In late April and early May, some days have excellent hawk flights best seen from the bank above the sea at headquarters.

Winter is a quiet time for birding. During a good cone crop year, winter finches will come in numbers. Check the bird feeders in Alma for rarities.

Probably the most sought-after bird is the Black-backed Woodpecker. The foraging area of this bird shifts as conditions change. Concentrate on sites where spruce and fir are dying or very recently dead, with bark still tight.

During the breeding season from mid-May to early July, the woodland species are of most interest. Rise before dawn and take the trails to spot them. Favourite summer spots include: Wolfe Lake, Caribou Plain Trail, the park headquarters area including the mouth of the Alma River, Maple Grove Rd. and Coppermine Trail. A few Gray-cheeked Thrushes nest near the first two brooks crossed by the Coppermine Trail.

DAVID CHRISTIE

Saint John

Clinging to the shores of the Bay of Fundy, Saint John is one of the oldest cities in Canada. Nesting gulls and cormorants, combined with coastal marshes and a ferry trip across the bay, result in a checklist of 212 regular species, of which 110 are nesters.

T.J.THORNIN/82

Great Cormorant

Champlain anchored in the bay and named the river in 1604. A small trading post built in 1631 mushroomed into an instant city with the influx of a few thousand Loyalists in 1783. The city was in its heyday during the wooden ship–building era of the nineteenth century. Today a visitor can explore those earlier days with a stroll along the 5-km "Loyalist Trail" through downtown Saint John and view houses, stores, churches an a market over a hundred years old.

Lying on Highway 1, Saint John is served by air, bus and poor passenger rail service. A visitor has a large selection of accommodations, including campsites. One of these sites lies in Rockwood Park, a pleasant birding location with an extensive trail system.

The provincial museum has published *Finding Birds Around Saint John*, a booklet by D.S. Christie that includes a comprehensive checklist. The Natural Science Department of the museum serves as a data base for birders. Contact Gayl Hipperson at the museum (506) 693-1196 or at home (506) 693-5093 for current birding trips. Refer above for contacts in Saint John and Rothesay.

Birding Features

The habitats range from deep and shallow sea, sandy sea beach, salt- and fresh-water marshes, to coniferous and deciduous woods and open fields. The above-mentioned booklet briefly covers the following areas, plus others within 50 km of the city.

Saints' Rest Marsh and Sewage Lagoon lie on the western outskirts of the city south of Highway 1. Stop on the shoulder of the eastbound lane for a quick scan over the marsh and ponds for herons, ducks, shorebirds and gulls. About 0.5 km east, an elevated travel information centre (where a local checklist is available) provides a good view of the central portion of the marsh. About 0.6 km east of the centre, pull over at the entrance to the sewage facility; scan for waterfowl. If it is productive, park out of the way of city vehicles and walk in. Pedestrian birders are tolerated by staff.

To visit the beach and south side of the marsh, take Exit 107A, Catherwood Drive, south from Route 1. Turn right on Sand Cove Road, 0.5 km off the highway. Park at the end of Sand Cove Road and don't drive out onto the sand beach. From here you can explore the marsh on foot. Scan seaward to Manawagonish Island where Double-crested Cormorant, Great Blue Heron, and Great Black-backed and Herring Gulls nest. High tide brings migrating shorebirds to the upper beach and marsh. At low tide they feed on a large mudflat to the west of Taylors Island, a wooded peninsula at the far end of the beach.

Reversing Falls. Take Reversing Falls exit off Highway 1 to the falls. There is a travel information centre at the western end of Reversing Falls Bridge, but the best place to watch is Falls View Park. Cross the bridge to the east, turn left on Douglas Ave. and take the next left onto Falls View Ave. to the park.

In summer, many Double-crested Cormorants feed in the rapids and fly up and down the river. Study the three small islands in the rapids for eggs and chicks of Great Black-backed and Herring Gulls that nest here.

Great Black-backed Gull

In winter, scrutinize for Common Goldeneye and Common Merganser. Walk to the right along the shore for American Black Ducks and Mallards resting on the upper island. Continue on 50 m to see into Marble Cove, a shallow cove above the rapids used as a roost by various gulls. Off the edge of the ice, Bufflehead and other ducks feed.

Marsh Creek, at the end of Hanover Street, lies three streets beyond the causeway. It is the best vantage spot in the area to examine both subspecies of Iceland Gull at close range.

Red Head Marsh. The marsh, on the eastern side of Saint John Harbour, is 3.3 km south of the Courtenay Causeway. Drive south on Bayside Dr. and turn right onto Red Head Road. Park by the sea wall at the marsh. Observe from the road or hike the sometimes rough trail along the south edge of the marshes. Stay in heavy cat-tail areas or on shore to avoid falling through treacherous mats of floating vegetation. The marsh interior can be explored by canoe along creek channels.

This is the northern breeding limit of several species. Look for a nesting Green-backed Heron, Least Bittern, Common Moorhen and Marsh Wren. The site is best visited from early May to late June and mid-August to mid-October. Come in early morning to hear rails call. Check the sea side of the road for water birds.

Ferry ride: Saint John to Digby, Nova Scotia. To reach the CN Marine terminal, take Exit 109 off Route 1 in West Saint John. This is not a consistently good pelagic trip, but from July through October you should see shearwaters and other deep-sea species. From November through January, look for Black-legged Kittiwake and other gulls, Atlantic Puffin, Razorbill and maybe one of the murres.

DAVID CHRISTIE, CECIL JOHNSTON, JAMES WILSON

St. Andrews

Visitors to St. Andrews can expect to enjoy late 1700s architecture as well as a good variety of shorebirds on migration. Overwintering waterfowl include eiders, scoters and scaups. Brant are numerous in spring.

After the American Revolution, many Loyalists fled from Maine to settle here. Several brought houses by barge, section by section, and rebuilt these "prefabricated units." Check at the tourist office for examples of late eighteenth century and early nineteenth century buildings. Don't miss the Greenock Presbyterian Church, built in 1824, the best of them all.

St. Andrews lies about 17 km south of Highway 1, in southwestern New Brunswick. It is a tourist area with lots of accommodation, including a campground at Indian Point. Public nature trails with potential for songbirds occur at Huntsman Marine Laboratory, at Pottery Cove on Joes Point Rd. and at Wren Lake, north of Route 1 between Digdeguash and Waweig (24 km from St. Andrews).

A pamphlet produced by the cws, *Birds of the Passamaquoddy Area*, and a checklist, are available at Sunbury Shores Arts and Nature Centre. Refer above for contacts in St. Andrews and St. Stephen.

Birding Features
Indian Point is about 1.5 km from downtown, south along Water Street. The beach and water attract a variety of species. A salt marsh, at the O'Neill farm, is about 1.2 km north from the trailer camp along the eastern end of the beach.

Shorebirds come in late May and from late July to mid-September. They gather on the intertidal zone of bedrock, sand and mud. Purple Sandpipers are here in winter. The inshore salt water attracts a variety of water birds such as loons, eiders and scoters from fall through spring. Brant are numerous in March and April. Check the nearby bushes and woods for songbirds during migration.

The Bar Road. This road to Ministers Island lies just over 2 km northeast from St. Andrews on Route 127. Turn east on the Bar Road to the intertidal gravel bar. The bar is submerged at high tide, so park your car above the high tide mark and remember about the tide when walking. This is an attractive area for loons, grebes, cormorants and ducks, with a few shorebirds. The protected salt-water and gravelly tidal flats, with trees and shrubs along the road, make a visit from October to late May worthwhile.

DARYL LINTON

Deer Island and Campobello Island

The rich marine resources at the entrance to Passamaquoddy Bay attract up to two million Red-necked Phalaropes in August, the largest known concentration in eastern North America. Bonaparte's Gull gatherings reach 30,000, the largest on the Atlantic coast of Canada.

A free ferry service to Deer Island operates hourly during daylight from Letete, on Route 772, off Highway 1 at St. George. In summer only, you can reach Campobello Island from Deer Island, on a commercially operated ferry. Campobello is also accessible by bridge from Lubec, Maine (on State Route 189, off U.S. 1).

Birding Features
The most attractive elements of this spot are the turbulent deep passages between islands, the sheltered coves and harbours, rocky intertidal sites, and coniferous and mixed woods.

Come from late July to mid-September for Red-necked Phalarope; August to October to see Bonaparte's Gull; mid-October to early January for kittiwakes. Common eider, large gulls and Black Guillemot are present all year. The concentration of gulls attracts such scarce or vagrant species as Common Black-headed, Little, Franklin's and Laughing Gulls in the fall.

The ferry from Letete to Deer Island crosses Letete Passage, where there are several small islands. Black Guillemot are often seen very near the boat. Common Eider, Surf and White-winged Scoters and Red-breasted Merganser are present from fall through spring. Bald Eagle is frequently observed.

Once on Deer Island, go south to the park at Deer Island Point, an excellent viewing area for the gulls and phalaropes which congregate in Head Harbour Passage. If the birds are too far away, check to see if the commercial ferry will take you over to Campobello and back as a foot passenger without the loss of too much time. These birds shift back and forth with the currents bringing food supplies to the surface. A patient wait of an hour may bring the birds right back to you on the point. A winter trip should include the sheltered harbours at each village for Bufflehead and other ducks.

Campobello Island also gives good views of the birds in Head Harbour Passage. The best spots are at the northwestern end, between Wilsons Beach and East Quoddy Head (Head Harbour Light). At the latter exposed site, the Harlequin Duck is frequently seen in winter. The deep water here attracts many species at any time of the year.

DAVID CHRISTIE

Grand Manan Archipelago

New Brunswick's most widely known birding area, Grand Manan, awed John James Audubon when he saw thousands of nesting seabirds here in 1813. The colonies on the offshore islands and pelagic birds in the surrounding waters have contributed to the more than 275 species of birds seen in the archipelago. Many firsts for the province have been reported from this area.

Settled for about 200 years, the island shows the results of varied uses by man. Today the land is a complex of young woodlands, brushy fields and settlements. At Dark Harbour on the northwest side, thirty-six tonnes a year of dulse, a seaweed delicacy, are harvested at low tide and dried in the sun. The product is shipped across North America.

The main island of 25 by 11 km has about twenty smaller islands along the east side. The archipelago is reached by car ferry from Blacks Harbour, off Route 1, on Route 776. The ferry runs one to three times daily depending on the weather and season. The fares are reasonable. Arrive sixty to ninety minutes ahead of sailing time. On the return trip from the island, it is often difficult to get a vehicle on the ferry of your choice unless you are prepared to wait. Once-a-day bus service to Blacks Harbour from Saint John may allow a connection with the last ferry of the day during the summer. Alternatively, take a taxi to the ferry from Pennfield, a small community on the Saint John–St. Stephen bus route. Charter air service, by small plane, is often available from the Saint John East Airport. Bicycles and limited car rentals are available on the island.

The Anchorage Provincial Park provides camping facilities on the island. There is a variety of hotel accommodation and cabins.

No keen birders are known to reside on Grand Manan. For help contact the Grand Manan Museum in Grand Harbour, and stop in to see their major collection of birds. Brian Dalzell (of Moncton, refer above for phone numbers) may be at Grand Manan on a weekend.

Birding Features
The habitat is extremely varied, including coniferous and mixed woodlands; brushy fields and headlands; cliffs and rocky intertidal areas; mud and sand flats; shallow inshore waters principally along the eastern side of the island; and deeper marine waters off the western and northern sides several km to the south. April and May, plus August through October, are best for small migrant land birds and others; mid-May through July for breeding seabirds; August through October for pelagic species; November through February for wintering water birds.

There are numerous spots to explore on and near the island, but the main places are as follows:

Grand Manan Channel is crossed by ferry from Blacks Harbour. The 35-km passage of about two hours offers possibilities of seeing a variety of pelagic species. These birds shift about the bay, so the chances range from very good to nil. Black-legged Kittiwakes are best from August through March; mid-August through September is good for the much sought after shearwaters and jaegers; murres and Razorbill are found from November through January. Crossing during the middle or later stages of a rising tide will be more productive than during a falling tide.

The Whistle. Lying at the northern tip of Grand Manan, about 5 km from the village of North Head, this location is good for migrant passerines. Activity is usually greatest during early morning, along the edges of woods and lawns around the lighthouse and the keeper's home. At the lighthouse, scan the sea from the clifftop for shearwaters, Double-crested Cormorant, jaegers, gulls and terns feeding in the Long Eddy, a pronounced tidal current not far offshore. Rising tide is the best time to spot them. In winter, large numbers of Black-legged Kittiwakes and Razorbills may be found here.

Swallow Tail. This narrow rocky point lies within walking distance north and east of the centre of the village of North Head. The bushy areas and low coniferous forests provide a haven for migrant songbirds in spring and fall. Check the small bushes on the lee side of the point for sparrows. The end of the Swallow Tail is also a good site for kittiwakes in fall and winter. The point is one of the best-known scenic areas on the island.

Castalia Marsh. The tidal marsh at Castalia is good for herons, ducks, shorebirds, gulls and a variety of small birds. It offers great diversity of habitat within a relatively small area. The marsh lies east of the main island road, 8 km south of the ferry terminal. The entrance is about 200 m south of the Castalia post office.

Begin at the north end where the road breaks out onto the sea wall; proceed along the road by car or foot to the comfort stations. Check the beach grass and upper edges of the marsh for sparrows; scan the sea for ducks and cormorants, the flats for shorebirds and gulls. At the picnic shelter, wander out on the inner marsh (with caution at low tide — there are soft spots) to search for shorebirds. Continue on past the picnic shelters to the wild rose clump. Leave the car here, as the rest of the road is too sandy for vehicles. Check the other side of the outlet run for shorebirds. The marsh can also be entered from the main road on the west side or farther south off the Bancroft Point Road. The south end is privately held, so request permission before leaving the road.

Grand Manan Migratory Bird Sanctuary. Three km southwest of Grand Harbour, take the road to the south to The Anchorage Provincial Park picnic area and campsite. The sanctuary, to the east of the park, includes Long Pond on the west, Great Pond to the east and Long Pond Beach. A sand road takes you between the low dune and the ponds. Drive along to the warden's cabin; park the car and explore. The sandy beach hosts flocks of Sanderlings in late summer and fall. Check the ponds for Pied-billed Grebe, herons, dabbling ducks, Ring-necked Duck and gulls bathing in the fresh water; check the sea for eiders and cormorants. The best spot for marsh birds is at the eastern end of Great Pond. Scout out the spruce and fir woodlands for breeding warblers including Blackpoll.

Southwest Head. The southern tip of the island is a beautiful spot. Basalt cliffs over 60 m high drop to the sea. Sunsets are spectacular! In summer look for the Black Guillemots that nest in the cliffs. In fall take the clifftop path west from the lighthouse on the trail to Bradford Pond. The woods are often full of elusive warblers and sparrows that sometimes dive over the cliff to a shrub just below your view — frustrating but fascinating. In September and October, this headland is a good spot.

Kent Island. This small island off the eastern side of Grand Manan supports a variety of nesting birds, including Leach's Storm-Petrel, eiders, guillemots and gulls. Reach the island by chartering the boat of a local fisherman. Owned by Bowdoin College, the island is operated as a summer research station. Permission to visit must be arranged through the Biology Department, Bowdoin College, Brunswick, Maine.

BRIAN DALZELL, DAVID CHRISTIE, MARY MAJKA, HENRIK DEICHMANN

Machias Seal Island Migratory Bird Sanctuary

Machias (ma-CHY-es) Seal Island, 18 km south of Grand Manan Island and 16 km off the coast of Maine, has an interesting seabird colony. Nesting species include Common and Arctic Terns, Razorbill, Atlantic Puffin and Leach's Storm-Petrel. Over 140 species of birds have been recorded. The island was a serious threat to shipping until a permanent lighthouse eased the danger in 1832. In 1944, the island became a federal migratory bird sanctuary.

The 11 ha of land is composed of a turf-covered central station and rocky granite shoreline. Access is by chartered or private boat, with imposed limits on the numbers of visitors to the island each day. Charters are available from: Preston Wilcox, Seal Cove, N.B. E0G 3B0, Telephone: (506) 662-8296; or from Barna Norton, Jonesport, Maine, U.S.A., Telephone: (207) 497-5933.

The CWS administers the sanctuary. No overnight visits are allowed. A warden-caretaker controls the number of visitors on land at any one time. For more information, request a copy of their pamphlet and bird checklist from the CWS in Sackville, N.B.

Birding Features
On the way out from either Grand Manan or Maine, watch for pelagic species. The summer resident birds are seen in greatest abundance from early June to mid-August. Don't be surprised to find a new or unexpected species during migration, as islands are known as landfalls for rarities.

The visitor is required to remain in a relatively small area. The CWS has provided three blinds to assist you.

Leach's Storm-Petrel nest here but hide in their well-concealed burrows during daylight. There are about 100 pairs of Common Terns and over 1300 pairs of Arctic Terns. Their nesting activities are well underway by the end of May. Roseate Terns have also bred here. There are about 50 pairs of Razorbills but the 800 pairs of Atlantic Puffins are the highlight. This is near the southern limit of their breeding range. They arrive offshore in late April, but don't come ashore for some time. The peak of hatching occurs in mid-June, with adults and young departing in August.

RICHARD BLACQUIERE, MARY MAJKA, CWS STAFF, ATLANTIC REGION

Fredericton

Nature is still relatively unspoiled in and around this university and capital city of 50,000. A stroll through Odell Park or a walk along the river in the Fredericton Game Management Area can be a very pleasant experience.

The area was settled in the 1700s. A college was founded which later became the provincial university, the oldest in Canada. Fredericton became a city in 1845 and obtained the first astronomical observatory in Canada in 1851 and first engineering school in 1854. The oldest dwelling still used was erected in 1785 and reflects a city that cherishes its past. Kings Landing, a restored historical village, lies 34 km west on Highway 2. The city contains all tourist amenities, together with an excellent collection of art in the Beaverbrook Art Gallery.

Birding Features

Odell Park. The 1 km^2 wooded park is reached at its northern end on Rookwood Avenue, the north-south street between Hanwell Road and Smythe Street. If you come off the Trans-Canada No. 2, exit onto Hanwell Road north. The walking trails pass through mixed deciduous and coniferous woods. They are best used in the early morning from mid-May to late June for viewing an excellent collection of woodpeckers and other woodland species such as Great Crested Flycatcher, Wood Thrush, Northern Oriole, Scarlet Tanager and warblers.

Fredericton Game Management Area. This site lies just east of the downtown area, along the river side of Waterloo Row (Route 102) between the railway bridge and the Princess Margaret Bridge. It was made a game management area in 1962 to prohibit trapping. There is good cover and food for migrant land birds, especially in fall. The tangles of grasses and weeds along the shore, and the bushes and trees are the most productive. You may wish to park off Waterloo Row on the green, about halfway between the two bridges. Walk south to the sewage treatment building through woods. At the end of the trail, check the mouth of the small brook for ducks. If the water level is down, cut back along the shore. Low water brings shorebirds to the opposite side of the river.

University of New Brunswick Forest. This mainly coniferous forest lies south of the centre of town about 3 km along Route 101. Access is from several points. A good network of roads and trails and a variety of smaller habitats, including ponds, renders the area attractive to bird watchers, particularly in spring. The Faculty of Forestry, University of New Brunswick, Fredericton, has a map of the trails, as has the Maritimes Forest Ranger School, R.R. 5, Fredericton.

DAVID CHRISTIE, PETER PEARCE

Driving Loop: Maugerville to Gagetown

A trip along the floodplain country east of Fredericton is very good for geese and ducks in the spring, and for marsh and floodplain species breeding in early summer. The fertile floodplain has been cultivated for a long time. Today vegetable crops and hay are the main produce.

The route begins about 20 km east of Fredericton at Maugerville on Trans-Canada No. 2. Visitors can stay in several communities along the way or in Fredericton. Information on the Portobello National Wildlife Area (NWA) is available from the Canadian Wildlife Service at Fredericton and Sackville. For help, contact Owen Washburn in Fredericton (see above).

Birding Features

The floodplain deciduous forest is mixed with meadows and farm fields. Marshes, the Saint John River, creeks and ponds add to the diversity. The Saint John River floods the lowlands to varying degrees each spring, sometimes enough to close the highway. Levels usually peak in early to mid-May and gradually recede over the summer. Make a visit in April and May for migrant waterfowl; June and July to see breeding marsh and land birds; or November and December for hawks.

Start at Maugerville. If you have a canoe, turn north on Church Road to reach Portobello Creek and the NWA, 3.5 km north. Before launching the canoe, make sure you have Topo Map 21 G/16 West and East, Grand Lake, N.B., to avoid getting lost. Go back to Highway 2 and continue east. Watch the creeks and any flooded fields for waterfowl. Scan the Saint John River, especially at Middle Island, about 3 km below the Burton Bridge connection to Route 102.

At McGowans Corner, about 10 km farther, take the pleasant side trip on Route 690 to Lakeville Corner. This 5-km road passes through floodplain hardwoods by a sheltered creek. Check the larger trees for Warbling Vireo. Just before Lakeville, signs on the left outline the eastern boundary of Portobello NWA. Access to this area is by boat. Return to the Trans-Canada.

From McGowans Corner continue east to Jemseg. This stretch usually provides good bird watching in the floodplain fields and marshy spots. Attractive wet sites are near the highway even in mid-summer. Come here for hawks in fall and winter if the mouse population is high. As you approach the Jemseg River Bridge, watch for Osprey. They often nest nearby.

On the east side of the bridge, turn right into Jemseg and then right again on the Lower Jemseg Road leading to the Gagetown ferry, 13 km away. This pretty drive usually provides interesting birds, especially in spring. Cross the ferry to Gagetown and proceed north through the village along Gagetown Creek. Stop and listen for Sora and possibly Virginia Rail calling from the marsh above the ferry during late May and June. Both species also frequent Grimross Neck, across the creek from the village.

Return to the ferry and drive south on Route 102 for about 3 km, then turn left to Upper Hampstead; follow this road south and then west to Elm Hill and back to Route 102; turn north towards Fredericton; about 7.5 km north of the Gagetown ferry, bear right on the road to Coytown, which will bring you back to 102 about 5 km ahead. This loop south and back is good from early spring through fall for a variety of birds.

ENID INCH, MELVIN B. MOORE

Mount Carleton Provincial Park

Set in the northern forested and unpopulated section of New Brunswick, Mount Carleton Provincial Park includes relatively high country with several hard-to-find species, such as both species of three-toed woodpeckers, Gray-cheeked Thrush and Fox Sparrow, all nesting here. About 130 species of birds have been reported, with 105 as confirmed nesters.

The 181-km^2 wilderness park includes Mount Carleton, at 820 m the highest point in the Maritimes. Headquarters is at Nictau Lake, 52.5 km east from Saint-Quentin on Highway 17; or 115 km northeast of Plaster Rock on Route 108. Nearest gas, food and other services are at Saint-Quentin to the west and Riley Brook, 75 km south. Camping space is available at Nictau Lake. There is no commercial transportation into the park. In summer, most of the park is accessible by canoe on the lakes or by hiking the numerous trails. Some roads are usable by car. In winter, park headquarters is reached by car and then access to the remainder is by snowmobile, cross-country skis and snowshoes. The park is staffed year-round. For detailed information, including a checklist, contact Tourism New Brunswick (see above). For help, refer to contacts in Plaster Rock (see above).

Birding Features

A 1923 fire burned much of the park. Today it is dominated by birch and aspen. Unburned portions are covered in spruce-fir-pine and birch. Come from the last full week of May to mid-July. Blackpoll Warbler, Pine Grosbeak and Fox Sparrow are found near the lake at park headquarters. The trail to the top of Mount Carleton penetrates scrubby forest at high elevations. These upper forests on Carleton, Sagamook Mountain and other high points are likely places to see a Gray-cheeked Thrush. The bird may also occur at lower elevations with open conifer growth and low birches along streams. Most boreal species are widespread in the park, whereas more southern ones are limited to favourable locations near rivers and lakes. Check with park staff for specific species' locations.

The Tobique River, which drains into Nictau Lake, can offer interesting canoeing but the water level is usually too low in mid- to late summer. Pleasant canoeing and birding are more easily combined further south, in the area of Nictau and Riley Brook.

R.P. RICHTER, ERWIN LANDAUER, K.H. DEICHMANN, WILMA MILLER

Nova Scotia

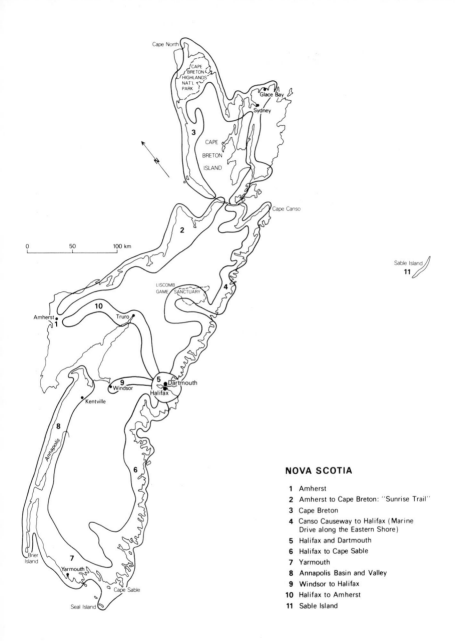

NOVA SCOTIA

1 Amherst
2 Amherst to Cape Breton: "Sunrise Trail"
3 Cape Breton
4 Canso Causeway to Halifax (Marine Drive along the Eastern Shore)
5 Halifax and Dartmouth
6 Halifax to Cape Sable
7 Yarmouth
8 Annapolis Basin and Valley
9 Windsor to Halifax
10 Halifax to Amherst
11 Sable Island

Nova Scotia

Canada's most southeasterly province contains several habitats, ranging from high, nearly tundra lands to lowland valleys. The high country is inhabited by such boreal birds as Spruce Grouse, Gray Jay and Pine Grosbeak. In the lowlands, look for Gray Catbird, Bobolink and Rose-breasted Grosbeak. A selective but undefined barrier for the dispersal of certain birds, other animals and plants exists in the New Brunswick–Nova Scotia boundary area. Hence many birds found nesting in eastern Canada west of Nova Scotia have not been recorded breeding in this province. These include (as of 1972) Red-shouldered Hawk, Eastern Screech-Owl, Three-toed Woodpecker, House Wren, Scarlet Tanager and Rufous-sided Towhee. Still others have just recently entered the province to breed. Being so far south and east, Nova Scotia tends to be visited by many species rare to Canada. People from Sable Island, part of the province but 150 km to the east, consistently report new birds for the province, Canada, and even North America. Small islands (some are sanctuaries) adjacent to the southern and eastern shores are used as nesting havens for seabirds.

The 34,280-km² province has a population of 851,600, mostly concentrated along the coasts and in the fertile Annapolis Valley. Early settlers, particularly in the north near New Brunswick, diked up the long inland bays. These marshlands were reclaimed and converted to hay crop production. With the demise of the horse as a major factor in our society, the lands became vacant and reverted to marshes. Today they are major sites for production of waterfowl and land birds.

The southern half of Nova Scotia rises gently from the sea on the south side to between 30 and 150 m near the north highlands. Topography of the south area is of slight relief and contains innumerable lakes, streams, bogs and barrens. The northern half of the province, including Cape Breton, consists of true uplands. Ranges of hills, mountains and plateaus reach elevations of over 300 m, and in Cape Breton, heights of over 425 m are attained. The hills are covered mainly with deciduous forest and White Spruce, with Balsam Fir and heath shrub barrens found on the highlands of Cape Breton.

A visitor to Nova Scotia should avoid the freeways and use the country roads, to experience the local atmosphere and to see many more birds. Ducks begin incubating in April. There are 22 warbler species found nesting here. Come in June to find them. However, this month tends to be cool, with high water in creeks and swamps. Use rubber boots and bring fly repellent. July is hot during the day and cool in the evening. Plan a trip to the Bird Islands off the east coast of Cape Breton, and islands on the eastern shore, for early July. You can then spot the petrels, cormorants, eiders, Razorbill, Black Guillemot and Atlantic Puffin young, half grown and nearly ready to fend for themselves. By mid-July, shorebirds begin returning. August weather becomes more settled and remains so through October. In late August and September you should have good birding, particularly on the islands off the southwestern tip, including Bon Portage, Seal and Brier. This season and later are the times to set up your telescope on the beaches and headlands to scan for gulls. The Ring-billed Gull appears September through October; the Common Black-headed Gull may appear in September and stays all winter, particularly in Halifax Harbour and Cole Harbour; it is most abundant at Glace Bay, in Cape Breton. The Bonaparte's Gull gathers in the surf from late August through November. Glaucous and Iceland Gulls are around from November to March. An offshore trip should produce Black-legged Kittiwake. Leach's Storm-Petrels are also found far out to sea in this late season.

At the north end, Amherst, with its diked lands, probably contains the widest diversity of species in the province. Around Halifax, be certain to spend at least half a day on a short loop from Dartmouth to Chezzetcook Inlet on Highway 207 looking for marsh and sea birds. Boreal species are seen easily along the short stretch north of Halifax to Windsor. The rarity seeker should try and get out to Sable Island. The Bird Islands (off Cape Breton), the southeast coast and the southwest side will give you the seabirds you want.

A visitor to Halifax should go to the harbour, then east on the Highway 207 loop, and finally north towards Windsor. This can all be done in a day. The marshes at Amherst, Cape Breton or the southwest each take two to three days. In a week of long days, you can cover the province. However, there will be little time to see such places as the Fortress of Louisbourg (one of the best historical parks in the world), the Miners' Museum at Sydney, and the Alexander Graham Bell National Historic Park at Baddeck. All of these places should be visited, since they represent key chapters in Canadian history.

The main birders' group in the province is the Nova Scotia Bird Society, c/o The Nova Scotia Provincial Museum, 1747 Summer Street, Halifax, N.S. B3H 3A6. They hold monthly meetings at the museum and publish *Nova Scotia Birds* three times a year, plus a fall flyer of announcements and sightings. Write for their excellent booklet, *Where to Find the Birds in Nova Scotia*, edited by P. R. Dobson, rev. ed. 1976. It has been a major source of the information for this chapter.

For a road map and other material, write: Department of Tourism, P.O. Box 130, Halifax, N.S. B3J 2M7.

Many visitors to Nova Scotia arrive by car at Amherst, heading for Cape Breton and the Cabot Trail. This chapter has been arranged to suit such an itinerary: along the Northumberland shore, a full circle along the Cabot Trail, then down the mainland shore from Canso around to Truro.

J. WOLFORD

Amherst

The ponds managed by Ducks Unlimited and the Chignecto National Wildlife Area (NWA) at Amherst are full of various marsh birds. With over 200 species reported from these sites, there is more diversity here than at any other location in Nova Scotia. The New Brunswick–Nova Scotia border region also supports one of the densest populations of breeding Northern Harrier ever reported. The underlying gypsum deposits here have provided a soil base, which results in an interesting assortment of uncommon ferns and other plants.

European settlers arrived in the seventeenth century and began diking the salt marshes. For centuries these converted lands were used for hay and pasture, at least until the 1940s, when the use of the horse declined and the market for hay faded. The area became a sanctuary in 1947, and the Chignecto NWA resulted from federal government acquisition of lands in the 1970s. Ducks Unlimited (Canada) constructed an impoundment on the Amherst Marshes (just north of Amherst) in the mid 1970s.

The ponds lie 1.8 km south of the New Brunswick border. Look for the Chignecto NWA (Amherst Point Migratory Bird Sanctuary and John Lusby Marsh) approximately 2 km from the Trans-Canada Highway at Amherst. Amherst contains all regular amenities, with bus and rail service too.

Information for this region was gathered from a variety of sources. The Canadian Wildlife Service produced a comprehensive brochure, map and checklist for the Chignecto NWA. For more information contact them at: Chignecto National Wildlife Area, P.O. Box 1590, Sackville, N.B. E0A 3C0.

Birding Features

The woodlands of the area are dominated by conifers, including spruce, Balsam Fir and Larch. Eastern Hemlock occurs on the slopes and ridges. A few Sugar Maple and Yellow Birch are all that remain of the once-dense hardwood stands. The old farmsteads range from open fields covered by goldenrod to growths of rose, alder and young conifers. The wetlands are managed carefully to provide maximum production of water birds. The dikes have impounded water to create shallow fresh-water marshes. Water draw-down, mechanical removal of dense vegetation, periodic mowing of old farm fields, and selective cutting of trees are all undertaken to further enhance wildlife production.

Amherst Marsh is located just off the Trans-Canada Highway, 1.8 km south of the New Brunswick border. To view the area, leave the highway at LaPlanche Street, or the first exit into Amherst, and loop around to rejoin the Trans-Canada heading back to New Brunswick. This will allow you to park on the gravel shoulder on the marsh side of the road, nearest the impoundment ponds. Scan the area for breeding Pied-billed Grebe, Northern Pintail, Blue-winged and Green-winged Teals, American Wigeon, Northern Shoveler, Wood Duck, Redhead, Ruddy Duck, Sora, American Coot and a colony of Black Terns. Walk along the dikes for a better look.

Chignecto NWA. This wildlife area consists of the Amherst Point Migratory Bird Sanctuary on the south side of the road and the John Lusby Marsh on the north side. Leave the Trans-Canada Highway at the Victoria Street exit in Amherst and head southwest for about 2 km; park on the left. Take time to walk around in both the sanctuary and the salt marsh. The birds here are similar to those of the Amherst Marsh. Note American Coot and Common Moorhen, both of which have nested. The variety of habitat caused by eroding gypsum sinkholes brings all sorts of different birds, particularly during migration in May and September.

J. WOLFORD

Amherst to Cape Breton: "Sunrise Trail"

On leaving Amherst, the traveller should take Highway 6 to Pictou. The birding is usually excellent along the Northumberland Strait in all seasons. The shore is easily accessible in several spots, or may be reached using side roads which are usually gravelled. There are several campsites and a variety of motels, hotels and restaurants from which to choose. The area retains a strong Scottish flavour. A visitor should try to take in one or more local fairs or gatherings that each community sponsors in the summer.

Birding Features
On the drive southeast, take one or more of the side roads to the sea, as they often traverse salt marshes or skirt brackish lagoons. The mudflats at the mouth of Wallace Bay, 16 km east of Pugwash, should be visited for shorebirds from mid-July into September. Look for Hudsonian Godwit.

Scan the sea at any likely viewpoint in the fall for Canada Goose, Greater Scaup and both goldeneyes. In late summer look for Bonaparte's Gull. In spring, transient Brants often rest on the sea.

At Pictou, along the causeway across the harbour on Highway 2, you will see some old wharf pilings that support a very visible and thriving nesting colony of Double-crested Cormorants. Just east of New Glasgow, instead of taking the main highway east, take the more interesting Highway 245 at Exit 27 just east of Sutherland River. The drive around the tip of Cape George, on a gravel road, is worth the time. About 12 km east of the turnoff from the freeway, beyond Merigomish and about 1.8 km from Barneys River Bridge, watch for the turn towards the sea and Merigomish Island. Drive to the end of the road. Migrating geese and ducks rest in the shallow water and shorebirds can be found on the beach south of the sandspit leading to the island. Particularly check for Whimbrel, which come regularly in August. Beware of soft sand on the shoulder of the road.

Continue around Cape George Point and head south. Beyond Morristown about 3.5 km, watch for the side road down to the water at Jimtown. Look for large numbers of cormorants, as they have a big colony near the community. Avoid a visit to the colony in May or June as gulls and ravens will take eggs and chicks if the parents are disturbed.

Continue on towards Antigonish. Watch the power poles along the roads near this community, as Ospreys nest semi-colonially on the tops of the poles. In Antigonish you will find St. Francis Xavier University, established in 1853; the oldest continuing newspaper in the Maritimes, *The Casket*; and Canada's oldest Highland games. Go down to the harbour to check the tidal marsh. During spring and fall migration many waterfowl rest here. Several species also breed in this secluded area. Look for Bald Eagle and a hunting Osprey. In late summer the variety of shorebirds should add a few to your list.

J. WOLFORD

Cape Breton

Bras d'Or Lake, an inland body of salt water, and its surrounding shores contain one of the largest concentrations of Bald Eagle in northeastern North America. The adjacent Bird Islands, with colonies of Leach's Storm-Petrel, Razorbill and other seabirds, add to the experience. The area abounds in history: the Fortress of Louisbourg, one of the largest and most realistic restoration sites in the world; the Alexander Graham Bell National Historic Park, displaying inventions from the telephone to aviation technology developed by this genius; local activities that are more Scottish than the Highlands of Scotland.

History began here with Portuguese settlers, about twenty-five years after the landing of John Cabot in 1497, followed by colonists from France and Scotland over the next three centuries. Today, numerous museums, and the coal miners' story told at Glace Bay, all add to an in-depth look at the region's past.

The one land entrance to Cape Breton is the 1.4-km-long Canso Causeway, opened in 1955. The causeway has the deepest base in the world. It prevents ice from entering the strait, thus creating an ice-free harbour 16 km long. Watch for the giant supertankers, some larger than three football fields, discharging oil at Point Tupper. A bus from Sydney services the area. Accommodation and services are available at any of the larger centres.

Information, including a bird checklist, is obtainable from: The Superintendent, Cape Breton Highlands National Park, Ingonish Beach, Cape Breton, N.S. B0C 1L0, Telephone: (902) 285-2270.

Birding Features

Once across the causeway, head towards Sydney and the Fortress of Louisbourg. Turn south immediately after the causeway and drive about 5 km to Point Tupper. Turn east and then south onto 104 and continue for about 40 km to St. Peters. Take a side road, 247, south to Point Michaud, one of the best spots for migrating shorebirds from mid-July to September. Return to Highway 4 and continue east towards Sydney, where you can take the ferry from North Sydney to Newfoundland. If you stay, then continue on to Glace Bay and the Miners' Museum. Common Black-headed Gulls are usually at Glace Bay from September through the winter. Go south on 255 towards Donkin and Port Morien, to the sanctuary (ask locally for exact location). Here from November to April you can spot the Common Black-headed Gull in fair numbers, together with Canada Goose and many ducks. From mid-July into fall, watch for a variety of shorebirds, including Willet

Willet

and Common and Arctic Terns. Continue south and west on 255 to Louis-bourg. On the way, stop and scan for gulls and shorebirds.

Head towards Sydney on 22; loop around it via North Sydney, on 125 and 105. At either Exit 17 or 15, go northeast to Big Bras d'Or, the departure point to the Bird Islands. On these islands you'll find thousands of seabirds from May to mid-August. Different operators will take you out; inquire locally. According to a 1980 newspaper article, "Hi Mills runs a twice-daily service from Seal Island Camping and Recreation Park near Big Bras d'Or Bridge. . . . You board the Seal Island Cruiser, a large comfortable launch with a capacity of 32 passengers for the 45-minute voyage. . . . It is forbidden to go ashore [but] the boat moves quite close to the cliffs and, with the aid of binoculars, one can observe very well." Allowing one and a half hours to cruise around the islands, the return trip takes a total of three hours and costs (in 1980) $7.50 per adult and $3.75 per child. Tours go out only during fair weather. Accommodation is available at Seal Island Campground and nearby motels just across the Big Bras d'Or Bridge. Look for colonies of Leach's Storm-Petrel (they come in only at night), Great and Double-crested Cormorants, gulls, Razorbill, Common Murre and Black Guillemot. Watch for Gray Seals and the odd Bald Eagle too.

Return to Highway 105, continue west to Exit 12 and turn right to Englishtown. At this community, the spit bars the mouth of St. Ann's Bay, providing a good resting spot for Bald Eagle, shorebirds, gulls and terns.

Back on 105, continue to Exit 11. You now have the choice of going north along the Cabot Trail or taking a jaunt west to Baddeck, the former summer home of Alexander Graham Bell and now site of a museum of his inventions; there is also a birding spot at nearby Nyanza, 14 km to the west.

Scan the water here for Great Blue Heron, nine species of duck, Bald Eagle, Osprey and Common Tern.

Now retrace your route east on Highway 105 to Exit 11 and turn left onto the Cabot Trail, around the north end of Cape Breton. Stop at park headquarters to consult with a naturalist. Try the nature trail at the southeast end of the park, behind Keltic Lodge. You may find several boreal species, including Spruce Grouse, warblers and an Evening Grosbeak in summer.

Established in 1936, Cape Breton Highlands National Park covers 950 km², and forms part of the upper tableland of Cape Breton. The highest point in Nova Scotia, 532 m, occurs here. The western coast has spectacular cliffs that rise nearly 300 m above the sea. Tree cover includes Hemlock, White Pine, and Balsam Fir on the higher elevations. Large areas of the central plateau are devoid of trees. Over 180 species of birds have been recorded. Watch for a Northern Gannet diving off the coast. Great and Double-crested Cormorants, Great Black-backed and Herring Gulls, Common and Arctic Terns, Black Guillemot and Common Raven all nest along here. American Black and Ring-necked Ducks, Common and Red-breasted Mergansers and Common Goldeneye breed on the inland ponds. Northern Goshawk, Bald Eagle, and Spruce and Ruffed Grouse are common. A variety of shorebirds migrate through from late July to November, including Black-bellied Plover, Ruddy Turnstone, Whimbrel and White-rumped Sandpiper. Listen for the relatively common Barred Owl in May and June. The park marks the southern limit of breeding for Boreal Chickadee, Blackburnian, Bay-breasted, Blackpoll and Mourning Warblers, Pine Grosbeak, Pine Siskin, Red and White-winged Crossbills, and Lincoln's and Fox Sparrows. Woodland Caribou were flown into the park in 1968 to join Moose, Lynx, Black Bear and Beaver.

There are over twenty hiking trails at Warren Lake and Black Brook on the eastern side and the Cheticamp area at the southwest corner. Camping is available at seven campgrounds from mid-May to late October.

As you proceed north of the park, watch for the gravel road branching off the Cabot Trail on the right, just beyond the village of Cape North. Take this side road north for about 12 km and then the right fork to Bay St. Lawrence. Park the car and walk east to Money Point in late September or October. Birds rest on the point on their way south. You could spot Northern Shrike, American Tree, White-crowned and Fox Sparrows, and others. Return to the car and the Cabot Trail; work your way along the park and then along the west shore to Cheticamp River, the southwest entrance to the park. Take the trail behind the campsite and follow it along the river. In May and June, watch for Yellow-bellied Flycatcher, Blackburnian and Blackpoll Warblers and Northern Waterthrush. The steep cliffs on the seaward southwest end of nearby Cheticamp Island have nesting colonies of Great and Double-crested Cormorants.

Follow the Cabot Trail south through Margaree Forks, then east to North East Margaree. From here, proceed north through Margaree Valley; drive for about 1.5 km north and turn right off the paved road; follow this gravel road about 12 km north through Rivulet to Kingross and Big Intervale, 1 km west. You may wish to return on the much more primitive "wagon trail" south of Big Intervale to the pavement at Portree, thence to North East Margaree and

Margaree Forks, and onto Route 19. The road up the river valley to Kingross and Big Intervale goes around Sugarloaf Mountain, with these hills rising 487 m. Above you will be spectacular though remote scenery and good woodland birding.

Continue south on Highway 19 to Harbourview, 3 km south of Port Hood. At this point, leave 19 for the road that runs along the beach through Maryville then back to Highway 19, about 8 km south of where you left it. This side road takes you by the Judique, Catherine and McKay's ponds. These barrier beach ponds provide havens for ducks and shorebirds. Watch for Bald Eagle.

J. WOLFORD

Canso Causeway to Halifax
(Marine Drive along the Eastern Shore)

The drive from the Canso Causeway to Halifax combines natural history, history and magnificent scenery. Nova Scotians call this stretch the "Eastern Shore." You will find a region of sheltered coves, friendly villages and quiet woodlands. The boreal habitat is mixed with seaside marshes. Look for a good variety of warblers, including Blackpoll, and shorebirds in mid- to late summer. You can also take a launch across to the Eastern Shore Bird Sanctuary to look for Leach's Storm-Petrel and other species.

Canso, founded in 1518, survived Indian raids, capture by the French, and attacks by pirates. The other communities in the area were established much later.

The Marine Drive, skirting the shore from the Canso Causeway to Dartmouth-Halifax, covers nearly 370 km of twisting roads. There are many communities and services along the way. Information may be obtained from the Department of Tourism in Halifax (see above).

Birding Features
Once off the Canso Causeway, turn left, or southeast, onto Highway 344 and follow it around to Boylston. Turn northwest onto 16 and then immediately west onto a gravel road that loops around the Guysborough Intervale and back down to join 16 on the other side. Birds of the water, marsh and upland are usually quite abundant along this short loop.

Follow Highway 16 south and east out to Canso. The barren headlands around this area are covered with Crowberry. Flocks of Whimbrel stop and feed on their way south from mid-July to September. Retrace your route to the junction with Highway 316 and take this road southwest along the shore to New Harbour. The estuary provides easy observation of migrating water and shore birds. Scan for Baird's and Buff-breasted Sandpipers, and godwits in late summer. Continue on to Isaacs Harbour and across on the ferry; swing west to join Highway 7 just beyond Jordanville; turn south on 7 to Sherbrooke. The town's oldest section, Sherbrooke Village, has been restored to its condition of about a hundred years ago, when it was a boom

259

community. Go in and observe carding and spinning, weaving on antique looms and blacksmithing.

Follow 7 south to the rugged coast adjacent to boreal forest. These woods have a variety of northern bird species, including Blackpoll Warbler on the outer wooded headlands and Lincoln's Sparrow in the Black Spruce bogs. The Common Eider is often seen in June and July with young. The numerous inlets may contain flocks of all three scoters on their way south in the fall.

Continue on about 4 km beyond Ecum Secum to the side road heading north. Check the marshes along the Ecum Secum River at Fleet Settlement on the east side of the river (1 km north and then branch to the right for another km), and at New Chester (go back south to the Y junction, take the northwest road on the west side of the river and drive about 5 km north). You should spot a variety of water birds, including Great Blue Heron, American Bittern and Common Snipe. Little Blue Heron, egrets and Common Moorhen have been noted here.

Return to the highway and continue west. At the next community, Necum Teuch, and at Harrigan Cove, 12 km farther, you may charter a boat to the offshore islands. Some of these havens for seabirds are owned and managed as a bird sanctuary by the Nova Scotia Bird Society. In summer, special tours are led to these spots by the society. Contact them in Halifax (see above). The society employs two wardens, one stationed at Necum Teuch and the other at Harrigan Cove. The wardens will also take parties out by previous arrangement. In May and early June and again in September and early October, water birds congregate here on their way south. Breeding birds on the islands include Leach's Storm-Petrel, Double-crested Cormorant, Common Eider, Herring Gull, Common, Arctic and Roseate Terns, and Black Guillemot. You may also spot a Fox Sparrow.

To sample some excellent back-country woodland birding, take the loop north through Liscomb Game Sanctuary, west to Highway 224 and then back south to Highway 7 near Sheet Harbour. The circle begins just over 20 km west of Harrigan Cove, and immediately east of Sheet Harbour. The first 10 km are paved but the rest is gravel. When you drive north of the pavement into the sanctuary, take note of which way you go, as there are many side trails. Keep heading north along the lake and then follow the river. Angle a bit northwest to Trafalgar. The numerous lakes, streams and virgin Nova Scotia forest in this 453-km^2 game sanctuary have abundant wildlife and good fishing. Nesting boreal species of birds are everywhere from mid-May through June. At Trafalgar, drive southwest to join Highway 336 at Dean.

From Sheet Harbour, continue along the shore drive for another 41 km to Ship Harbour. Just beyond this community, take the loop road southeast along the bay down to the point at Little Harbour. Retrace your route about 3 km north and then proceed west to Clam Harbour. Continue for 2 km and take the left fork through Clam Bay, then north to regain Highway 7 just east of Lake Charlotte. During late April and May, and again from mid-July through September, shorebirds rest and feed along these beaches. The nearby forested areas contain Spruce Grouse.

At Musquodoboit Harbour, about 18 km beyond Lake Charlotte, take the road south to Martinique Beach and the game sanctuary. The trip of approximately 12 km is worthwhile for the numerous Great Blue Herons, variety of ducks, nesting Osprey and large numbers of shorebirds.

Return to Highway 7, where you may continue on to Dartmouth-Halifax or take a side trip north in a country rich in woodland birds. For the side trip, leave Musquodoboit Harbour north on Highway 357. You'll follow the Musquodoboit River for about 40 km to Middle Musquodoboit and the junction with Highway 224. Take 224 west to Highway 102 and then south to Halifax. From mid-May through June, you should add several woodland species to your list.

If you decide to continue west on Highway 7, turn south onto Highway 207; it lies about 13 km west of Musquodoboit Harbour (just prior to meeting Highway 107). This section of road provides a comprehensive look at a wide variety of Nova Scotia land birds. If time is limited, this is one area not to miss. You'll see Bald Eagle, nesting Osprey, a variety of shorebirds including Purple Sandpiper (in late fall to early spring), plus many others (refer to Halifax area).

J. WOLFORD

Halifax and Dartmouth

Near this centre of Canadian history, a bird watcher can find over 60 species during an easy day in June. Take a trip out to sea, watch for the Common Black-headed Gull in the harbour, find boreal species like kinglets just north of the city, and locate 15 breeding species of warbler plus the "Ipswich Sparrow" (a race of Savannah Sparrow) from Sable Island during migration. A short distance north of these twin cities, the Waverley Game Sanctuary hosts Black Bear, Moose and deer.

Halifax was founded in 1749. The two cities are full of echoes of our past, from press gangs who walked the street, through privateers who auctioned off their goods from a warehouse, to the home of one of the Fathers of Confederation. The modern city of high-rises still retains streets where Wolfe and Captain James Cook walked. The latter supervised the construction of the oldest naval dockyard in North America, begun in 1759. Seven years before, in 1752, the oldest salt-water ferry system in Canada was established between Halifax and Dartmouth. Canada's first responsible government met in the sandstone Province House on February 2, 1848. Bedford Basin, between the two cities, is large enough to hold the combined world navies. Dartmouth Park was built by New England Quakers who revised the first town plan to include a common (grassy opening) in 1785. The many parks in both cities, and the twenty-six lakes in Dartmouth, provide havens for birdlife.

Accommodation is readily available in Halifax, the largest city in the Maritimes. The international airport lies northeast of the city complex, just east of Highway 102.

Information on this and other areas in Nova Scotia, together with a variety of publications and a bird checklist, is readily available from the Nova Scotia Provincial Museum (see above).

The Nova Scotia Bird Society (headquarters in the museum) offers periodic field trips to various sites in the Dartmouth/Halifax area and many spots around the province.

Birding Features

Halifax. If you come here from late fall to early spring, go down to the docks along the waterfront or to the city dump on the south shore of Bedford Basin. You will spot a variety of gulls, including Glaucous, Iceland, Great Black-backed, Herring, Ring-billed and Common Black-headed. The Common Black-headed may appear in September and remains all winter in Halifax Harbour.

Boats may be rented in Halifax Harbour to find pelagic birds. Check with the museum for places to go and contacts for boat rentals. You might find shearwaters, petrels, Northern Gannet, diving ducks, phalaropes, jaegers, gulls, terns and alcids.

Dartmouth. The immediate Dartmouth area has several sites to examine: Sullivan Pond, about six blocks north of Dartmouth Shipyards, lies on the south end of Prince Albert road. The pond is excellent for waterfowl. To reach Russell Lake, on the east side of Dartmouth, take Portland Street (Highway 207) at Exit 7, east from Highway 111 for one block and then south on Baker Drive. The lake is about 200 to 400 m east of here. Scan for waterfowl. Bell Lake lies further east along Portland Street to Bayswater Road (west side of the lake), or Ayr Avenue (east side). Follow either of these streets around the lake to Dorthea Drive on the north side of the marshy end to find a variety of waterfowl.

Hartlen Point. The patient observer may wish to take a side trip south of Dartmouth, on Highway 322 through Eastern Passage south to Hartlen Point. The point is a good spot to scan for offshore seabirds such as gannets, shearwaters and petrels.

Dartmouth to Chezzetcook. Highway 207 east from Dartmouth to Head of Chezzetcook passes through practically every kind of habitat in Nova Scotia. From May through early July, look for American Bittern nesting in the marshes, with American Black Duck, Green-winged and Blue-winged Teals, and Ring-necked Duck. The Osprey and Bald Eagle both nest in this area; the latter may be seen throughout the year. The Short-eared Owl is found in the open dune areas at Conrad and Lawrencetown beaches. Stop at the White and Black Spruce forests for boreal species. Listen and look for Yellow-bellied and other flycatchers; Gray Jays are quite numerous; four species of swallow can be spotted; Black-capped and Boreal Chickadees and the kinglets are abundant; about 15 species of warbler may be seen, the most common being Black-and-white, Nashville, Northern Parula, Magnolia, Yellow-rumped, Chestnut-sided, Blackpoll and Common Yellowthroat. Look for the Ipswich Sparrow during spring and fall migration in the dunes close to shore; this area is the closest to their breeding ground on Sable

Island. The Sharp-tailed Sparrow nests in salt marshes whereas the Savannah Sparrow is more likely along the drier margins.

In the fall and winter, look for Common and Red-throated Loons and Red-necked and Horned Grebes feeding close to shore. You may spot up to 100 Great Blue Herons feeding in shallow inlets at low tide during migration in the fall. Large flocks of Canada Goose and Black Duck appear in the fall and remain all winter. Common Goldeneye, Bufflehead, Oldsquaw, Common Eider, and Common and Red-breasted Mergansers are winter residents. The Common Black-headed Gull may appear in September in Cole Harbour, just east of Dartmouth. The Purple Sandpiper is a regular winter bird on Fox Island off Conrad Beach. From October to April check the upper part of Chezzetcook Inlet for Bufflehead and Ring-billed Gull in the extensive salt marshes. The Snowy Owl is usually found in the open dune country at Conrad and Lawrencetown beaches. At Lawrencetown Beach, check the fresh-water and salt-water marshes. Further east about 5 km, at Three Fathom Harbour, scan for more waterfowl. This stretch of coast also is a good site to watch large movements of Horned Lark, Water Pipit, Lapland Longspur and Snow Bunting during the fall.

Halifax West. Take Route 333 southwest of the city to Peggys Cove and then north along the shore to Highway 3 west. This half-circle will bring you in contact with mainly boreal species. A visit to the inshore waters should provide Herring and Greater Black-backed Gulls, and Common and Arctic Terns. In late summer and fall, scan the ocean for numbers of loons, grebes, cormorants, alcids and sea ducks.

J. WOLFORD

Halifax to Cape Sable

The "South Shore," as Nova Scotians call the strip from Halifax to Cape Sable, was home to the mariners who dominated the region in the 1800s to early 1900s. The people of Lunenburg once owned the largest deep-sea fleet fishing the Grand Banks off Newfoundland. The pride of their fleet, *Bluenose*, was the fastest sailing ship afloat in the 1920s and 1930s.

Settled by Germans, Swiss and United Empire Loyalists, the area today retains some fine examples of small fishing communities, including Peggys Cove at the southeast corner of St. Margarets Bay. Birding is fair along this stretch of coast, but the atmosphere to be had in the communities is worth the trip. In Liverpool, you can imagine you are back in the late 1700s fighting to save your home from French, Spanish and Yankee privateers, or getting ready to sail to the Caribbean in retaliation for a raid on your ships down there.

This approximately 250-km stretch of road utilizes major highway 103, with additional side loops. Accommodation abounds, together with other amenities.

Birding Features
Proceed west of Halifax on Highway 103 to avoid the suburban area

adjacent to the city. Take Highway 3 from Interchange 4, west along the northern shore of St. Margarets Bay to Hubbards. The best time to visit the bay is from late fall through winter, to look for Red-throated Loon, Red-necked and Horned Grebes, Great Cormorant, goldeneyes, Oldsquaw, mergansers, Thick-billed Murre and Dovekie. In the colder months, head south of Hubbards on Highway 329, loop around the Aspotogan Peninsula and back north to Highway 3 at East River. Scan the waters for seabirds.

At East River, watch for the highway sign which says "East River Point." At 3.4 km west of this sign, look for the abandoned road on the north side of Highway 3. This old road, which leads to an abandoned power dam, should be hiked for a km or more upstream along the East River to spot a good collection of warblers from late May to early July.

Proceed west on Highway 3 and follow it down to Lunenburg. Take Route 332 to Kingsburg, on the tip of the peninsula, for ducks and shore-birds in early spring and late fall. Loop back on 332 northwest to Bridge-water. This community is the centre of a network of roads good for spotting flycatchers, warblers and finches in the varied woodland habitat. If you arrive here in late July or August, you may be lucky enough to experience the often spectacular Common Nighthawk migration that follows the course of the La Have River.

At Bridgewater, turn southeast onto Highway 331, which follows the west bank of La Have River. Turn southeast at La Have and follow 331 for about 8 km to Crescent Beach. This is one of the best sites along the South Shore for migrating ducks and shorebirds. The woodlands along this route also abound in birds. About 4 km west of Crescent Beach, in and around the estuary of Petite Riviere, look for nesting Spotted Sandpiper, Willet, Belted Kingfisher and Bank Swallow. Continue on 331 to rejoin 103 and on to Liverpool, where Highway 8 heads north to Kejimkujik National Park (see below).

Farther along Route 103, turn off to the south at Sable River. This road begins as pavement but soon becomes gravel. Follow the *east* bank of Sable River to the far south and then turn northeast and north to the sanctuary at Port Hebert. In spring and fall migration, thousands of water birds rest and feed. You should be able to spot cormorants, Great Blue Heron, Canada Goose, Brant, American Black Duck, Northern Pintail, Green-winged and Blue-winged Teals, Greater Scaup and mergansers, often in large flocks.

Return to Highway 103. Immediately west of Sable River, turn south along Highway 3 for about 3 km; branch off to the southeast on the road to West Middle Sand; follow it south along the west side of Sable River. Stop several times, particularly at Louis Head Beach, to explore habitats and paths. In winter, thousands of Canada Geese remain here. The nearby woods are a wintering area for the Yellow-rumped Warbler (myrtle race), abundant in this season. Continue southeast just over 2 km to Little Harbour; swing straight south towards Arnold. This dirt road terminates in a large open field on Hemeon's Head, with the sea in sight to the east, south and west. Park the car and walk along the clearly marked path heading west along the beach. Look for a Whimbrel on the uplands. The other shorebirds concentrate about 2.4 km from the parking area on the flats. To reach these, continue beyond the point where the sea and lake nearly join, to the flats where shorebirds gather at low tide. Find the narrow crossing, where you can wade across. After you've scanned the shorebirds, follow the channel to its mouth on the main beach. You may sight Ruddy Turnstone and Red Knot. To return to the car, follow the beach back for 3.2 km. If you come in September or October look for Northern Wheatear, especially around the piles of driftwood.

Return to Highway 3 and follow it north to Jordan Falls to rejoin 103. Continue west to Exit 26 at Shelburne. Turn north and follow the Ohio road for about 8 km of pavement and 18 km of gravel to the Indian Fields road sign. From here on, the road becomes uncertain. Proceed at your own risk. If you turn back, go to Lower Ohio and then swing west to the Clyde River road. If you go north to Upper Clyde River, the road heads west for about 4 km and then loops south for over 30 km to Port Clyde and Highway 103. Alternatively, just west of Lower Ohio, a turn south will bring you back to Highway 103 in about 8 km. The woodlands consist of Red Maple, Rowan and poplar, with some pine and hemlock farther north. Birders have found more than 100 species during the summer in here. These include Black-backed Woodpecker, Boreal Chickadee and 23 species of warbler.

Continue west from Shelburne to Clyde River; swing south through Port Clyde; then southeast through Port Saxon, North West Harbour and North East Harbour to Ingomar, where the pavement ends. Take the dirt road south to East Point, a good spot for watching migrants of both land and water birds, particularly during bad weather.

Return to Port Clyde and head south again to Baccaro Point. This headland is also a good place for migrating birds. Return north, and just beyond Port La Tour swing west and north up to Barrington and Highway 3. Follow 3 south and then cross over to Cape Sable Island on Highway 330. Proceed south to Clark's Harbour and Lower Clark's Harbour and beyond to The Hawk. Ask at the post office for the small boat to the island. Depending on the weather and tide, get dropped off at one end of the island and picked up at the other (about a 5-km walk). This hike will provide opportunities to see a wide variety of either migrating or nesting shorebirds; breeders include Piping Plover, a Bank Swallow colony and Savannah and Song Sparrows. At Black Point, on the south end, look for nest holes of the Bank Swallow on the seaward side. On the inner side, you may spot sandpipers and other species. The cobblestone sea wall is a useful path at high tide. Look for nesting Common and Arctic Terns in June and July. From mid-July to late August, there should be hundreds of shorebirds along the beaches.

The island widens on the southeast to an open swampy upland which attracts stray egrets, Black-crowned Night-Heron and other large wading birds. The brackish pond brings in teal, both species of yellowlegs and all three phalaropes.

The lighthouse is the most southerly on Canada's coast. These tall buildings and the light bring in a wide variety of birds. Over 30 species of warbler have been seen hawking insects around the building. Brown Thrasher, thrushes, Yellow-breasted Chat and Rufous-sided Towhee all can be seen in the grasses along the sea wall. The numerous flies over the kelp beds attract swallows.

Steven's Point Landing, the pick-up spot, can be reached by hiking across on the tractor road or continuing along the sea wall, where you may spot shearwaters and gulls. The eastern shore of rocks is home to Ruddy Turnstone, Willet, Red Knot and plovers.

If you come in winter, look for grebes, diving ducks (including Common Goldeneye, Bufflehead, Oldsquaw, all three scoters and mergansers), gulls, murres, Dovekie, Black Guillemot, Horned Lark, Dark-eyed Junco and other sparrows, Lapland Longspur and Snow Bunting.

Off from Cape Sable Island, two small islands, Bon Portage and Seal, have been studied extensively for birds over many years. Bon Portage Island lies 7.5 km straight west of Cape Sable Island and 4 km southwest of Shag Harbour. Bon Portage is owned by Acadia University at Wolfville, N.S. Seal Island is partly owned by the Canadian government and partly by an individual who resides there. Permission to land must be obtained from the owner. These islands are best visited in late April to mid-June, and late July through mid-October. For rare birds, Cape Sable Island is the best site; Seal Island would rank second; Brier Island (see Annapolis Basin) would be third, but it is very accessible and so usually the first choice for visitors. Both Bon Portage and Seal require hiring a fishing boat for access.

J. WOLFORD

Yarmouth

Long points of land extend south into that area between the Bay of Fundy and the Atlantic Ocean. Here, at the extremity of Nova Scotia, are ideal landing and departure sites for birds. Shallow bays between these points offer sanctuary to overwintering loons, grebes, geese and ducks; and feeding sites for migrating herons and stray egrets. The wooded back country attracts a wide variety of nesting land birds, including at least 15 species of warbler.

Acadians settled here in 1768, after they had been expelled by the English. In the late nineteenth century, shipbuilding flourished in Yarmouth; Nova Scotia's 3000 sailing ships made up one of the largest merchant fleets in the world, and made Yarmouth the richest port on the Atlantic coast. Today many of the farms are abandoned and Yarmouth thrives on an active tourist trade.

Birding Features
In winter, a visitor should spot the usual finches, plus Yellow-rumped Warbler, Horned Lark, American Goldfinch, American Tree Sparrow, an occasional Lapland Longspur and Snow Bunting.

Yarmouth. From mid-July to early September, a drive around town should produce a number of species. The flats and beaches on both sides of Yarmouth Harbour are resting and feeding sites for Semipalmated and Black-bellied Plovers, Ruddy Turnstone, Willet, both species of yellowlegs, Short-billed Dowitcher and others. At the mid-August height of migration, the Dunlin is abundant; later in September and October, look for Pectoral Sandpiper.

Ferry Crossing from Portland, Maine, and from Bar Harbor, Maine.
These crossings, to or from Yarmouth, are particularly good for seabirds if the day is free of fog. From spring to fall, look for Greater and Sooty Shearwaters, Leach's and Wilson's Storm-Petrels and Northern Gannet, the latter mostly immature. From late fall to spring, scan for other pelagic species, including Northern Fulmar, Red and Red-necked Phalaropes, Black-legged Kittiwake, Razorbill, Common and Thick-billed Murres, Dovekie and Atlantic Puffin.

Shorebird Route. Proceed south from Yarmouth on Main Street. At the head of Kelly Cove, about 2.5 km south of the railway level crossing at the edge of town, take the narrow track to the right, southwest over a low hill and down to a small sand beach and tidal marsh. At low tide, look for a variety of water birds. This is also a good spot for the late-arriving Sharp-tailed Sparrow (after June 1). Parking can be difficult. You may want to leave the car on the paved road and hike down the several hundred metres to the beach.

Continue south on the paved road, and then turn sharp south to reach Chebogue Point. Park at the end of the road and hike along the pebbled ridge to the drumlins, about 1 km east. Expect a wide collection of ducks and shorebirds in spring and fall. In late fall, look for Horned Lark, Lapland Longspur and Snow Bunting. If you come at high tide, check the gravel spits fringing the lower salt marsh near the end of the road for large numbers of Black-bellied Plover, Greater and Lesser Yellowlegs, Red Knot and smaller shorebirds too. Nearby fields host Lesser Golden-Plover in August and September.

Return north, and then swing northeast through Central Chebogue to Highway 3. Proceed east on it for about 2 km, then turn south on 334; leave 334 and take the road south to Pinkney Point. About 2 km south from the fork off 334, you will find the Melbourne Bird Sanctuary.

The large shallow inlet is used as a staging and wintering area for thousands of Canada Geese, American Black Ducks and a wide variety of other water birds. This is a favourite fall and winter spot for Ring-billed and Common Black-headed Gulls. Continue south to Cook's Beach; it serves as a fine roosting site for sandpipers at high tide. South towards Pinkney Point, the extensive marshes and shallow pools provide excellent habitat for Great Blue Heron, Black-bellied Plover, yellowlegs and other species, including large flocks of Willet in the fall.

Return to Highway 334, and then go south on it through Wedgeport and Lower Wedgeport to Wedge Point. You are now on the extreme tip of Tusket Wedge, where migrants congregate while waiting for good weather.

Inland Exploration. This trip is best from late May to very early July to spot or hear land birds on territory. You may see a pair of Common Loons on each lake. Take Highway 1 from Yarmouth about 4 km to Hebron. Turn northeast onto 340, where the sign says Carleton-Deerfield. From here it is about 10.5 km to Ellenwood Lake Provincial Park, past Deerfield. Turn right at the Braemar and park signs; follow these signs in. At the entrance, ask the attendants about local birds, including Barred Owl.

After checking out the park, take the shortest road back south to Highway 103. To get there, follow Pleasant Lake Trunk 3 from the sign at the park entrance. At Pleasant Lake on 3, turn right and head back to Yarmouth.

Bartlet's Beach. This good shore and marsh bird habitat is reached from Highways 101 or 1. The beach is about 1 km south of Beaver River on Highway 1 and about 24 km north of Yarmouth. Similar marshes and beaches lie north of here along the Bay of Fundy and St. Mary's Bay to Weymouth and beyond. Come at high tide.

Offshore Islands. The Nova Scotia Bird Society owns some islands off the southwestern tip of Nova Scotia. Visits to these sanctuaries are prohibited during the breeding season, but are excellent in September and early October. Contact the society (see above) or inquire at the local Yarmouth museum or tourist office for help. These islands are often swarming with birds getting ready for the large hop to southern wintering spots.

J. WOLFORD

Annapolis Basin and Valley

This fertile valley produces apples that are famous across Canada. Forested hills lie adjacent. Varied habitats provide havens for everything from seabirds to the Bald Eagle.

Nova Scotia's first permanent European settlers arrived from France with Champlain in 1605 at Port Royal (now re-created in a historic park that is worth a visit). The valley was settled by French-speaking Acadians, who were later expelled by the British and replaced by New Englanders and then United Empire Loyalists. The area breathes history at such sites as Port Royal, just west of Annapolis, and a "living museum" of Nova Scotia's agricultural history at the New Ross Farm, 40 km south of Kentville.

Highways 1 and 101 run through the region, with numerous side roads providing access to the Bay of Fundy and the nearby hills. Tourism is a major industry, with widespread services of all types.

A visitor to Wolfville, at the east end of the valley, should contact the Biology Department at Acadia University for information and/or guides for local bird watching.

Birding Features
Digby Neck and Brier Island. Route 217 off Highway 1 is considered by many to be one of the finest birding spots in the province, particularly Brier Island at the tip. Sites for camping are available, and Westport has a couple of general stores. The best time to come is Labour Day weekend in early September, when members of the Nova Scotia Bird Society often have a popular field trip. A bird-banding site on the island may allow the visitor to

TWThorMiN/83   *Laughing Gull*

have a close look at hard-to-identify songbirds. Mist netting and banding takes place on a strip of land owned by Acadia University (near the North Light). Trips out to sea may also be included in the weekend. On these sea excursions, Red Phalarope often seem to cover the water for long distances and Greater Shearwater can be abundant; Sooty Shearwater and Red-necked Phalarope are also present. Additional thrills are the Humpback and Finback Whales, and porpoises that may play around the boats. Other pelagic birds include Northern Gannet, petrels, jaegers, Black-legged Kittiwake, terns and Atlantic Puffin. Some of these can be spotted from land, at either the North Light or the West Light (scan the horizon and watch for passing fishing boats). Near shore, watch loons, cormorants and eiders feeding. On land, the masses of smaller birds change daily as flocks pass south. Shorebirds line the beaches, especially at Pond Cove, at the southern end of the island.

Peter Island lies between Brier Island and Freeport. Peter is a nesting site of Common and Arctic Terns; both species can be clearly viewed in summer from the Westport ferry wharf.

Digby. The town sits in the Annapolis Basin, with nearby woodlands worth exploring. Check for Bald Eagle near Bear River, 7.5 km east and 5 km south of Digby. A main ferry crosses to and from Digby and Saint John, New

Brunswick. The trip provides ready access to pelagic birds similar to those seen on the ferry off Yarmouth (see above). Exploring around the town often proves productive for shorebirds. Digby Harbour (Annapolis Basin) in winter is an excellent locale for seabirds, gulls and diverse diving ducks.

The Valley and North and South Mountains. The agricultural flatlands are bounded on either side by a range of hills 185 to 260 m high. These hills are covered with a mixed forest of conifers and deciduous trees. They harbour a wide collection of woodland bird species. The long prominent ridge adjacent to the Bay of Fundy, called the North Mountain, is continuous with Digby Neck. This piece of highland appears to be a main launching strip for migrating hawks, especially Broad-winged and Sharp-shinned on their way south in late September and October.

Walk up the North Mountain near Granville Ferry, just north of Annapolis Royal, on an evening in June and listen for Veery. After dark, try hooting to hear the Barred Owl reply. You may even bring in a Pileated Woodpecker to your call — it has happened several times.

The valley lowlands with farms and orchards are havens for man-oriented species such as Killdeer, and three common species of swallow (Bank is especially abundant throughout the valley, particularly at the eastern end), with Barn and Tree being numerous; Ring-necked Pheasant, Cedar Waxwing, Eastern Kingbird and Purple Finch are present also.

Evangeline Beach. Lying on the east end of the valley, this is a very good spot for fall shorebirds. To get there, drive 9 km east of Wolfville on Highway 1 to Grand Pre. Turn north on the paved road, across the dikelands to Evangeline Beach. To the east of the public beach, tens of thousands of smaller shorebirds congregate from late July through August. They are dominantly Semipalmated Sandpiper, but scan the flocks for Semipalmated Plover, White-rumped and Least Sandpipers and Sanderling. If you come in July, look for gatherings of Red Knot and Hudsonian Godwit along the beach; later there will be a variety of other shorebirds, especially Black-bellied Plover and Short-billed Dowitcher. All of these shorebirds are present because of the extensive mudflats of the Minas Basin. Look for these birds at *high tide*, when they roost in concentrated flocks along the beaches or in open plowed fields of the dikelands.

In October and November, check the dikeland for flocks of Horned Lark, Lapland Longspur and Snow Bunting. If there are numerous mice, watch for a Short-eared Owl and, in winter, a Rough-legged Hawk.

Just east of Evangeline Beach is Boot Island, which can be reached by boat to see nesting colonies of Herring and Greater Black-backed Gulls, Double-crested Cormorant, Great Blue Heron and an occasional pair of Long-eared Owls. This island, from fall to spring, is a roosting site for up to 30,000 American Crows. Their flights to the island at dusk are truly spectacular.

Gaspereau River Valley. The Grand Pre dikelands, along with the Gaspereau River Valley just to the south, are excellent for overwintering Bald Eagles, especially from December through February. Common Ravens are also numerous and often conspicuous all year. Cyril Coldwell has a farm along the Gaspereau River where he had been trapping and banding ravens, year-round from 1965 to 1982. He continues to put out food which attracts ravens and Bald Eagle, crows and gulls. Fifty-two eagles were seen at once in 1981. The best time to see these birds is early morning from December through February and part of March. Most of the birds spread out each day over the Wolfville-Canning-Avonport area where they rest in big trees. Be prepared to observe all plumage variations and gradations leading up to fully adult colouration after five years of age. To reach the Coldwell place, take Gaspereau Avenue in Wolfville south over the ridge into Gaspereau Valley, to White Rock Road and then east about 1.5 km to the farm on the north side of the road, along the river. Another major site for wintering Bald Eagle is the west end of the Shubenacadie River Valley, west of Truro (see below).

J. WOLFORD

Windsor to Halifax

Birding Features
Highways 1 and 101 cross the province to Halifax. This approximately 60-km trip will take you into a range of woodlands from mixed forests to conifers. Take Highway 1 south and east of Windsor, cross over 101 near St. Croix and continue east on 1, through Newport Corner. As you approach the higher country, the trees change from mixed woods to coniferous forest. Stop, listen and look for Gray Jay, Boreal Chickadee and Pine Grosbeak. The Black-backed Woodpecker and Spruce Grouse are often spotted. Watch for the checkerboard sign just beyond the fire tower at the top of Ardoise Hill. Turn right at this sign and park the car. This dirt road is better for hiking than driving. From here it is about 4 km to Stillwater Siding, a good place to look for Red Crossbill. Cross 101 (it is hard to find this road from the freeway), and then encounter the siding. The crossbills may be found in a clearing at the end of the road, where it meets the railway tracks. As you hike along keep alert for Northern Goshawk, Sharp-shinned Hawk, Yellow-bellied and Olive-sided Flycatchers and the Mourning Warbler in June.

Halifax to Amherst

Birding Features
Highways 2 and 102 will take you from Halifax almost straight north to Truro and beyond to New Brunswick. A side trip would be to turn left onto 214 at Interchange 8, about 35 km north of Halifax near Elmsdale. Follow 214 north for 5 km to Route 14. Take 14 northwest for about 15 km to Highway 354 and then go north on 354 to Noel and Route 215. Follow 215 east along the coast and then south back to Highway 102, or turn on Highway 236 to get to Truro. West of here, on the lower Shubenacadie River Valley, is an important site for overwintering Bald Eagle, as is the Gaspereau Valley near Wolfville (see above). The area is almost certain to produce Red-

tailed Hawk. Ruffed Grouse, Ring-necked Pheasant and Gray Partridge are abundant in the uplands on this looped trip. In wet areas, watch for American Bittern, American Black Duck, Green-winged and Blue-winged Teals and Sora. The Yellow Rail has been reported at Noel near the coast. Check the few lakes for nesting Pied-billed Grebe and Ring-necked Duck. American Woodcock breed in the alder thickets, and the Common Snipe can be heard displaying on spring evenings. Open fields hold Bobolink. At the salt marshes listen carefully for Sharp-tailed Sparrow.

In fall and winter, the trip almost certainly will produce large flocks of Horned Lark and Snow Bunting. Watch for scattered Lapland Longspur in these flocks. In some years, Common Redpoll may also be abundant.

Another interesting looped trip takes you east of Highway 102 in a circle. Leave 102 at Interchange 9 and proceed northeast to meet Route 224 about 1 km north of Shubenacadie. Follow 224 about 50 km to Upper Musquodoboit; proceed north on Route 336 to meet 289. Follow 289 back west and north to Highway 102 at Interchange 12, just west of Brookfield. The drive passes through a mixture of farm and woodland. In the forests keep alert for Pileated and Black-backed Woodpeckers. Check out Lake Egmont, 2 km straight south of Cooks Brook on a side road, for the Wood Ducks that use the houses set out for them. Search in hardwood forests in June for the Black-throated Blue Warbler and Ovenbird. If you find a stand of mature conifers, stop and listen for Bay-breasted Warbler.

At Truro, you have a choice of travelling straight northwest to New Brunswick on 104 or the longer route on 2. Highway 104 proceeds through the Wentworth Valley between hardwood-covered hills. Watch for Red-tailed Hawk, Great Horned Owl and Pileated Woodpecker. The Purple Martin retains a last stronghold in Nova Scotia at Oxford and Amherst. Try the colony at 150 Victoria Street on Highway 6.

J. WOLFORD

Sable Island

Lying 150 km straight east of Nova Scotia, Sable Island has hosted about 325 species of birds, of which 25 have nested, with 18 of these still producing young each year. The most famous, the endemic "Ipswich Sparrow," a race of the Savannah Sparrow, has between 1150 and 3300 adults returning each year since 1967. They produce populations of 3500 to 14,000 in late summer.

The island attracts a wide variety of rare species. Eighty-five vagrant species for Nova Scotia have been reported here. These rare birds include two first records for North America, four for Canada and twenty-four for Nova Scotia. A number of northern or arctic species have visited in summer. An additional attraction is the horses, decendants of those from early shipwrecks, and the seals. Visitors interested in plants can explore the dunes for a variety of hardy species.

Champlain described the island in his *Voyages*. The first white settlement on the island was established almost four hundred years ago. Since then, many people have written about its animals and plants. The Bouteillier brothers, James and Richard, made a very detailed study and kept extensive records in the late 1800s and early 1900s (refer to McLaren's paper, below). The most recent and by far the best description of the birdlife, with both historical records and up-to-date studies, has been prepared by Ian A. McLaren in "The Birds of Sable Island, Nova Scotia," Proceedings of Nova Scotia Institute of Science, 1981; Vol. 31 (1) pp. 1–84. Information for this site has been taken from this publication. For further reference, obtain a copy.

Sable Island lies nearly 300 km east of Halifax, the major port of departure for a site visit. The island is difficult and expensive to visit. You must obtain government permission to stay on the island. The best way to go is through a tour. These are offered regularly by nature-oriented travel agents working with the Canadian Nature Federation and the Federation of Ontario Naturalists (refer to *Nature Canada* magazine for tours offered by these organizations). There is no accommodation on the island, but you may camp if permission has been given.

Birding Features
This treeless sand bar, approximately 34 km long, with a maximum width of about 1.5 km, offers a stopover for migrating waterfowl and shorebirds. It is an unexpected landfall for migrating land birds; they come in droves! Rarities have included Little Shearwater, British Storm-Petrel, Roseate Spoonbill, Cave Swallow, Worm-eating Warbler and Hermit Warbler. Come from early to mid-May and mid-August to mid-September for migrants; nesters are best in June.

Pelagic species can be spotted from your boat, helicopter or plane, as you arrive or depart, and at the island's tips. The Northern Fulmar is regular in May and June and in September; Cory's Shearwater is most common in July; watch for Greater Shearwater at the tips in summer, especially when winds are easterly; Sooty and Manx Shearwaters are most numerous in early summer; Northern Gannet is regular too. At the tip, these species may be watched rounding the ends or feeding in the turbulent shallow waters. Also look for Black-legged Kittiwake, rare gulls and terns.

Wallace Lake, a once-extensive body of fresh water, is now reduced to a small pond. Here you should see a few cormorants, herons, sea ducks and rails. Large concentrations of shorebirds gather here in spring and fall. The series of ponds about 0.5 km and 2 km east of the westernmost basin on Wallace Lake do attract some rarities at times. These shorebirds occur also along the island's edges.

Another good spot for water birds is the complex of ponds between the West Light and the meteorological station. Here and at Wallace Lake look for nesting American Black Ducks, which are common; a few nesting Northern Pintails, Green-winged and Blue-winged Teals and several pairs of Red-breasted Mergansers occur. Other nesting species around these water bodies include a few Semipalmated Plovers, Spotted Sandpipers and fairly numerous Least Sandpipers.

A dike has been built southwest of the West Light to hold back incursion of salt water. Look there for shorebirds, including from 100 to over 1000 Black-bellied Plovers in late August and early September, plus 50 or more Ruddy Turnstones at the same time. Other shorebirds include Pectoral

Northern Parula

Sandpiper in late September and early October, White-rumped Sandpiper in late August to mid-September, Semipalmated Sandpiper and perhaps Ruff. The Short-billed Dowitcher is regular in spring and abundant in fall.

Near the old No. 3 lifesaving station, the brackish ponds draw in shorebirds. Proceed to the relatively deep one 1.3 km west of this station to find water birds. About 0.3 km northwest of the station there is a very small, shallow, vegetationally diverse pond which has produced a number of rare herons and rails. However, it is filling in with sand and may soon be gone.

The extensive beaches at the tips of the island should be searched for gull and tern nesting colonies. There are over 1000 nesting Great Black-backed Gulls, with twice as many Herring Gulls; and over 2000 nesting terns, with about 60 per cent Arctic, 30 per cent Common and 10 per cent Roseate. There is a good possibility you will spot an Iceland Gull, now fairly regular; Black-legged Kittiwake usually occurs at least once a month.

Search for land birds in the more densely vegetated areas. Look around the above-mentioned ponds and in the higher shrubs. By late summer Marram Grass, Beach Pea and Seaside Goldenrod cover the tops of the dunes. These insect-rich "thickets" attract the migrants, including hordes of recently fledged young Ipswich Sparrow from late August to November.

Black-and-white Warbler is regular and common in spring and fall. The Northern Parula is regular in spring, but decidedly rare in fall. Cape May Warbler is scarce most springs but sporadically common in fall. Blackburnian Warbler is a quite regular migrant. Blackpoll Warbler is most common between May 24 and June 12 and between September 5 and October 16. Prairie Warbler comes in the fall. Palm Warbler passes through in spring, as does the Ovenbird. Indigo Bunting occurs most springs and occasionally in the fall. Pine Siskin arrives in spring and often stays through June.

The long easternmost dune is an excellent spot for recently landed migrants. Another site is at the flanks of the dunes 0.5 km southwest of the West Light.

Be sure to inspect the man-made structures, including towers, buildings and the rose garden. Many of the most interesting rarities have occurred on and around the house nearest the West Light. Examine the collapsing buildings at Old Main Station and the nearby rose garden that was planted in 1901.

Prince Edward Island

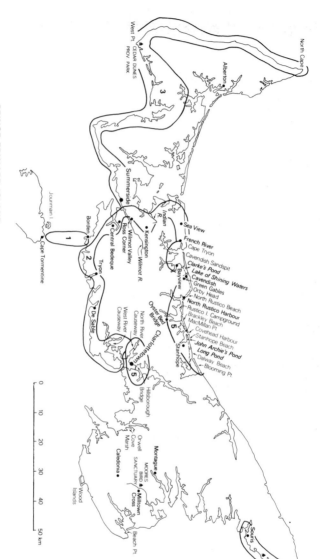

PRINCE EDWARD ISLAND

1 The Ferries and Arrival in P.E.I.
2 Blue Heron Drive (Central P.E.I.)
3 Lady Slipper Drive (West P.E.I.)

4 Prince Edward Island National Park
5 Charlottetown
6 Kings Byway (East P.E.I.)

Prince Edward Island

Our smallest province draws visitors to experience its quiet, beautiful, long sand beaches and pleasant pastoral landscapes. The Great Blue Heron is one of the most commonly sighted birds; Great and Double-crested Cormorants fly from their nesting cliffs within close view; Piping Plovers nest in fair number on some of the beaches.

Micmac Indians named it Abegweit — Cradled on the Waves. Jacques Cartier renamed it Ile Saint-Jean when he landed in 1534. The British later christened it in honour of Prince Edward, Duke of Kent, in 1798. Covering 5656 km², with a population of 124,000, the lands rise as high as 142 m from the sea. The underlying bedrock is red sandstone, resulting in red soil. About half of P.E.I. is covered in woodland; the remainder is cleared, much of it in agriculture. A variety of crops is produced, including potatoes, tobacco and grain. Most farm units contain at least one woodlot, leaving a patchwork of fields and woods, with no extensive tracts of uninterrupted woods. A band of low hills traverses the central part of the island in a north-south direction. A second hilly area is found around Caledonia. The rest of the province is quite level to gently rolling. Shorelines consist of red sandstone cliffs, barrier sand dune systems sheltering salt-water bays, and salt marshes with estuaries. Most of the bays are shallow, with many sand bars. Most of the larger rivers are tidal for a considerable length. A number of small ponds are present, but no actual lakes are found.

Water birds are common because of the nearness to the sea. Warblers move through in early June; shorebirds come south in late July and August. Piping Plover may be found on territory from May to July. Check offshore for migrating Northern Gannet in October. Wintering ducks are most numerous from December to March.

Prince Edward Island National Park is considered the best birding site in the province. Different species are found at all seasons in this area of woodlots, sand beaches and marshes. The park and the cormorant colony at Cape Tryon, west of the park, can be visited in a half to a full day. Most of the spots in this province can be covered in two days to a week, depending upon how fast you move.

No rare bird alert telephone number exists. Visiting birders should write ahead to the main natural history society for help: Natural History Society of P.E.I., Box 2346, Charlottetown, P.E.I. The provincial Department of Tourism provides a detailed map of the province, showing the different drives and loops mentioned below. For a copy write: Prince Edward Island Tourist Information Centre, P.O. Box 940, Charlottetown, P.E.I. C1A 7M5, Telephone: (902) 892-2457.

WINIFRED CAIRNS

The Ferries and Arrival in P.E.I.

Car ferries link P.E.I. with New Brunswick, Nova Scotia and the Iles de la

Madeleine in Quebec. Only the New Brunswick connection remains open in winter. This service is operated by CN Marine off Highway 16, from Cape Tormentine, N.B., to Borden, P.E.I. The 14-km trip takes three-quarters of an hour and runs every hour or so in the summer. The Nova Scotia link, operated by Northumberland Ferries, is 22 km off Highway 106, at Caribou. The trip to Wood Islands, P.E.I., lasts ninety minutes; there is regular service from spring through fall. The third ferry carries visitors from the Iles de la Madeleine to Souris, near the northeastern shore of P.E.I., a 134-km ride. Schedules and rates are available from the P.E.I. Tourist Information Centre (see above).

A bus provides service from New Brunswick to Charlottetown. Within P.E.I., there is no public transit system. However, during the summer, a double-decker bus takes guided tours from Charlottetown to the north shore. If you talk to the driver, it is sometimes possible to be dropped off at the far end and picked up a few hours later on the return ride to town.

To do any serious exploring, a car is a necessity. There are numerous car rental agencies on the island, as well as a variety of accommodation.

Birding Features
The ferries provide opportunities to spot sea ducks and Northern Gannet, especially in the fall. In winter, a ride on the New Brunswick ferry usually produces Common Goldeneye, Oldsquaw, Common Merganser, plus a regular following of gulls, especially Iceland.

WINIFRED CAIRNS

Blue Heron Drive (Central P.E.I.)

Upon arrival at Borden, drive the 3 km to Carleton and turn left onto Blue Heron Drive (Route 10). This loop around the perimeter of central P.E.I. provides a scenic drive along the coast. The Great Blue Heron is quite abundant, with up to a dozen often spotted in one area. Canada Geese feed in the grain and potato fields and rest on bays and estuaries. Caspian Tern and Osprey are occasionally spotted.

Birding Features
Almost all of P.E.I.'s fifteen or so Great Blue Heron colonies are found on offshore islands. The birds come to the estuaries, river mouths, ponds and marshes to feed. These heronries are believed to have some of the largest populations in eastern Canada. In spring and fall migration, watch for Canada Goose at Central Bedeque, near the junction with 1A, about 13 km along Route 10 from Carleton. You may see geese at Ross' Corners, 2 km farther on, or at Wilmot Valley, 3 km farther; then turn right on 107 for 2 km. The Wilmot River, with bordering farmland, is a favourite stopover for migrating Canada Geese in March and April. Later in the season look here for Caspian Tern. After continuing another 6 km along Blue Heron Drive, through Kensington, stop at Indian River and the adjacent salt marshes along the river proper. You should be able to spot more waterfowl species here

than anywhere else on P.E.I. Scan for numerous Canada Geese, American Black Ducks, some Gadwalls, Blue-winged Teal, Northern Shoveler, Greater Scaup and Ruddy Duck.

Once on the north shore, you can't miss the high and stable red sandstone cliffs. At Cape Tryon these cliffs support a large colony of cormorants, the best and most easily accessible in the Maritimes. The upper sites are primarily home to Great Cormorant; those lower and nearer the sea house mostly Double-crested. To reach the cape and colony, proceed through French River and turn left off Blue Heron Drive, towards the sea; proceed on the paved road for about 1.5 km to the T-intersection; turn left onto the unpaved road and drive about 0.5 km; turn right down a farm lane to the sea. You'll spot No Trespassing signs on the fields on either side. They do not apply to the lane you are on, only to the adjacent land. Continue past the house to the lighthouse at the end. The colony occupies beautiful sandstone cliffs from the lighthouse westward for 0.25 to 0.5 km.

Return to Blue Heron Drive and continue south to New London. Take time to visit the green-trimmed white cottage, the birthplace of L. M. Montgomery, author of *Anne of Green Gables*.

During summer and fall, the drive along this north shore should produce Caspian Tern, particularly around the mouths of bays. There are about forty pairs of Ospreys nesting in the province. Watch them fishing in the coastal bays and rivers.

If you are in this area in winter, look for sea ducks on open water under bridges, such as at Bayview, 2 km north of Stanley Bridge. At Stanley Bridge, drop into the Manor of Birds, a museum with more than 700 mounted birds and butterflies from around the world. At nearby Marineland you will see exhibits of P.E.I. fish, marine life and live seals. Continuing northeast, you arrive at Cavendish, where Green Gables, the old farmhouse, was immortalized in *Anne of Green Gables* and other novels. Visit the restored Green Gables House at Prince Edward Island National Park. This is also the first of several entrances into the park, the best birding area in the province (see below).

After continuing along Blue Heron Drive another 18 km, you will arrive at Oyster Bed Bridge, where sea ducks gather on the open water in winter. After 3 more km, turn straight south toward Charlottetown, 20 km away.

To complete the loop, leave Charlottetown on Highway 1 west, also called Blue Heron Road, which proceeds north, west, then south for a short distance. The North River Causeway lies 5 km from Charlottetown along this route. Watch for wintering sea ducks on the open water under the bridge. You should be able to spot American Black Duck, Common Goldeneye and Common Merganser. Ten km farther on Blue Heron Drive (don't forget to leave Highway 1 at Cornwall), you will pass over the West River Causeway. Look for the largest concentration of wintering sea ducks in the province. These include American Black Duck, Common and Barrow's Goldeneyes and Common Merganser. Also watch for wintering Bald Eagle.

Continue along this shoreline route another 38 km to DeSable, where Canada Geese are usually spotted. They'll also be seen at Tryon, another 11 km. Drive a further 11 km to reach Carleton and the ferry.

WINIFRED CAIRNS

Great Blue Heron

Lady Slipper Drive (West P.E.I.)

To explore the west end of P.E.I., where half the province's potatoes are grown, proceed west from Summerside. Follow Highway 11 around the shore or cut across country on 2; transfer onto 14 and drive west down to West Point and Cedar Dunes Provincial Park. Eastern White Cedar and White Spruce grow over low rolling dunes in the area. Warblers are abundant in the forests; sea ducks, gulls and terns are found near the sea; the beaches may be occupied by Piping Plover at times. Check out the wooden lighthouse that is over a century old and still in use.

Continue up the west side along 14, and then turn off near the tip, on Highway 12, to North Cape. You can drive right to the point. The land here consists of open exposed cliffs. This is a good spot to observe sea ducks, especially in late summer and fall. Look for Common Eider, scoters and gulls. If you are lucky you may spot a Northern Gannet too. In late summer watch the local people who come here to gather Irish Moss from the shores. They continue the practice of their forefathers, unchanged for generations, of pulling metal baskets through the water to harvest the moss.

WINIFRED CAIRNS

Prince Edward Island National Park

The park is a favourite birding spot on the island, with over 210 species recorded. Rustico Island, in the park, is home to hundreds of Great Blue

Herons. Twenty or more of these birds may often be spotted simultaneously as they forage in the marshes and on beaches along park roads. Piping Plovers nest at several places along the sand beaches.

The long sand beaches on the north shore of P.E.I. have been a popular playground for over a hundred years. Dalvay-by-the-Sea, an elegant historic summer hotel, was constructed in 1895 as a summer home. Today visitors can enjoy its beauty during an overnight stay.

The approximately 26-km^2 strip of land making up the park stretches 40 km along the north central coastline. Charlottetown lies 24 km south on Highways 6 or 15. There are several access points to enter the park, with Highway 6 the main trunk corridor, lying parallel to, and south of, the shore. A park brochure shows the different access points, beaches and hiking areas. Three park campgrounds are provided. Commercial accommodation may be obtained both within and outside the boundaries.

The CWS has a 231-page report, *Avifaunal Survey of P.E.I. National Park*, by K. Martin and W. Cairns, published in 1979. For more information, contact: The Superintendent, Prince Edward Island National Park, Box 487, Charlottetown, P.E.I. C1A 7L1, Telephone: (902) 672-2211.

Birding Features

The park consists of red sandstone cliffs, barrier beach and dune systems; shallow salt-water bays bordered by salt marshes; cranberry bogs, ponds, mixed deciduous and coniferous woodlands, and old fields now largely grown up into White Spruce. The outstanding features are the great dune lands. Each dune looks like a strip from the Sahara Desert. The dunes are held stable by Marram Grass, with roots penetrating down 3 m in search of water. However, heavy human traffic spells doom to these grass patches, so take care and avoid walking on them.

Spring brings Great and Double-crested Cormorants back to the area and their nesting cliff west of the park at Cape Tryon (see above). These birds feed in the gulf and bays near the park all summer. A hike out to the far western tip of the park, east of Cape Tryon, onto Cavendish sandspit, should produce Piping Plover nesting along the beach, together with a colony of Common Tern. Visitors must have a park official accompany them in this specially protected nesting area. A few Arctic Terns may also nest here. After moving east of the west end of the spit for about 2 km along the beach road, you will arrive at Clarke's Pond. This is a favourite area for nesting and summering ducks. Look for Mallard, American Black Duck, Northern Pintail, Green-winged and Blue-winged Teals, American Wigeon, Ring-necked Duck and Red-breasted Merganser. The Lake of Shining Waters, on the west side of the road immediately north of Cavendish, is good for summering ducks. Check out the woodlots for warblers and other woodland species, as this is one of the better spots for land birds.

After moving east about 3 km along the beach road to Orby Head, you arrive at a small colony of Black Guillemot in the cliffs. Continue east to North Rustico Beach at the point where the road jogs south to North Rustico. Check North Rustico Beach for Caspian Terns; they regularly occur here during late summer and fall. At the community of North Rustico you'll find the P.E.I. Wildlife Park, with animals native to the Maritimes on display.

Follow Highway 6, Blue Heron Drive, down and around to the intersection with Highway 15; take the latter road north to the beach road and then straight west by Rustico Island Campground to the end of the road on Rustico Island. Stop and scan the trees at the western end of the campground for the Great Blue Heron colony. Piping Plover nest along this causeway, so keep a careful watch. The woodlot around the campground should produce warblers and other land birds in fair numbers from late May to July.

Now proceed east along the beach road to Brackley Beach, which lies at the T-junction with Highway 15. This is a good area for migrating waterfowl. Scan the sea for Common Eider and the three scoter species. After continuing along the beach east another 4 km or more from the T-junction, you come upon Covehead Bay to the south of the road and Covehead Harbour. There is an extensive marsh here, plus open water in winter. In spring, look in the harbour for Canada Goose, Brant and a variety of ducks. Later in summer, check this marsh beside the road between Brackley Beach and Covehead Harbour for migrating shorebirds. The site is the best one known in the area to find these birds on migration. Scan the sea again for the same species as found off Brackley Beach. Look along the edges of the marsh for nesting Spotted Sandpiper and Willet. Piping Plover also nest at Covehead Harbour. At the bridge across the harbour, check the tern colony where there are abundant Common and a few Arctic. Caspian Terns are also sometimes observed in the harbour.

Now proceed to John Archie's Pond on the sea side of the beach road, about 1 km east of the harbour bridge. Look for the variety of summering ducks mentioned previously. Stanhope Beach is a good spot to look for the Bank Swallows which nest in the adjacent cliffs. Continue along the beach road about 5 km from the Covehead Harbour bridge to search for Long Pond, a fairly large pond on the landward side. Waters here hold a variety of the same summering ducks mentioned previously.

Head south and then back along the road to Stanhope. Check the woods for warblers and other woodland species from late May into July.

Piping Plover

The final spot to explore from spring through early fall is Blooming Point, the finger of land farthest east. You can reach this point by boat or by following Highway 6 east, 8 km from Stanhope to Mill Cove, and then on 219 for 6 km to 218; follow 218 north through Blooming Point, approximately 3 km to the end of pavement. Drive down to the beach (about 2 km), and then west along the long spit of land, about 6 km one way to the far west end. This is a beautiful, peaceful walk, but hot in the summer. Take plenty of drinking water and make sure you have sun protection to avoid sunburn. Watch for the numerous animal tracks in the dunes and colonies of Piping Plover and terns. The latter are the same as mentioned above. You should see swallows roosting along this beach in late summer.

The Osprey nests in the general vicinity of these beaches and sometimes is spotted hunting over the ponds and salt-water bays. Watch for Northern Harrier, the commonest raptor, cruising over the dunes and marshes.

Come in August to watch large flocks of migrating swallows roosting all along the beaches. The shorebirds begin appearing in early August and increase in numbers as fall progresses. Scrutinize each flock for Semipalmated Plover, Black-bellied Plover, Ruddy Turnstone, Whimbrel, Spotted Sandpiper, Greater and Lesser Yellowlegs, Red Knot, Pectoral Sandpiper, White-rumped Sandpiper, Least Sandpiper, Dunlin, Short-billed Dowitcher, Semipalmated Sandpiper, Hudsonian Godwit and Sanderling. The best spot to see these shorebirds lies in the marsh between Covehead Harbour and Brackley Beach (see above). Inspect the small marshy ponds and sandy shores throughout the park for these birds. Gulls are regular fall visitors along the sand bars and bays. Study them for Great Black-backed, Herring, Ring-billed and Bonaparte's.

If you are a winter visitor, check for open water at Covehead Harbour. Look just south of the park at the Oyster Bed Bridge causeway south of Rustico Bay. Examine MacMillan Point, reached by driving along Route 6 from Stanhope, southwest through Covehead to West Covehead (about 5 km from Stanhope). Take the narrow road north from West Covehead to near the point. These three spots should produce a complete collection of wintering ducks, including American Black Duck, Common and Barrow's Goldeneyes, Oldsquaw and Common Merganser.

WINIFRED CAIRNS

Charlottetown

Charlottetown, the smallest provincial capital and only city in Prince Edward Island, is the birthplace of Canada. Here, in September 1864, the Fathers of Confederation met and signed articles that led to our nation forming in 1867.

Prince Edward Island was first settled by 300 Acadians in 1720; Port la Joie, at Rocky Point, is now the site of Fort Amherst National Historic Park. The French colony was captured in 1758 by the British, who then moved across the harbour and established Charlottetown in 1764. Several downtown buildings date from the mid-1800s, giving a special character to the community.

Birding Features
In the southwest corner, Victoria Park, consisting of about 200 ha, overlooks the harbour. The park is a mixture of hardwoods and open spaces with a variety of woodland birds. At the east end of the city, close to Hillsborough Bridge spanning the Hillsborough River, open water in the winter attracts sea ducks plus large numbers of American Black Ducks. Check the stone pilings on this bridge from May to July for Common Tern nests. Cormorants also regularly roost along this bridge.

WINIFRED CAIRNS

Kings Byway (East P.E.I.)

This loop on the eastern shore of P.E.I. begins on the wharf at Wood Islands. This is the docking site for the ferries to Nova Scotia. The sand islands and shallow marshes constitute a good place to look for birds while waiting for the ferry. Scan for the Common Tern colony, Great Blue Heron, American Black Duck, a variety of gulls and, in the fall, migrating shorebirds.

If you are heading to Charlottetown, stop at the salt marshes of Orwell Cove Wildlife Management Area. This site, 32 km north of Wood Islands, can be seen readily from the road running off the highway into Orwell Cove and out to the point (about 3 km from the highway). Stop here, especially during spring and fall migration, for geese and ducks.

Now return through Wood Islands and continue east on Routes 4 and 18 out to Beach Point, about 25 km east. Check the harbour at Beach Point for cormorants, Red-breasted Merganser, and Great Black-backed, Herring and Ring-billed Gulls, all of which nest in this area. Continue around the point to Murray River and then take Highway 4 across to Milltown Cross, 10 km north of Murray River. At Milltown Cross, you will find the Sturgeon River and the Harvey Moore Migratory Bird Sanctuary. This spot, 5 km south of Montague, is a haven for Canada Geese and ducks that frequent the ponds. A variety of upland birds may be spotted along the hiking trails. The rivers and bays around Montague are home to the Bald Eagle. The province's only known nesting pair reside in this area.

From Montague take Routes 4, 5, 2 and 16 out to East Point, the eastern limit of the province. Come to the point in late September and early October to watch the variety of migrating raptors. Scan the open sea at all seasons for Northern Gannet, cormorants, Common Eider and scoters.

WINIFRED CAIRNS

Newfoundland

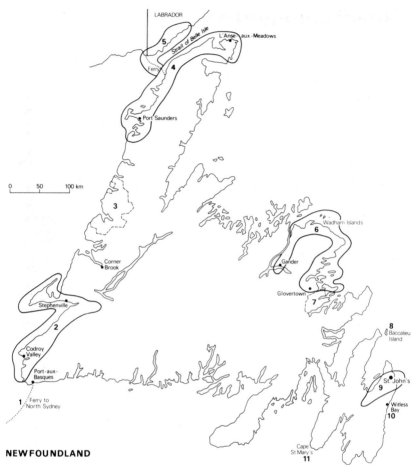

NEWFOUNDLAND

1 The ferries
2 Codroy Valley and southwest Newfoundland
3 Gros Morne National Park
4 Northern Peninsula and L'Anse-aux-Meadows
5 Strait of Belle Isle and south Labrador coast
6 Gander and Glovertown (northeast)
7 Terra Nova National Park
8 Baccalieu Island
9 St. John's
10 Witless Bay Seabird Sanctuary
11 Cape St. Mary's Seabird Sanctuary

Newfoundland

Our closest point of land to Europe, Newfoundland, is half island and half mainland. Birds to look for include pelagic species such as shearwaters, storm-petrels and other migrating seabirds, as well as Northern Gannet, sea ducks and alcids, notably Common and Thick-billed Murres, Atlantic Puffin, Razorbill and Black Guillemot. Coastal boats, ferries and hikes along the coast are the best ways to get to see these birds. Inland, the boreal forest contains many interesting passerine species, a large number of which actually nest. The barren ground on the west coast, especially the highlands of Gros Morne, is an excellent place to search for Rock Ptarmigan. The northern tip of the island is a good area to look for arctic species which come south in the winter, notably Gyrfalcon and Ivory Gull, although they are by no means guaranteed.

Birders who visit Newfoundland should note that there is not a large number of birds in the province compared to other areas of North America. Moreover, many species are seen only occasionally or in very small areas, and those who gauge their success by the daily numbers of species seen should be highly satisfied with 70 to 75 species.

A rough triangle of land consisting of 112,733 km^2 makes up the island of Newfoundland. The greatly indented eastern shore contains numerous sheltered harbours and large bays. Forest covers about half of the interior; the remainder is barrens and bog. The Long Range Mountains rise to 762 m along the west coast. Their valleys contain large timber of commercial value.

The Grand Banks on the southeast form a large underwater shelf, rich in plankton and fish and thus drawing numerous seabirds. The meeting of the warm Gulf Stream of the south and the colder Labrador Current results in highly productive waters full of food for birds.

The narrow Strait of Belle Isle separates the island from Labrador, a roughly triangular section of mainland 293,348 km^2. Labrador includes all those lands which have rivers flowing eastward towards the Atlantic. The interior of Labrador rises in a series of plateaus, with the Torngat Mountains rising steadily from south to north, reaching a height of 1500 m.

June to mid-July is the best time for nesting seabirds and forest and highland species. Storms in spring and fall bring in strays from the south and Europe. Shorebirds begin returning from the arctic in July and August. September brings the hawks and the rest of the shorebirds.

Cape St. Mary's Seabird Sanctuary is one of the highlights of the province, with Northern Gannet and other coastal nesting birds. A boat is not required to see the birds at this spot. Shorebirds are numerous in the fall here, as are hawks, accidental mainland species, and warblers. The cape provides a good landfall for storm-driven species. Witless Bay Sea Bird Sanctuary is much closer to St. John's but one needs a boat to experience all the birds. The area around L'Anse-aux-Meadows National Historic Park, on the far northern peninsula, provides excellent birding, particularly in the town and nearby sites. Rarities include European Redwing and Pink-footed

Rock Ptarmigan

Goose, which have been spotted in St. Anthony in the past three years. The Codroy Valley to the southwest has good hawk migration, with one of the best shorebird concentrations in the province in the fall. Terra Nova National Park, north of St. John's, will produce warblers, thrushes and seabirds offshore. Gros Morne National Park should be visited for northern species, including Rock Ptarmigan and redpolls.

If your time here is limited, begin at St. John's. A long half-day can be spent checking Bowring Park and/or Pippy Park in the city for land birds; Cape Spear to the southeast should be examined for seabirds. A full day of birding should begin at Cape St. Mary's, the best accessible spot in the province for seabirds and some land birds. Another day could be spent at Terra Nova National Park for both land and sea birds. A visitor to Gander should grab a car and slip east to Terra Nova for a half-day of worthwhile birding. When on the southwest side of Corner Brook, drive south to the Codroy Valley for a good half-day or, if time permits, north to Gros Morne National Park.

A two-day to one-week stay in Newfoundland can best be spent by starting in St. John's and checking out Quidi Vidi Lake for gulls and shorebirds; Long Pond for ducks, hawks, an occasional heron, rails and other waders; Pippy Park and Oxen Pond Botanic Park for nesting land birds; Bowring Park for migrating land birds and nesting species. Then drive southeast to Cape St. Mary's for seabirds in all seasons and shorebirds in the fall. A trip to Witless Bay might produce Atlantic Puffins, murres and other alcids, as well as gulls, shearwaters and Leach's Storm-Petrel. A boat must be hired to explore around the three-island sanctuary.

During a two-day visit to Gander, make sure you go north to Gander Bay and loop south to Glovertown. This trip will take about a half to three-quarters of a day, leaving the rest of your stay to explore Terra Nova National Park for ducks, eagles and other birds of prey, seabirds, shorebirds and upland species.

You need almost a week to explore around and to the north of Stephenville and Corner Brook. Begin down at Cape Ray and John T. Cheeseman Provincial Park, where summer naturalists will help you get started. Head up the Codroy Valley. Shorebirds in the fall are best located at Stephenville Crossing. Spend the bulk of your time at Gros Morne National Park, where you can hike to the best spots. It takes at least three days return for L'Anse-aux-Meadows. If you have enough time, drive this stretch for the beauty of the mountains and the northern species you will spot there.

To date, no rare bird alert telephone number is available. Contact people include Roger Burrows, the author of *A Birdwatcher's Guide to Atlantic Canada; Vol. 1, Newfoundland and Labrador, Pelagic Ferries and Offshore Islands*. This book is available for $5.00 from Avid Services, P.O. Box 73, Glovertown, Newfoundland A0G 2L0, Telephone: (709) 533-6641. Mr. Burrows may be contacted at this address. Material from this book has been used extensively throughout this chapter.

Another very helpful individual, John Pratt, may be contacted at: 12 Highland Park, Box 108, Holyrood, C.B., Newfoundland A0A 2R0, Telephone: (709) 229-6423.

The Newfoundland Natural History Society meets monthly at Coughlan College in winter and Oxen Pond in the summer. Names and addresses of the current executive and key club members may be located in their publication, *The Osprey*.

The Newfoundland and Labrador, Atlantic Canada, Official Road Map and other information should be acquired for your visit. Contact: Newfoundland and Labrador Department of Development and Tourism, Information Office, P.O. Box 4750, St. John's, Newfoundland A1C 5T7.

The Ferries

The trip from the mainland provides ample opportunities to spot many seabirds. Scan the waters for Northern Fulmar, a variety of shearwaters, storm-petrels, Northern Gannet, phalaropes, gulls and murres. Land birds stop to rest on the boat riggings while moving through.

The Cabot Strait ferry (year-round service) leaves North Sydney, Nova Scotia, and six hours later arrives at Port-aux-Basques, Newfoundland. The other ferry, also from Sydney, but going to and from Argentia, Newfoundland, takes more than twenty-two hours but saves twelve hours on the drive to St. John's. The Argentia ferry operates only from the third week of June to September and may be closed down in 1985 because of limited use. Either ferry trip should be reserved in advance. The Port-aux-Basques service usually has short lineups, with extra sailings in summer eliminating delays, except on weekends. The longer crossing usually has lineups for cabins. For information on both ferries, contact: CN Marine, P.O. Box 250, North Sydney, N.S. B2A 3M3, any CN Marine ferry terminal or VIA Rail station. Telephone: (709) 794-7203 when in Newfoundland, 1-800-565-9470 in the other maritime provinces, 1-800-565-9411 in Ontario, Quebec, Newfoundland and Labrador, 1-800-432-7344 in Maine, 1-800-341-7981 in other northeast states. CN Marine also operates a Coastal Boat Service to local outports. Vehicles are carried on the North Coast Service from Lewisporte to Goose Bay and to Battle Harbour, both in Labrador.

Birding Features

The continental shelf, off Newfoundland, is covered with waters full of fish and pelagic birds. Winter is the best season, when bird species from the Arctic move south to feed.

Cabot Strait Ferry. A crossing anytime from December to April should produce many hundreds of Iceland (more common) and Glaucous Gulls, and Black-legged Kittiwakes. Watch for Thick-billed Murre, Dovekie and Black Guillemot close to shore. Razorbill, Atlantic Puffin and Common Murre are likely possibilities. Remember to watch for Northern Fulmar, which can be seen year-round but is especially common in winter. An Ivory Gull is not an impossibility. A trip in May should produce alcids. Late in the month you might encounter a few phalaropes and Arctic Tern. In June, numbers again increase with excellent chances of spotting Greater, Sooty and Manx Shearwaters and a possible Cory's off Cape Breton. From late June to late August, scrutinize for Northern Fulmar, Leach's and Wilson's Storm-Petrels, Northern Gannet, Common Murre and Atlantic Puffin; Pomarine Jaeger appears from May through October. By early August, you again encounter Greater and Sooty Shearwaters in rafts, particularly off the North Sydney shore. You may even spot Manx Shearwaters in low numbers, with a very rare Cory's. Survey the birds in this area for Black-legged Kittiwake and Arctic and Common Terns. From May through September, look for Parasitic Jaeger. The fall runs are most remembered for the large number of Greater Shearwaters, with up to 3000 encountered in late October. They and other shearwaters disappear shortly after this date. By midwinter, Northern Fulmars are still in numbers up to 100. The Dovekies arrive from November through April with up to 1250 reported on a Christmas run. These winter birds, together with Iceland and Glaucous Gulls and Black-legged Kittiwake, remain high in numbers from December to March.

Argentia Ferry. This run is considered by some to be the best ocean trip for birds in the northwest Atlantic. The weather can be a problem, with rough seas and thick fog not uncommon. By late June when the service begins, you will spot Northern Fulmar, possibly a Cory's Shearwater, up to 500 or more Greater and Sooty Shearwaters with a few Manx too. By July, these numbers increase considerably. Later in July, look for flocks of Black-legged Kittiwake, which are common in summer. Along the coast of Cape Breton, watch for shearwaters. The most shearwaters are again seen a few hours out of Argentia. Between three and four hours from landing there, scan the waters for large numbers of Leach's Storm-Petrel and a few Wilson's Storm-Petrel. As you pull into Placentia Bay, just before Argentia, the waters become quite productive, with a few Manx Shearwaters, Common Murre and Atlantic Puffin. The Whimbrel appears regularly in mid-July. By early August, Pomarine and Parasitic Jaegers appear, and by the end of the month there is a better chance of seeing them and Red-throated Loon, and Greater and Sooty Shearwaters. Black-legged Kittiwakes are present here all summer. You may even spot a Sabine's Gull. By the last sailing in September, numbers are reduced.

Coastal Boats. Coastal boats run from Port-aux-Basques along the south coast. Check with the CN ferry schedules. If you have lots of time, use these boats to enjoy spotting seabirds and eagles and to explore a part of Newfoundland seldom seen by outsiders.

JOHN PRATT

Codroy Valley and Southwest Newfoundland

Set between the extreme southwest coastal Anguille Mountains and the inland South Long Range Mountains, the Codroy Valley, with its adjacent birch-fir forests and rivers, has some of the best birding habitats in the province. Water birds are particularly numerous on migration. The woodlands contain Blackpoll and Mourning Warblers, Lincoln's and Fox Sparrows. Farmlands provide homes for Gray Catbird, Bobolink and Dickcissel.

The first report of this coast was in 1594, when a British ship noted an Indian village, several shipwrecks, and a dramatic rescue of Spanish seamen from their captors. The area was settled over two hundred years ago. The names along the coast reflect the Scottish and French backgrounds of these early people.

Travel by automobile is a must, as commercial transportation is very limited. Make certain you have a full tank of gasoline when you leave the ferry, since many service stations close early and are off the highway and hard to find. There is bus service at least once a day from Port-aux-Basques and other centres to St. John's. Check with your travel agent or CN–Terra Transport for a schedule. Numerous provincial campgrounds are located along the way. Commercial accommodation is available in major centres such as Corner Brook.

Information for this section is from the above-mentioned birding guide.

Birding Features
Upon arriving at Port-aux-Basques, if you have lots of time consider taking one of the coastal boats that run out of this port. Such a trip will provide you with a good look at this seldom-visited part of Newfoundland plus provide opportunities to spot a variety of seabirds and eagles.

This southwestern area can be explored using the John T. Cheeseman Provincial Park, or another park farther along, as a base.

Cape Ray. Start your trip by moving down to Cape Ray, about 3 km west of Cheeseman Park, or southwest of the community of Red Rocks. This "landfall" point brings in the migrators and also is a good spot to watch for hawks. The beach provides a resting site for shorebirds. Check into Cheeseman for other species. The summer interpretive naturalists on duty will help.

Mummichog Provincial Park. A small killifish, found in brackish water in the nearby lagoon, provides the name for the park. Set at the mouth of the

Little Codroy River, the park offers excellent birding chances. The 2-km-long Sandpiper Walk along the shoreline should be taken in spring and fall migration periods. Great Blue Heron is a regular visitor. American Woodcock has nested here, one of the few provincial breeding records. In August you may spot migrating American Goldfinch. Boreal species such as the Three-toed Woodpecker have been spotted.

Grand Codroy. The tidal estuary and mouth of the Grand Codroy River provide the best fall waterfowl birding area in Newfoundland. Come during the week. Summer naturalists are on duty. Great Blue Heron is a regular. Summer nesters include Northern Pintail, American Wigeon and Green-winged Teal. August through October offers the most birds, but hunters arrive in October. Red-throated Loon and Red-necked and Pied-billed Grebes have been seen in small numbers in mid-October. Canada Geese may appear in flocks up to 2000 as they pass through. Mallards are noted; American Black Ducks are very common; Ring-necked Duck, Greater and Lesser Scaups and Red-breasted Merganser are seen; Green-winged Teals have been sighted in groups of up to 500, with a few Blue-winged present. The above-mentioned breeders are also around. Northern Goshawk, Bald Eagle, Northern Harrier and Peregrine Falcon all occur occasionally. Shorebirds are not as numerous as at Stephenville Crossing and St. Pauls Flats to the north. Here on the Codroy in September and October, ferret out Semipalmated and Black-bellied Plovers and Lesser Yellowlegs; a Willet was sighted on the beach in 1981; other shorebirds include Red Knot, Pectoral and White-rumped Sandpipers, Dunlin, Semipalmated Sandpiper, Hudsonian Godwit and Sanderling. Grasslands behind the estuary provide another place to check for shorebirds, including Least and Spotted Sandpipers and Common Snipe. The Caspian Tern is a regular visitor. At Upper Ferry (check local road map), look for concentrations of migrating snipe and flocks of Red-winged Blackbird. The Doyle area has had American Coot in the fall. Hooded Mergansers are more likely seen here than anywhere else in Newfoundland, but they are still rare. The Rough-legged Hawk now arrives on its way through, followed by a possible Gyrfalcon and a Snowy Owl.

Great Codroy and Cape Anguille. Fall is the best time to come here. Common and Red-throated Loons, Red-necked Grebe, Black Guillemot and many other species are seen off the headland at the cape in October. Check the woods for warblers and vireos, which have included Warbling Vireo. You may come upon numerous Fox and White-throated Sparrows in the weedy fields.

Codroy Valley. Yellow Birch is unusually common along this valley. Other trees such as White Birch and Balsam Fir provide good cover for woodland birds. Inspect these forests for the uncommon Red-eyed Vireo, Nashville Warbler and Rose-breasted Grosbeak. Softwood stands are to be inspected for Yellow-bellied Flycatcher, Blackpoll and Mourning Warblers, Hermit Thrush and Lincoln's Sparrow. The farmlands should be reconnoitred for Bobolink and American Goldfinch. Don't forget the river marshes for Sora and migrating waterfowl in the fall.

Crabbes River Provincial Park. Located on the bank of a salmon river, this park sometimes has a few boreal species. Look for the Great Horned Owl, Gray Jay, Boreal Chickadee and Pine Grosbeak in all seasons. From mid-May to early June or August, search for migrating warblers on their way through. The salmon fishing is recommended highly.

Barachois Pond Provincial Park. If you are a salmon fisherman, try the several rivers flowing into the bay near St. George's on the way to the park. Barachois Park, one of the largest in the province, has an area of virgin forest unsurpassed on the island. Stands of Black Ash are worth the visit. There is a great variety of flowering plants, including many rare orchids seen in June and July. These forests are the last stronghold for the Pine Marten. Red Squirrel and Eastern Chipmunk were introduced to help feed this large predator. These small mammals, and the increase in Ruffed Grouse, have aided the birds of prey that hunt in the park. The 5-km Erwin Mountain Trail, beginning near the campground, provides access to the top of the 305-m-high peak. On the plateau you'll often spot part of the herd of 7000 Caribou. The park contains 6 woodpecker species, including the Three-toed. You can sometimes hear the songs of the Gray-cheeked Thrush and Veery. Warblers are common; look for Black-throated Green and Black-and-white, which may be at their northeastern limits.

Stephenville Crossing. The community was originally established as a rail-road distribution centre for the Port-au-Port Peninsula in the late 1800s. You may spot a Common Black-headed Gull nesting, as they have bred here in the past. The extensive mudflats, with some salt marshes, are accessible from Route 461 just south of the village, across the railway tracks by the road. Check the east side of the causeway at low tide for gulls and shore-birds. The gulf shore is also rewarding, particularly in late winter, when seabirds are blown inshore. Killdeer have nested here, the second spot on the island; Lesser Golden-Plover have been seen in May; from late July on, come to watch migrating shorebirds, including Red Knot, Pectoral Sandpiper and Dunlin; Buff-breasted and Baird's Sandpipers, Hudsonian Godwit and Wilson's Phalarope have all been reported. The Pomarine Jaeger is sometimes swept in during a fall storm. This is one of the few places in the province where Bonaparte's Gull and Caspian Tern can be spotted during migration. In September, when gulls are most numerous, Common Black-headed Gull numbers often reach fifty. Several rare land birds have been spotted here too. Look for Osprey and Bank Swallow. Search the area for Eastern Wood-Pewee, Alder, Yellow-bellied and Olive-sided Flycatchers. Merlins are fairly easy to find. Bobolink, Rose-breasted Grosbeak and Indigo Bunting are not regular but are worth looking for. Flocks of Snow Buntings are very common in spring and fall, and are sometimes accompanied by a few Lapland Longspurs.

Port-au-Port Peninsula. This arrow-shaped peninsula has been occupied since 1712, when French fishermen settled. From then on, a flourishing French–Micmac Indian culture grew that today makes the area a unique attraction. The oldest wooden building on the island is here at Aguathana.

The limestone deposits at this community contain brachiopod fossils and barite crystals. Piccadilly Head Provincial Park provides an attractive campground; the Bird Blind Walk of 1.5 km, along the shore, is best visited in mid-September for flocks of Black-bellied Plover and Red Knot. From early May to late September, check the telephone wires for American Kestrel. Begin the stay by driving out on Route 460 and then northeast on 464 to the end of the 17-km Long Point. The final stretch of 8 km, with scrubby spruce and fir, concentrates land migrants in such heavy densities that up to 6 species of birds of prey may be spotted hunting songbirds, with Sharp-shinned Hawk and Merlin especially common in August. The best way to fully experience the point is either to park and walk the last 8 km, or to take turns in driving short lengths while the others in your group hike. Flycatchers to be seen include Alder, Yellow-bellied and Olive-sided; most vireos are present; warblers are numerous, with rarer species for the island fairly regular, including Cape May and Canada. Bobolink, Rose-breasted Grosbeak and Indigo Bunting are regular. The common breeding sparrows are present too. Explore the rest of the peninsula along 463 and 460.

Gros Morne National Park

Set on the western coast of Newfoundland, near the base of the Great Northern Peninsula, Gros Morne National Park provides a rich variety of things to see, including 207 species of birds listed on their checklist. The stunted spruce and fir, called tuckamore, provides habitat for songbirds; a number of lakes host Common Loon, Ring-necked Duck, Harlequin Duck and Red-breasted Merganser. The Rough-legged Hawk breeds in the park. The upper heathlands host year-round Willow and Rock Ptarmigans. Shorelines provide nesting sites for scattered Killdeer; Arctic Tern also nests on the coast. Gray-cheeked Thrush is locally common, together with a good collection of warblers, including Wilson's, Blackpoll, Mourning and Common Yellowthroat. Common Redpolls nest around the base and lower slopes of Gros Morne in June. The park is one of the few places in Canada where American Tree Sparrows can be found nesting near a settled area. The unique green serpentine rock on the tableland makes the visit worthwhile. Come to see Arctic Hare and the Newfoundland Caribou, one of the world's largest subspecies of this ungulate.

The early Native peoples lived mainly on marine mammals and made carvings of them. Next came the Dorset Eskimo, who also lived on marine mammals. Finally, the Beothuk Indians arrived about 800 A.D. and were later exterminated by early whites. Jacques Cartier landed at Cow Head to avoid a storm in 1534.

Recent settlement of the area was delayed by a series of treaties and agreements between the French and the British. As in the other parts of Newfoundland, there is a strong sense of community.

The 1943-km^2 park lies 126 km north on Highways 1 and 430 from Corner Brook. The main entrance on Route 430 lies 40 km north of Deer

Lake; the scenic route is by way of 431 to Woody Point and the Bonne Bay ferry. Regular air passenger flights operate into Deer Lake. Several small communities exist within the park. There is an excellent interpretive centre at Rocky Harbour. Hiking and interpretive trails are spread throughout. An excellent trail brochure provides information. In addition, the park brochure shows communities, topography, interpretive features and other amenities.

Three campgrounds, one fully serviced with 156 sites at Berry Hill, are available for your use. Commercial accommodation is found at Deer Lake, 72 km southeast; within the park at Woody Point near the ferry launch in the southwest side of Bonne Bay; at Rocky Harbour on the north side of Bonne Bay; and at Cow Head on the northwest corner of the park.

Write for information, including a bird checklist: The Superintendent, Gros Morne National Park, Box 130, Rocky Harbour, Bonne Bay, Newfoundland A0K 4N0, Telephone: (709) 458-2417.

Birding Features
The slopes of the west side of the Northern Long Range Mountains support good stands of Balsam Fir. White Birch is present in places. Eastern White Pine grows well in the Bonne Bay area. The heathland provides year-round habitat throughout the park for Willow Ptarmigan.

Trout River Area. Drive to the end of Route 431 at Trout River. The braided stream at the mouth of the river is best visited by boat; hire one at the dock. The luxuriant ferns and shrubs between the various stream courses provide a jungle-like environment. You'll find Alder and Yellow-bellied Flycatchers, Red-eyed Vireo and Pine Grosbeak nesting in these lowlands. The beaches have regular broods of Spotted Sandpiper. Higher up the slope, open sites are home to Black-and-white and Black-throated Green Warblers.

Serpentine Tableland. As you drive beyond Woody Point or Glenburnie on 431, you will come upon this unique green barren rock. No trees and few plants grow on these serpentine outcrops, which lack many essential nutrients. Rock Ptarmigan is fairly common. A few pairs of Greater Yellowlegs nest near a lowland pond.

Bonne Bay Area. Both Highways 431 and 430 provide excellent views of the two long arms of the sea extending inland. The community of Lomond at the end of the South Arm is a good spot to find such strays as Solitary Vireo and Bay-breasted Warbler. The marshes attract American Bittern. Osprey hunts over the water; Willow Ptarmigan nests on the Lookout Hills. In June and early July, stop at second-growth spots along the road to ferret out the Mourning Warbler. Northern Harrier occasionally hunts over the land; Merlin and American Kestrel perch on wires. Chipping Sparrow uses the groves of spruce along the manicured lawns at the visitor centre.

Rocky Harbour. Located just off 430, this community has much to offer. Bonne Bay contains most salt-water fish, salmon and sea trout. You can purchase these as well as lobster, crab, scallops, mussels and clams at the community wharf. Whales, porpoises and seals appear close to shore. Birds seen in the area in spring and summer include Ruby-throated Hummingbird, Gray-cheeked and Swainson's Thrushes, Eastern Kingbird, Least Flycatcher, Barn Swallow, Red-eyed Vireo, Mourning, Wilson's and Blackpoll Warblers, Northern Waterthrush, Rose-breasted Grosbeak, Swamp, Lincoln's and Fox Sparrows, Purple Finch and American Goldfinch. Some pelagic species will appear after a storm.

Lobster Cove. Just off 430, at the end of the point overlooking Rocky Harbour, the lighthouse area provides another spot to do coastal birding. Park staff are present in the refurbished lighthouse to talk about local history and give guided walks. Check the bushes in spring and fall for small birds resting on their way by. The meadow north of the building is used by Bobolink. Watch for White-throated, Fox and Lincoln's Sparrows in this clearing too. Sharp-shinned Hawk, Merlin and American Kestrel are numerous and prey on these small birds.

Green Point and Baker Brook. Drive to the primitive campground at Green Point and spend at least a day in early to mid-summer. Take the trail from the campground through tuckamore and taller firs. Watch for Moose tracks on your way by the marshes of Bakers Brook to the shore. Scan the sea for gulls, terns and other water birds. If you spot a flock of Common Eider, check for King Eider, a species which has been spotted here. In spring, the Short-billed Dowitcher has been noted. American Kestrel and Short-eared Owl nest along here. Look for Swainson's and Gray-cheeked Thrushes, Magnolia and Blackpoll Warblers, Northern Waterthrush, Mourning Warbler, Common Yellowthroat, Wilson's Warbler and American Redstart. Walk into the bog for dewberries and other bog plants and a nesting Savannah Sparrow. Check the beach for salt-spray plants and shells.

Gros Morne Plateau. Drive southeast about 3 km from the visitor reception centre, to the parking lot and the head of the trail to the top of this plateau. Take either the 4- or 7-km hike along the James Callaghan Trail to the base, both easy walks. The total trail, including the climb up, takes about six or seven hours for a return hike. It is about an hour walk to the base of the mountain. The mountain rises 806 m above sea level, making it the second-highest in Newfoundland. On the way in, carefully examine the woods for Three-toed Woodpecker, Olive-sided Flycatcher and Cape May Warbler. Make sure to stop at the beaver ponds at the base of the hill for Willow Ptarmigan, Common Snipe, Spotted Sandpiper, a wide selection of thrushes and warblers in the dense growth, plus Swamp Sparrow. As you go down into Ferry Gulch, just before the base of the mountain, look for a nesting American Tree Sparrow and White-crowned Sparrow. Look in the tuckamore around the base and the lower slopes for nesting Common Redpoll in June. On the way up, take the longer route up Ferry Gulch and then climb up the back slope, an easier route than the one by which you'll return. On top, check the gullies for resident Rock Ptarmigan. An occasional Common Raven will appear. Flocks of Water Pipit and Horned Lark may flush as you explore. Far below on the ponds, you'll spot a Common Loon. The tundra attracts Lesser Golden-Plover in fall.

From the top, take the shorter, steeper trail down through the tuck-amore and watch for American Tree and White-crowned Sparrows. You'll spot Common Redpolls at the bottom of the climb if you missed them going up.

St. Pauls Bay. Some people say this area is better for shorebirds than Stephenville Crossing, in the southwestern area of the province (see above). Located near the northern end of the park, the tidal flats and marshes attract a wide variety of birds at low tide to feed, and to roost on the rocky shoreline at high tide. The nearby farmland provides habitat for Lesser Golden-Plover and Black-bellied Plover, and Pectoral and Buff-breasted Sandpipers in September. On the flats in late July, Least Sandpiper outnumbers all other species. But look for Semipalmated Plover, Common Snipe, Ruddy Turnstone and Pectoral Sandpiper. Then others come in, including Whimbrel, Red Knot and Short-billed Dowitcher. White-rumped and Semipalmated Sandpipers form the highest numbers on the mudflats. The regular Dunlin appears, as do a few Baird's Sandpiper in September.

In June and July, search for Killdeer and Hudsonian Godwit. Common and Arctic Terns nest nearby. They are joined by Caspian Tern in July and August. Horned Lark nests by the mudflats. The Song Sparrow breeds in the tuckamore nearby. Search for Tree, Bank, Barn and Cliff Swallows, Eastern Kingbird and Alder Flycatcher, together with some blackbirds.

In winter, waterfowl are plentiful. You may spot Glaucous and Iceland Gulls, plus a possible Ivory Gull. Flocks of Lapland Longspur and Snow Bunting use the beaches, as do a few other sparrows.

Cow Head and Shallow Bay. At the last stop at the north end of the park, come to scan for sea ducks in spring and late fall. In late May and early June, you will see some White-winged and Black Scoters, together with a few Harlequins and Oldsquaws. Barrow's Goldeneye and Bufflehead may appear in spring too. Go out onto Belldowns Point to view Ring-billed Gull and Black-legged Kittiwake during the run of capelin in late June. You may spot a jaeger. However they and other pelagic species usually come a couple of months later. From late July watch for Black-bellied Plover and Ruddy Turnstone. In September, White-winged and Surf Scoters and Black Guillemot appear. In winter the dunes may have Snowy Owl.

BLAKE MAYBANK, WILLIAM THRELFALL

Northern Peninsula and L'Anse-aux-Meadows

On the tip of this peninsula, Vikings landed at L'Anse-aux-Meadows about a thousand years ago. Today, at this world heritage site, you can visit the remains of their seven buildings plus a smithy and two cook pits. Displays at the interpretive centre show a variety of articles found, including a soapstone wheel used for spinning wool. This flywheel, the earliest European household implement found in North America, is identical to items found at Viking sites in Greenland, Iceland, Sweden and Norway.

Highway 430 north to the tip is approximately 360 km one way from Gros Morne National Park. Labrador Airways services St. Anthony on a year-round basis. However, bad weather often interrupts air service, so if you use it be prepared to stay a few days longer than expected. If you drive, there are a couple of campgrounds along the way, at River of Ponds Provincial Park and Pistolet Bay Provincial Park. Commercial accommodation is available at scattered communities along the route. Starting just north of Gros Morne National Park, they include Daniel's Harbour, Hawkes Bay, Port au Choix, Roddicton, Main Brook, Plum Point, St. Barbe, Pistolet Bay and St. Anthony.

Material for this section is from the birding guide mentioned above.

Birding Features

On the way look at the good stands of Balsam Fir on the west-facing slopes, together with White Spruce. White Birch groves are scattered among these evergreens. At the northern tip, the forests grade into open woodland with traces of tundra. The soil is minimal, with extensive peatlands prevailing. Watch for ponds that host Northern Pintail and Green-winged Teal.

At River of Ponds Provincial Park, about 80 km north of Gros Morne National Park, stop and look at the displays of early artifacts. Farther north about 40 km, stop at Port au Choix National Historic Park to see artifacts from the Indian people of 2400 B.C. The visitor centre has excellent displays.

If you come in the spring or fall migration period, go out to the Ferolle Peninsula, about 60 km north of Port au Choix. This point is a landfall for land birds. Look for warblers and sparrows, plus shorebirds. The shoreline north of here to Flower's Cove has numerous bays and coves that attract shorebirds and gulls. You'll see huge ships passing offshore in the Strait of Belle Isle from here.

Near the north end, stop in at Eddies Cove, the last community on the shore before Route 430 turns inland. The cove is about 120 km north of Port au Choix. The Strait of Belle Isle between Labrador and Newfoundland provides access to pelagic birds, which come in close during storms. Sea winds from north and south should drop birds on this landfall. Late July, August and into September you should see a variety of shorebirds. Another nearby site to check out is Green Island Cove, about 12 km west of Eddies Cove along 430. The Short-eared Owl has been seen near Green Island, as have a variety of shorebirds.

Cape Norman, at the end of Route 435, just north of Cooks Harbour, is a natural landfall. It catches ocean wanderers and windblown migrant land birds. Come here on a windy or foggy day for Greater, Sooty and a few Manx Shearwaters, Leach's Storm-Petrel and Northern Gannet, which are all regular. Scrutinize the gulls for Iceland, Ring-billed, Common Black-headed and Sabine's. Watch for Black-legged Kittiwake. All three jaegers have been spotted in the fall. Shorebirds are usually noted at this rocky point, with Ruddy Turnstone and Whimbrel common in August. Don't forget the nearby marshes for ducks on migration and a possible Northern Harrier or Short-eared Owl.

Drive back down and across to Route 437. Then proceed north on it towards Pistolet Bay Provincial Park. If you have a canoe, it would help you get around to spot such breeders as Common Redpoll and White-crowned Sparrow. Drive down to the end of the road at Cape Onion and Ship Cove to

spot pelagic species in late summer. Hope that a northeast gale will blow
good numbers of shearwaters and jaegers into the inner bay. Shorebirds
include the regular numerous White-rumped Sandpipers in the fall. You may
spot Red and Red-necked Phalaropes at this time too. Land birds are usually
few.

Reached from Route 436, by the shore, L'Anse-aux-Meadows is a major
landfall, attracting a variety of migrants. The site has become one of the
province's birding hot spots. Bird watching is most productive in early
winter, but there is a wealth of birdlife year-round. In April to early May,
Greater Golden-Plovers have occurred. The Ivory Gull also comes through
off the point after northeast storms from December through March. May
winds have brought in a Black-tailed Godwit and Eurasian Wigeon. A few
pairs of Common Loons nest inland, as do American Bittern, Canada Goose,
American Black Duck, Green-winged Teal, Greater Scaup, Common Eider
and Red-breasted Merganser. The Rough-legged Hawk breeds in the offshore islands and may come in, as may Northern Harrier. In the uplands you
should locate Willow Ptarmigan. Common Snipe, and Spotted and Least
Sandpipers breed here. Common and Arctic Terns have nesting colonies
along this area. You may possibly see Caspian Tern, particularly in mid- to
late summer. Other breeders to search for include Horned Lark, Gray-
cheeked Thrush, Ruby-crowned Kinglet, Water Pipit, northern warblers
mentioned in other areas (see above), Rusty Blackbird, large numbers of
Common Redpolls, some Savannah Sparrows, numerous White-crowned
Sparrows and scattered Swamp Sparrows. Razorbill, Common Murre and
Atlantic Puffin sometimes come inshore from mid-June to early August.
Black Guillemot breed on the nearby islands.

Greater and Sooty Shearwaters come in because of fog. You are almost
certain to find Northern Fulmar and Northern Gannet in summer. In late
summer, Manx Shearwater and Wilson's Storm-Petrel often appear. Cory's
Shearwater is not common, but is always worth looking for. Fall is the time
to see large numbers of jaegers and gulls. Up to 10,000 Black-legged
Kittiwakes have appeared offshore in late August to early September.

Greater Shearwater

Attendant jaegers also appear in numbers, with all three species present, together with a few Great Skua. The Ring-billed Gull may come in from more western colonies. Migrant shorebirds stop, with the best site to observe them located along the beach among the kelp near the historic site. Whimbrel is the most numerous shorebird in August to early September. Survey each flock for Red Knot, Pectoral and Baird's Sandpipers, Dunlin, Short-billed Dowitcher, White-rumped and Buff-breasted Sandpiper. Winter is the best season for your visit. You could be rewarded with species seldom seen in Atlantic Canada. Thick-billed Murre and Dovekie regularly occur. King Eider is irregular, along with Common Eider. In the harbour you'll find Glaucous and Iceland Gulls.

Go to Round Head from mid-October to early May for Gyrfalcon. The dark phase is common from late October on, and the white phase in March and April. The Snowy Owl is best seen in half and fading light or on dull days as they sit on the barrens. Some also regularly fly out to sea at about a 100-m height, presumably to prey on seabirds. The Short-eared Owl is also present. There are rare but regular records of Northern Wheatear.

A continuation of the trip could be a drive down to St. Anthony. If you use the air service in or out of this community, check the weather and airline offices before making final plans, as flights are often cancelled. The coastal lands around St. Anthony are mainly barrens and tuckamore. Willow Ptarmigan, Horned Lark and Water Pipit are common and widespread breeders, as are Common Redpoll and White-crowned Sparrow. They all breed on the barrens or in the scrub growth. The mature forest holds Mourning Warbler, Common Yellowthroat and year-round Gray Jay and Boreal Chickadee. Look for Lincoln's and Fox Sparrows in the open areas. European wanderers often show up.

A few Northern Wheatears appear regularly. A Pink-footed Goose was confirmed, as was the Redwing from Europe. Fall migration at St. Anthony is not as good as at L'Anse-aux-Meadows. Fishing Point Lighthouse, Saint Anthony Bight and Goose Cove are the good spots to observe from, particularly in winter, when the Ivory Gull may come in close to shore. Large flocks of Common and King Eiders, Glaucous Gull and Black Guillemot appear in mid-winter. The Dovekie often appears in large numbers. The Gyrfalcon is a regular visitor. A Snowy Owl may show up too.

If you have an extra week, you may want to take the ferry between St. Anthony and Goose Bay, Labrador, across the Strait of Belle Isle. Another similar ride is from St. Barbe across to Blanc-Sablon, Quebec. There is a chance to spot whales too. Summer birds include Northern Fulmar, Greater and Sooty Shearwaters, and Leach's Storm-Petrel; look for large flocks of Black-legged Kittiwake, scoters, Razorbill, Thick-billed and Common Murres, Black Guillemot and Atlantic Puffin (fairly common). In the fall, watch for all three jaegers, a possible Ivory Gull, Dovekie, the odd Gyrfalcon and Snowy Owl, and a few Lapland Longspurs within flocks of Snow Bunting.

Strait of Belle Isle and South Labrador Coast

The narrow Strait of Belle Isle is crossed on an 18-km ferry trip from St.

Atlantic Puffins

Barbe on Newfoundland, to Blanc-Sablon in Labrador. You will see a variety of pelagics on this little-over-an-hour trip. If you are short of time, stay on for a return ride, a total of four hours. The ferry runs from June to freeze-up in November/December, with no service on Sunday. The road on the Labrador side is about 70 km long from the ferry landing at Blanc-Sablon north to Red Bay. The rest of this eastern shore region is connected by boat and ferry.

If you decide to remain with your car on the Labrador side, you will find commercial accommodation at L'Anse-au-Clair, Forteau and L'Anse-au-Loup. Refer to the birding guide for more information (see above).

Birding Features

On the trip over, scan for Northern Fulmar, which are fairly common; Greater and Sooty Shearwaters, numerous from June to late September; Manx Shearwater is a regular late summer to early fall bird. You should see Leach's Storm-Petrel; Oldsquaw and Common Eider are regularly seen in spring and fall; look for several hundred Red and Red-necked Phalaropes from August through October. Pomarine and Parasitic Jaegers often are spotted from mid-May to October. Long-tailed Jaeger is occasionally present in August and early September. Look for the large flocks of immature Black-legged Kittiwakes that gather in late summer. Very rarely a Sabine's Gull turns up from late July to September. You should spot a few Razorbills, and Common and Thick-billed Murres; Atlantic Puffins are usually seen off Blanc-Sablon with young birds close to the boat in August.

Blanc-Sablon. Although in Quebec, this community serves as the link between Newfoundland and Labrador. On the ferry run look for the following birds. Red-throated Loon is noted in numbers up to 100 in mid- to late August. Greater and Sooty Shearwaters move inshore in early summer during the capelin run. Manx Shearwater can be seen in small numbers in summer. A few water birds, including Blue-winged Teal and American Bittern, are noted. In late July, look for large numbers of Northern Phalarope. Small flocks of other shorebirds appear, including Least Sandpiper and Short-billed Dowitcher. Check out the gulls for a few Pomarine and Long-tailed Jaegers in the harbour at this time. In late summer Black-legged Kittiwakes are the most numerous. A few Common Black-headed Gulls are present in mid- to late summer. Shorebirds in early fall include White-rumped and Semipalmated Sandpipers.

Red Bay. At the end of the road, this community is the site of the recent discovery of the Basque whaling galleon. This discovery, and detailed archival checking, has proven that these sailors lived here fifty years before Champlain. The boat sank in 1565, with insurance paid the following year to the owners in Spain. Whale oil recovered in 1978 was still in good condition. The ship is the earliest found in Canadian waters. Look for breeding Red-throated Loon and also Harlequin Duck, Oldsquaw and Common Eider in large numbers.

Spot all three scoters in summer. Other birds seen are similar to those mentioned above. However, also search for Northern Hawk-Owl and Boreal Owl, and Great Horned and Short-eared Owls from further south, all nesters at times. Black-backed and Three-toed Woodpeckers are common. The Gray-cheeked Thrush is found in the forests, with the Horned Lark and Savannah Sparrow in open country. American Tree and White-crowned Sparrows are common.

Henley Harbour to Cartwright. This eastern coast of Labrador is served by the CN Marine Coastal Boat. The ride to the several communities on the way offers a good glimpse into fishing lifestyles before the modern world came along. The shore is very barren and windswept, with steep cliffs. Water birds are the main attraction. You should find flocks of Greater and Sooty Shearwaters. Scan for breeding Red-throated Loon. Flocks of ducks, including Oldsquaw, Common Eider, scoters and Red-breasted Merganser are regulars. Scan the sky for a Rough-legged Hawk; Golden and Bald Eagles are usually present in summer. Search the bays for Red Phalarope; the shores should be examined for sandpipers and plovers. The Northern Wheatear is a very local breeder on the Labrador coast from Cartwright north.

Gander and Glovertown (Northeast)

Several villages and communities along the northeast coast of the province provide interesting locations to explore. Highway 1 cuts inland through

Gander, away from the coast. Time permitting, go north and east from Gander on 330 and back south on 320 to join the Trans-Canada at Gambo. The loop takes you through a mix of communities that depend on the sea for existence. Islands in Bonavista Bay to the south and east support a relatively large population of Bald Eagle and Osprey. Watch for them as you skirt the coast. At Gambo, the Trans-Canada Highway is built on a huge glacial deposit, skirting Freshwater Bay.

Highway 310 goes east from 1 at Glovertown. Take it to visit Salvage. It was isolated for nearly 300 years until a road was built in the late 1940s. Local artifacts can be viewed in the museum.

Glovertown has become the main service area for visitors to Terra Nova National Park to the immediate south. There are several good craft shops in the community, plus an active group of birders. Roger Burrows, who kindly supplied much material for this province, resides here. He can provide you with a copy of his book, detailed information and people to contact. For his address, see above.

Birding Features
Gander Bay. The road north from Gander, Highway 330, takes you through varying habitat to the sea. Stop at a couple of sites and explore for a wide variety of species. When you reach the bay scan out to sea for seabirds; then continue following the coast to Musgrave Harbour.

Wadham Islands. Set out in the Atlantic, southeast of Fogo Island, these islands are good spots for seabirds. Boats are available out of Musgrave Harbour. The islands contain Leach's Storm-Petrel, Arctic Tern and Atlantic Puffin in summer.

Glovertown area. Fire has raged over this area at times during the past thirty years. There are still a few stands of spruce, fir and birch left, together with pockets of Tamarack, which are good places to look for Palm Warbler. Begin your visit along Station Road, the best birding site. The birch, cherry and alder thickets attract a wide and numerous collection of land birds in late summer. Move to the boggy spot behind the school where the scattered Tamarack and shrubs host Wilson's Warbler and Swamp Sparrow in summer. Explore the shrubs and low growth by the Shore Road in South Glovertown. Look for warblers and sparrows, with a possible Chipping Sparrow. Stop along the edge of Spenser Bridge, where Route 1 crosses the Terra Nova River. Survey the meadows for American Kestrel. A Rough-legged Hawk is possible in spring and winter. A walk along the river should produce warblers, and a Ruby-throated Hummingbird has been sighted. You may also find a Red-winged Blackbird, with the Rusty Blackbird the most common. Check the adjacent spruce for Red Crossbill and Pine Grosbeak.

The water at the mouth of the Terra Nova River is good for Double-crested Cormorants in spring, before they move over to Traytown. In late summer and fall, watch for flocks of Common Goldeneye, with one or more Barrow's among them in late fall and winter. White-winged and Black Scoters also appear here at South Glovertown, near the river. Look for a

303

Red-winged Blackbird and waxwings. Both Cedar and Bohemian have been spotted here in one year.

A winter visitor should check the feeders for Blue Jay and a few stray Dickcissels among wintering sparrows. Northern Shrikes come in November, and are found in the spruce along the river.

Traytown and Cull's Harbour are connected by a single-lane causeway. The fast current keeps an expanse of bay open all year. Look for Double-crested Cormorant from late spring on. Shorebirds appear in spring and should be checked on the mudflats near the causeway. Gulls also use these mudflats. The mid-summer flocks of Greater Yellowlegs are added to by Semipalmated Plover and White-rumped Sandpiper in mid- to late fall. Scan for hunting Bald Eagle and Osprey and a possible Northern Goshawk.

Now move on to the Shore Road and woods for Tennessee Warbler and kinglets in the alders and spruce-fir complex. Look for the few Bank Swallows, with a possible Barn Swallow around the quarry. You should see the Belted Kingfisher, which nests here and is conspicuous along the shoreline from May to September. The adjacent highlands contain a few resident Willow Ptarmigans.

JOHN PRATT

Terra Nova National Park

Terra Nova, on the east coast of Newfoundland, hosts an excellent mix of birds. Look for Common Loon nesting, summering Leach's Storm-Petrel, Northern Gannet, wintering Barrow's Goldeneye, numerous breeding Bald Eagle and Osprey, and up to a dozen species of shorebirds, including occasional strays. Spotted Redshank has been noted a few times. Other birds to be seen include several gulls and terns, with a few Arctic that breed at a Common Tern colony, Black Guillemot, resident Great Horned and Boreal Owls, a good chance for Black-backed Woodpecker, Least and Alder Fly-catchers that nest, Gray-cheeked Thrush and Veery, and several warblers, including Tennessee, American Redstart, Black-throated Green, Ovenbird, Northern Waterthrush, Magnolia, Palm and Blackpoll; Red and White-winged Crossbills are widespread year-round. Then to top it off you can whale watch for up to five species in the peak period from late June to early August. Shore hikes almost certainly will bring you numerous tracks of River Otter and Mink; whereas Moose, Black Bear and Lynx are often spotted in the uplands. Fishermen, or those who like fresh fish, can find places to catch or buy a great variety from fresh-water trout and salmon to cod, mackerel, herring, squid and capelin. Sandy Pond is a popular swimming area.

The 398-km² park lies at the head of Bonavista Bay. It can be reached by the Trans-Canada Highway or by water through Newman Sound into the middle, or Clode Sound, which reaches to the southwest corner. Buses operate twice a day from the ferry at Port-aux-Basques and St. John's. Rental car and road cruiser services are available in St. John's. There are several wharves for docking and numerous trails and interpretive loops, all shown on park brochures. Accommodation is plentiful within the park, with a large campground of over 400 serviced sites on Newman Sound near headquarters; another one with 165 serviced sites is 3 km from the north gate. Of the five smaller spots, two are winterized, one fully, and the other is a primitive one. Supplies and commercial accommodation are available in Musgravetown, Bunyan's Cove, Port Blandford, Terra Nova, Charlottetown, Glovertown, Traytown and other nearby communities.

The park contains an information centre with interpreters stationed in headquarters at the head of Newman Sound. Write: The Superintendent, Terra Nova National Park, Glovertown, Newfoundland A0G 2L0, Telephone: (709) 533-2801.

Roger Burrows prepared a comprehensive avifaunal survey of the park and produced a detailed checklist and a bird-finding guide used in preparing this section. Ask for a copy.

Birding Features

The landforms are gently rolling, with a good collection of ponds and streams. The forests are Black Spruce and Balsam Fir with groves of Tamarack and White Birch. Open bog and fen communities are scattered with some local *Cladonia* parkland. Rock barrens and bogs tend to dominate the highlands. The major water features, the sounds, are former deep glaciated valleys with narrow restrictions at their mouths. The reduced salt water flow caused by these restrictions tends to produce conditions with unique marine life.

Malady Head. Take the hiking trail from Site 62 in the campground up to a lookout point near the top of Malady Head. On the way, you should find Gray-cheeked Thrush. If you go in early morning or evening, listen to the flute-like songs of Hermit, Swainson's and Gray-cheeked Thrushes. On top, on the barrens, inspect for Blackpoll Warbler and Fox Sparrow. You should see at least one Bald Eagle and an Osprey from the lookout point.

Louil Hills and Burnt Point. Located in the northwest section of the park, the hills have been burned over and now the lower slopes are covered with heath and blueberries. Near the shore look for Belted Kingfisher and Swamp Sparrow. Shorebirds can be found in mid- to late summer on the beach. Common Loon and Double-crested Cormorant occur on the water in summer and fall. Warblers found in these woodlands are more abundant than elsewhere in the park, and include Yellow, Ovenbird, Mourning, Wilson's and American Redstart. West of the turnoff to Burnt Point, look for the Yellow-bellied Flycatcher; east of this turnoff you will find an Alder Flycatcher in the dense roadside cover. You could see a Purple Finch or a Common Redpoll on the road. Look for both crossbills on the Louil Hills trail.

Blue Hill Trailhead. Come here to find that elusive Black-backed Woodpecker, all year. You will probably spot Northern Goshawk, Merlin, Ruffed Grouse and maybe a Great Horned Owl. Red Fox and Lynx are regulars.

Salton's Brook and Buckley's Cove. Beyond Highway 1, a bog and fen system is used by breeding Canada Geese and Greater Yellowlegs. Check Salton's Beach or the wharf and bridge area for River Otter and Mink. At the wharf in winter, search the flocks of ducks for Greater Scaup, Barrow's Goldeneye, Common Murre and Black Guillemot. Make sure you follow the trail east towards Buckley's Cove to find warblers and Red and White-winged Crossbills. Take the hike in early fall for shorebirds and a possible Bald Eagle.

Headquarters Wharf to Newman Sound Day Area. This coastal trail is one of the best year-round birding hikes in eastern Newfoundland. The variety of habitat, nearby facilities and short length (2 km) make it a pleasant interlude. Vegetation includes a forest of Balsam Fir, clumps of Red Maple, elderberry and alders. Several sand spits and rocky shores add to the habitat. August and early September are the best times for Northern Goshawk and Bald Eagle. Also look for Semipalmated Plover and Semipalmated Sandpiper at the campfire circle. Least Sandpiper will be near the tiny salt marsh just below the parking lot. White-rumped Sandpipers are found on the rocky and pebbly beaches in early October. They move to the lower margins near Big Brook Flats later on. Gulls of several species are on Rocky Point at high tide and on the boulders in midchannel at other times. Wintering waterfowl are numerous and varied. Watch for the River Otter at this season.

Big Brook Flats. This area has recently gained status as a bird sanctuary and international biological preserve. Waterfowl are very common. Shorebirds are not as numerous here as on the west coast, but diversity makes up for numbers. Gulls appear in large flocks. Nearby woods have Yellow-bellied Flycatcher and Ruby-crowned Kinglet. Go to the Newman Sound campground to listen for Great Horned and Boreal Owls. Riverside bushes and marshes host Alder and Olive-sided Flycatchers, a few Palm Warblers, American Redstart, and Swamp and Lincoln's Sparrows.

Puzzle Pond Trail. Take this trail from Big Brook to Ochre Hill. Become acquainted with boreal forest. It provides everything from *Cladonia* parkland near Rocky Pond to fens, bogs and ponds. Spot breeding Ring-necked Duck, Northern Goshawk, Boreal Owl, Black-backed Woodpecker, Palm and Mourning Warblers, and Lincoln's and Swamp Sparrows. Explore the large bog close to the Ochre Hill Trail intersection for a Three-toed Woodpecker. The nearby woods hold several Ruby-crowned Kinglets, Northern Waterthrush and Dark-eyed Junco. You may see a Moose as you stroll.

Bread Cove Trails. To reach the bogs and softwood forests north and east of Ochre Hill, take the trail beyond the Puzzle Pond turnoff and proceed east. You should find Yellow-bellied Flycatcher, Hermit Thrush, Golden-crowned and Ruby-crowned Kinglets, and several warblers including Magnolia, Yellow-rumped, Blackpoll and Palm. There is a possibility of a Winter Wren on this or adjoining trails. The bogs and fens that dot the area house Swamp and Lincoln's Sparrows.

Sandy Pond Trail. Begin beyond the last parking lot and look at the variety of plants. Note the Spruce Budworm and Birch Casebearer damage to the trees. This abundant insect life attracts Yellow-bellied and Least Flycatchers, Tree Swallow, and Blackpoll, Black-and-white and Palm Warblers. The wet areas are favourites for American Bittern, a few ducks including nesting Ring-necked, and Swamp and Lincoln's Sparrows.

Outer Newman Sound. If whale watching appeals to you, take a boat tour. A Bald Eagle is likely to be around. Copper Island has a large gull colony. It also has the only known Oldsquaw nest site along the east coast of Newfoundland. You should see a few seabirds, such as Northern Gannet and Black Guillemot. Dovekies are abundant in winter.

Clode Sound Beaches. Try Tidewater (marked on park maps as Platter('s) Cove) first; it lies south of Charlottetown at the spot where the road drops sharply towards the shore, past a huge rockface. Take the trail through fir and alder between two streams. Bald Eagle and Osprey are usually here close at hand. Flocks of American Black Duck, Common Goldeneye and Red-breasted Merganser are close to shore. Try nearby woods for warblers.

Proceed a little farther south to Cobbler's Beach and the parking lot and picnic area. Common Loon is especially plentiful in September and may be joined by Leach's Storm-Petrel. Bald Eagle, Osprey and a migrant Sharp-shinned Hawk and Merlin are almost a certainty here and at Northwest River, a little farther along.

Baccalieu Island

Lying almost due north of St. John's, the island is reached via Highway 80 on the east side of Trinity Bay, or 70 on the west side of Conception Bay. Seabirds abound! Whales, especially Humpbacks, are common in summer around the island. Boats are available from Bay de Verde.

Birding Features
Nesting species include Leach's Storm-Petrel, Northern Gannet, Great Black-backed and Herring Gulls, Black-legged Kittiwake, Razorbill, Common and Thick-billed Murres and Atlantic Puffin.

WILLIAM THRELFALL

St. John's

The capital and only city in the province, St. John's mixes homes built over a century ago with new high rises. The early spring weather and activity in the harbour attract a lot of birdlife. Rarities are continually appearing: everything from Northern Lapwing to Purple Gallinule.

On June 24, 1997, the city will celebrate the five hundredth anniversary of John Cabot's sighting land here. Newfoundland became the first overseas British colony in 1583. Residents successfully defended their city from the French and pirates more than once. Fire ravaged the community at least five times in the 1800s, with 70 per cent destruction in the 1892 blaze. The excellent landlocked harbour has provided a berth for ships from many nations for hundreds of years. Water Street continues to host seamen from numerous overseas nations.

A variety of services and accommodation outlets are available in the city. A major airport provides ready access and car rentals are available. Buses serve the two major ferry terminals.

The Newfoundland Museum has a natural history section. The Memorial University biology department may also provide help. The nearby Salmonier Nature Park has some very keen birders associated with it. Drop any of the above a note, or telephone when you arrive. The Newfoundland Natural History Society meets monthly at Coughlan College in winter and Oxen Pond in summer.

Birding Features

Like all urban centres, St. John's has its collection of bird feeders. The best ones are in the Pine Bud Avenue part of the city near the Memorial University campus. These feeders have attracted such species as Northern Mockingbird, Brown Thrasher, Northern Oriole and sparrows during a winter. Spring begins early in the city. There are often very unusual visitors in April, including Black-crowned Night-Heron, Ruff or Northern Wheatear. Nesting birds are fairly few in the summer, but Cedar Waxwing and Blue Jay are noted. A fall visit is the most rewarding, with everything from a Yellow-billed Cuckoo to Indigo Bunting and Grasshopper Sparrow observed.

Oxen Pond Botanic Park. Begun in 1973, this naturalists' haven has quickly become a hub for interpretive and resource people in the city. The over 200 species of flowers are worth a visit. The park will eventually consist of 32.3 ha of land and lies alongside Mount Scio Road. Habitat consists of mature and regenerating spruce-fir forest, bogs and fens, heathlands, alder thickets, rock gardens and lakeshore. This is a site you should visit first upon arrival in the city. You'll see a diversity of birdlife. In the short time the area has been developing, over 100 bird species have been spotted. Spring and fall are the best times.

Long Pond. Located opposite Memorial University campus, the pond is a haven for water birds in spring and fall. Pied-billed Grebe is uncommon until freeze-up; look for a variety of ducks; the Sora is a regular. Spring brings in such species as Little Blue Heron and Ruff as rarities. Check the Ring-billed Gull flock for a Common Black-headed Gull.

The Harbour. This body of water naturally attracts numerous water birds. Look for up to seventy Common Black-headed Gulls plus some Lesser

Black-backed Gulls by Christmas. These birds remain all winter. Go to Pier 17 at the National Harbours Office at the base of Hill O'Chips to spot these species. Black-legged Kittiwake appears, as well as Iceland and Herring Gulls. A few Bald Eagles are regular.

Robin Hood Bay Sanitary Landfill Site. Go north on Logy Bay Road to Robin Hood Bay Road, then down to the city dump. Many gulls are to be seen, together with raptors. Search the area for Merlin, Northern Goshawk, Rough-legged Hawk and Bald Eagle. A Red-tailed Hawk was seen the winter of 1982–83, a rare sighting for Newfoundland.

Quidi Vidi Lake. This lake is the home of the oldest continuous sporting event in North America, the St. John's Regatta, begun in 1826 and still held today. The lake lies in the eastern part of the city, below Pleasantville. This water body is near enough to the sea to attract a good collection of shorebirds, especially in fall. Check the muddy shoreline from late July to mid-October. This is a good spot for Eurasian species along the east coast, including Ruff and Northern Lapwing. Regulars include Lesser Golden-Plover, Black-bellied and Semipalmated Plovers, and Spotted and White-rumped Sandpipers. Previous late fall sightings have included Blue-winged Teal, Canvasback, American Wigeon, Greater Scaup, Tufted Duck and Ruddy Duck. Gulls winter here in large numbers, including Iceland, Great Black-backed and Herring. Also look for Glaucous, Ring-billed and Common Black-headed Gulls, with a possible Lesser Black-backed, Mew or Laughing Gull. The area is also good for Merlin and Kestrel.

Mundy Pond. This body of water sits just north of Topsail Road off Blackmarsh Road. The pond lies within a residential area that contains a few low shrubs and trees. Visit here in the fall and early winter for Green-winged Teal and a possible Ruddy Duck. Come in mid- to late October, when you can spot Lesser Golden-Plover too. As to be expected, there is a regular gull flock with a few Ring-billed and a possible Common Black-headed. Upland birds are generally absent.

Pippy Park. The park was established to preserve land in a new residential area in 1968. Lying in the north of the city, natural woodlands, ravines, grasslands and water occur. A series of trails plus a campground are set in a secluded wooded valley. The park borders Long Pond. Come here for thrushes, warblers and sparrows on migration, together with several breeding species in summer.

Cape Spear. Lying about 12 km southeast of St. John's, this sea cape is a good place to observe a few shearwaters, puffins and Common Murres in summer.

Butter Pot Provincial Park. Located 32 km southwest of St. John's on the Trans-Canada, this park contains Willow Ptarmigan, found on the barrens all year.

Holyrood Area. Holyrood is located at the base of Conception Bay, about forty minutes' drive from St. John's. Take the Trans-Canada west to the Witless Bay Line and proceed to your right for about 4 km to a T-intersection. Turn left for a good view of the beach. While in this area contact John Pratt at (709) 229-6423. Holyrood is a good place to head for if you have only a short time, especially in winter. Birds to be seen in the area include, in summer, Common and Arctic Terns, Ruffed Grouse, Barn Swallow and Mourning Warbler. In fall you'll see a good assortment of shorebirds, and after a northerly gale you may find hundreds of Leach's Storm-Petrels very close to land. In winter, the same storms bring in Dovekie, Thick-billed Murre, Black-legged Kittiwake and most of the local gulls, plus Black-headed Gull. This site is a good spot to find wintering Belted Kingfisher, American Robin and White-throated Sparrow. A few Northern Shrikes have been reported, along with Common Grackle, Pine Siskin, Common Redpoll, Red and White-winged Crossbills, Pine and Evening Grosbeaks and Purple Finch. Red-necked and Horned Grebes are reported from single sightings. Common Eider, scoters and Oldsquaw can be expected off the headland when conditions are right.

Salmonier Nature Park. Located about 11 km south of the Trans-Canada Highway on Route 90, this park is a good place to start a trip around St. Mary's Bay or to spend the afternoon. It is only a forty-five-minute drive from St. John's. Birds include Ruffed Grouse, Black-backed and Three-toed Woodpeckers, Tree Swallow, an occasional Bank Swallow, Merlin, Kestrel, Pine Grosbeak, Purple Finch, White-winged Crossbill, Gray Jay, Ovenbird and Wilson's Warbler. Oddities have been seen here over the years, including a pair of Wood Ducks one summer. It is possible that captive Canada Geese attract passing ducks to come in and land. Nearby ponds almost always have breeding Ring-necked Duck and Green-winged Teal each spring. The Ring-necked Ducks stay through the summer and are very easy to observe. Other area birds include American Bittern. Several unusual herons have been seen in the Salmonier River Valley, including Snowy Egret, Little Blue Heron and Least Bittern. Other oddities to wander into this fir-forested valley include Eastern Kingbird, Northern Parula, Mockingbird and Ruby-throated Hummingbird. All of these records are one time only affairs, but one never knows what will turn up next. At Trepassey, a Gray Catbird was seen in 1982.

Salmonier Nature Park also has a few captive species of birds on public display. Snowy and Boreal Owls are displayed separately in large domes covered in nylon mesh. The Boreal Owls are particularly interesting; they blend into the background, illustrating why it is so easy to miss them in the wild!

JOHN PRATT, WILLIAM THRELFALL

Witless Bay Seabird Sanctuary

This is probably the best-known seabird colony in Atlantic Canada. Come to see or hear Leach's Storm-Petrel, Great Black-backed and Herring Gulls, some Razorbills, a large colony of Common Murres, some Thick-billed Murres and many Atlantic Puffins. A winter visit should be productive for large numbers of Common Eider, a variety of gulls and numerous Black Guillemot. Whales are often present in late June and July.

Sometimes called the Bird Islands, the three islands are, from north to south, Gull, Green and Great. They lie 33 km south of St. John's on Highway 10, and 27 km south of the international airport. Access is very restricted for boat landing. It may be possible to obtain a permit to land on Gull Island if your visit is considered scientific. Casual visits are not allowed! Permits can be obtained from the Department of Tourism offices at the Confederation Building in St. John's. You can reach Gull Island from Witless Bay by boat. Charters may be had from Jim Russell or other fishermen in Witless Bay or Bay Bulls. John Reddick, Box 2, Tors Cove, charters his boat around Great Island. It is about a 4-km run and costs approximately $25 per visit. Come here during the last two weeks of June and first two in July. The islands are managed by the Provincial Wildlife Division, which also has offices in the Confederation Building and at Building 810 in Pleasantville.

Birding Features

The birds begin arriving in April. They do not go in to breed until about late May and remain until mid-July in large numbers. By early August, most adults have left the islands, with the few remaining young to depart soon. Offshore in August, many are present fishing.

In winter, visit the coast and search the sea for large flocks of Common Eider, Oldsquaw and Black Guillemot.

Gull Island is heavily wooded with Balsam Fir. The shoreline has precipitous cliffs. The interior is riddled with burrows of Leach's Storm-Petrel, with thousands of them coming in at night. Great Black-backed Gull nests on the south end of the promontory projecting south. Herring Gull nests here and along the south, southeast and northeast shores. Black-legged Kittiwake breeds all around. Razorbills have their colony on the west side of the south projection. Common Murre is on the west side of the south projection and on the northeast side of the island. Black Guillemot is found in the two bay areas on the north end, towards the west side.

Green Island, with its steep cliffs and grassy top, has a large colony of Common Murre. There are some Great Black-backed and Herring Gulls, Razorbill, Thick-billed Murre and many Atlantic Puffins. You can also observe this colony from Witless Point off Highway 10.

Great Island, the southernmost of the three, has spectacular scenic cliffs and the same bird species as Green Island. You can view Great Island from Tors Cove and rent a boat here.

WILLIAM THRELFALL

Cape St. Mary's Seabird Sanctuary

Lying southwest of St. John's, Cape St. Mary's is one of the most accessible seabird colonies on the western Atlantic. Several thousand pairs of Northern Gannet, Black-legged Kittiwake, and Common and Thick-billed Murres provide an experience which encompasses all the senses. Finback and Humpback Whales are common below the cliffs in search of capelin.

Cape St. Mary's lies along Highway 100, mainly paved, southwest of its junction with the Trans-Canada near Whitbourne. The birds crowd onto the cliffs of Bird Island, a 90-m-high sea stack. They may be seen after an easy 1-km walk from the lighthouse, where you can park, to the viewpoint. To examine the colony and to see pelagic species offshore, hire a boat for $50 a day at St. Brides, 7 km north, when the fishing is slack. Good observations can be had from the cape and at St. Brides.

Camping is allowed at the cape. The nearest campground is at Fitzgerald's Pond Provincial Park, about 15 km west of the junction of Highways 100 and 1. Other accommodation is very limited. A visitor would be advised to make St. John's the home base if motel or hotel accommodation is required.

The sanctuary is operated and protected by the Wildlife Division, Government of Newfoundland. They have an office and sleeping space for rotating staff at the cape. Sign in here on arrival and get the latest information; staff here are among the best birder guides in Newfoundland.

Birding Features

Fog is possible at any time and may last for several days, so check the weather before coming. The best conditions occur when the wind is from the north, west, southwest and northwest, which clears the fog away. Walk down to the viewpoint, an easy 1-km hike, where you can use your telephoto lens to obtain excellent pictures with minimum disturbance to the birds. Northern Gannet, Black-legged Kittiwake and Common Murre are there in thousands from mid-June to late July. Thick-billed Murre and Black Guillemot are present in hundreds.

By mid-July to August, the shorebirds come in. Expect Lesser Golden-Plover and Whimbrel. For other shorebirds, go to the beach on Point Lance at the end of a spur road off Highway 100. From late July to mid-October at Point Lance Beach, you should spot several species, including Sanderling, Ruddy Turnstone, White-rumped, Spotted and Semipalmated Sandpipers and Greater Yellowlegs. Purple Sandpiper appears in winter.

By early November you will note a collection of migrating waterfowl. Scan for a few loons, sometimes a Red-necked Grebe, Harlequin Duck, Common and a few King Eiders, Black Scoter, and an occasional Surf and White-winged Scoter. Thick-billed Murre, Dovekie and Black Guillemot are regulars. Golden Bay is the best spot for these birds, which usually remain until March. In late March the first Northern Gannets and Black-legged Kittiwakes arrive.

At nearby Island Head, ferret out a small mixed colony of Great and Double-crested Cormorants, one of the few places in Newfoundland where the Great nests.

Atlantic Puffin is uncommon on the cliffs of Cape St. Mary's. While at the cape, take time to explore inland. Look near the cliffs for Water Pipits, which are common all around these cliffs. The nearby heaths and bogs are home to Horned Lark and Savannah Sparrow. In stunted trees, look for a Gray-cheeked Thrush or a stray migrant. A walk further back in the bogs and fens will almost certainly produce a Willow Ptarmigan.

If you take a boat to look at the colony from the sea side, continue about 15 to 20 km farther out to sea for pelagics. You can expect Northern Fulmar, Greater, Sooty and Manx Shearwaters, and Leach's and Wilson's Storm-Petrels. The phalaropes may appear in mid-summer. These birds also draw in all three jaegers and a few Great Skuas. Take your spotting scope and scan the waters from the viewpoint. If you are lucky, you may see most of the above.

To the north, near the ferry terminal at Argentia, reconnoitre for shorebirds, gulls and pelagics. The mix of warm and cold waters, with the resultant fog and high food content, brings in many species. If you use the ferry, either into or out from Argentia, watch for Northern Fulmar, Greater and Sooty Shearwaters and Wilson's Storm-Petrel from June through August. In early fall, search for a Red-throated Loon.

WILLIAM THRELFALL

Yukon

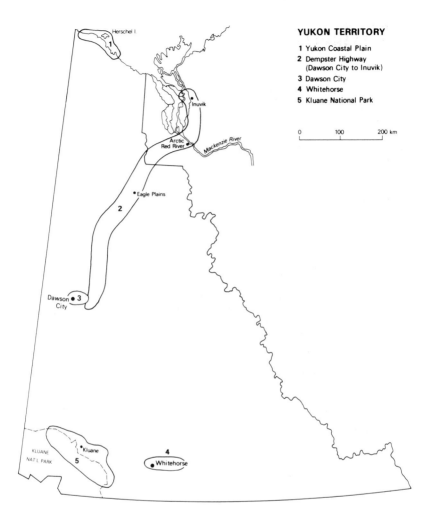

YUKON TERRITORY

1 Yukon Coastal Plain
2 Dempster Highway
  (Dawson City to Inuvik)
3 Dawson City
4 Whitehorse
5 Kluane National Park

0   100   200 km

Herschel I

Inuvik

Arctic
Red River

Mackenzie River

• Eagle Plains

2

Dawson • 3
City

KLUANE
NAT'L PARK

• Kluane

5

4
• Whitehorse

Yukon

Land of the Midnight Sun, the Yukon contains arctic and subarctic species of birds on their breeding grounds. Recently some far-northwestern birds, including mainly Eurasian species, have been spotted. Key breeding birds include Yellow-billed Loon, on the far Arctic coastal area around Herschel Island; Brant on the coast; Greater White-fronted Goose on Eagle River; Common and King Eiders on the coast; Tundra Swan on the coast, Old Crow Flats and possibly south of there; Trumpeter Swan in Kluane National Park, southeastern Yukon, and perhaps centrally and north to the coast; Rough-legged Hawk north of latitude 67°; Ruddy Turnstone, probably on the coast; Semipalmated, Pectoral, Buff-breasted Sandpipers, also inland on the North Slope; Red Phalarope, Parasitic Jaeger and Glaucous Gull, on the coast; Black Guillemot on Herschel Island on the coast; a few Snowy Owls on the coast; Great Gray Owl along the Ogilvie, Peel and Porcupine rivers; Boreal Owl can be quite common; Siberian Tit, which most likely breeds in the far north, has provided a few records widely spread over the Yukon, including west of the Dempster Highway; Yellow Wagtail on the coast. Other rarities that have been seen include Steller's and Spectacled Eiders, Ivory and Ross' Gulls, and Bluethroat. Robert Frisch has now tracked down the elusive Surfbird in the Richardsons and Ogilvies, those mountains west of Dawson at the U.S. border, and in the Dawson Range near Carmacks.

The 482,515 km² that make up the Yukon contain fewer than 25,000 people. Key habitats consist of subarctic to arctic alpine, together with the North Slope and arctic maritime, including Herschel Island. Subarctic taiga forests are found in the valleys north of latitude 65°. Typical boreal forests cover the valleys throughout the territory.

The best time to visit is from mid-May through June for migrants and breeders. Spring migration lasts from late April to early June and is more striking everywhere than fall migration. Spring migration on the far northern coast peaks in early June.

The top birding spot for arctic-subarctic terrain in the Yukon (the top such spot in North America, some say) and certainly rivalling Churchill, is the Dempster Highway. This road leads smack through the best area in the entire Yukon, south of the extreme northern fringe, and takes you near to the Arctic Ocean, the only road to do so in North America.

Other key spots to visit include Marsh Lake, southeast of Whitehorse, just off the Alaska Highway, for spring migrants; Lake Laberge, just north of Whitehorse, for spring migrants including nesting Short-billed Dowitcher; Kluane National Park and the adjacent Burwash Uplands, for typical south Yukon mountain birds; Yukon Coastal Plain for high-arctic species, such as Yellow Wagtail and Red-throated Pipit. If you wish to make a river trip for birds, try the Ogilvie, Peel and Old Crow through Old Crow Flats; and the Nisling, White and Yukon rivers to Dawson.

Time restraints are always hard to satisfy. You could do the Yukon Coastal Plain in a full day. Kluane Park and the adjacent Burwash Uplands take two to three days to sample. A motorist with up to a week to spend should take the Dempster Highway, both for representative and key species. The really keen lister would be best satisfied on the Coastal Plain, where a single day may suffice for a good sample, but it will be an expensive day. You may wish to go instead to Churchill, Manitoba, at less cost. The Dempster road is probably the number one site because of such special birds as Surfbird, Wandering Tattler, Northern Wheatear, Rock Ptarmigan, Long-tailed Jaeger, Gyrfalcon, Siberian Tit and others.

There are no bird alert numbers to call. For special tips, contact Helmut Grunberg, regional editor for *American Birds*, at: Yukon Conservation Society, 308 Steele Street, Whitehorse, Yukon Y1A 2C5, Telephone: (403) 667-4510. Helmut may also be reached at the school where he teaches. Telephone: (403) 667-6703.

Another contact is the Resource Management Division, Department of Renewable Resources, Box 2703, Whitehorse, Yukon Y1A 2C6, Telephone: (403) 667-5711. Senior Wildlife Management Biologist (Small Game) Dave Mossop can be telephoned at (403) 667-5766.

Robert Frisch may be contacted by writing: P.O. Box 558, Dawson, Yukon Y0B 1G0.

The above have prepared a checklist of Yukon birds. Write for a copy.

The Yukon government supplies a good road map, available by writing: Tourism Yukon, Whitehorse, Yukon Y1A 2C6. The American Automobile Association also has a good map. Special expeditions to find wanted species should acquire topographic maps from: Canada Map Office, Department of Energy, Mines and Resources, 615 Booth St., Ottawa, Ontario K1A 0E9.

ROBERT FRISCH

Yukon Coastal Plain

The strip of land from the mountains down to the coast at the northern edge of the Yukon has produced 122 species of birds with nearly 60 nesting. As the main fall staging area for the Snow Goose of the western Canadian Arctic, the North Slope also plays host to far-western species, including the Northern Wheatear, Bluethroat and Yellow and White (very rare) Wagtails. Arctic and Red-throated Loons nest too.

Until very recently, knowledge of this land was limited to the coast. With the advent of helicopters and wide-tired aircraft, plus the need to assess the impact on wildlife by the proposed construction of a major pipeline, detailed studies have now been done on this unique strip of northern Canada. Northern and eastern range extensions have thus been established.

Access to these plains is by air, usually out of Inuvik. To arrange a trip write: Airport Manager, Inuvik, NWT X0E 0T0, or one of the following three companies, operating out of this airport: Ram Air, Aklak Air Service and Aklavik Flying Service.

The best landing spots are Stokes Point, midway between Alaska and the Mackenzie Delta; Herschel Island, farther west; and Clarence Lagoon on the far western boundary, adjacent to Alaska.

Information for this section was obtained with the help of Tom Barry and from a major article: "Distribution and Abundance of Birds on the Arctic Coastal Plain of Northern Yukon and Adjacent Northwest Territories 1971–1976," by Richard F. Salter, Michael A. Gollop, Stephen R. Johnson, William R. Koski and C. Eric Tull in *Canadian Field-Naturalist*, Vol. 94, No. 3, July–September 1980, pp.219–237. The national natural history museum in Ottawa has sent parties into this area. Check with them.

Birding Features

The North Slope plains occur as low arctic tundra north of the mountains, adjacent to the Beaufort Sea. Birds to be found include those inhabiting northern woodlands, tundra and marine habitats. The flat landscape contains a few incised river valleys and is underlain by continuous permafrost. Polygonal ground and permafrost-related features are everywhere. Small lakes abound, particularly on the eastern side and near the coast. The vegetation consists of a mosaic of dry tussock, wet sedge and low willow shrubbery. Tall bushes grow along rivers and some lakes.

The low, sandy and silty cliffs and narrow beaches of the Beaufort Sea coast are separated by river deltas, barrier islands, spits and lagoons. There are two permanent settlements, Komankuk, 30 km from the Alaska border, and Shingle Point (DEW-line sites), near the west side of the Mackenzie Delta. Herschel Island, 3 km off the coast, was once a major whaling base in the early 1900s, and until recently an RCMP outpost.

Open water appears as early as mid-May on some of the deltas. Lakes begin to have some meltwater by late May, with most of them ice-free by late June. Coastline open water first shows in late May or early June, with cracks in the sea ice opening up by mid-June. The ice pack leaves the shore area by mid-July and returns by October to November.

Mid-June would be the best time to come, since all breeding birds are on territory and a few far-northern species are still coming through. Search for the four loon species: Common and Yellow-billed are very rare but may be seen; Arctic and Red-throated breed along here. The Tundra Swan nests near tundra lakes. Brant pass through in early June and again in September. The coastal plain appears to be the major fall staging site for the Snow Goose of the western Arctic. They begin arriving in mid-August and quickly build up to numbers often exceeding 200,000. Departure is around mid-September. The Oldsquaw is the most numerous duck on the plain. Common Eider is a breeder on the barrier beaches. King Eider is a migrant from mid-May to mid-June.

Rough-legged Hawk and Golden Eagle may be seen nesting on river cliffs. Gyrfalcon and Peregrine Falcon are fairly numerous, with the former remaining all year. Willow Ptarmigan is the more abundant, but Rock Ptarmigan also is fairly plentiful in the more barren areas. Breeding shore-birds are fairly common and include Semipalmated Plover, Lesser Golden-Plover, Whimbrel, Pectoral Sandpiper, Semipalmated Sandpiper, Long-billed Dowitcher, Stilt Sandpiper, Buff-breasted Sandpiper, and Red and Red-necked Phalaropes. Pomarine Jaeger breeds, with some Parasitic and a few Long-tailed Jaegers also. Glaucous Gull raises young here as does the Arctic Tern. Black Guillemot is limited to the coast, on, and west of

Herschel Island. Look in the buildings on the island for some nests. The Snowy Owl is present but there is no evidence of breeding, whereas the Short-eared Owl breeds throughout the area. Northern Wheatear is found nesting. The Bluethroat has nested. The Yellow Wagtail was noted by the above study as nesting; more recent work by the National Museum of Canada indicates that the Red-throated Pipit nests too. American Tree and White-crowned Sparrows breed, as do Lapland Longspur and Snow Bunting.

Dempster Highway (Dawson City to Inuvik)

The ribbon of gravel that runs from the boreal interior of the Yukon, across the Arctic Circle, to the Mackenzie Delta on the edge of the vast arctic tundra, is the only road in North America which gives access to this representative section of our subarctic. Over 160 bird species have been sighted. The contrasting landforms and vegetational diversity are remarkable in any context, passing from mountains and highlands in the Yukon to the flat forests of the delta; rich, wooded valleys alternate with bare, rock-strewn slopes and alpine barren; timberline is rarely far from the road; tundra ponds, numerous creeks, and several major rivers add to the diversity. This trip allows sight of the far-northern birds you've watched on migration, here on their breeding grounds. Most of them are observed from the car window. Along the way look for Arctic and Red-throated Loons, numerous Golden Eagles, Gyrfalcon, Willow and Rock Ptarmigans, Lesser Golden-Plover, Surfbird, Upland Sandpiper, Wandering Tattler, Baird's Sandpiper, Long-tailed Jaeger, Northern Hawk-Owl, Gray-cheeked Thrush, Northern Wheatear, Harris' Sparrow, Lapland and Smith's Longspurs, and a few pairs of Snow Bunting. This is *the* region for Siberian Tit. You will pass near a major Dall Sheep lambing range and possibly even spot a Grizzly going rapidly away.

The 721-km good gravel road begins 40 km east of Dawson City, or 481 km north of the Alaska Highway, just west of Whitehorse. A bus runs several times a week from Whitehorse to Dawson. There are five government-operated campsites along the way: Tombstone Mountain at Km 74.5; Engineer Creek at Km 195; Richardson Mountains at Km 465; Nutuiluie Campground and Information Centre at Km 543; Happy Valley at Inuvik. Commercial accommodation can be found at Eagle Plains Hotel and Campsite at Km 368. The country is very fragile, with camping at other than designated spots discouraged. Gasoline may be purchased at Km 0 (turnoff), Km 368 (Eagle Plains Hotel), Km 556 (Fort McPherson), and at the end, at Inuvik at Km 721. If you are really stuck, you may be able to obtain gas from the highway maintenance camp at Ogilvie River, Km 198 (afternoons only).

This far-northern drive has special conditions to keep in mind. Weather can change rapidly — generally for the worse — as you move from a mountain range to a valley or back into plateau country. From early June to mid-August snowfall is rare, except above 1370 m, and usually melts almost immediately. The snow cover is gone by mid- to late May at the highway level. Persistent snow cover returns in mid-September to October. The ice on the Peel and Mackenzie rivers usually goes out in mid-May and on the Ogilvie and Blackstone rivers in late April to early May. There are several year-round open water spots on the Blackstone and North Klondike rivers. Warm Creek at Km 212 is the most prominent creek that remains unfrozen even at – 40°C for long periods. The mosquito season runs from mid-June to early August, with greatest numbers in July. They are not very thick in the Southern Ogilvie Mountains at that time, but come in hordes north of there, even on high ridges. Stay on the road is the best advice. Walking in vegetation stirs them up. Blackflies appear in late July but are never too bad except across in the Mackenzie Valley and sometimes in the Richardson Mountains.

Traffic and services are sparse along this route. Make certain you have two spare tires, extra gasoline, oil, a spare fan belt, plus a good set of tools that you know how to use! Extra food and a first-aid kit is a must. A parka, hat, wool pullover sweater, warm footwear, mitts, rainwear and mosquito repellent should be carried. Plastic headlight covers should be acquired. The road is open all year, so if you travel on it in winter have a full complement of winter outdoor clothing plus a sleeping bag for each person.

Hiking in the lower country off the road can be a hazard, particularly in the hummocks and tussocks of the upland tundra. Progress is 1 to 2 km per hour. Most birds can usually be seen from the road anyway. Alpine hiking is easier. Several of the high-country birds can be seen only away from the road. On your walks, look for Rock Ptarmigan; White-tailed Ptarmigan and Surfbird are found only away from the road; Baird's Sandpiper, Horned Lark, Northern Wheatear, Water Pipit, Rosy Finch, Golden-crowned Sparrow and Snow Bunting are all seen best on territory away from the highway in the breeding season.

Caution regarding the animals. The slopes above North Fork Pass are critical to the lambing of Dall Sheep. Don't climb there until after mid-June when the sheep have withdrawn deeper into the mountains. The Porcupine herd of Caribou crosses the highway each spring and fall in migration to and from the Arctic Ocean coast. Some traffic control is undertaken at this time. If you see them, stay well away so as not to frighten them. Stay away from the several Golden Eagle eyries in your hikes. There are a few Peregrine Falcons ranging the high country. Because of the danger these birds are in from DDT still being used in the southern countries where they winter, leave them alone if you spot one.

The government has imposed a no hunting zone of 8 km on either side of the highway. This 16-km strip offers the observer a unique chance to avoid any conflict with hunters.

The information for this major route has been borrowed from an excellent, comprehensive, and thoroughly interesting booklet, *Birds by the Dempster Highway*, by Robert Frisch, 1982. This guide includes a great number of helpful hints, ranging from how to identify small birds on the wing, to breeding areas (he has noted extensions north and south from the usual published accounts). His list of "Dempster Specials" illustrates the uniqueness of this road, with many wanted birds easily available. Included also is a detailed species account for the 164 birds to be found. Anyone planning the trip should obtain a copy ($3.50 plus postage) to supplement the information supplied here. Write: Yukon Conservation Society, 308 Steele Street, Whitehorse, Yukon Territory Y1A 2C5, or Dawson Museum, Dawson City, Yukon Territory.

Birding Features
The road crosses a great variety of habitat. Several far-northern breeders nest along it, particularly in the bare tussock-hummock tundra far south of its usual occurrence. If you are short of time and don't wish to make the whole trip, then a drive north as far as the Blackstone Uplands, from Km 87 to Km 132 in the Southern Ogilvie Mountains, will provide most of the boreal, alpine and arctic species. Bird activity along the highway peaks in late May to early June. At that time the breeders are on territory and the species that nest far to the north are still passing through. By mid-May spring is well on its way, and by the end of June to early July bird activity falls off sharply. Mosquitoes are also few in number from mid-May to mid-June, when they increase. In fall, from mid-August to mid-September, the country is beautiful, with yellows and reds predominating, but there are few birds except along the Peel and Mackenzie rivers, where large numbers pass through. Shorebirds come in August, with waterfowl in September.

Tintina Valley or Trench along the Lower North Klondike River, Km 0 – 50, elevation 460 – 885 m. The habitat includes boreal forest of spruce, poplar and birch, including muskeg forest. There are extensive burns and willow thickets. Near the river, tall White Spruce and poplar with willow thickets prevail. Sloughs and swamps lie near the Klondike River. From Km 25 onward, look for the spurs of the Ogilvie Mountains. This is the only typical boreal forest with pronounced aspen succession that you will encounter, so check it out. A number of forest birds reach their northern breeding limits here, including Ruffed Grouse, Yellow-bellied Sapsucker, Hairy Woodpecker, Western Wood-Pewee, Hermit Thrush, Townsend's Warbler and Common Nighthawk. Boreal Owl is a year-round resident in tall dense spruce in the valley bottom. Listen for the call from midwinter to mid-April. Hammond's and Alder Flycatchers are common in the deciduous woods and thickets. Violet-green and Tree Swallows are around clearings and habitations. In winter, American Dipper is found on the open water of the North Klondike River at Km 10. Orange-crowned Warbler is common from Km 0 to Km 73 at timberline. Look for it in deciduous trees and tall shrubbery. Lincoln's and Fox Sparrows are also found in this area.

Upper North Klondike River Valley, Km 50 – 72, elevation 885 – 1035 m. This stretch is in montane spruce forests with a few aspen and scrub birch in the understory. The forests grade into the timberline of scrubby trees and bushes at Km 68. The public campsite is situated in the last woods at Km 72. You'll begin encountering birds of the subarctic mountains, such as Wilson's Warbler and American Tree Sparrow. With luck, you may spot Wandering Tattler. The Northern Goshawk is often sighted south of here and along the valley to timberline. The over-mature stands of spruce here, and those to the south, often have Three-toed Woodpecker. American Dipper occurs in the Upper Klondike River and its tributaries. Fox Sparrows are fairly common in the valley.

Southern Ogilvie Mountains — North Fork Pass, Km 72 – 87, elevation 1035 – 1310 m. Vegetation consists of scrubby tundra with some bare tussock tundra. Ponds are found in the East Blackstone valley. You are near the alpine tundra; look up from the highway above 1370 m for the rich meadows, heath and tussocks. The pass forms the divide between the Klondike-Yukon river systems of the Pacific, and the Blackstone-Peel river systems of the arctic watersheds. To the east rise the Sheep Mountains, where you may spot Dall Sheep. West of the road is the Cloudy Range. You have entered the richest alpine birding area on the route, the Southern Ogilvie Mountains. To reach this "birders' dreamland," from the pass at Km 80 – 83, hike up the west flanks of Sheep Mountain, which the road skirts. These mountains rise another 610 m; though rather steep, they are climbed easily. These slopes are the lambing grounds of Dall Sheep, so stay off until the second week of June. Look for all the alpine birds, regularly located here, and also Surfbird and Baird's Sandpiper, which are seen only occasionally. The Golden Eagle is a regular sight along the highway. Willow and Rock Ptarmigans are spotted higher up. This is the best area in which to find White-tailed Ptarmigan, but you'll have to go into these mountains east or west of the pass. In ponds you should see Red-necked Phalaropes, which are common. The Northern Wheatear is most common in these Southern Ogilvie Mountains. Look for them in cliffs and rock rubble on the Sheep Mountains to the east of the pass. Townsend's Solitaire occurs on rocky slopes. The Northern Shrike is most often seen here, especially in the valley to the west, near the source of the East Blackstone River. You will encounter redpolls. There is a problem of identification between Common and Hoary in this country, so don't be surprised and confused as to which you are watching. The "experts" are not sure either! American Tree and White-crowned Sparrows are common to abundant. You should spot a Golden-crowned Sparrow in the shrubby gullies above Km 81 – 82 as this is the most likely spot on the route. The Fox Sparrow is common in bushy areas lower down in valleys. On your hike east and west of the pass, look for Snow Bunting in rock debris near remnant snowbeds. The recently discovered nesting sites of these birds in the Sheep Mountains are within an easy one day's excursion from North Fork Pass. To get there, hike up the valley east of about Km 90 and then up a tributary valley from the south. On the trip you should be able to locate Golden Eagle, Rock and White-tailed Ptarmigans, Wandering Tattler, Northern Wheatear, pipits and Rosy Finch, together with Arctic Ground Squirrel, Pika, marmot and some sheep.

Blackstone Uplands, Km 87 – 132, elevation 915 – 1035 m. The landscape consists of bare tussock and shrubby tundra, with some fen. There are many lakes and ponds, including Moose Lake at Km 105; Chapman Lake at Km 120 and some kettle ponds at Km 120 – 125. The rivers include the East, West and Main Blackstone, with wide gravel pans. There are groves of spruce and cottonwood along the river. This site is the climax of the trip for numbers

Lesser Golden-Plover

and diversity of birds. Here you may spot nesting Red-throated Loon, Oldsquaw, Golden Eagle, Gyrfalcon, Willow and Rock Ptarmigan, Lesser Golden-Plover and other shorebirds, Long-tailed Jaeger, Short-eared Owl, redpolls (mainly Common), and Smith's and Lapland Longspurs. There are also many breeding woodland species in the timberline trees and groves of willows along the Blackstone River. The adjacent mountains contain nesting Townsend's Solitaire on rocky slopes, Surfbird, Water Pipit, Rosy Finch, Golden-crowned Sparrow and Snow Bunting. Spring migrants, particularly water birds, come in large numbers. Moose Lake, at Km 105, is usually ice-free by late May, with Chapman Lake, at Km 120, icebound until well into June. In both bodies and other smaller ones, there is usually open water along the edges from early May on. Such habitat draws in water birds like a magnet.

The Red-throated Loon nests by ponds and smaller lakes in open country around Blackstone Forks at Km 117. This is probably the most accessible spot in Canada at which these birds can be seen on territory. The Tundra Swan is seen regularly in spring at Moose Lake. The Oldsquaw is a regular breeder on the numerous ponds near the Upper Blackstone River east and west branches. The Golden Eagle is usually around from late March onward. Northern Harrier swoops low in the Upper Blackstone valleys. Gyrfalcon will be back up in the mountains, hunting low down, or perched on a tussock. Willow and Rock Ptarmigans are common, with Willow the more numerous. A Lesser Golden-Plover is usually noticed from the road as it defends a territory. The Whimbrel nests in open tundra along valleys and on low ridges. It is usually spotted between Km 90 and Km 100. An Upland Sandpiper may be spotted from clearings in open taiga forest to tussock tundra with some shrub and a few spruce. At Km 132, Cache Creek, check carefully for a Wandering Tattler in the gravel along the creek, or for an American Dipper on the water. You may sight a Pectoral Sandpiper on migration. Many of the ponds should have a Red-necked Phalarope spinning around as it feeds. The Long-tailed Jaeger is fairly common in the open tussock tundra. Mew Gull, the common gull along here, breeds by braided streams and tarns. Bonaparte's Gull has a breeding site in trees just west of Km 119 – 122 by the ponds lined with spruce. Arctic Tern also breed here in braided stream areas near the Blackstone River at Km 118. The Short-eared Owl flits its wings as it flies by. Near timberline, look in tall willows for a

Gray-cheeked Thrush. In the mountains nearby, you'll find Northern Wheatear in the cliffs and rock rubble. The highland warbler singing in the bushes is probably a Wilson's.

West of here some 100 km, Dr. Theo Hotmann found six Siberian Tits in August 1982. His group drove to Km 119 and then paddled upstream on the Blackstone River to 65°42' north latitude and 137°25' west longitude; they then climbed a ridge about 457 m above the river to find the birds in a very open stand of spruce fairly close to the tree line. The spot is about 20 km from the highway as the crow flies (from the point where the road runs north of the Ogilvie River, about 100 km south of Eagle Plains). Use maps 116H and 116G and F of Mines and Technical Surveys. Refer to *Birdfinding in Canada*, Vol. 3, No. 3, May 1983.

Common Redpoll, or Hoary (see above for difficulty in distinguishing them here), occur along the road as fairly common summer residents throughout the subalpine shrubs. You may also spot a Golden-crowned Sparrow. The Lapland Longspur is an abundant bird in bare tussock tundra in the highlands and mountains.

Northern Ogilvie Mountains, Km 132 – 197, elevation 610 – 1005 m. This stretch consists of discontinuous subarctic taiga forest of White Spruce, with cottonwoods along streams up to the timberline around 915 m. You'll also see much Black Spruce muskeg grading into tussock tundra. The main streams are the Blackstone River and Engineer (Big) Creek. There are no lakes and only one pond at Windy Pass, Km 155. Your second choice of campsites is at Km 195. These mountains are known more for their beautiful scenery than as a birding area. Townsend's Solitaire is common at timberline. The Wandering Tattler breeds at Windy Pass. There is a known Baird's Sandpiper breeding site close to and south of the highway at Windy Pass. As you drive, watch for a Gyrfalcon. You may spot a Willow or a Rock

Gyrfalcon

Lapland Longspur

Ptarmigan too. Check the treetops for Northern Hawk-Owl, seen from here north. As in the previous sites, the Wilson's Warbler is the typical highland species.

Ogilvie River Valley, Km 197 – 248, elevation around 610 m. The valley contains taiga-type forest with much cottonwood and some Tamarack. Extensive willow thickets occur with no open tundra near the highway. There are several creeks, including Warm Creek at Km 212, which are open year-round. Check this valley for a nesting Great Gray Owl. Warm Creek hosts the American Dipper in winter.

Eagle Plains, Km 248 – 410, elevation 610 – 915 + m. The lands are covered with continuous low hummocky Black Spruce taiga, which thins northward to Black Spruce–Tamarack forest tundra. Taller White Spruce and poplar are along the Eagle River with open tundra ridge tops at Km 255 – 280 and northeast of Eagle River. No lakes are found, but there are oxbow ponds along the river. The one hotel and service stop on the route, Eagle Plains, is at Km 368. This is the area of the fewest birds, including a virtual absence of eagles. A few woodland species occur, including the odd Spruce Grouse, Northern Hawk-Owl, Gray Jay, Gray-cheeked Thrush, Yellow-rumped Warbler and a very few Blackpoll Warblers. The one consolation is that the Eagle Plains are the driest for rainfall on the Yukon side. Rock Ptarmigans occur on bare ridges on the southern rim from Km 265 – 280. Swainson's Hawk may breed near Km 280. The Gray-cheeked Thrush is quite common from here north, both at the timberline and in shrubby taiga.

Southern Richardson Mountains and Foothills, Km 410 – 450, elevation 460 – 760 m. The highway cuts through hummock-tussock tundra with intermittent woods along streams and a few patches elsewhere. Many creeks are located here, with the main ones Rock, at Km 433, and Cornwall at Km 448. No lakes are found. Aside from the lack of waterfowl and a few missing species of shorebirds, these mountains are prime birding territory. This area just north of the Arctic Circle is the best place to study Rock Ptarmigan, Lesser Golden-Plover, Long-tailed Jaeger, Gray-cheeked Thrush and Smith's Longspur. Back in the mountains you'll find Surfbird. Watch for Gyrfalcon as you drive, and Upland Sandpiper may be spotted if you are lucky. Short-eared Owl occurs along here. Rosy Finches are fairly common in the high alpine rocky area. Near Rock River at Km 437, look for Golden-crowned Sparrow at timberline. At Km 448 on the Cornwall River, look for a Harlequin Duck on the water and a nearby Lapland Longspur.

Northern Richardson Mountains, Km 450 – 492, elevation 460 – 915 m. The road approaches the mountains through bare tussock-hummocky tundra. It crosses into the Northwest Territories on the crest at Km 467. Tundra occurs in the mountains with much rocky terrain. There are no woods, except in the gullies of Cornwall River and its tributaries. The lower courses of the creeks are deeply incised with gorges, including James Creek at Km 480. There are some lakes and ponds on the NWT side. This is the area most arctic in character, with continuous permafrost present. A campground occurs at Km 465. Larks, pipits and Northern Wheatears are best observed along here at the border and around Km 490. Baird's Sandpiper is also found at the border in saddles along the mountain spine. The high country from Km 467 – 490 is probably the most convenient along the route for alpine birding. There are no steep ascents and the country is the nearest to the arctic you will see along the route. Most mountain species occur here, as do Northern Wheatears. Scan the hills and roadside for Willow Ptarmigan, Lesser Golden-Plover, Baird's Sandpiper west of Km 480, Long-tailed Jaeger, Rosy Finch and Lapland Longspur.

Peel Plateau, Km 492 – 541, elevation 90 – 610 m. The plateau consists of a partially wooded sloping upland dissected by many streams. The land is covered with sparse hummocky taiga and hummock-tussock tundra. Taller spruce, birch and poplar grow in the valleys. The two streams, Vittrekwa River and Stony Creek, are steeply incised and muddy. Many lakes and ponds occur. On open ridges, look for Willow Ptarmigan. In streamside thickets in the uplands you should spot a Wilson's Warbler. The woods from timberline into shrubby tundra may produce a Gray-cheeked Thrush. At Km 510, Halfway Lake is the spot to locate both a Harris' and a Golden-crowned Sparrow. As you drive east towards the Peel River, watch the lakes and ponds for Tundra Swan. The woods usually have Blackpoll Warbler. As you approach the Peel River, scan any water for an Arctic Loon.

Peel River Valley, Km 541 – 543. This river bench contains a White Spruce forest; birch grow on the valley slopes with a dense willow-alder understory. The banks and river are muddy. There are many oxbow lakes. Free ferry services are available from spring to fall. The NWT government operates a campground and information centre on the east side of the river. Nearby Fort McPherson was established by the Hudson's Bay Company in 1848. Trappers continue to use it today as their home base. There are no services at Fort McPherson. Look for Arctic Loon on the river and Sandhill

Crane on the east side. The luxuriant vegetation in the valley is alive with bird song in late May and early June. See what you can locate. Migrants use the valley, particularly shorebirds in August and waterfowl in September.

Peel River to Mackenzie River, Km 543 – 609, elevation around 90 m. The habitat is mainly low muskeg taiga, with White Spruce and birch on better-drained sites and ridges. There are many lakes and a few creeks, such as Frog Creek at Km 590. Scan the lakes and shores for Arctic Loon, Sandhill Crane and Semipalmated Plover. The latter is often found in gravel pits along the highway and by the Peel and Mackenzie rivers. A Blackpoll Warbler should be heard and seen in the woods along here.

Mackenzie River Valley, Km 609 – 615. Some moderately tall White Spruce and birch grow on the slopes. High, steep banks occur in places such as the Lower Ramparts. The small community of Arctic Red River lies at the crossing of the Mackenzie. Arctic Red River was first settled permanently as a Catholic mission in 1868; a trading post followed shortly thereafter. Free ferry service is available across the Mackenzie from spring to fall. The Blackpoll Warbler sings in nearby woods and Lincoln's Sparrow occurs near the river crossing in tall dense shrub. This is the last known sighting of the bird. The gulls on the river are probably Glaucous, as they are common at the dump in Inuvik.

Mackenzie River to Inuvik, Km 615 – 726, elevation 10 – 90 m. This last stretch tends to be low muskeg–thin taiga, swampy and shrubby. There are a few creeks; the largest, Rengleng River, lies near Km 650. Lakes occur along the highway, particularly near the northern end. Some rocky scarps and hills are found near Inuvik, including the Campbell Hills. There are several public campsites near Inuvik. Birdlife is similar to that reported at Inuvik (see below in NWT). Look for Harris' Sparrow in the discontinuous Black Spruce taiga as you approach town.

BIRDS BY THE DEMPSTER HIGHWAY AND ADDITIONAL UNPUBLISHED NOTES
BY ROBERT FRISCH

Dawson City

Headquarters for the famous Gold Rush of 1898, Dawson City has now been restored in places to recapture the flavour of '98. Visitors flock to this northern community, once touted as "the largest city west of Chicago and north of San Francisco." These lands had been explored very little until on August 17, 1896, gold was found in Bonanza Creek, a tributary of the Klondike River. News leaked out and when, in the summer of 1897, miners from Dawson arrived in Portland, Oregon, and San Francisco with nearly $2 million (1897 dollars!) to a world deep in a depression, the rush was on. By the following spring, about 60,000 women and men had passed through Dawson on their way to riches at the Klondike. Dawson City sprang up at the confluence of the Yukon and Klondike rivers. By summer's end in 1898, some 30,000 people called it home. By the following spring, all creeks in the area were staked. Between 1896 and 1904, creeks in the area produced more than $100 million in gold. Jack London, Robert W. Service and others wrote colourful tales of their personal experiences. Later, Pierre Berton, raised there, added to these stories. Today, an actor gives readings from Service's works daily in the original cabin each summer. Several historical buildings have been restored by the National Historic Sites Service, which operates them with daily shows, productions and activities all summer. Interpreters of human history are located at various centres in the community throughout the summer. The post office, built in 1900, serves as the interpretive centre for Klondike Gold Rush International Historic Park.

Most visitors arrive via the Alaska Highway to Whitehorse, then the Klondike Highway No. 2 northwest for 481 km; alternatively, take the Alaska Highway into Alaska to the Tetlini Junction and proceed northeast 201 km into Dawson. The latter road is closed in winter. Regular bus service departs Edmonton twice a week year-round. Major airlines fly daily into Whitehorse with smaller lines flying from there into Dawson. Campgrounds are available along the highways and near Dawson. Commercial accommodation is often at a premium in July and August; book ahead.

Much has been written about the Klondike, particularly on the Gold Rush. Information may be obtained from: The Interpretive Service, Klondike Gold Rush International Historic Park, Dawson City, Yukon.

Birding Features
Within the town limits, abandoned lots with shrubs provide rich habitats for an abundance of birds. The town's Common Ravens are always entertaining, with a pair utilizing a nest in a cottonwood by the museum in the city core. Forests, meadows and mountainsides outside the city are host to many birds.

Owls are calling in April. A Northern Hawk-Owl has nested recently near the airport. Later in April, Swainson's and Rough-legged Hawks appear. The Harlan's colour phase of the Red-tailed Hawk is not uncommon nesting in the valleys, as is the Northern Harrier. At this time, some Northern Shrikes pass through along the Klondike Highway. May is the migrant month and also the time when nesting species come in numbers. Check the Yukon River for Red-throated Loon and especially Km 694 of the Klondike Highway, where sloughs and flooded hayfields draw Sandhill Crane, Tundra Swan, the small race of Canada Geese, Lesser Golden-Plover, Whimbrel, Pectoral, Baird's and Least Sandpipers, Long-billed Dowitcher and Semipalmated Sandpiper. From early May you will find numerous Hammond's Flycatchers; Alder Flycatchers arrive to breed in late May. Say's Phoebes pass through from mid-May to early June. The downstream end of town and also the "Slide" from late April onward are places to locate a Townsend's Solitaire that stays to breed. Pipits are common in spring. American Tree and Fox Sparrows are plentiful in town during May.

In June to mid-July, breeding populations are most dense. Within the community, you should have no trouble finding such species as Violet-green and Cliff, the most common swallows; Tree and Bank Swallows are also present. Townsend's Solitaires are still on territory. While in the downstream end of town, check out the numerous Fox Sparrows, mainly in this area. Look in spruce woods wherever you find them, for Varied and Swainson's Thrushes, and Yellow-rumped and Townsend's Warblers. Hermit Thrushes are likely to be ferreted out in the aspen bluffs around town; listen also for Orange-crowned and Yellow Warblers. You may sight a Wilson's Warbler migrating through. Common Redpolls breed in or very near town. White-winged Crossbill is usually found breeding most years. Lincoln's Sparrow is common, the most active singer in the "night." The commonest sparrow, White-crowned, adds to the diversity.

Outside of Dawson in June and early July, watch the Klondike River for Red-throated Loon and a fair number of Common Mergansers. Ducks are not too numerous, with Bufflehead the only common species in the Klondike Valley. The American Kestrel is the most common breeding raptor throughout the area.

In fall, late July to October, there is nothing too exciting; some Sandhill Cranes and Canada Geese pass through. Waterfowl migration and wader movement is minimal.

ROBERT FRISCH

Whitehorse

As capital of the Yukon, Whitehorse is the thriving community of northwestern Canada. Golden Eagles nest within 8 km of the city. The Harlan's Hawk (a colour phase of the Red-tailed) is the most common bird of prey in the valley. Gyrfalcon and Peregrine Falcon are seen regularly.

At the time of the '98 Gold Rush, thousands of prospectors journeyed up from the south by boat to Skagway, Alaska, then climbed the rugged mountain passes to reach the Yukon River and a natural waterway to Dawson. Whitehorse was born on the banks of the Yukon at the head of the steamboat travel. Stern-wheeler boats were soon plying between Whitehorse and Dawson — two days down and five days return. Rails were needed to speed up the journey from Skagway; construction on the White Pass and Yukon Railway commenced in May 1898 with the 177-km line through to Whitehorse opening in 1900. When the war between the U.S.A. and Japan began, men and machines flocked in to build the Alaska Highway. Military and civilian workers pushed through 2200 km over a great variety of terrain in eight months (a feat that was estimated would take five years) to open the highway on November 20, 1942. Today the population of nearly 17,000 caters to government personnel as the headquarters of the Yukon, and hordes of summer visitors searching for that elusive Klondike spirit.

Daily air services to Edmonton and Alaska are provided. Buses run along the Alaska Highway year-round. Rental cars are available in Whitehorse, but book ahead in summer.

Whitehorse, at Km 1480 on the Alaska Highway, has a wide collection of motels, hotels and campgrounds, and all the amenities of a southern city. A small group of very dedicated naturalists and environmentalists operate the Yukon Conservation Society. They have an office where most birders meet (refer above).

The Yukon Department of Renewable Resources administers a Small Game branch as part of its Wildlife Management Section. The small game staff has undertaken many studies of birds for the territory. Dave Mossop heads up the team. He is considered the leading ornithologist of the Yukon and has supplied the information used for this site. Refer above for his address and telephone number.

Birding Features

Set in the valley, near a major river and lake, the city has varied habitats, attracting a wide collection of birds. Trumpeter Swans pass through to nest not far away. Numerous birds of prey use the Yukon Valley as a migration funnel; a high concentration of these birds nest in the surroundings. Five areas to search during a stay include:

Haeckel Hill, lying 915 m above Whitehorse, provides a splendid view of the city and also hosts tundra bird species. Ask local people for directions to the Fish Lake Road and then find your way up the forestry road to the top. Willow Ptarmigans raise broods up here each year. Golden Eagle and Gyrfalcon often cruise by. Small tundra birds are to be expected.

Old Dump Site. No longer used as a refuse deposit, this area is worth a birding visit. Again, ask a local person how to reach the site by taking the Range Road. Keep driving until you reach the opposite side of the beautiful ravine into which, until recently, garbage was dumped. Turn right, stop and explore on foot. Hike roughly parallel to the top of the ravine, along to the Yukon River. Continue along the cliffs of the river bank as far as you wish. A trail runs along its entire length. The views along the Yukon Valley are spectacular. Herring and Mew Gulls are present in abundance, with a Glaucous Gull often to be found. A jaeger sometimes flies by. McIntyre Creek hosts American Dipper. In mid- to late May, the backwaters of the Yukon River along here are used by water and shore birds as a staging area. The woods along the cliff are passageways for migrating land birds. Air currents along the cliffs help the many hawks move up the valley.

Schwatka Lake–Miles Canyon walk. This hike provides a variety of habitat, pleasant scenery and a good, level trail. To reach it, take the turnoff from the south access road to Whitehorse. Continue halfway around Lake Schwatka, a hydro reservoir, and park at the turnoff. Hike along the shore on the old historic roadbed into Miles Canyon. Retrace your steps on return or come back on the gravel road. Scan the lake for loons, grebes and ducks. Canvasback, an uncommon Yukon duck, is sometimes present. Go into the adjacent woods to ferret out Swainson's Thrush and warblers that have a slightly different song to those from down south.

Yukon Game Farm property. These lands provide probably the finest birding in the Whitehorse area. If time is limited, then try and make this

330

stroll top priority. However, the property is privately owned. Please request permission from the owners, who reside on site, before entering. Once permission has been received, park your vehicle at the edge of the property and walk the entire circuit for best results. The walk is a fairly long one; allow at least a half day. You will pass through woodland, wet and dry meadow, wet and dry shrubland, marsh and open wood. Migration time brings a wide collection of water birds, including Sandhill Crane, shorebirds and the accompanying birds of prey. Breeding shorebirds include Semipalmated Plover, Killdeer at their northern breeding limits, Greater Yellowlegs and Least Sandpiper.

Shallow Bay, a shallow south extension of Lake Laberge, near the inlet of the Yukon River, provides another chance to pick up water birds. Proceed north of town on the Klondike Highway, for 20 km from its junction with the Alaska Highway. Depart from the highway at the marsh. During migration, a wide variety of water and shore birds use this area as a staging site. Even in summer you should be satisfied with the diversity of species ferreted out, including nesting shorebirds.

Swan Lake. This shallow, marshy boreal lake is located about 20 km north-northwest of Whitehorse. The area is well worth a day's birding. You reach the lake via a *dry-weather* road beginning at the Whitehorse Hospital (ask for directions to the Long Lake Road). Proceed along the old wood-cutting roads towards the north-northwest (local instructions may be required to keep from getting lost!!). Bald Eagles nest in the muskeg areas. The region is used for staging during spring and fall. Water birds, including Trumpeter Swan, and shorebirds are common on migration. Shorebirds nest in the area. Some of the most remarkable sightings in the Whitehorse area are made here.

DAVE MOSSOP

Kluane National Park

More than half covered by snow and ice year-round, and containing Mount Logan, Canada's highest peak, Kluane National Park also hosts over 180 species of birds. There are 88 species confirmed as nesters, with an additional 23 probables. Trumpeter Swans are likely breeders with Tundra passing through. Golden and Bald Eagles, Gyrfalcon, Peregrine Falcon, the 3 ptarmigan species, including Willow, Rock and White-tailed, are all confirmed nesters, as are Wandering Tattler, Northern Hawk-Owl, Gray-cheeked Thrush, Mountain Bluebird, Northern Wheatear and Snow Bunting. The largest subspecies of Moose in North America is quite common in the wooded valleys, and Dall Sheep graze the slopes of Sheep Mountain. Other mammals to be watched for include Grizzly and Black Bears, Wolf, Coyote, Red Fox, Wolverine, Lynx, Marmot and Arctic Ground Squirrel.

The oldest archaeological evidence of man in this area has been dated to 8000 years ago, near the end of the last ice age. Early explorers noted that according to legends, some of the Indian villages have been occupied continuously for at least 1000 years. The Kluane area was not explored until late in the 1800s, with recorded history not beginning until 1890. The Gold Rush of 1898 and later discoveries in the park in 1903 at Sheep and Bullion creeks, near the south end of Kluane Lake, brought hordes of people. Some of the buildings of this once-active Silver City may still be seen at the east end of the lake, together with the remains of an Indian village and graveyard. Other discoveries of gold and copper in the park area resulted in numerous roads, now used as hiking trails.

The Alaska Highway opened up the region. During its completion in 1942, a recommendation was made to set aside Kluane as a park. On December 8, 1942, a protected reserve of 16,000 km² was established for the protection of wildlife. Two years later, lands around Kluane Lake and potential mineral-producing properties along the highway were deleted, with some other land added in as compensation. Later the same year, mineral explorations were allowed and mining rights granted in the park. To provide for the ever-increasing numbers of people who wanted to live in the area "away from civilization," a strip 309 m wide along the west side of the highway was withdrawn in 1962, to allow for settlement. Finally, in 1972, a block of land 13,500 km² became a national park reserve.

To mountaineers, Kluane means adventure and challenge, with several peaks over 5000 m and Mount Logan at 5950 m. The first reference to these heights was made by Bering, the famous Russian explorer, to a European audience in 1741, when he described Mount St. Elias. Finally in 1897, an Italian, H.R.H. Prince Luigi Amedeio Dei Savoia, Duke of Abruzzi, challenged Mount St. Elias. Canadian climbers ascended Mount Logan in 1925 and other peaks have been "conquered" since.

Haines Junction hosts the park administration office. Located at the junction of the Alaska and Haines highways, the two main arteries connecting the Yukon to Alaska and southern Canada, this community at Km 1640 is a good base, providing most visitor services. Other commercial accommodation and campgrounds occur on both highways, north and south.

Weather is a major factor restricting outdoor activity. Suitable times for camping and hiking occur between June 15 and September 15. Ski touring and winter camping are possible; however, take the usual precautions regarding clothing and emergency gear.

Approximately 250 km of hiking trails are provided, with some leading to remote areas and others ideal for day trips. A map showing these and other interpretive features is available from the main office. Suggested trips are listed under birding features.

Interpreters are employed all year. Staff have prepared an excellent bird list together with comments; they also have a good history of the area and a detailed vegetation description. Ask for them. There are two information centres: park headquarters at Km 1640 and Sheep Mountain at Km 1707. The Sheep Mountain Information Centre will be closed permanently in 1985 or 1986. The information service will then be covered by a new facility at the site where visitors will begin the "bus" trip to the Kaskawulsh Glacier. For further help write: The Superintendent, Kluane National Park, Haines Junction, Yukon Y0B 1L0, Telephone: (403) 634-2251. More information on this spectacular park can be found in *Kluane/Pinnacle of the Yukon*, ed. J.B. Theberge (Toronto: Doubleday, 1980). This 175-page book contains a chapter on birds.

Birding Features

Valleys in the park are at about 590 m (Haines Junction is 588 m) above sea level.

The park includes three main vegetation zones: montane, consisting of White Spruce forest in the lower valleys and up to 800 – 1100 m; subalpine, with tall shrubs, mostly willow with scattered individual White Spruce, extending up to 1400 m; and a lower alpine zone of small shrubs, extending upward into the alpine tundra with dwarfed plants.

Beginning at Haines Junction, park headquarters, there are several trails to explore. Obtain a map from the information office. Before starting out check with the park naturalists at headquarters in Haines Junction or at the information office at Sheep Mountain. They often lead hikes along some of the trails and you may be able to join one. If not, they will show you the most productive birding trips and tell you what recent sightings have been made.

Most of the hikes are along valleys. Special birds to look out for are a possible Trumpeter Swan, which likely nests, and a variety of breeding ducks, including both goldeneyes. Watch for soaring Golden and Bald Eagles, both nesting here. You may be lucky and spot a Gyrfalcon or Peregrine Falcon, as they also breed in the park. On your trip up to the higher country, look for all three species of ptarmigan, which nest. Shorebirds around lakes and on the tundra during the breeding season include Lesser Golden-Plover, Wandering Tattler and Red-necked Phalarope. Long-tailed Jaegers may be harassing the smaller birds seeking food for their own young. The forests contain nesting Northern Hawk-Owl, and probably Great Gray and Boreal. Breeding thrushes include Gray-cheeked, Mountain Bluebird and the elusive Northern Wheatear. Listen for Orange-crowned Warbler in the woods, as well as for the Blackpoll. Rosy Finch breeds high up in the hills, whereas American Tree Sparrows are lower down. Smith's Longspur and Snow Bunting are also breeding on the tundra.

STAFF OF KLUANE NATIONAL PARK

Northwest Territories

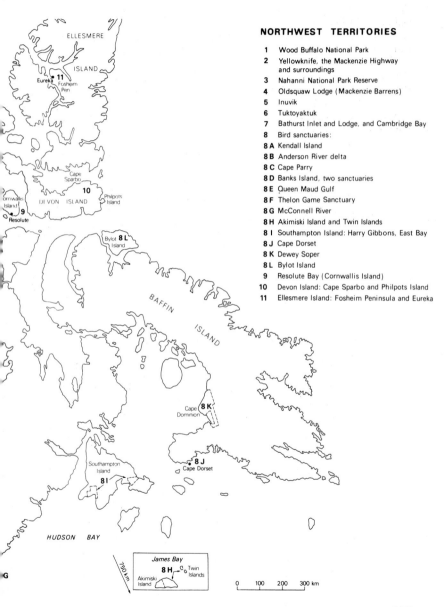

NORTHWEST TERRITORIES

1   Wood Buffalo National Park
2   Yellowknife, the Mackenzie Highway and surroundings
3   Nahanni National Park Reserve
4   Oldsquaw Lodge (Mackenzie Barrens)
5   Inuvik
6   Tuktoyaktuk
7   Bathurst Inlet and Lodge, and Cambridge Bay
8   Bird sanctuaries:
8 A   Kendall Island
8 B   Anderson River delta
8 C   Cape Parry
8 D   Banks Island, two sanctuaries
8 E   Queen Maud Gulf
8 F   Thelon Game Sanctuary
8 G   McConnell River
8 H   Akimiski Island and Twin Islands
8 I   Southampton Island: Harry Gibbons, East Bay
8 J   Cape Dorset
8 K   Dewey Soper
8 L   Bylot Island
9   Resolute Bay (Cornwallis Island)
10   Devon Island: Cape Sparbo and Philpots Island
11   Ellesmere Island: Fosheim Peninsula and Eureka

335

Northwest Territories

Covering one-third of the lands and fresh waters of Canada, the Northwest Territories contain 3,340,552 km² and stretch from Ellesmere Island in the north at 82° north latitude, south to the islands in James Bay at 52°. From east to west, lands include 80° of longitude. About 46,500 people reside in three districts: Mackenzie, the mainlands west of 102° west longitude; Keewatin, generally the mainlands east of 102°, as well as the islands in Hudson Bay; and Franklin, the Arctic islands, together with Melville and Boothia peninsulas.

These northern lands host colonies of waterfowl, plus breeding land and shore birds seen only on migration in the south. A visit up here will be rewarded by watching sandpipers, plovers and other species doing their territorial defence activities and displays.

The boreal forest extends down the Mackenzie River almost to the coast. This tree line angles southeast, skirting the northern end of Great Bear and Great Slave lakes and intersecting Hudson Bay at Fort Churchill. This approximate line is shown on the "Official Explorers' Map, Northwest Territories." This excellent all-round map is available from: TravelArctic, Government of the Northwest Territories, Yellowknife, NWT, X1A 2L9.

Arctic tundra consisting of scrub willow, dwarf birch, grasses, sedge or heath occurs mostly north of the tree line. Bedrock or sands and gravel are often exposed.

Spring is the best time for birding. Depending on latitude, this occurs between the first of May and the first of July, or at least before the mosquitoes and blackflies appear. A good supply of insect repellent is recommended, especially if one travels by canoe. Insects can be very bothersome at temperatures as low as 4°C. Courtship displays and songs of shorebirds are at their peak between May 28 and June 15, depending on latitude, geography and weather.

When you travel in the North by light aircraft, boat, snowmobile or dog team, it is best to allow one or two "weather days" per week, especially in coastal regions.

Fall migration can begin as early as July 1 for male eiders, followed by shorebirds in late July and August. Geese begin accumulating in staging areas by mid-August, and some nonbreeding Greater White-fronted Geese may have headed south by then. September is the best time to look for fall migrants of most water birds. Occasionally some species, such as Black Guillemot, eider, Oldsquaw, Ross' Gull and Ivory Gull, are seen along open leads in November.

All sites in the territories are far away from major centres. Wood Buffalo Park is probably the easiest and most rewarding, particularly in May and June, on the Peace-Athabasca Delta when waterfowl move through.

For comfort, good food and excellent guides, plus lots of arctic species, the two lodges — Bathurst Inlet, on the Arctic Ocean coast, plus nearby Banks Island or Oldsquaw Lodge in the Mackenzie Barrens — are the best

Ross' Gull

sites. You need three days to a week to cover the area around these lodges thoroughly. Other sites are provided at communities, or you can indulge in primitive camping on the tundra. A canoe trip down the Thelon River or a visit to the Mackenzie Delta from Inuvik are well worth the time and expense. If Churchill, Manitoba (see under that area) is on your itinerary, you may also wish to visit the Snow Goose colony at La Perouse Bay to the east on Cape Churchill, by charter plane.

There are no special telephone numbers or bird clubs to contact. However, you will find most people of the North very friendly. Most of the biologists working in the Arctic operate out of the Canadian Wildlife Service Office in Edmonton. Contact them, including Tom Barry, who was instrumental in setting up many of the bird sanctuaries. Dr. Barry supplied much of the resource data for this chapter. Their address is: Canadian Wildlife Service, Department of the Environment, 9942 — 108 Street, Edmonton, Alberta.

T.W. BARRY

Wood Buffalo National Park

Home of the Wood Buffalo, nesting grounds for the Whooping Crane and host to over a million swans, geese and ducks during migration, this park is one of the largest and most special in the world. All of the continent's major migrational flyways overlap here. Of the 227 species of birds noted within its boundaries, 142 nest, with only 25 species overwintering. Forty-six mammal species have been recorded, including Moose, Woodland Caribou, Black Bear and Wolf. Several species of frogs and the Boreal Toad are present. The most northerly hibernacula of the Red-sided Garter Snake in North America are found in the karst topography of the Salt River area.

Soon after the glacial ice receded, about nine thousand years ago, man moved in. Native peoples speaking the Cree, Chipewyan and Beaver languages still inhabit the area today. The first European recorded to have arrived here was Samuel Hearne, in the winter of 1771–72. In his words, the buffalo were "plentiful." Fort Chipewyan is the oldest continuously inhabited settlement in Alberta. Established in 1788, "Fort Chip" was the centre for the extensive fur trade in the entire northwest.

In 1789 Alexander Mackenzie reported large herds of buffalo along the Slave River. Fifty years later they were seldom seen and by 1888 the population had been reduced to small bands, with a maximum of several hundred left. From 1877 onward the government has attempted to protect these animals, the largest mammal in North America. By the end of 1922, when the park was established, herds of Wood Buffalo had increased to an estimated 1500.

Under the pressure of up to 1000 calves being born each year to the protected Plains Buffalo down south at Wainwright, Alberta, the government made a controversial decision to move 6600 of these plains mammals north between 1925 and 1928. Plains and Wood Bison interbred and today the bison in the park are probably hybrids. A pocket of presumably pure Wood Bison was located in a far corner of the park in the early 1960s. Twenty-four of these were moved south to Elk Island National Park in 1965 to found the only large confined herd of Wood Bison in the world. Today, this southern herd has increased to over 100, and animals are shipped to zoos in many places, together with some now being introduced back into the wild (*i.e.*, Nahanni and Jasper).

The search for the nesting grounds of the Whooping Crane had been going on for years. These birds once numbered several thousand and were spread across the plains of North America. Land clearing and hunting reduced the population to less than 100 in the 1920s. By the early 1940s, the bird appeared to be headed for extinction. From 1922 until 1954, not a single active nest was found. In 1937, the United States government established the wildlife refuge at Aransas, Texas, to protect the last wintering grounds of these birds. Men scoured the country to discover where the few remaining birds nested during the summer. On a helicopter trip during forest fire suppression activities, in 1954, G.M. Wilson, Superintendent of Forestry at Fort Smith, spotted two adult white birds and a young one in an area south of Great Slave Lake. The next day, Dr. W.A. Fuller, then the regional biologist for the CWS and now a professor at the University of Alberta, identified them as Whooping Cranes. The nesting grounds were confirmed after a very difficult ground search in 1955. Their nesting territory lies between the headwaters of the Nyarling, Sass and Klewi rivers in the northeast corner of the park. CAUTION!: you are *not* allowed into this area from spring until fall. A 600-m height restriction exists for aircraft flying over the park north of Highway 5, as further protection for the birds.

As one of the largest in the world, the park covers 48,807 km^2, straddling the Northwest Territories and Alberta border. Fort Smith, the park headquarters, sits just north of the Alberta border on Highway 5, in the NWT. This community is a 30-km drive from the park. Pacific Western Airlines provides scheduled jet service to and from Edmonton and Fort Chipewyan. To reach the park by car take one of the several roads in Alberta to the town of Peace River; then drive west 21 km to Highway 35 and north on 35 into the NWT. Proceed east on Highway 5 to Fort Smith and south into the park.

The Peace-Athabasca Delta is the best park birding area. Access is difficult. By car, drive 145 km south from Fort Smith on a gravel and dirt road; take a canoe or powerboat up the Peace River for 8 km; hike about 15 km down an old road to get to the best areas. Or start from Fort Chipewyan and go into this and other delta areas. But it is worth it! For detailed directions, a map and a list of professional guides and tour companies, contact the park naturalists. In the delta a guide is almost indispensible. Several gravel roads provide ready access to parts of the park. Hiking trails have been constructed to allow additional exploration. The roadways, trails, rivers and lakes to explore are shown on special brochures available at the park office and information outlets.

No commercial accommodation exists within the park; however, Fort Smith contains hotels, as does Fort Chipewyan, near the southeast end of the park. Pine Lake, a lovely spot 66 km south of Fort Smith, has a thirty-six-site campground and a group site. Tenting and other primitive camping is allowed anywhere in the park as long as the site is beyond 1.5 km from Pine Lake or any road or trail. There is a campsite in the town of Fort Smith.

Park staff have prepared a checklist of the birds of Wood Buffalo, together with several brochures. For copies write: The Superintendent, Wood Buffalo National Park, Box 750, Fort Smith, NWT X0E 0P0, Telephone: (403) 872-2349 or 872-2237. Park naturalists are on duty all year to offer assistance.

Birding Features

Located in boreal forest with numerous bogs, muskegs and prairies, the park provides good birding opportunities. In addition, the underground salt and gypsum deposits illustrate some of the best gypsum karst landscape in North America. The salt leaches out at the base of a low escarpment and flows across flat open areas, producing major changes in the plant communities.

Part of the high hills of the Caribou Mountains occur within the southwest corner of the park. The Birch Hills lie on the far southern boundary. Both of these highlands are very inaccessible and hence little is known of their birdlife even today. Rising to 420 m above the surrounding plain, they have the potential to add new northern bird species to Alberta's list.

Finally, the Peace-Athabasca Delta is one of the largest inland deltas in the world. Waters from the Peace, Athabasca and Birch rivers converge here. Serious birders should endeavour to travel into it. This biologically rich area attracts hundreds of thousands of migrating birds from all four North American flyways each year. No other area in the park can compete with the delta for sheer numbers and variety of birdlife. Look for Great Blue Heron, almost all of the northern nesting species of geese, ducks, Golden and Bald Eagles, Osprey, possibly Peregrine Falcon and owls, including the Short-eared. The recommended time to come to the delta, in fact to the whole park, is the last two weeks of May, before the bugs and leaves are out, and the middle weeks of September.

The most northerly colony of American White Pelican in North America occurs on rocky islands in the Slave River, near the town of Fort Smith. Be sure to include these birds in your visit to the area.

BOB LEWIS

Yellowknife, the Mackenzie Highway and Surroundings

With a population of nearly 10,000, Yellowknife is both the largest community in and, as of 1967, the capital of the NWT. This city provides a good base for a variety of side trips.

The first recorded visit to the area was by Samuel Hearne in 1771. Gold was discovered on the shores of Great Slave Lake in 1934 and the city was born as a boom town. The population crashed during the Second World War, when six of the operating mines closed. A second major gold discovery in 1945 started another gold rush. Two large gold mines offer tours in the summer, but book early, as they are usually filled.

Road access into the area is via the Mackenzie Highway north from Peace River, Alberta. A new road linking Fort Nelson on the Alaska Highway to the Mackenzie Highway south of Fort Simpson opened in 1983. This route will provide a long circle tour of the region. Bus connections to Edmonton depart from Hay River three days a week. Scheduled daily air service links Edmonton to Yellowknife.

Three hotels and three motels offer accommodation and meals. Campgrounds are present along the highways. A traveller into the area should carry extra gasoline, tires, fan belt and sleeping bag, since service centres are far apart.

Information on the area is available by writing TravelArctic (see above).

Birding Features
When you reach Hay River, going north on the Mackenzie Highway, you

Parasitic Jaeger and Red-necked Phalarope

may go east to Fort Smith and Wood Buffalo Park (see above), or west. An easterly excursion will take you to the south of the Whooping Crane nesting area (no entrance is allowed during breeding time) down to near the south end of the park. Don't forget the American White Pelican colony at Fort Smith (see above).

West from Hay River along the Mackenzie Highway, you will pass along the escarpment to Fort Simpson.

Liard Highway. This road south to Fort Nelson leaves the Mackenzie Highway just south of Fort Simpson and opens up areas in which you can spot boreal species. Look for Northern Hawk-Owl, often seen on dead spires in spruce muskeg; Great Gray Owl near Tamarack stands; and Boreal Owl looking out of holes in mature Aspen Poplar. Other species to watch for as you drive include Spruce Grouse, both three-toed woodpeckers, Gray Jay, Bohemian Waxwing, grosbeaks and both crossbills.

Fort Providence lies on the north bank of the Mackenzie River. Cross on the ferry in summer and on an ice bridge in winter. From Fort Providence you can take your canoe, boat or a bush road west, downstream to Mills Lake, at the junction of the Horn River. Mills Lake, a widening of the Mackenzie River, contains a large marsh and willow clumps on the north bank. In August and early September fall warblers abound here; waterfowl arrive in September and October on their way south.

East from Fort Providence by boat, you can reach Beaver Lake and the beginning of the Mackenzie River at Great Slave Lake. This eastward trip should produce Red-necked Grebe and other water birds, Bald Eagle and Osprey. Concentrations of migrant Tundra Swan, Canvasback and other diving ducks gather at Beaver Lake and Deep Bay of Great Slave Lake in September and early October.

Yellowknife. When you arrive in Yellowknife, look for the ever-present Common Raven, the official bird of this city. In spring and summer, it is mostly nonbreeders that remain in town. Winter, when the adults and young arrive, is the best time to observe their antics. Use Yellowknife as a base for other boat trips such as down the Thelon River (refer to Thelon under Bird Sanctuaries).

West Mirage Islands. The Mackenzie Highway enters the Precambrian Shield country of rocks and lakes near Rae and Edzo on the North Arm of Great Slave Lake. Twenty-one km south-southwest of Yellowknife, the West Mirage Islands are accessible by boat. These ninety-seven rocky outcrops contain a variety of terrestrial and lake habitats that result in a wide diversity of breeding birds. Sixty-five species have been reported from these islands. The cold waters of Great Slave Lake result in subarctic conditions and encourage more northerly species to occur. Look for the Red-throated Loon, Greater Scaup, Red-breasted Merganser, Red-necked Phalarope, Parasitic Jaeger and Arctic Tern. California Gull and Caspian Tern occur here at the northern limit of their ranges.

T.W. BARRY

Nahanni National Park Reserve

This valley of legends contains 91.5-m-high Virginia Falls and hosts at least 170 species of birds, of which 22 are year-round residents. A few Trumpeter Swans nest in the park, as do Golden and Bald Eagles. Gyrfalcon, Spruce, Blue and Ruffed Grouse, White-tailed Ptarmigan, Northern Hawk-Owl, Boreal Owl and both species of three-toed woodpeckers are permanent residents. Thirty-one mammal species have been recorded in the park. Grizzly and Black Bear are common; Moose occur in the valleys; Dall Sheep are found sporadically in the alpine tundra areas with the densest population around Deadmen Valley; Woodland Caribou occupy the upper valleys of both the Flat and South Nahanni rivers.

In contrast to most of Canada, parts of the Nahanni Valley were not covered by ice during the last ice advance, which ended about 8000 years ago. The area was cold but insufficient precipitation restricted the formation and movement of glaciers. Unlike most of Canada's other mountain valleys, glaciers have been absent here for at least 100,000 years. River valley features such as deltas and fans therefore have been developing for at least ten times longer than those found elsewhere. Man arrived, and by the early 1700s Slavey Indians roamed and hunted in the area. Fur-trading posts were built by white traders. The Crees moved in and pushed the more submissive Slaveys westward. The word Nahanni was used by these Athapaskan-speaking people to refer to others living in areas not normally visited. A literal translation is "people-over-there-far-away." Gold brought prospectors into the region in the very early 1900s following the huge strike in the Yukon to the west. The headless bodies of prospectors and brothers William and Frank McLeod were discovered in 1908; subsequent mysterious disappearances of other prospectors, combined with stories of fierce natives and mythical mountain men, resulted in the legends of the Nahanni. A few people have lived here. Mary and Gus Kraus stayed intermittently from 1940 to 1971. They all searched for that elusive mother lode of gold.

A federal order in council in 1971 resulted in these lands being withdrawn from other potential uses; three years later Nahanni National Park Reserve was created.

Covering 4766 km² of the Northwest Territories, the park lies just east of the Yukon border. Access is by boat or float plane. Charter planes fly out of Fort Simpson, NWT (308 km east of Rabbit Kettle Lake), Watson Lake, Yukon (224 km southwest), and Fort Nelson, B.C., straight south. Information on these charter companies and outfitters operating in the park may be obtained by writing the park superintendent (see below). An alternative source of assistance is TravelArctic (see above).

Canoeing the South Nahanni and Flat rivers has recently become a popular activity. To assist hardy, adventuresome people, Parks Canada has prepared an excellent booklet dealing with the 300-km section of the South Nahanni that lies within the park. This material also describes a 128-km section of the Flat River from Seaplane Lake to its junction with the South Nahanni. Brief notes are provided on the human history, natural history and river characteristics such as gradients and canoeing grade.

Several hot springs, with accompanying beautiful tufa deposits and "exotic" vegetation, enhance the picture. Mean water temperatures in these pools are around 21°C, with seasonal variations. The Kraus Hot Springs beside Clausen Creek, near the eastern boundary of the park, contain two source pools where water as hot as 35 or 36°C bubbles up through fine mud.

Hiking trips in the park are increasing in popularity. Excursions range from a one-day outing to a week or more. Almost any tributary creek valley can be taken to explore wilderness. Higher elevation explorations can also be made. High-country trips include the tundra-like Tlogotsho and Nahanni plateaus and ridge walking, with the latter being some of the finest in Canada. Visitors also take the excellent excursion to Sunblood Mountain.

Canoeists and hikers should be prepared for a wide range of weather conditions. Summers may be hot and dry, but it can also snow in any month of the year. Bad weather is to be expected, particularly in the high country. Low clouds may make flying in the narrow valleys impossible for several days. Flexibility of time must be built into your schedule when entering and leaving the area. You may wait a week or more before a pick-up is possible!

Park staff have prepared a brochure and bird list on the park. For this information, a list of outfitters and boating guides operating in the park, together with a list of charter companies to fly you in, write to: The Superintendent, Nahanni National Park, Postal Bag 300, Fort Simpson, NWT X0E 0N0, Telephone: (403) 695-3151.

Birding Features
The Nahanni contains birds from the more southerly Great Plains and foothills, such as Blue Grouse and Black Tern, and such northern species as Gyrfalcon and Arctic Tern. Trumpeter Swans have nested at Yohin Lake. Look for Bald Eagle near this lake too. You may also spot Arctic and Red-throated Loons, a wide variety of ducks, including such prairie species as Northern Shoveler and Redhead. Both goldeneye species are seen together with Osprey, and four species of grouse (Spruce, Blue, Ruffed and Sharp-tailed) nest here. Boreal species that breed in the park include Northern Hawk-Owl and Boreal Owl, both species of three-toed woodpeckers, Common Raven, Boreal Chickadee and Gray-cheeked Thrush. When travelling through or near the deep canyons watch for Peregrine Falcon and Black Swift, which are noted regularly. The American Dipper can be spotted around white water.

Much of the birding information on the Nahanni has been collected in conjunction with other major environmental studies. As a consequence, not too much is known of the birds. Information on areas away from the rivers, particularly in the highlands, is lacking. If you do any hiking, keep notes and forward them to the superintendent at the above address.

Oldsquaw Lodge (Mackenzie Barrens)

At this guest lodge constructed by Sam Miller on the old Canol Road, you can spot Lesser Golden-Plover, Red-necked Phalarope, Gyrfalcon, Long-tailed Jaeger, the odd Wandering Tattler, Lapland Longspur and Snow Bunting. Of course, Oldsquaw nest here.

You have to fly in, from Whitehorse. The two-storey log lodge has several heated cabins as outbuildings for visitor accommodation. Wall tents are provided for excursions by trail or canoe. Visitors are encouraged to select their choice of horse trips, canoe rides along 320 km or more of rivers, or nature walks on the Mackenzie Barrens to look for Woodland Caribou and Dall Sheep. Group size is small to allow personal attention. For further information write: Oldsquaw Lodge, Suite 8A, 4048 — 4th Avenue, White-horse, Yukon Y1A 4K8, Telephone: (403) 667-4033.

Birding Features
Set on a plateau known as the Mackenzie Barrens, with isolated ranges and adjacent continuous mountains extending from the Yukon border some 32 km east, the area ranges from 1370 to 1675 m above sea level. Vegetation consists of shrub tundra with some bare tundra. Some wetlands and small lakes and creeks are also present. There are a surprising number of high-arctic birds nesting this far south. Refer above for some of the key species.

ROBERT FRISCH

Inuvik

Near the mouth of the Mackenzie River on the northern edge of the boreal forest and adjacent to arctic tundra, Inuvik certainly has a diversity of birdlife. Species usually spotted not too far away include Rough-legged Hawk, Golden and Bald Eagles, Peregrine Falcon, six gull species and Northern Hawk-Owl; Northern Wheatear and Yellow Wagtail nest to the west and sometimes come into Inuvik; redpolls and Lapland Longspur are usually around.

The Mackenzie Delta has long been a meeting place for the Dene and Inuit peoples, who searched for food, and later for furs to fill the needs of the white traders. The first permanent settlement, Aklavik, was established on the west side of the delta in 1915 at the opening of a fur-trading post. However, because of unstable soil conditions, a new community, Inuvik, meaning "place of man," was carved out of the wilderness in 1955. The site, originally called East-3, had many factors in its favour: good river access, flat upland suitable for an airport, freedom from flooding, low ice content or permafrost in the soil, a good gravel deposit for road building and ready availability of fresh drinking water. Today the community is a major base for oil exploration, a transportation and communication centre, and the terminal point of the Dempster Highway, the first North American public road to cross the Arctic Circle. Utility lines are all above ground in a large boxlike structure called a utilidor.

The community of nearly 3000 people is one of the largest in the NWT. Edmonton, the main jumping-off point to the western Arctic, lies 1966 km southeast. Pacific Western Airlines provides the main link to Edmonton.

Other charter services fly into various communities from Inuvik. Boats can come down the Mackenzie River via the "east branch" of the delta. The hardy can arrive via the Alaska and Dempster highways (see above). Four hotels, restaurants, stores, gas stations, a garage, hospital, telephone and telex connections to the outside world are here for your use. There are many companies operating from the community in the summer, so book well in advance if you require accommodation. In-town and near-town campgrounds offer alternative resting places for the hardy who wish to combat the mosquitoes and blackflies. These warriors come out in late June and are very aggressive until September, after the first frost.

Further help or information is available from: Inuvik Research Laboratory, Box 1430, Inuvik, NWT X0E 0T0, Telephone: (403) 979-3838. Write to TravelArctic for additional information (see above).

If you are on site, local maps can be obtained from the village office.

Inuvik can function as the jumping-off point for the far western Arctic, including Sachs Harbour with the two Banks Island bird sanctuaries, about 525 km northeast; Cape Parry Bird Sanctuary 410 km northeast; Anderson River Delta Bird Sanctuary about 240 km northeast; Kendall Island Bird Sanctuary about 140 km straight north on the coast (see below for descriptions); and, of course, the Yukon Arctic coast to the west, with several Asiatic nesting species (refer to the Yukon chapter). If you plan to visit any of the above, except the Yukon coast, you must have permission of the Canadian Wildlife Service at least forty-five days ahead. Contact them at Edmonton (see above).

Birding Features

Inuvik sits near the northern limit of the trees in the Mackenzie Valley, with tundra close by. The valley acts as a migration corridor for northern species. A variety of habitats, including the open green spaces within the town and in the vicinity, bring in the birds. Visitors are usually impressed with the antics of the Common Raven, probably the most obvious bird year-round and the most abundant in winter. Visit the town dump at the east end, off the airport road in May and early June to check the six gull species: Glaucous, Herring, Thayer's, Mew, Bonaparte's and Sabine's. A trip to the sewage lagoon at the west end of town should produce 20 or more different species of shorebirds, especially in late May and June. Along the waterfront, from the "in-town" airstrip next to the sewage lagoon, upstream of the commercial docks, you should expect a variety of large and small land birds. Many of these species are near the northern limit of their range. Varied Thrush, White-crowned and Fox Sparrows are heard here in spring.

Hike to the tundra above the northeast side of town for Hoary and Common Redpolls and Lapland Longspur nesting sites.

Take a cab or convince a local birder to take you along the airport road and out to the Dempster Highway, then to Campbell Lake and beyond, even to Arctic Red River, 132 km south, for Northern Goshawk, Rough-legged Hawk, Golden and Bald Eagles, Peregrine Falcon, Merlin and Northern Hawk-Owl.

With the delta so near the Arctic coast, Alaska and Asia, there is an excellent chance of seeing rarities. In the past, species reported have included Ruff, Bar-tailed Godwit, Yellow and White Wagtail and the Northern Wheatear. Refer to Dempster Highway and Yukon coast accounts for these species and others.

T.W. BARRY

Tuktoyaktuk

Situated on the Arctic coast, Tuktoyaktuk (Tuk) allows a visitor to observe two, and sometimes three, loon species, numerous geese and ducks, including Common (Pacific race) and King Eiders, abundant shorebirds in spring, three species of jaeger, a variety of gulls and a diverse collection of land birds.

Tuk was established by "free traders," who eventually sold out to the Hudson's Bay Company. Located just east of the Mackenzie Delta, Tuk has an excellent harbour. Transportation companies long recognized the advantage of bringing goods down the Mackenzie River on barges and then transferring them to sea-going ships servicing the Arctic coast communities. With the construction of the DEW-line site, and the school and nursing station in the mid-1950s, families from the region moved into the village. Oil exploration brought a boom economy, with Dome Petroleum, Esso Resources Canada and Gulf Canada setting up their base camps here to explore the Beaufort Sea. Today the community contains about 700 natives plus various numbers of whites employed with the above operations.

Limited accommodation and meals may be had at the Beaufort Inn. Book well in advance. Tenting is permitted near the airport and along the beaches. The community contains a nursing station, RCMP detachment, Hudson's Bay Company store, and telephone service (403 area code) to the "outside."

Airplane is generally the way in, via Inuvik. Contact the airport manager at Inuvik or Tuk for a list of charter companies that service the community, using the 1525-m airstrip. Boat access is also possible from Inuvik. Additional information may be obtained from employees of these companies. There is a good map entitled "Mackenzie Delta 1:250,000." Other information and help are available from: Village Manager, Tuktoyaktuk, NWT X0E 1C0. Guides and boats for a charter trip along the Beaufort Sea coast or into the Mackenzie Delta are available through the president of the Tuktoyaktuk Hunters and Trappers Association in Tuk. These people still hunt the Beluga or White Whale during July and August.

Birding Features
The area in and around Tuk represents coastal tundra. Come in late May through the first three-quarters of June, to observe both migrants and local breeders at their peak. The sea ice generally goes out in late June. Prior to that time, the tundra ponds are filled with meltwater, as are most of the lagoons along the beaches. Shorebirds arrive in their full breeding plumage then. You can witness their elaborate aerial courtships and hear them call,

using sounds only heard on the breeding grounds — an experience never to be forgotten. Ponds and lakes hold Arctic and Red-throated Loons, with the occasional Yellow-billed Loon offshore to add to your list. Tundra Swan, geese and a variety of ducks are also present; Pomarine, Parasitic and Long-tailed Jaegers, Glaucous and Sabine's Gulls and Arctic Tern are all observed moving through, around Tuk. From a charter plane or helicopter you can spot Common and King Eiders along the edge of the shorefast ice, migrating in May and June.

The radar or microwave structures of the DEW-line site are sometimes used for nesting by Rough-legged Hawk, an occasional Gyrfalcon and Common Raven. June and July are best for tundra-nesting land birds. Check for the "common" species, including Willow Ptarmigan, Semipalmated Plover, Whimbrel, Pectoral Sandpiper, Semipalmated Sandpiper, Hudsonian Godwit, Hoary and Common Redpolls and Lapland Longspur. Ponds around Tuk accumulate moulting waterfowl in July and August. Lagoons and ponds next to the airport often have Tundra Swan. Coastal lakes and lagoons near Toker Point, north of Tuk, host scaup, Oldsquaw and White-winged and Surf Scoters.

By early August, fall migration is well underway. Some species, such as Lesser Golden-Plover and Pectoral Sandpiper, migrate east along the coast; Red Phalaropes move west instead. Late August and September bring Brant and Snow Goose past Tuk, on their way to staging areas in the Mackenzie and further west to the Yukon coast.

T.W. BARRY

Bathurst Inlet and Lodge, and Cambridge Bay

Situated 64 km north of the Arctic Circle, Bathurst Inlet has Yellow-billed Loon, Tundra Swan, Oldsquaw, both eiders, Gyrfalcon, Peregrine Falcon, Willow Ptarmigan, Glaucous Gull, Red Phalarope, Hoary Redpoll, Harris' Sparrow and Lapland Longspur, all near the lodge. Arctic Wolf, Caribou and Musk Oxen are spotted regularly. Lodge staff are interested in early explorers and hence sometimes take trips to former campsites of the ill-fated Franklin Expedition, which travelled across the tundra 160 years ago.

The community was established in 1929 by prospectors and abandoned in 1964. Five years later, the Warners (Trish and Glenn) took over the old Hudson's Bay Company buildings as a lodge for naturalists. They use local Inuit people as staff and guides. Experts also come in from the south to assist and to explore their own interests, such as plants, Caribou, wolves and history.

Chartered aircraft from Yellowknife, 544 km south, is the way in. The lodge has hot and cold running water and home-cooked meals. However, all supplies must be flown in and thus costs are fairly high. While here, you may want to jump across to Cambridge Bay on the south side of Victoria Island (approximately 200 km north). The community of Cambridge, over 900 people, has a hotel with dining room and scheduled air service from Yellowknife. Lodge-based aircraft are available for charter.

For information on both Bathurst Lodge and Cambridge Bay write TravelArctic (see above for address). The lodge address is: Bathurst Inlet Lodge, Box 820, Yellowknife, NWT X1A 2H2, Telephone: (403) 873-2595. The big advantage of the lodge is the hospitality and the excellent tour guides combined with contact with the Inuit peoples to discuss their lifeskills.

Birding Features

The lodge at Bathurst Inlet offers chances to observe, in the immediate vicinity of the buildings, nesting Willow Ptarmigan, Gray-cheeked Thrush, Hoary and Common Redpolls, and the Gamble's subspecies of White-crowned Sparrow. Nearby you will encounter Yellow-billed Loon, breeding Tundra Swan, and Gyrfalcons, which are slowly becoming more common, as are Peregrine Falcons. A few nesting Rough-legged Hawks are spotted regularly, together with the odd Golden Eagle, Rock Ptarmigan, and Pectoral, Baird's and Least Sandpipers. Jaegers of all three species abound; Glaucous and Thayer's Gulls nest not too far away, as do Lapland Longspur and Snow Bunting.

Across at Cambridge Bay you can photograph Buff-breasted Sandpiper, Red Phalarope and Sabine's Gull.

TRISH AND GLENN WARNER, ESTHER BRADEN

Bird Sanctuaries

The Canadian Wildlife Service, Department of the Environment, has set aside several Migratory Bird and Game Sanctuaries in the NWT. *Caution:* these areas have restrictions on access during parts of the season. All of them are very inaccessible and terribly expensive to reach. For more details than provided below, together with how to obtain permission to visit them, write the Canadian Wildlife Service in Edmonton (see above).

Birding Features

These sanctuaries in the NWT lie either on the Arctic coast or on the Arctic islands. From west to east they include:

Kendall Island Bird Sanctuary. Located about 120 km straight north of Inuvik, the sanctuary hosts numbers of breeding Tundra Swan and Lesser Snow Geese. The delta habitat is ideal for a great variety of other arctic species, especially other waterfowl.

Anderson River Delta Bird Sanctuary. Lying about 240 km northeast of Inuvik, at the mouth of the Anderson River, the area contains the nesting grounds of an excellent collection of waterfowl and other water birds. These include Arctic and Red-throated Loons, Tundra Swan, Greater White-fronted Goose, Snow Goose, Brant, and a variety of ducks, including Oldsquaw. Land birds include Rough-legged Hawk, Golden and Bald Eagles,

Gyrfalcon and Willow Ptarmigan. Shorebirds have ideal breeding habitat and include Common Ringed Plover and Whimbrel. The European Starling first reached the Arctic coast at this site in 1963. Hoary and Common Redpolls are common nesters, together with other species.

Cape Parry Bird Sanctuary. Approximately 400 km north and mainly east of Inuvik, the site sits out on the end of the cape. The area protects a colony of Thick-billed Murre, the only colony known in the western Canadian Arctic. Birds appear to be attracted here because of the breakup of sea ice in June near the nesting cliffs. The open water also draws in migrating loons, Oldsquaw and eiders.

Banks Island's Two Sanctuaries. On the west side is the larger sanctuary, the one at the north end being a thin sliver; between them these two sanctuaries, 480 km north of the Arctic Circle, host a large segment of waterfowl similar to those at Kendall Island and Anderson River. A recent breakthrough for exploring this area has come in linking of the birding tours at Bathurst Inlet Lodge with those of Banks Island Lodge at Sachs Harbour on the south side of Banks Island. The community of Sachs Harbour, 200 Inuit and white residents, is a perfect base to search for nesting Snow Goose, three jaeger species and Snowy Owl. Common mammals include Polar Bear, Musk Ox, Peary's Caribou and Wolf. The flora north of the 72nd parallel is unsurpassed. For further information contact: Nature Travel Service Ltd., c/o Canadian Nature Federation, 75 Albert Street, Ottawa, Ontario K1P 6G1, or Banks Island Lodge, P.O. Box 820, Yellowknife, NWT X0E 1H0, Telephone: (403) 873-2595.

Snowy Owl

Queen Maud Gulf Bird Sanctuary. Sitting on the coast nearly 1000 km northeast of Yellowknife, this 62,000-km² reserve contains several extensive nesting colonies of breeding Snow and Ross' Geese. Recent counts have indicated more than 9000 Snow and 30,000 Ross' on the site. They nest in colonies on islands in shallow lakes. Forty-seven bird species and six mammal species have been spotted. The Ellice River area on the west side is a critical calving site for the Bathurst herd of Caribou. Musk Oxen are common.

Thelon Game Sanctuary. Located northeast about 600 km from Yellowknife, this sanctuary can be reached by canoe. Fly in from Yellowknife and float down the Thelon River. Charter companies may be contacted by writing the manager of the Yellowknife Airport. For information on "put in" and "pick up" spots on the river write TravelArctic (see above). On a trip on the river in late June and July, if you are lucky, you may spot all four species of loon. In addition, you should be able to locate Tundra Swan, the larger and smaller races of Canada Goose, Greater White-fronted Goose, both the white and blue colour phases of Snow Goose, Rough-legged Hawk, Golden and Bald Eagles, Gyrfalcon, Peregrine Falcon, Merlin and a possible American Kestrel. A surprisingly wide variety of tundra and tree-line bird species are also observed on such a voyage.

McConnell River Bird Sanctuary. Located on the west central shore of Hudson Bay, about 90 km north of the Manitoba border, this reserve of 32,800 ha is only 27 km south of Eskimo Point and 230 km north of Churchill. Eskimo Point is the home of the Inuit Cultural Institute, established to preserve Inuit culture. One motel services the centre, with meals provided to guests. A separate restaurant lies in the village, population 980. Scheduled air service is provided to Churchill. The Snow Goose colony at McConnell River has undergone rapid growth. First reports of geese nesting here were in 1930; in 1975 their numbers were estimated at 320,000 breeding birds. The area has now become the largest nesting colony of the Lesser Snow Goose in the Canadian Arctic and has spread beyond the boundaries of the sanctuary. Other abundant nesting species include Oldsquaw and Common and King Eiders; Willow Ptarmigan breed and Rock Ptarmigan are winter migrants; all three jaegers are common breeders; several other land birds nest, including Lapland Longspur and Snow Bunting.

Akimiski Island Bird Sanctuary and Twin Islands Game Sanctuary. Sitting in the midst of James Bay, these havens for birds lie about 175 km north of Moose Factory in Ontario. Check with the Edmonton office of the Canadian Wildlife Service for details as to nesting birdlife preserved on the east half of Akimiski and on the Twin Islands.

Southampton Island (Harry Gibbons Bird Sanctuary and East Bay Sanctuary). Sitting at about the middle of the north end of Hudson Bay, Southampton Island contains one community, Coral Harbour. The two sanctuaries lie 130 km straight west and about 60 km straight east, respectively, from this village. The local Katudqivik Co-op operates the hotel. Scheduled air service operates from Rankin Inlet to the west on the west side of Hudson Bay, and from Frobisher Bay to the east. As at several of the other sanctuaries, Tundra Swan, Snow Goose and Brant (Atlantic race) are common breeders. Old-squaw and King Eider are also common nesters. All three jaegers nest on the island. Some of the other common breeders include Arctic Tern, Snowy Owl, Lapland Longspur and Snow Bunting.

Cape Dorset Bird Sanctuary. At the southwest tip of Baffin Island, this reserve consists of three islands. The community of Cape Dorset is nearby, on the mainland of Baffin Island. Cape Dorset has gained worldwide fame as the home of soapstone carvings, prints and lithographs. Scheduled air service runs twice a week from Frobisher Bay or Timmins, Ontario. One inn services visitors. For details on birdlife, contact the CWS office in Edmonton (see above).

Dewey Soper Bird Sanctuary. Sitting on the southwest side of Baffin Island, this 815,900-ha reserve is named after the man who first found the nesting grounds of the blue phase of the Snow Goose. The reserve lies about 340 km northwest of Frobisher Bay. Three large colonies of Snow Goose occur, with nearly half a million individuals counted in 1973. Make the trip here after the birds have completed nesting and are moving around to feed and build up strength for their southern flight. Mid-July is the time to arrive. You won't disturb their nesting, but rather will see the families feeding on the plateau. At the same time, you will observe what is probably the most important nesting area for Brant in the eastern Arctic. Other numerous species include the Canada Goose, Oldsquaw, eiders and several species of shorebirds. They are concentrated on the west side of the sanctuary around Cape Dominion. Some of the other birds to look for include Arctic and Red-throated Loons, Tundra Swan, both eiders, Willow and Rock Ptarmigans, a variety of shorebirds including Purple Sandpiper, three jaeger species and the normal upland birds as mentioned in other spots above.

Bylot Island Bird Sanctuary. This reserve lies off the northeast end of Baffin Island. The community of Resolute lies about 550 km straight west of Bylot Island. Snow Geese (greater race) congregate here in summer to nest. Some of the other species that breed on the island include Northern Fulmar, King Eider, Gyrfalcon, Rock Ptarmigan, Common Ringed Plover, Semipalmated Plover, Purple Sandpiper, Black Guillemot, Snowy Owl and Snow Bunting.

T.W. BARRY

Resolute Bay (Cornwallis Island)

With the increased world demand for oil and the potential of major oil pools within the Arctic basin (Arctic islands), companies are exploring these islands on the top of the world. Large colonies of seabirds utilize the cliffs.

Ivory and Ross' Gulls have nested near Resolute Bay. A trip here, combined with chartering a plane for exploration, is very expensive. If money is no problem, you can come and see large numbers of Northern Fulmar, Greater Snow Goose, Thick-billed Murre, Glaucous and Thayer's Gulls, Black-legged Kittiwake and Black Guillemot.

Resolute, the nearest community to the north magnetic pole, served as a harbour during the Franklin searches of the mid-1800s. A joint U.S.–Canadian airstrip and weather station was opened in 1947. Inuit were relocated from other parts of the Arctic to this site in 1953. Today the community of less than 200 people serves as a staging area for oil and gas exploration and scientific expeditions in the Arctic islands.

Accommodation and meals are available in three hotels and a tourist home. Services include RCMP, radio, TV, nursing station and a licensed club accessible to the general public and visitors. Aircraft is the only way in: Nordair from Montreal, 3470 km away; and Pacific Western Airlines from Edmonton, 2561 km away. Contact the airport manager for names of aircraft charter companies currently operating out of Resolute and be prepared for some very expensive but enjoyable bird watching. The village manager or the Resolute Bay Inuit Co-op can assist with guides and other local help. Telephone area code 819 and advise the operator to route "via Ottawa."

Birding Features

Birds at Resolute Bay are typical of the high Arctic. Expected species include King Eider, Gyrfalcon, Rock Ptarmigan, Ruddy Turnstone, Purple Sandpiper, Sanderling, three species of jaeger and Snowy Owl. To view the uniqueness of the high Arctic, charter an aircraft to visit the seabird colonies, east on Lancaster Sound. The closest site to Resolute Bay, Prince Leopold Island, lies about 160 km east and a bit south, off the northeastern coast of Somerset Island. Sheer cliffs on Prince Leopold contain colonies of Northern Fulmar, Black-legged Kittiwake and Thick-billed Murre; talus slopes are the nest sites for Black Guillemot; crests of cliffs contain Glaucous and Thayer's Gulls. Now fly south to Cresswell Bay on nearby Somerset Island for the Greater Snow Goose breeding grounds. Further east, around the north end of Baffin Island and Bylot Island, you will find large seabird colonies. The colonies on Bylot are part of the Bylot Island Bird Sanctuary. Permission to visit this sanctuary must be obtained at least forty-five days ahead from the Canadian Wildlife Service in Edmonton (see above for address). Other colonies occur on the south side of Devon Island, north of Lancaster Sound.

Check the open water, called a "polinya," of Hell's Gate at the northwest end of Jones Sound, about 250 km north of Resolute Bay, for Common Eider that nest on small islets.

Ivory Gulls have been reported from northern Baffin Island and nesting on nanataks (portions of land above a glacier) in the icefields of Devon and Ellesmere islands. Ross' Gull has been recorded nesting on low islets in the vicinity of Resolute Bay, with sight records a possibility as you move around.

T.W. BARRY

Devon Island: Cape Sparbo and Philpots Island

Sparbo-Hardy Lowland
Lying east of Resolute Bay, Devon Island has a major research station operated by the Arctic Institute. Key birds that are seen regularly include Snow Goose, Common and King Eiders, Peregrine Falcon, Rock Ptarmigan, Glaucous Gull, and a variety of shorebirds, including Baird's Sandpiper, Black-bellied Plover and Common Raven. Mammals include Musk Ox, Arctic Fox, Arctic Hare and the occasional Polar Bear and Wolf.

Access is generally by charter aircraft from Resolute Bay; alternatively, a ride may be arranged as a diversion flight from Grise Fiord, 70 km north, or from Pond Inlet, about 400 km southeast. Most of the planes used in the area are de Havilland Twin Otters, with about a 1200-kg load capacity. Carry a two-way radio for emergencies. Permission to visit the area should be requested by mail at least six months in advance from: Grise Fiord Trappers' Association, Grise Fiord, NWT.

To use the research station camp at Truelove, about 40 km southwest of Cape Sparbo, request permission from: Arctic Institute of North America, University of Calgary, Calgary, Alberta T2N 1N4. Work has been carried on here for several years. Dr. D.L. Pattie has done research each season since 1970 and has offered to provide detailed information. Contact him at: Northern Alberta Institute of Technology, 11762 — 106 Street, Edmonton, Alberta T5G 2R1, Telephone: (403) 427-9161.

Birding Features
The lowlands, about 40 km long and between a few metres to 8 km wide, form one of those arctic oases relatively rich in both species and densities of arctic breeding birds. Try to arrange a visit from mid-June through July, when bird densities of thirty to fifty per square kilometre may be expected. Regular breeders include Red-throated Loon, Snow Goose, Oldsquaw, Common and King Eiders, Peregrine Falcon, Rock Ptarmigan, Lesser Golden- and Black-bellied Plovers, White-rumped and Baird's Sandpipers, Glaucous Gull, Arctic Tern, Parasitic and Long-tailed Jaegers, Lapland Longspur and Snow Bunting. Occasional breeders include Piping Plover, Ruddy Turnstone, Red Knot, Red Phalarope, Horned Lark and Northern Wheatear. Visitors include Brant, Red-breasted Merganser, Purple Sandpiper, Sanderling, Sabine's Gull, Snowy Owl and Hoary Redpoll.

Philpots Island
Located off the southeast corner of Devon Island, Philpots is an excellent spot to come for Northern Fulmar, Ivory Gull and others mentioned above. A short distance north, Coburg Island contains an estimated quarter million breeding Thick-billed Murre, together with some Northern Fulmar and Black Guillemot.

Access, as for the previous spot on Devon, is by chartered aircraft or a diversion flight. Permission to visit should be requested at least six months ahead from the Grise Fiord Trappers' Association. Be prepared to wait out storms that sometimes last a week while you remain in your tent! The area is apt to be cold, windy and foggy. Polar Bears frequent the area, searching for seals. Walrus and whales are common sights.

Birding Features

This wildly beautiful iceberg-riddled spot offers tremendous opportunities for photographers. The area from Cape Cockburn, the extreme east point, to Beatrice Point on the south side, is particularly rich in marine bird and mammal life. You will likely spot Red-throated Loon, Northern Fulmar, Oldsquaw, Common and King Eiders, Glaucous and Ivory Gulls, murres, Purple Sandpiper, Arctic Tern, guillemots and Snow Bunting.

D.L. PATTIE

Ellesmere Island: Fosheim Peninsula and Eureka

Concentrations of forty to sixty birds per square kilometre occur here in July. Species are similar to those at the other sites mentioned on the Arctic islands.

Access is generally by plane from Resolute Bay to Eureka, about 630 km. Refer to Devon Island or Resolute areas for details on chartering flights in. Then take a 50-km hike southeast to near the base of the Sawtooth Mountains. You will note Musk Ox, Caribou, Wolf, Arctic Fox and Arctic Hare as you stroll along.

Birding Features

The area has, for the Arctic, a dense concentration of birds. Come in late June to early August. You should be able to spot Snow Goose, Oldsquaw, Red Knot, Baird's and White-rumped Sandpipers, Red Phalarope, Parasitic and Long-tailed Jaegers, Arctic Tern, Snowy Owl, Common Raven, Lapland Longspur and Snow Bunting.

D.L. PATTIE

Provincial and Territorial Checklists for Canada

	BC	ALTA	SASK	MAN
Number of Species	426	341	334	353
Red-throated Loon	B	B	B	B
Arctic Loon	X	B	*	B
Common Loon	B	B	B	B
Yellow-billed Loon	X	X	*	*
Pied-billed Grebe	B	B	B	B
Horned Grebe	B	B	B	B
Red-necked Grebe	B	B	B	B
Eared Grebe	B	B	B	B
Western Grebe	B	B	B	B
Short-tailed Albatross	*			
Black-footed Albatross	X			
Laysan Albatross	*			
Black-browed Albatross				
Yellow-nosed Albatross				
Northern Fulmar	X			
Black-capped Petrel				
Mottled Petrel	*			
Cory's Shearwater				
Pink-footed Shearwater	X			
Flesh-footed Shearwater	X			
Greater Shearwater				
Buller's Shearwater	X			
Sooty Shearwater	X			
Short-tailed Shearwater	X			
Manx Shearwater				
Black-vented Shearwater	*			
Little Shearwater				
Audubon's Shearwater				
Wilson's Storm-Petrel				
British Storm-Petrel				
Fork-tailed Storm-Petrel	B			
Leach's Storm-Petrel	B			
Band-rumped Storm-Petrel				
White-tailed Tropicbird				
Red-billed Tropicbird				

Legend

B — Breeding
X — Present and usually migrant
* — Vagrant, accidental or *very few* records

ONT	QUE	NB	NS	PEI	NFLD	YUK	NWT
419	350	356	370	295	327	233	249
B	B	X	X	X	X	B	B
B	*B			X	*	B	B
B	B	B	B	X	B	B	B
*						B?	B
B	B	B	B	B	X	*	B
B	B	X	X	X	X	B	B
B	X	X	X	X	X	B	B
X				*			B
*						*	
					*		
					*		
	*	*					
*	X	X	X	*	X	*	B
*							
			*		X		
	X	X	X	X	X		
	X	X	X	X	X		
	*	X	*		X		
			*		*		
*							
*	X	X	X	X	X		
			*				
*	B	B	B	X	B		
*							
			*				
					*		

357

	BC	ALTA	SASK	MAN
Number of Species	426	341	334	353
Brown Booby				
Northern Gannet				
American White Pelican	B	B	B	B
Brown Pelican	X			
Great Cormorant				
Double-crested Cormorant	B	B	B	B
Brandt's Cormorant	B			
Pelagic Cormorant	B			
Anhinga				
Magnificent Frigatebird	*			
American Bittern	B	B	B	B
Least Bittern	*		*	B
Great Blue Heron	B	B	B	B
Great Egret	*	*	B	B
Little Egret				
Snowy Egret	*	*	*	X
Little Blue Heron	*		*	*
Tricolored Heron				*
Reddish Egret				
Cattle Egret	X	*	B	X
Green-backed Heron	B		*	X
Black-crowned Night-Heron	X	B	B	B
Yellow-crowned Night-Heron				X
White Ibis				
Glossy Ibis				
White-faced Ibis	*	B?	*	*
Wood Stork	*			
Greater Flamingo				
Fulvous Whistling-Duck	*			
Tundra Swan	X	X	B	B
Trumpeter Swan	B	B	B	X
Mute Swan	B		B	
Pink-footed Goose				
Greater White-fronted Goose	X	X	X	X
Snow Goose	X	X	X	B
Ross' Goose	X	X	X	X
Emperor Goose	X			

ONT	QUE	NB	NS	PEI	NFLD	YUK	NWT
419	350	356	370	295	327	233	249
			*				
*	B	X	X	X	B		
B	*	*	*				B
*			*				
*	B	X	B	B	B		
B	B	B	B	B	B	*	
*							
			*		*		
B	B	B	B	B	B		B
B	B	B	*B		X		
B	B	B	B	B	X	*	B
B	*	X	*	X	X		
					*		
X	*	X	*	*	X		
X	*	X	*	X	X		
X	*	*	*		*		
				X			
B	*	X	*	X	X		
B	B	B	*	*	X		
B	B	B	*B	X	X		
X	*	*	*	*	X		
*	*	*	*		*		
X	*	X	*	X	X		
*		*					
		*	*		*		
X		*	*	X			
B	B	*	*	X	*	B	B
*						B	B
B							
					*		
X	*	*	*	X	X	B	B
B	X	X	*	X	X	X	X
X	X						B

	BC	ALTA	SASK	MAN
Number of Species	426	341	334	353
Brant	X	*	*	X
Barnacle Goose				
Canada Goose	B	B	B	B
Wood Duck	B	B	B	B
Green-winged Teal	B	B	B	B
Baikal Teal	*			
Falcated Teal	*			
American Black Duck	B	B	B	B
Mallard	B	B	B	B
Northern Pintail	B	B	B	B
Garganey	*	*		*
Blue-winged Teal	B	B	B	B
Cinnamon Teal	B	B	B	X
Northern Shoveler	B	B	B	B
Gadwall	B	B	B	B
Eurasian Wigeon	X	*		X
American Wigeon	B	B	B	B
Canvasback	B	B	B	B
Redhead	B	B	B	B
Ring-necked Duck	B	B	B	B
Tufted Duck	X			
Greater Scaup	X	B?	B	B
Lesser Scaup	B	B	B	B
Common Eider	*			B
King Eider	*	*		B
Spectacled Eider	*			
Steller's Eider	*			
Harlequin Duck	B	B	*	X
Oldsquaw	B	X	*	B
Black Scoter	X	*	*	X
Surf Scoter	X	B	B	B
White-winged Scoter	B	B	B	B
Common Goldeneye	B	B	B	B
Barrow's Goldeneye	B	B		X
Bufflehead	B	B	B	B
Smew	*			
Hooded Merganser	B	B	B	B
Common Merganser	B	B	B	B
Red-breasted Merganser	B	B	B	B
Ruddy Duck	B	B	B	B

Legend

B — Breeding
X — Present and usually migrant
* — Vagrant, accidental or *very few* records

ONT	QUE	NB	NS	PEI	NFLD	YUK	NWT
419	350	356	370	295	327	233	249
X	X	X	X	X	X	B	B
		*			*		
B	B	B	X	B	B	B	B
B	B	B	B	B	X		
B	B	B	B	B	B	B	B
B	B	B	B	B	B	*	
B	B	B	B	B	X	B	B
B	B	B	B	B	B	B	B
		*		*			
B	B	B	B	B	B	B	B
*		*				*	
B	B	B	*B	B	X	B	B
B	B	X	*B	B	*	*	B
X	*	*	*	X	X	*	
B	B	B	B	B	B	B	B
X	X	*	*	*	X	B	B
B	B	*	*B?	B?	X	X	B
B	B	B	B	B	B	B?	B
*					*		
B	B	X	X	X	B	B	B
B	B	X	*	X	X	B	B
B	B	B	B	X	X	B	B
B	B	X	*	X	X	X	B
	*						
X	B	X	*	X	X	B	B
B	B	X	X	X	X	B	B
X	B	X	X	X	X	X	
B	B	X	X	X	X	B?	B
B	X	X	X	X	X	B?	B
B	B	B	B	X	B	B	B
X	B	X	*	X	X	B	B
B	X	X	X	X	X		B
*	*						
B	B	B	B	B	X	*	
B	B	B	B	B	B	B	B
B	B	B	B	B	B	B	B
B	B	X	*B?	X	X	*	B

	BC	ALTA	SASK	MAN
Number of Species	426	341	334	353
Black Vulture				
Turkey Vulture	B	B	B	B
Osprey	B	B	B	B
American Swallow-tailed Kite				
Mississippi Kite				
Bald Eagle	B	B	B	B
Northern Harrier	B	B	B	B
Sharp-shinned Hawk	B	B	B	B
Cooper's Hawk	B	B	B	B
Northern Goshawk	B	B	B	B
Red-shouldered Hawk	*			*
Broad-winged Hawk	*	B	B	B
Swainson's Hawk	B	B	B	B
Zone-tailed Hawk				
Red-tailed Hawk	B	B	B	B
Ferruginous Hawk	*	B	B	X
Rough-legged Hawk	X	X	X	B
Golden Eagle	B	B	B	B
American Kestrel	B	B	B	B
Merlin	B	B	B	B
Peregrine Falcon	B	B	X	X
Gyrfalcon	B	X	X	X
Prairie Falcon	B	B	B	X
Gray Partridge	B	B	B	B
Chukar	B		B	
Ring-necked Pheasant	B	B	B	B
Spruce Grouse	B	B	B	B
Blue Grouse	B	B		
Willow Ptarmigan	B	B	*	B
Rock Ptarmigan	B		*	X
White-tailed Ptarmigan	B	B		
Ruffed Grouse	B	B	B	B
Sage Grouse	X	B	B	
Greater Prairie-Chicken			*	
Sharp-tailed Grouse	B	B	B	B
Wild Turkey	X	B	B	B
Northern Bobwhite	B			
California Quail	B			
Mountain Quail	B			

ONT	QUE	NB	NS	PEI	NFLD	YUK	NWT
419	350	356	370	295	327	233	249
*	*	*	*	*		*	
B	*	*	*	X	X		
B	B	B	B	B	B	B	B
*			*				
*							
B	B	B	B	B	B	B	B
B	B	B	B	B	X	B	B
B	B	B	B	B	X	B	B
B	B	B?	*B	X	X		
B	B	B	B	B	X	B	B
B	B	B	*		X		
B	B	B	B				
*	*					B	B
			*				
B	B	B	B	B	X	B	B
B	B	X	X	X	X	B	B
B	B	X	*	X	X	B	B
B	B	B	B	B	B	B	B
B	B	B	B	B	B	B	B
B	B	X	*	X	X	B	B
X	B	X	*	X	X	B	B
B	B	B	B	B			
B	B	B	B	B	B		
B	B	B	B		B	B	B
						B	B
B	B	*	*B		B	B	B
*	B		*		B	B	B
						B	B
B	B	B	B	B	B	B	B
B*						B	B
B	B						
B							
B							

	BC	ALTA	SASK	MAN
Number of Species	426	341	334	353
Yellow Rail				
Corn Crake		B	B	B
Clapper Rail				
King Rail				*
Virginia Rail	B	B	B	B
Sora	B	B	B	B
Purple Gallinule				
Common Moorhen				*
Eurasian Coot				
American Coot	B	B	B	B
Sandhill Crane	B	B	B	B
Common Crane		*		
Whooping Crane	*	B	X	X
Northern Lapwing				
Black-bellied Plover	X	X	X	X
Greater Golden-Plover				
Lesser Golden-Plover	B	X	X	B
Snowy Plover	*		*	
Wilson's Plover				
Common Ringed Plover				
Semipalmated Plover	*	B	B	B
Piping Plover	X	B	B	B
Killdeer	B	B	B	B
Mountain Plover		B		
American Oystercatcher				
American Black Oystercatcher	B			
Black-necked Stilt	*	*B		*
American Avocet	B	B	B	B
Greater Yellowlegs	B	B	B	B
Lesser Yellowlegs	B	B	B	B
Spotted Redshank	*			
Solitary Sandpiper	B	B	B	B
Willet	X	B	B	B
Wandering Tattler	B	*		*
Spotted Sandpiper	B	B	B	B
Upland Sandpiper	B	B	B	B
Eskimo Curlew				
Whimbrel	X	X	X	B
Bristle-thighed Curlew	*			
Slender-billed Curlew				
Long-billed Curlew	B	B	B	X

ONT	QUE	NB	NS	PEI	NFLD	YUK	NWT
419	350	356	370	295	327	233	249
B	B	B	*				B
			*		*		
		*	*	*	*		
B	*	*			*		
B	B	B	*B	B	B		X
B	B	B	B	B	B	B	B
B		*	*B		X		
X	B	B	*B	X	X		
					*		
B	B	B	B	B	X	X	B
B	*		*	*	*	B	B
*							B
	*	*	*	*	X		
X	X	X	X	X	X	X	B
					X		
B	X	X	X	X	X	B	B
*							
			*		X		
					X		B
B	B	B	B	B	X	B	B
B	*B	B	B	B	B		
B	B	B	B	B	B	B	B
*		*					
*		*			*		
X	*	*	*	*			
X	B	X	B	X	B	X	B
B	B	X	X	X	X	B	B
*					*		
B	B	X	X	X	X		B
X	*	B	B	B	X		
*						B	B
B	B	B	B	B	B	B	B
B	B	B	*	B		B	B
*							B
B	X	X	X	X	X	B	B
*							
		*		*			

	BC	ALTA	SASK	MAN
Number of Species	426	341	334	353
Black-tailed Godwit				
Hudsonian Godwit	B	X	X	B
Bar-tailed Godwit	*			
Marbled Godwit	X	B	B	B
Ruddy Turnstone	X	X	X	X
Black Turnstone	X			
Surfbird	X	*		
Red Knot	X	X	X	X
Sanderling	X	X	X	X
Semipalmated Sandpiper	X	X	X	B
Western Sandpiper	X	*		*
Little Stint				
Temminck's Stint	*			
Least Sandpiper	B	B	B	B
White-rumped Sandpiper	*	X	X	X
Baird's Sandpiper	X	X	X	X
Pectoral Sandpiper	X	X	X	X
Sharp-tailed Sandpiper	X	*		
Purple Sandpiper				*
Rock Sandpiper	X			
Dunlin	X	X	X	B
Curlew Sandpiper	*	*		
Stilt Sandpiper	X	X	X	B
Spoonbill Sandpiper	*			
Buff-breasted Sandpiper	X	X	X	X
Ruff	*	*	*	*
Short-billed Dowitcher	B	B	B	B
Long-billed Dowitcher	B	X	X	X
Common Snipe	B	B	B	B
Eurasian Woodcock				
American Woodcock				B
Wilson's Phalarope	B	B	B	B
Red-necked Phalarope	B	*	B	B
Red Phalarope	X	X	*	X
Pomarine Jaeger	X		*	X
Parasitic Jaeger	X	X	*	B
Long-tailed Jaeger	X	*	*	X
Great Skua	X			
South Polar Skua				

Legend

B — Breeding
X — Present and usually migrant
* — Vagrant, accidental or *very few* records

ONT	QUE	NB	NS	PEI	NFLD	YUK	NWT
419	350	356	370	295	327	233	249
					X		
B	X	X	X	X	X	X	B
					*		
B	*	*	*	X	*		
X	X	X	X	X	X	B?	B
						*	
					B		
X	X	X	X	X	X	X	B
X	X	X	X	X	X	X	B
B	B	X	X	X	X	B	B
B		X	X	X	X	B	B
*						*	
X	X	X	X	X	X		B
B	X	X	X	X	X	X	B
*		*				*	
B	X	X	X	X	*	B	B
X	X	X	X	*	X	B	B
B		*	*	X	X		
X	B	X	X	X	X	B	B
X	*	*	X			B	B
B	B	B	B	B	B	B	B
					*		
B	B	B	B	B	B		
B	B	X	X	X	*	B	
B	B	X	X	X	X	X	B
X	B	X	X	*	X	X	B
X	B	X	*	*	X	X	B
B	B	X	*	*	X	B	B
*	B	*	*		X	B	B
	*	*	*		X		
					*		

	BC	ALTA	SASK	MAN
Number of Species	426	341	334	353
Laughing Gull				*
Franklin's Gull	X	B	B	B
Little Gull	X		*	*B
Common Black-headed Gull	*			*
Bonaparte's Gull	B	B	B	B
Heermann's Gull	X			
Mew Gull	B	X	B	*B
Ring-billed Gull	B	B	B	B
California Gull	B	B	B	B
Herring Gull	B	B	B	B
Thayer's Gull	X	*	X	X
Iceland Gull		*		X
Lesser Black-backed Gull				*
Slaty-backed Gull	*			
Western Gull	B			
Glaucous-winged Gull	B	*		
Glaucous Gull	X	*	*	X
Great Black-backed Gull				*
Black-legged Kittiwake	X	*		*
Ross' Gull	*			*B
Sabine's Gull	X	*	*	X
Ivory Gull	*			*
Gull-billed Tern				
Caspian Tern	X	B	B	B
Royal Tern				
Sandwich Tern				
Roseate Tern				
Common Tern	X	B	B	B
Arctic Tern	B	*	B	B
Forster's Tern	B	B	B	B
Least Tern				
Bridled Tern				
Sooty Tern				
White-winged Tern				
Black Tern	B	B	B	B
Black Skimmer				
Dovekie				*
Common Murre	B			
Thick-billed Murre	*			
Razorbill				
Black Guillemot				X
Pigeon Guillemot	B			

ONT	QUE	NB	NS	PEI	NFLD	YUK	NWT
419	350	356	370	295	327	233	249
X	*	B	*	*	X		
X	*	*	*		*		B
B	*B	X	*	X	X	*	
X	*B	X	X	X	X		
B	B	X	X	X	X	B	B
*	*	*	*		X	B	B
B	B	B	X	B	B	*	B
*						*	B
B	B	B	B	B	B	B	B
X	*		X	X	X	X	B
X	B	X	X	X	X		B
X	*	*	*	*	X		
		X	X	X		*	B
X	B				X	B	B
B	B	B	B	B	B		
X	B	X	B	X	B	*	B
					*		B
X	*	*	*	*	X	X	B
*	X	*	*	*	X		B
		*	*				
B	*B	X	*	X	X		B
*			*				
	*B	B	*B	*			
B	B	B	B	B	B		B
B	B	B	B	B	B	B	B
B	X	*	*				
		*	*	*			
					*		
			*				
		*					
B	B	B	*B	*	X	*	B
*	*	*	*	*	*		
*	X	X	X	X	X		
	B	B?	X	X	B		
*	B	X	X	X	B		B
*	B	B	B		B		B
B	B	B	B	B	B	B	B

	BC	ALTA	SASK	MAN
Number of Species	426	341	334	353
Marbled Murrelet	B			
Kittlitz's Murrelet	*			
Xantus' Murrelet	*			
Ancient Murrelet	B	*		*
Cassin's Auklet	B			
Parakeet Auklet	*			
Rhinoceros Auklet	B			
Tufted Puffin	B			
Atlantic Puffin				
Horned Puffin	B			
Rock Dove	B	B	B	B
Band-tailed Pigeon	B	*		*
White-winged Dove	*			
Mourning Dove	B	B	B	B
Common Ground Dove				
Black-billed Cuckoo	B	X	B	B
Yellow-billed Cuckoo	*	*		*B
Groove-billed Ani				
Common Barn-Owl	B		*	*
Flammulated Owl	B			
Eastern Screech-Owl				B
Western Screech-Owl	B	B	B	
Great Horned Owl	B	B	B	B
Snowy Owl	X	X	X	B
Northern Hawk-Owl	B	B	B	B
Northern Pygmy-Owl	B	B		
Burrowing Owl	B	B	B	B
Spotted Owl	B			
Barred Owl	B	B	B	B
Great Gray Owl	B	B	B	B
Long-eared Owl	B	B	B	B
Short-eared Owl	B	B	B	B
Boreal Owl	B	B	B	B
Northern Saw-whet Owl	B	B	B	B
Lesser Nighthawk				
Common Nighthawk	B	B	B	B
Common Poorwill	B	*	B	
Chuck-will's-widow				
Whip-poor-will			B	B

ONT	QUE	NB	NS	PEI	NFLD	YUK	NWT
419	350	356	370	295	327	233	249
	*					*	
*							
	B	B	B	*	B		
B	B	B	B	B	B	B	B
*		*	*				
*		*	*				
B	B	B	B	B	X	X	X
*							
B	B	B	*B	X	X		
B	*B	X	*	X	X		
*							
B	*	*	*		*		
B	B	*	*				
B	B	B	B	B	B	B	B
X	B	X	*	X	X	B	B
B	B	B	*	X	B	B	B
*	*	*					
B	B	B	B	B		B	B
B	X	*	*			B	B
B	B	B	*B	B	*	*	X
B	B	B	B	B	B	B	B
B	B	*	*	X	X	B	B
B	B	B	B	B	X		
*							
B	B	B	B	B	X	B	B
*							
B		*	*				
B	B	B	*B	X			

	BC	ALTA	SASK	MAN
Number of Species	426	341	334	353
Black Swift	B	B		
Chimney Swift			B	B
Vaux's Swift	B			
White-throated Swift	B			
Ruby-throated Hummingbird		B	B	B
Black-chinned Hummingbird	B	*		
Anna's Hummingbird	X	*		
Costa's Hummingbird	*			
Calliope Hummingbird	B	B	*	
Rufous Hummingbird	B	B	*	*
Belted Kingfisher	B	B	B	B
Lewis' Woodpecker	B	B?	*	X
Red-headed Woodpecker	*	*	B	B
Red-bellied Woodpecker			*	*B
Yellow-bellied Sapsucker	B	B	B	B
Red-breasted Sapsucker	B	*		
Williamson's Sapsucker	B		*	
Downy Woodpecker	B	B	B	B
Hairy Woodpecker	B	B	B	B
White-headed Woodpecker	B			
Three-toed Woodpecker	B	B	B	B
Black-backed Woodpecker	B	B	B	B
Northern Flicker	B	B	B	B
Pileated Woodpecker	B	B	B	B
Olive-sided Flycatcher	B	B	B	B
Western Wood-Pewee	B	B	B	B
Eastern Wood-Pewee			B	B
Yellow-bellied Flycatcher	X	B	B	B
Acadian Flycatcher	*			
Alder Flycatcher	B	B	B	B
Willow Flycatcher	B	B	B	X
Least Flycatcher	B	B	B	B
Hammond's Flycatcher	B	B		
Dusky Flycatcher	B	B	B	
Gray Flycatcher				
Western Flycatcher	B	B		
Black Phoebe	*			
Eastern Phoebe	B	B	B	B
Say's Phoebe	B	B	B	B
Vermilion Flycatcher				
Ash-throated Flycatcher	X			

ONT	QUE	NB	NS	PEI	NFLD	YUK	NWT
419	350	356	370	295	327	233	249
							X
B	B	B	B	X	X		
B	B	B	B	B	B		B
*						X	
B	B	B	B	B	B	B	B
*							
B	B	X	*				
B	*		*				
B	B	B	B	B	B	B	B
B	B	B	B	B	B	B	B
B	B	B	B	B	B	B	B
B	B	B	*	*	B	B	B
B	B	B	B	B	B	B	B
B	B	B	B	B	B	B	B
B	B	B	B	X	X		B
B	B	B	B	B	B	B	B
						B	B
B	B	B	B	B	X		
B	B	B	B	X	B	*	B
B	*						
B	B	B	B	X	B	B	B
B	B	*	B				
B	B	B	B	B	X	B?	B
						B	
						X	
*							
B	B	B	B	X	X		B
*	*		*			B	B
*							
*							

	BC	ALTA	SASK	MAN
Number of Species	426	341	334	353
Wied's Crested Flycatcher	*			
Great Crested Flycatcher		B	B	B
Tropical Kingbird	*			
Cassin's Kingbird				
Thick-billed Kingbird	*			
Western Kingbird	B	B	B	B
Eastern Kingbird	B	B	B	B
Gray Kingbird	*			
Scissor-tailed Flycatcher	*	*	*	X
Fork-tailed Flycatcher				
Eurasian Skylark	B			
Horned Lark	B	B	B	B
Purple Martin	B	B	B	B
Tree Swallow	B	B	B	B
Violet-green Swallow	B	B	B	*
Northern Rough-winged Swallow	B	B	B	B
Bank Swallow	B	B	B	B
Cliff Swallow	B	B	B	B
Cave Swallow				
Barn Swallow	B	B	B	B
Gray Jay	B	B	B	B
Steller's Jay	B	B	*	
Blue Jay	X	B	B	B
Clark's Nutcracker	B	B	*	X
Black-billed Magpie	B	B	B	B
American Crow	B	B	B	B
Northwestern Crow	B			
Fish Crow				
Common Raven	B	B	B	B
Black-capped Chickadee	B	B	B	B
Mountain Chickadee	B	B		
Siberian Tit				
Boreal Chickadee	B	B	B	B
Chestnut-backed Chickadee	B	*		
Tufted Titmouse				
Bushtit	B			
Red-breasted Nuthatch	B	B	B	B
White-breasted Nuthatch	B	B	B	B
Pygmy Nuthatch	B			
Brown Creeper	B	B	B	B

Legend
B — Breeding
X — Present and usually migrant
* — Vagrant, accidental or *very few* records

ONT	QUE	NB	NS	PEI	NFLD	YUK	NWT
419	350	356	370	295	327	233	249
B	B	B	*B	*	X		
*							
X	*	X	*	*	X		
B	B	B	B	B	X	*	B
*							
X	*	*	*				
*		*	*				
B	B	B	B	B	B	B	B
B	B	B	B	X	X	*	
B	B	B	B	B	B	B	B
						B	B
B	B	B	*		X	*	
B	B	B	B	B	B	B	B
B	B	B	B	B	X	B	B
			*				
B	B	B	B	B	B	B	B
B	B	B	B	B	B	B	B
						*	
B	B	B	B	B	B		
*						*	B
X		*	*		*	B	B
B	B	B	B	B	B	*	B
*							
B	B	B	B	B	B	B	B
B	B	B	B	B	B	B	B
						X	
						B	B?
B	B	B	B	B	B	B	B
						*	
B	*	*					
B	B	B	B	B	B	B	B
B	B	B	B	X			
B	B	B	B	B	B	*	

	BC	ALTA	SASK	MAN
Number of Species	426	341	334	353
Rock Wren	B	B	B	*
Canyon Wren	B			
Carolina Wren				*
Bewick's Wren	B			
House Wren	B	B	B	B
Winter Wren	B	B	B	B
Sedge Wren		B	B	B
Marsh Wren	B	B	B	B
American Dipper	B	B		
Golden-crowned Kinglet	B	B	B	B
Ruby-crowned Kinglet	B	B	B	B
Blue-gray Gnatcatcher	*			*
Bluethroat				
Northern Wheatear	B			*
Eastern Bluebird		*	B	B
Western Bluebird	B			
Mountain Bluebird	B	B	B	B
Townsend's Solitaire	B	B	B	X
Veery	B	B	B	B
Gray-cheeked Thrush	B	B	B	B
Swainson's Thrush	B	B	B	B
Hermit Thrush	B	B	B	B
Wood Thrush			*	B
Fieldfare				
Redwing				
American Robin	B	B	B	B
Varied Thrush	B	B	X	X
Gray Catbird	B	B	B	B
Northern Mockingbird	B	B	*B	B
Sage Thrasher	B	*	*B	
Brown Thrasher	*	B	B	B
Yellow Wagtail				
White Wagtail	*			
Red-throated Pipit				
Water Pipit	B	B	X	B
Sprague's Pipit		B	B	B
Bohemian Waxwing	B	B	B	B
Cedar Waxwing	B	B	B	B
Phainopepla				

Legend
B — Breeding
X — Present and usually migrant
* — Vagrant, accidental or *very few* records

ONT	QUE	NB	NS	PEI	NFLD	YUK	NWT
419	350	356	370	295	327	233	249
*							
B	B	*					
B							
B	B	B	*	*			B
B	B	B	B	B	B		B
B	B	B?	*	*			
B	B	B	*B	*			B
						B	B
B	B	B	B	B	B	B	B
B	B	B	B	B	B	B	B
B	B	X	*	X	*		
						*	*
X	B	*	*		X	B	B
B	B	B	*B	*	*		
*						B	B
*	*	*	*			B	B
B	B	B	B	X	B		
B	B	B	B	X	B	B	B
B	B	B	B	B	B	B	B
B	B	B	B	B	B	B	B
B	B	B	*B	*			
*	*				*		
					*		
B	B	B	B	B	B	B	B
X	*	*	*			B	B
B	B	B	B	B	X		
B	B	B	B	X	X		
*							
B	B	B	*	X	X		
						B	B
							*
						B	
B	B	X	X	X	B	B	B
*							
X	B	X	X	X	X	B	B
B	B	B	B	B	B	*?	B
*							

	BC	ALTA	SASK	MAN
Number of Species	426	341	334	353
Northern Shrike	B	B	X	B
Loggerhead Shrike	X	B	B	B
European Starling	B	B	B	B
Crested Myna	B			
White-eyed Vireo				*
Bell's Vireo				
Solitary Vireo	B	B	B	B
Yellow-throated Vireo			X	B
Hutton's Vireo	B			
Warbling Vireo	B	B	B	B
Philadelphia Vireo	B	B	B	B
Red-eyed Vireo	B	B	B	B
Blue-winged Warbler			*	
Golden-winged Warbler			*	B
Tennessee Warbler	B	B	B	B
Orange-crowned Warbler	B	B	B	B
Nashville Warbler	B	B	B	B
Virginia's Warbler				
Northern Parula		*	*	B
Yellow Warbler	B	B	B	B
Chestnut-sided Warbler	X	B	B	B
Magnolia Warbler	B	B	B	B
Cape May Warbler	B	B	B	B
Black-throated Blue Warbler		*	*	X
Yellow-rumped Warbler	B	B	B	B
Black-throated Gray Warbler	B	*	*	
Townsend's Warbler	B	B	B	
Hermit Warbler	*			
Black-throated Green Warbler	B	B	B	B
Blackburnian Warbler		B	B	B
Yellow-throated Warbler				
Pine Warbler		*	*	B
Kirtland's Warbler				
Prairie Warbler				
Palm Warbler	B	B	B	B
Bay-breasted Warbler	X	B	B	B
Blackpoll Warbler	B	B	B	B
Cerulean Warbler				*
Black-and-white Warbler	B	B	B	B
American Redstart	B	B	B	B
Prothonotary Warbler				
Worm-eating Warbler				

ONT	QUE	NB	NS	PEI	NFLD	YUK	NWT
419	350	356	370	295	327	233	249
X	B	X	X	X	X	B	B
B	B	B	*B	*			
B	B	B	B	B	B	B	B
B	*	*	*				
X							
B	B	B	B	X	B	*	B
B	B	*	*		X		
B	B	B	*	*	X	B?	B
B	B	B	X	X	X		B
B	B	B	B	B	B		B
B	*	*	*		X		
B	B	*	*				
B	B	B	B	B	B	B	B
B	B	*	*	*	X	B	B
B	B	B	B	B?	B		
*							
B	B	B	B	B	X		
B	B	B	B	B	B	B	B
B	B	B	B	X	X		
B	B	B	B	B	B		B
B	B	B	B	X	X		B
B	B	B	B	X	X		
B	B	B	B	B	B	B	B
*B			*				
*			*			B	
*	*		*				
B	B	B	B	B	B		B
B	B	B	B	X	B		
X	*	*	*	X	X		
B	B	X	*	*			
*	*						
B	*	X	*		*		
B	B	B	B	B	X	X	B
B	B	B	B	B?	X		B
B	B	B	B	B?	B	B	B
B	B	*	*				
B	B	B	B	B?	B		B
B	B	B	B	B	B	X	B
B	*	*	*				
B	*		*				

	BC	ALTA	SASK	MAN
Number of Species	426	341	334	353
Swainson's Warbler				
Ovenbird	B	B	B	B
Northern Waterthrush	B	B	B	B
Louisiana Waterthrush				
Kentucky Warbler				
Connecticut Warbler	B	B	B	B
Mourning Warbler	B	B	B	B
MacGillivray's Warbler	B	B	B	
Common Yellowthroat	B	B	B	B
Hooded Warbler				*
Wilson's Warbler	B	B	B	B
Canada Warbler	X	B	B	B
Painted Redstart	*			
Yellow-breasted Chat	B	B	B	*
Summer Tanager	*		*	*
Scarlet Tanager		*	B	B
Western Tanager	B	B	B	*
Northern Cardinal			*	B
Rose-breasted Grosbeak	B	B	B	B
Black-headed Grosbeak	B	B	B	X
Blue Grosbeak				
Lazuli Bunting	B	B	B	X
Indigo Bunting	*	*	B	B
Painted Bunting				
Dickcissel	*	*	*B	B
Green-tailed Towhee			*	*
Rufous-sided Towhee	B	B	B	B
Bachman's Sparrow				
Cassin's Sparrow				
American Tree Sparrow	B	X	B	B
Chipping Sparrow	B	B	B	B
Clay-colored Sparrow	B	B	B	B
Brewer's Sparrow	B	B	B	
Field Sparrow			*	B
Vesper Sparrow	B	B	B	B
Lark Sparrow	B	B	B	B
Black-throated Sparrow	*			
Sage Sparrow	*			
Lark Bunting	X	B	B	B
Savannah Sparrow	B	B	B	B
Baird's Sparrow		B	B	B
Grasshopper Sparrow	B	B	B	B

ONT	QUE	NB	NS	PEI	NFLD	YUK	NWT
419	350	356	370	295	327	233	249
			*				
B	B	B	B	B	B		B
B	B	B	B	X	B	B	B
B	*		*				
X	*	*	*		X		
X	B	*	*				
B	B	B	B	B	B		B
*						B	
B	B	B	B	B	B	B	B
B	*	*	*				
B	B	B	B	X	B	B	B
B	B	B	B	B	X		B
*							
B	*	X	*	X	X		
X	*	*	*		X		
B	B	B	*	X	X		
*	*	*	*				B
B	B	B	*B	X	X		
B	B	B	B	B	B		B
*		*	*				
X		*	*		X		
*							
B	B	B	*	*	X		
*							
B	*	X	*	X	X		
*			*				
B	B	X	*	*	X		
*							
*			*				
B	B	X	X	X	B	B	B
B	B	B	B	B	B	B	B
B	B	*	*			*	B
						B	
B	B	B	*	*	X		
B	B	B	*B	X	X		B
B		X	*	X	X		
*		*	*		*		
B	B	B	B	B	B	B	B
B	B	*	*	*	X		

	BC	ALTA	SASK	MAN
Number of Species	426	341	334	353
Henslow's Sparrow				
Le Conte's Sparrow	B	B	B	B
Sharp-tailed Sparrow	B	B	B	B
Seaside Sparrow				
Fox Sparrow	B	B	B	B
Song Sparrow	B	B	B	B
Lincoln's Sparrow	B	B	B	B
Swamp Sparrow	B	B	B	B
White-throated Sparrow	B	B	B	B
Golden-crowned Sparrow	B	B	*	
White-crowned Sparrow	B	B	B	B
Harris' Sparrow	X	X	B	B
Dark-eyed Junco	B	B	B	B
McCown's Longspur	*	B	B	X
Lapland Longspur	X	X	X	B
Smith's Longspur	X	X	X	B
Chestnut-collared Longspur	*	B	B	B
Snow Bunting	X	X	X	X
Bobolink	B	B	B	B
Red-winged Blackbird	B	B	B	B
Eastern Meadowlark				*
Western Meadowlark	B	B	B	B
Yellow-headed Blackbird	B	B	B	B
Rusty Blackbird	B	B	B	B
Brewer's Blackbird	B	B	B	B
Common Grackle	X	B	B	B
Brown-headed Cowbird	B	B	B	B
Orchard Oriole			*B	B
Northern Oriole	B	B	B	B
Scott's Oriole				
Common Chaffinch				
Brambling	*			
Rosy Finch	B	B	X	*
Pine Grosbeak	B	B	B	B
Purple Finch	B	B	B	B
Cassin's Finch	B	B		*
House Finch	B	*		
Red Crossbill	*	B	B	B
White-winged Crossbill	*	B	B	B
Common Redpoll	B	B	B	B
Hoary Redpoll	X	X	X	B

Legend
B — Breeding
X — Present and usually migrant
* — Vagrant, accidental or *very few* records

ONT	QUE	NB	NS	PEI	NFLD	YUK	NWT
419	350	356	370	295	327	233	249
B	*						
B	B				*		B
B	B	B	B	B			B
		*	*				
B	B	B	B	B?	B	B	B
B	B	B	B	B	B	X	B
B	B	B	B	B?	B	B	B
B		B	B	B	B	*	B
B	B	B	B	B	B	X	B
*			*			B	B
B	B	X	X	X	B	B	B
X	*		*			*	B
B	B	B	B	B	B	X	B
B	B	X	X	X	X	B	B
B						B	B
*		*	*		*		
X	B	X	X	X	X	B	B
B	B	B	B	B	B		
B	B	B	B	B	B	B	B
B	B	B	*B	X	X		
B	B						
B	*	*	*		X		B
B	B	B	B	X	B	B	B
B			*		*	B	
B	B	B	B	B	X		B
B	B	B	B	B	B	X	B
B	*	*	*	*			
B	B	B	B	B	X	*	
*							
					*		
*						B	B
B	B	B	B	X	B	B	B
B	B	B	B	B	B	B	B
B	*	X	*				
B	B	B	B	X	B	B	B
B	B	B	B	X	B	B	B
B	B	X	X	X	B	B	B
X	B	*	*	*	X	B	B

	BC	ALTA	SASK	MAN
Number of Species	426	341	334	353
Pine Siskin	B	B	B	B
Lesser Goldfinch	*			
American Goldfinch	B	B	B	B
Evening Grosbeak	B	B	B	B
House Sparrow	B	B	B	B

Information Provided By:

British Columbia: Yorke Edwards and *Checklist of B.C. Birds* (to June 1977) by R. Wayne Campbell, B.C. Prov. Museum.

Alberta: A. Wiseley, T. Thormin and *Checklist of Alberta Birds*, 4th Edition, 1981, Prov. Museum of Alberta.

Saskatchewan: J. Bernard Gollop and C. Stuart Houston.

Manitoba: Rudolf F. Koes and *Manitoba Birds Field Check List*, Man. Mus. of Man and Nature.

Ontario: According to *Checklist of the Birds of Ontario*, by R.D. James and A. Wormington, in press, 1983.

Quebec: Bob Barnhouse and *Field Checklist of Birds in the Montreal Area*, 1976, Prov. of Quebec Soc. for the Protection of Birds, Inc.; and *Oiseaux du Quebec*, 1977, Club des Ornithologues du Quebec.

New Brunswick: David Christie

Nova Scotia: J. Wolford and Ian McLaren

Prince Edward Island: Winifred Cairns and *Field Checklist of Birds, Prince Edward Island*, Dept. of Tourism, Parks and Conservation.

Newfoundland: John Pratt and *Field Checklist (1982) of the Birds of Insular Newfoundland*, Newfoundland Natural History Society.

Yukon: Robert Frisch and *Field Checklist of the Birds of the Yukon Territory*, Game Branch, Yukon Government.

Northwest Territories: *List of Birds; Wood Buffalo National Park*; Nahanni National Park; T.W. Barry; and *The Birds of Canada*, by W. Earl Godfrey, 1966, Nat. Mus. of Canada.

Legend
B — Breeding
X — Present and usually migrant
* — Vagrant, accidental or *very few* records

ONT	QUE	NB	NS	PEI	NFLD	YUK	NWT
419	350	356	370	295	327	233	249
B	B	B	B	B?	B	B	B
B	B	B	B	B	B		
B	B	B	B	X	X	*	B
B	B	B	B	B	B	B	B

Recent Name Changes Affecting Canadian Birds

Revised Name according to the 34th Supplement of the American Ornithologists' Union Check-List of North American Birds

Older Name	Revised Name
Scaled Petrel	Mottled Petrel
Pale-footed Shearwater	Flesh-footed Shearwater
New Zealand Shearwater	Buller's Shearwater
Slender-billed Shearwater	Short-tailed Shearwater
Manx Shearwater	{ Manx Shearwater / Black-vented Shearwater
Harcourt's Petrel	Band-rumped Storm-Petrel
White Pelican	American White Pelican
Common Egret	Great Egret
Louisiana Heron	Tricolored Heron
Green Heron	Green-backed Heron
Wood Ibis	Wood Stork
American Flamingo	Greater Flamingo
Fulvous Tree Duck	Fulvous Whistling-Duck
Whistling Swan / Bewick's Swan	Tundra Swan
White-fronted Goose	Greater White-fronted Goose
Black Duck	American Black Duck
Pintail	Northern Pintail
Shoveler	Northern Shoveler
European Wigeon	Eurasian Wigeon
Marsh Hawk	Northern Harrier
Goshawk	Northern Goshawk
Sparrow Hawk	American Kestrel
Pigeon Hawk	Merlin
Turkey	Wild Turkey
Bobwhite	Northern Bobwhite
Common Gallinule	Common Moorhen
Lapwing	Northern Lapwing
Eurasian Golden Plover	Greater Golden-Plover
American Golden Plover	Lesser Golden-Plover
Ringed Plover	Common Ringed Plover
Black Oystercatcher	American Black Oystercatcher
Upland Plover	Upland Sandpiper
Knot	Red Knot
Northern Phalarope	Red-necked Phalarope

Skua . . . . .Great Skua
Black-headed Gull . . . . .Common Black-headed Gull
Little Tern . . . . .Least Tern
Common Puffin. . . . . .Atlantic Puffin
Barn Owl . . . . .Common Barn-Owl
Screech Owl . . . . ⎰ Eastern Screech-Owl
⎱ Western Screech-Owl

Hawk Owl . . . . .Northern Hawk-Owl
Pygmy Owl . . . . .Northern Pygmy-Owl
Saw-whet Owl .Northern Saw-whet Owl
Poor-will . . . . .Common Poorwill

Yellow-bellied Sapsucker . . . . ⎰ Yellow-bellied Sapsucker
⎱ Red-breasted Sapsucker

Northern Three-toed Woodpecker . . . . .Three-toed Woodpecker
Black-backed Three-toed Woodpecker . .Black-backed Woodpecker

Yellow-shafted Flicker ⎱
Red-shafted Flicker   ⎬ . . . . .Northern Flicker
Common Flicker   ⎰

Kiskadie Flycatcher . . . . .Great Kiskadie
Skylark. . . . . .Eurasian Skylark
Rough-winged Swallow. . . . . .Northern Rough-winged Swallow

Canada Jay   ⎱
Whiskey Jack ⎰ . . . . .Gray Jay

Common Crow .American Crow
Gray-headed Chickadee . . . . .Siberian Tit
Common Bushtit . . . . .Bushtit
Short-billed Marsh Wren . . . . .Sedge Wren
Long-billed Marsh Wren . . . . .Marsh Wren
Dipper . . . . .American Dipper
Wheatear . . . . .Northern Wheatear
Mockingbird . . . . .Northern Mockingbird
Starling. . . . . .European Starling

Audubon's Warbler ⎱
Myrtle Warbler   ⎰ . . . . .Yellow-rumped Warbler

Parula Warbler. . . . . .Northern Parula
Cardinal . . . . .Northern Cardinal
Tree Sparrow. . . . . .American Tree Sparrow

Slate-colored Junco ⎱
Oregon Junco   ⎰ . . . . .Dark-eyed Junco

Baltimore Oriole ⎱
Bullock's Oriole ⎰ . . . . .Northern Oriole

Gray-crowned Rosy Finch ⎱
Black Rosy Finch   ⎬ . . . . .Rosy Finch
Brown-capped Rosy Finch ⎰

Printed in Canada